Sacco and Vanzetti

Also by Bruce Watson

*Bread & Roses: Mills, Migrants, and the Struggle for
the American Dream*

The Man Who Changed How Boys and Toys Were Made

Sacco and Vanzetti

The Men, the Murders, and
the Judgment of Mankind

Bruce Watson

Viking

VIKING
Published by the Penguin Group
Penguin Group (USA) Inc., 375 Hudson Street, New York, New York 10014, U.S.A.
Penguin Group (Canada), 90 Eglinton Avenue East, Suite 700, Toronto, Ontario,
Canada M4P 2Y3 (a division of Pearson Penguin Canada Inc.)
Penguin Books Ltd, 80 Strand, London WC2R 0RL, England
Penguin Ireland, 25 St Stephen's Green, Dublin 2, Ireland
(a division of Penguin Books Ltd)
Penguin Books Australia Ltd, 250 Camberwell Road, Camberwell, Victoria 3124,
Australia (a division of Pearson Australia Group Pty Ltd)
Penguin Books India Pvt Ltd, 11 Community Centre, Panchsheel Park, New Delhi —
110 017, India
Penguin Group (NZ), 67 Apollo Drive, Rosedale, North Shore 0745, Auckland,
New Zealand (a division of Pearson New Zealand Ltd)
Penguin Books (South Africa) (Pty) Ltd, 24 Sturdee Avenue, Rosebank, Johannesburg
2196, South Africa

Penguin Books Ltd, Registered Offices: 80 Strand, London WC2R 0RL, England

First Published in 2007 by Viking Penguin, a member of Penguin Group (USA) Inc.

1   3   5   7   9   10   8   6   4   2

Copyright © Bruce Watson, 2007
All rights reserved

Page 434 constitutes an extension of this copyright page.

LIBRARY OF CONGRESS CATALOGING-IN-PUBLICATION DATA
Watson, Bruce.
Sacco and Vanzetti : the judgment of mankind / Bruce Watson.
p. cm.
Includes bibliographical references and index.
ISBN 978-0-670-06353-6
1. Sacco-Vanzetti Trial, Dedham, Mass., 1921. 2. Sacco, Nicola, 1891–1927—Trials,
litigation, etc. 3. Vanzetti, Bartolomeo, 1888–1927—Trials, litigation, etc.
4. Trials (Murder)—Massachusetts. I. Title.
KF224.S2W38 2007
345.73'0252309744—dc22   2006103092

Printed in the United States of America

For all those struggling
to maintain a dauntless spirit
and an open mind

Why should there not be a patient confidence in the ultimate justice of the people? Is there any better or equal hope in the world?

—Abraham Lincoln

A Note on Quotations

Nicola Sacco, Bartolomeo Vanzetti, and several others in this book were far from proficient in English. Lest their writing be truncated by the Latin *"sic"* following each spelling or grammatical error, the author has taken extra care to reproduce their words precisely as written without noting them as such.

Contents

Sacco and Vanzetti

Late in the summer of 1927, a distant bell echoed throughout the world. Its tolling resounded from Europe to Australia, from Paraguay to Japan. And for one agonizing Monday in August, all talk of tomorrow ceased and all attention focused on a hulking granite prison in Massachusetts where Nicola Sacco and Bartolomeo Vanzetti were due to die at midnight.

Eulogized as "the good shoemaker and the poor fish peddler," they had become the most famous people on the planet. Some considered them demonic—murderers, anarchists, immigrants bent on savaging "all the institutions that Americans hold dear." Others saw them as "shining lights," gentle pacifists framed by a heartless judge and a ruthless prosecutor. Few knew them as men, one a dedicated father, the other a vagabond with the soul of a poet, both fierce militants. And at the approach of executions the whole world would witness, millions could not look but could not look away.

Outside the American embassy in Paris, tanks squared off against angry mobs. London's Hyde Park teemed with protesters. Across South America, widespread walkouts shut down factories and transportation. Restless crowds swarmed the streets of Sydney, Bucharest, Berlin, Amsterdam, Rome, Tokyo, Buenos Aires, Athens, Prague, Johannesburg, Marrakech . . .

Throughout America, the "Jazz Age" America of flappers and rumble seats, Babe Ruth and Charles Lindbergh, talk across back fences was of the two Italians, their eloquent pleas of innocence, the doubts clouding the verdict, the evidence of their guilt. Rank-and-file workers had contributed the modern equivalent of millions to free them. Now it all came down to midnight. Would there be another stay of execution? A last-minute pardon? Another bomb destroying a Manhattan subway or another juror's home? As darkness fell, lawyers raced to find a judge who might intervene. Radio stations promised to stay on the air late. Marchers outside the locked-down prison gazed at a watchtower where a light would dim when the switch was thrown.

The drama did not end that day, nor had it started with a 1920 gangland murder. The deepening saga of Sacco and Vanzetti, which descended into a deathwatch, opens like a package rigged with dynamite.

Book One

And so, I think it best you follow me
  for your own good, I shall be your guide
  and lead you out through an eternal place
Where you will hear desperate cries, and see
  tormented shades, some as old as Hell itself.

                  —Dante, *Inferno*

Prologue

Neatly wrapped and labeled, thirty identical bombs were mailed from Manhattan in late April 1919. Each was addressed to a prominent American—John D. Rockefeller, J. P. Morgan, Oliver Wendell Holmes—and each was a masterpiece of sinister intent. Enveloped in brown paper, the long, thin packages were marked GIMBEL BROTHERS, NEW YORK—SAMPLE and graced with a drawing of an Alpine mountaineer. Depending on their destinations, some bombs were mailed earlier than others so that all would be detonated in one devastating May Day demonstration.

Along with the more famous recipients, the targets of the plot included many prominent Americans singled out for suppressing radicals. Among these were Attorney General A. Mitchell Palmer, congressmen from both parties, and Judge Kenesaw Mountain Landis, the future baseball commissioner whose court had found scores of "Wobblies" from the Industrial Workers of the World guilty of sedition. Seattle's mayor, targeted for breaking a general strike that winter, received the first bomb.

Taking the tan package from the mayor's mail, a clerk unwrapped it upside down. A slim vial of acid fell to the floor, leaving hundreds of metal slugs packed around a stick of dynamite. The package was taken to the bomb squad, who admired its ingenuity. The following day in Georgia, an ex-senator received a Gimbel's package. His wife started to open it but, thinking it contained only pencils, told her maid to put the contents in a cabinet. Tearing off the paper, the maid unscrewed the top of the enclosed tube. Two screws punctured a glass phial, pouring acid onto cotton wadding. The acid soaked through the cotton. The bomb blew off the maid's hands. That afternoon, a dozen other Gimbel's packages arrived in post offices throughout the nation.

The broadest assassination plot in American history was foiled by a postal clerk. At 2:00 a.m. on April 30, Charles Kaplan was riding the El train home to Harlem. Weary from the night shift, he sat reading a newspaper. He was drawn to a story from Atlanta about a bomb blowing off a maid's hands. As the train rattled him toward home, Kaplan read about the "infernal machine" and the "Negro servant" it had nearly killed. The description of the package struck the clerk as familiar. In the bleary-eyed darkness, he hopped off the El and took a train back to his midtown post office, where he and a supervisor found sixteen identical packages in the parcel post room. All were marked GIMBEL BROTHERS, NEW YORK—SAMPLE. Neither caution nor carelessness explained why they had not been sent. Sealed with a red sticker denoting first-class mail, the bombs had been delayed for insufficient postage.

By the following noon, federal investigators were fanning out through post offices nationwide searching for more infernal machines. Bombs were intercepted in San Francisco, Washington, D.C., Chicago, Salt Lake City. "I do not recollect anything of the kind in our history more diabolical than this conspiracy," said Postmaster General Albert Burleson, another target of the plot. Federal agents quickly drew up a list of suspects, but did not round them up. Not yet.

No bombs exploded on May 1, 1919. In offices and boardrooms, May Day was quiet. On the street, however, something akin to a culture war raged as veterans back from the Great War slugged it out with their fellow Americans. In Boston, parading Socialists battled the flying fists of soldiers and sailors. More than a hundred people were arrested. In Manhattan, a mob ransacked the offices of a Socialist daily, smashing furniture, confiscating books and pamphlets. Vigilantes in Cleveland battled May Day paraders throughout the city. Lesser disturbances shook Chicago and Detroit. Meanwhile, accusations flew about who was to blame for the bombs. Rumors hinted of a German plot. Wobblies blamed "capitalist hirelings" trying to pin the crime on the IWW. The Georgia senator who had received a bomb accused "disgruntled anarchists [and] Bolshevik cussedness." As days passed and a final three bombs were found—one congressman tried to open his package but the lid jammed—the "Negro servant" remained the plot's only casualty, but a slow, creeping fear was its consequence.

On May 4, the *New York Times* urged "vigorous prosecution if the Bolshevist movement is to be held in check." Two days later in Washington, D.C., a pageant crowd rose for "The Star-Spangled Banner." When the final strains faded, three shots rang out. A sailor had killed a man who had refused to stand. The audience burst into applause. All that May, talk of terror spread, fanned by Seattle's mayor, Ole Hanson. "I trust Washington will buck up and clean up and either hang or incarcerate for life all the anarchists in the country," Hanson said. "If the government doesn't clean them up, I will." He soon resigned to embark on a nationwide tour warning Americans about the Red menace. He found an eager audience.

The year 1919 had begun in joy and mourning. The Great War was over. Ten million were dead, but at least no more would die in the trenches. The burden of killing had shifted from man to microbes. A deadly strain of Spanish flu was raging. Before the pandemic ebbed, it would kill fifty to one hundred million people, making it the worst plague in history, worse even than the Black Death of the Middle Ages. Advancing like an invading army, the flu swept through American cities and towns, killing 675,000, more than died in the Civil War. Tragic stories—of healthy people dying in a day, of entire companies of soldiers who survived the trenches only to be stricken down after the armistice—spread like the virus itself. The dead, their bodies turned a ghastly blue, were stacked like cordwood. Priests drove horse-drawn hacks through the streets calling people to bring out their dead. By that spring, the pestilence was waning, yet makeshift hospitals with starched white tents and Model T ambulances still dotted the country, and doctors warned that the virus could strike again the next winter.

The twin tolls of war and disease shaped 1919, the year Americans had longed for since the conflict began. Anticipated as a time of peace, it unfolded in pitched battles on the home front. After sacrificing 126,000 soldiers, America maintained a wartime mentality. The war had thrown the economy into overdrive, doubling prewar prices. Workers in every trade walked off the job. There were dressmakers' strikes, railway strikes, cigar makers' strikes, miners' strikes. Even police went on strike, leaving Boston to rampaging drunks and looters. That summer, savage race riots set off by white mobs broke out in Chicago, Washington, D.C., and two dozen other cities.

The war had finished off the Victorian age, yet no new ethos had taken its place. Each day Americans awoke to a strange new world. From the ashes of tottering empires rose fledgling nations whose names tripped the tongue—Yugoslavia, Czechoslovakia, and the Union of Soviet Socialist Republics. Not even the laws of science seemed immutable. In late May, Newtonian physics fell to the first concrete proof of Einstein's universe. A few weeks later, another tower toppled as Congress granted women the right to vote. Come fall, baseball's World Series concluded with rumors of a gambler's fix. The year was not over before Americans were shocked by an ad showing a woman holding a cigarette. By the dawn of 1920, the average citizen faced a nation he did not recognize in a world he did not know. And under Prohibition he could not even order a beer and laugh about the changes. Given the uncertainty, scapegoating was only natural. The search begun on that chaotic May Day quickened a month later when bombs came to American doorsteps. Taking no chances with postage this time, the bombers delivered their packages by hand.

Just after 11:00 p.m. on June 2, a tall man wearing a pinstriped suit, a polka-dot bow tie, and a derby strode briskly through a posh neighborhood in Washington, D.C. No one noticed the man or his flimsy suitcase. In it were a stack of flyers, two revolvers, an Italian-

English dictionary, and twenty pounds of dynamite. As the man strolled up the street, Franklin Roosevelt, then assistant secretary of the navy and not yet stricken by polio, parked his car and walked with his wife, Eleanor, into their home. Across the street, Attorney General A. Mitchell Palmer turned off the light in his library and went upstairs. He had just undressed when he heard a thump at his front door. The noise was followed by a deafening explosion. Windows shattered up and down the block. "The world is coming to an end!" the Roosevelts' cook shouted. Mansions shook on their foundations, throwing sleeping residents from their beds. Hurrying outside, pajama-clad people smelled a foul odor and saw pieces of flesh splattered through the treetops. Roosevelt rushed to Palmer's home to find his neighbor unhurt. Despite the force of the blast, its lone casualty was the bomber, who had tripped on the steps. But this was only a wake-up call.

For the next ninety minutes, explosions splintered the silence of several cities. In Philadelphia, two bombs caved in the porch of a Catholic church. In Cleveland, a pipe bomb blew off the front of the mayor's house. Midnight bombs destroyed homes in Pittsburgh, Boston, New York, and New Jersey. The targets had one thing in common—each had zealously suppressed radicals, especially anarchists. Lest anyone wonder who was responsible, copies of the same pink flyer were found scattered in the rubble. Beneath a headline—PLAIN WORDS—the flyer began:

> The powers that be make no secret of their will to stop here in America the worldwide spread of revolution. The powers that be must reckon that they will have to accept the fight they have provoked. . . .
>
> The challenge is an old one, O "democratic" lords of the autocratic republic. We have been dreaming of freedom, we have talked of liberty, we have aspired to a better world, and you jailed us, you clubbed us, you deported us, you murdered us. . . .
>
> There will have to be bloodshed; we will not dodge; there will have to be murder: we will kill, because it is

necessary; there will have to be destruction; we will destroy to rid the world of your tyrannical institutions.

Thirteen more paragraphs denounced the "capitalist" war in
Europe, the expulsion of radicals from America, and the enrich-
ment of a few at the expense of millions. Concluding with the cry
"Down with tyranny!" the pamphlet was signed THE ANARCHIST
FIGHTERS.

Over the next few weeks, police pieced together clues from the
flyers, the debris, and pieces of the man blown to bits on the attorney general's steps. The man's left leg was found on a nearby door-
step, and his torso was discovered a block away. Two boys found a
foot and kept it in their refrigerator until their mother came upon
it. When forensic experts gently lifted the man's scalp off a roof, a
hairdresser examined its thick black locks, identifying the bomber
as an Italian in his late twenties. While the hunt continued, the
press called for "a few free treatments in the electric chair." "If I
had my way," said the evangelist Billy Sunday, "I'd fill the jails so
full of them that their feet would stick out the windows. . . . Let
them rule? We'll swim our horses in blood up to the bridles first."

Ten days after the bombings, the raids began. Manhattan police
stormed the Russian Bolshevik Mission, took several prisoners, and
seized pamphlets calling for workers' soviets in America. A few
days later, they raided a Socialist school but found just a few men
playing cards. Wobblies were rounded up across the nation. As July
4 approached, Americans braced for more bombings. Police guarded
federal buildings and prominent homes. Headlines stoked the fear:
REIGN OF TERROR PLANNED (*Chicago Tribune*); PLANS FOR WIDE-
SPREAD VIOLENCE AND MURDER (*Cincinnati Enquirer*); CITIES
PREPARE FOR REDS (*Los Angeles Times*). The Fourth came and
went, but the only explosions were fireworks, the only fighting was
Jack Dempsey pummeling Jess Willard to win the heavyweight
championship. Yet as the summer dragged on, the alarm lingered.
"There is hardly a respectable citizen of my acquaintance who does
not believe that we are on the verge of armed conflict in this country," a West Virginia man told the attorney general.

Scarred by war, devastated by plague, terrorized by bombs, America lashed out against a new scapegoat, one that had surged to prominence during the 1917 Bolshevik Revolution. Reds had stirred up "the Negroes." Reds had caused all those strikes. Reds had infiltrated the schools, the government, the movies. America's first "Red Scare" was shorter than its McCarthy-era successor yet far more intense. Teachers were fired for merely mentioning Bolshevism. A Connecticut man was jailed for praising Lenin. Following a shoot-out in central Washington, one of the accused—both a Wobbly and a veteran—was dragged from jail, castrated with a razor, hung from a bridge, and riddled with bullets. Then the federal government took over.

That fall, Attorney General Palmer, criticized for being soft on subversives, cracked down. Palmer suddenly saw red everywhere, in "the sharp tongues of the Revolution's head licking the altars of the churches, leaping into the belfry of the school bell, crawling into the sacred corners of American homes and seeking to replace marriage vows with libertine laws." Courting public opinion as an election year approached, Palmer ordered the raids that would bear his name. In November, federal agents swarmed through labor halls, arresting hundreds guilty only of being present. Many were beaten or held for months without trial. Just before Christmas, a ship nicknamed "the Soviet Ark" sailed out of New York, taking 249 radicals to Russia. The press and the public cheered. Then on January 2, 1920, came the biggest of the "Palmer Raids," masterminded by Palmer's assistant, future FBI director J. Edgar Hoover. Bursting into meetings and arresting everyone in sight, agents rounded up four thousand aliens in thirty-three cities. Raids were especially intense in Massachusetts's industrial towns—Brockton, Bridgewater, Lawrence, and Lowell. Then, as the frenzy was fading, its ashes were stirred by the story of two Italian immigrants near Boston. On a dark night far from their homes, both were arrested while covering up for their friends, the Anarchist Fighters.

CHAPTER ONE

"Lambs and Wolves"

*I came to understand that each individual has two "I's,"
the real one and the ideal.*

—Bartolomeo Vanzetti

In their final months on the streets of their adopted country, Nicola Sacco and Bartolomeo Vanzetti led dual lives. For six days a week they were gentle, hardworking citizens, respected and admired throughout their communities. But each Sunday afternoon, they met with their fellow anarchists to discuss hiding the group's role in the recent bombing campaigns. By the spring of 1920, the schism within each man had come to a breaking point. No longer bearable, it had led both to consider returning to simpler lives in Italy. Sacco and Vanzetti suspected their remaining time in America might be short. Neither imagined it was his freedom, not his sojourn in this country, that had dwindled to a handful of days.

Sacco was up early each morning throughout that warm, blossoming April. A compact, energetic man, he rose at 4:00 a.m. to spend an hour in his garden behind his small bungalow in Stoughton, a factory town seventeen miles southwest of Boston. Planting the season's first seedlings, protecting them from New England's late frosts, Sacco tended his garden until sunrise. After breakfast with his wife, Rosina, and their seven-year-old son, Dante, he joined the jostle of the morning shift walking to the Three-K shoe factory. Sacco was an edge trimmer, one of the best in Massachusetts's thriving shoe industry. Taking a shoe other workers had cobbled together, he would run its sole along a whirring blade, slicing away excess leather before tossing the finished product into a bin and grabbing another. With his meager hourly wage bolstered by piecework, Sacco was earning eighty dollars a week in a time when the average worker took home a third as much. Throughout that spring he continued to make good money. Moonlighting as a night watchman at his factory, he sent his father a hundred dollars and pushed his savings above fifteen hundred, enough to return to the little town of Torremaggiore near Italy's southern Adriatic coast. "We always had the idea to go back to Italy," Rosina Sacco remembered. Early that spring, a letter hastened their plans.

On March 23, a black envelope arrived in Stoughton. Opening it, Sacco learned that his mother, Angelina, was dead. Prostrated with grief, he decided to end his youthful experiment in the country that, as a boy, had been "always in my dreams." In May he, Dante, and Rosina, now a few months pregnant, were to leave for Italy. Sacco had already visited the Italian consulate seeking travel papers. He was told to return with a family photo. He did so on April 15, or so he and several witnesses later testified.

After seven years of marriage, "Nick and Rosie" still acted like sweethearts. Having eloped over her father's protest of his radical views—"that one will end on the gallows!"—they had settled into a stable, loving marriage. Dante had been born a year later, followed in 1916 by a daughter who had lived only a month. Sacco was tightly bound to his family, drawing life from the lives around him. From prison, writing in his awkward English, he later recalled a typical scene:

> I remember when wi youst live in South Stoughton
> Mass in our little sweet home and frequently in evening
> Rosina, Dante and I, we youst go see a frend. . . . Dante
> in that time of hour hi was always sleeping, so I youst

bring him always in my arm away to home; some time
Rosina she youst halp me to carry him and in that same
time she youst get Dante in her arm both us we youst
give him a warm kisses on is rosy face. Those day . . . they
was a some happy day.

Vanzetti spent that spring in Plymouth, peddling fish. After a
dozen years of backbreaking labor—"I was a 'Dago,' to be worked
to death"—he had bought a two-wheeled fish peddler's cart from a
friend returning to Italy. A fishmonger's pay was meager, but the
outdoor work freed Vanzetti from the stuffy factories and kitchens
that had irritated his lungs. And a peddler's irregular hours gave
him free time to pursue his favorite pastimes—reading and dreaming of revolution, peaceful if possible, violent if necessary. Twice a
week he bought a barrel of fish, cleaned the catch, and placed it on
ice in his cart. Then, inhaling the stench of his wares, he strolled
through Plymouth's Italian and Portuguese neighborhoods, down
alleys strung with clotheslines, past the clutter of children playing,
calling *"Pesce! Pesce!"* Cutting off heads, weighing portions on
his scale, Vanzetti peddled cod, halibut, swordfish, and, on special
occasions, eel. When Boston fishermen had a lean week, he went
clamming near the Plymouth pier not far from the rock where the
Pilgrims had landed.

Along his route, Vanzetti was well-known and loved. He often
stopped in kitchens and sat drinking black coffee, the strongest
drink he allowed himself since swearing off alcohol several years
earlier. At ease among his customers, he talked incessantly about
life and literature. His huge, flowing mustache, expressive eyes,
and *simpatico* demeanor made him a favorite among children. At
thirty-one, he had no family of his own. "The thought of getting
married has never crossed my mind," he wrote an aunt. "I have
never had a girl friend, and if I have ever fallen in love, it has been
an impossible love, the kind that had to be stifled in my breast."
Gregarious but solitary, Vanzetti was devoted only to friends,
books, and his true "beloved"—anarchism. "A little roof, a field, a
few books and food is all what I need," he wrote. "I do not care for

money, for leisure, for mundane ambition." This world, he often said, was one of "lambs and wolves," though he never revealed which he considered himself.

Vanzetti had many friends but was closest to Vincenzo Brini and his children, with whom he had boarded upon arriving in Plymouth. The three Brini children adored "Bart," but he was especially fond of Beltrando. Calling the boy "my spiritual son," Vanzetti helped Beltrando with homework and took him for walks on the beach or in the woods, pointing out flora and fauna. Only days before his arrest, Vanzetti had seen Beltrando trample a garden in search of a baseball, then sass the neighbor who scolded him. Vanzetti had gotten down on one knee, telling the boy he had to apologize. Beltrando was devoted to the man who spent more time with him than his own father. "He was my ideal," Beltrando remembered. "For some boys it was Ty Cobb, but for me it was Bartolomeo Vanzetti."

Such were their serene weekdays, yet each Sunday afternoon Sacco and Vanzetti met with Gruppo Autonomo, a cell of Italian anarchists in East Boston. Circulating among skilled saboteurs, they discussed the group's recent bombings and the federal agents closing in. Although no evidence exists proving that either Sacco or Vanzetti made or planted the bombs that terrorized America in 1919, their ties to the bombers gave them inside information and may have rendered them legally complicit in the conspiracy. It was their friend Carlo Valdinoci who had blown himself to bits on the steps of the attorney general's home. Rosina Sacco regarded Valdinoci as "a great anarchist," and after his death invited his sister to move in with the Saccos. Another Gruppo Autonomo member, Mario Buda, had pulled off bombings in Milwaukee and probably, as he put it, "plant[ed] the poof" in Pittsburgh and Cleveland in June 1919. Buda considered Sacco and Vanzetti his best friends in America. Gruppo Autonomo loyalist Nicola Recchi, his left hand blown off by one of his homemade bombs, made many of the infernal devices and had the *Plain Words* pamphlet printed. An old Italian saying—*Chi va con lo zoppo impara a zoppicare* (He who travels with the lame man learns to limp)—suggests that Sacco and

Vanzetti did more than just take cover during the 1919 bombings. Did they help plan? Sit on the sidelines and say nothing? Argue against assassination? This mystery is the first of many.

All these anarchists were *Galleanisti,* disciples of Luigi Galleani, whom Vanzetti called "our master." Galleani's *La Salute è in voi!* (The Health Is Within You!) was a primer on bomb making. "Dynamite is a paste made from nitroglycerine and an absorbent powder," the pamphlet explained. "It is very easy to use, transport, and conserve. Since dynamite is by now quite common, it is usually very easy to obtain." A lawyer by training, the gentlemanly Galleani edited a newspaper, *Cronaca Sovversiva,* which he called "a rag of a paper that lives on crusts and bits of bread." The U.S. Bureau of Justice called *Cronaca* "the most rabid, seditious, and anarchistic sheet ever published in this country" and made subscribing to it grounds for deportation. Sacco and Vanzetti both subscribed. Vanzetti also wrote for the paper and distributed a hundred copies a week. A typical *Cronaca* editorial summed up Galleani's militancy: "To hell with the Constitution! Such is the shout of yesterday, of today, of tomorrow, of any day, of each conflict that brings forth rights and privileges, labor and capital, exploited and exploiters."

During the hysteria of the Red Scare, Sacco, Vanzetti, and other *Galleanisti* lay low. Galleani was deported in June 1919, leading his followers to issue another pamphlet warning, "We will dynamite you!" Other anarchists had been shipped back to Italy during the Palmer Raids, yet the core of Gruppo Autonomo remained in the Boston area and federal agents seemed no nearer to pinning the bomb plots on them. Then in February 1920, agents got a tip that made the group take cover. At Ellis Island, a New Jersey anarchist grilled by J. Edgar Hoover blamed the bombings on Boston-based *Galleanisti.* Another tip led agents to a Brooklyn print shop where they found pink paper and a font featuring a singular "s" that matched each "s" in the *Plain Words* flyer. Police arrested two printers, and by late March Vanzetti was growing worried about one of them, his good friend Andrea Salsedo. Salsedo had written Vanzetti that he was "under grave charges" and urgently needed money. He had already confessed to printing *Plain Words*. At their Sunday meetings, Sacco, Vanzetti, and other cell members worried: What else would Salsedo reveal? Where would the net close next? How could they raise money to defend their friends?

But another question echoes down through the decades. How could two modest gentlemen, each beloved and respected, each a loving parent or surrogate parent, be in the thick of bomb plots? Ever since Sacco and Vanzetti became world famous, the two sides of these two men have led to contrasting verdicts in history. Calling them "philosophical anarchists," defenders have pointed to their gentle dispositions. Roger Baldwin, cofounder of the American Civil Liberties Union, said both men were "about as far away from murderers and thieves as anyone you could think of." Sacco's factory boss added, "A man who is in his garden at four o'clock in the morning and at the factory at seven o'clock, and in his garden again after supper . . . that man is no holdup man."

More than one murderer has convinced admirers of his virtue, however, and their dueling personalities still cast doubt on Sacco and Vanzetti. If, as Vanzetti wrote, "each individual has two 'I's,' the real one and the ideal," then in these individuals the real and the ideal waged constant warfare. Like their fellow Anarchist Fighters, Sacco and Vanzetti believed in armed insurrection. They saw sporadic violence as righteous retaliation against those who had jailed, deported, and killed their comrades on picket lines and in protests. A few supporters were later disturbed by flashes of this darker "I." Sacco "loved flowers, he loved birds," recalled journalist Gardner Jackson, but "he was also a terrific hater." Yet Jackson, who worked tirelessly in their defense, never doubted the men's innocence. Nor did novelist Upton Sinclair, though he came to see that both men "believed in and taught violence." Vanzetti, Sinclair noted, "was not the pacifist he was reported under the necessity of defense propaganda. He was, like many fanatics, a dual personality, and when he was roused by the social conflict he was a very dangerous man."

Still, for all their militancy, would Sacco or Vanzetti gun down two payroll guards in broad daylight? The question has given the men parallel portraits. Those who branded them anarchists saw them guilty as charged. According to this reasoning, anarchists, with their history of assassinations and bombings, were capable of any crime. Others have refused to believe such peaceful souls capable of cold-blooded murder. Decades after the case, when confronted with evidence to the contrary, one woman said, "They *had* to be innocent."

To reconcile the men's character, it helps to see them as a study in chiaroscuro. Literally meaning "light/dark," *chiaroscuro* is the Italian word for high contrast in a sketch. Sacco and Vanzetti may have been lambs, but they belonged to a wolfpack. They were gentle dreamers whose dream included armed rebellion. Two mentalities coexisted inside each of the two men because each was formed by two nations—Italy and America. The former instilled a soft, sentimental side. The latter hardened them like iron in a foundry.

Thirteen years after leaving Italy and six months after landing in an American jail, Vanzetti wrote his life story. Arrested for murder and facing the electric chair, he did not consider his journey unusual. "My life cannot rise to any worthy example, however it is considered," he began *A Proletarian Life*. He was, he wrote, "anonymous in the anonymous crowd." Vanzetti's thirty-page memoir recounted jobs he had taken and insults he had borne, but an earlier letter had been more succinct: "We knocked down mountains, uprooted forests, built palaces, and ended up with nothing; that is my story."

The story began in the northern Italian town of Villafalletto where Vanzetti was born on June 11, 1888. Unlike the sizzling southern villages from which so many Italians fled to America, Vanzetti's birthplace was prosperous, even idyllic. Villafalletto's red tile roofs, sepia walls, and green fields sloping toward the snowy Alps provided all the beauty and comfort a young boy could want. Each morning, men and women set out for the fields beyond the town, often singing as they went. The Vanzettis were well-off, living in a large two-story home surrounding a garden so opulent "it takes a poet of first magnitude to worthy speak of it," Vanzetti remembered. The eldest of five children, Vanzetti later romanticized his youth as "unspeakably beautiful."

Bright and eloquent, young "Barto" was an outstanding student, yet his father, who ran a thriving farm, cared little for education. He yanked his thirteen-year-old son out of school and apprenticed him to a pastry chef in nearby Cuneo. There Vanzetti worked from sunup until midnight, seven days a week. "In the evening, when I quit work after eighteen hours of my long day," he wrote his parents, "I seem to have my feet in embers, so much do they burn. To tell the truth, I am tired of this miserable life." Praising God and occasionally fighting older workers who mocked his Catholic faith, Vanzetti continued his long, burning days until a bout of pleurisy sent him home.

While recuperating in the care of his mother, "the good, the worshipped mother," Vanzetti enjoyed the happiest time of his life. Resting, reading, walking with a cane, he found himself consumed with "the fever of knowledge" and soon took up a new apprenticeship—as a radical. Daily discussions in cafés convinced him that religion was a sham and society a palimpsest on which revolution would soon stamp a better world. The teenager who had defended Catholicism with his fists was becoming the stocky, hirsute man who would reject all religion and laws. "I came to understand that the plagues which most beset humanity were ignorance and the degeneration of natural sentiment," he remembered. "My religion no longer needed temples, altars, and formal prayers. God for me became a perfect spirit, stripped of any human quality."

Early in 1908, Vanzetti's flagging faith was demolished when his mother, Giovanna, contracted liver cancer. For three months he sat by her bed while his younger sister, Luigia, cared for the two children born while he had been off working. During his mother's final weeks, Vanzetti did not even change his clothes. When she died in his arms, he wandered for days in the woods, often considering suicide. He decided instead to emigrate. "There was nothing for me to do but come away," he remembered. "I had to put the seas between me and my grief." Vanzetti's father, who had journeyed to California as a young man, knew the lure of America but begged his son not to abandon him, a fifty-nine-year-old widower with two teenagers and two toddlers. Leaving father and family in mourning, bidding tearful good-byes to the crowd that accompanied him to the train station, Vanzetti made his way across the Alps and northward to Le Havre. From there, the steamer *La Provence* took him to a land where he could start again.

On June 19, 1908, the lyrical, bookish Italian who would become the greatest cause célèbre the world has ever known stood in the streets of Manhattan, suitcase in hand, looking into his new country. America was far from the dreamland he had expected. To his amazement and disgust, he saw people sleeping in alleys and scrounging in garbage cans for rotten lettuce and bad fruit. Manhattan teemed with gangs, prostitutes, and other by-products of the nation's relentless drive to industrialize. Tycoons bestrode the boulevards in top hats and tails, dined in fine restaurants, and summered in Newport, in Maine, in the Berkshires. Common laborers had to settle for cloth caps, hardscrabble home cooking, and sweaty summer afternoons at Coney Island. With one small percentile of Americans holding *half* the nation's wealth, the tension between social classes was explosive, and, as Vanzetti would learn, the divide turned many moderates into Socialists and some Socialists into anarchists.

A fellow Italian soon got Vanzetti a job as a dishwasher. For the next eight months, first at one restaurant, then another, he toiled for seventy hours a week in dark, smelly pantries where water dripped off the ceiling and a slimy offal spread across the floors. The heat and humidity aggravated his lungs, still scarred from pleurisy. Eating "rotten food hardly fit for dogs," earning five or six dollars a week, he finally quit for fear of contracting consumption. Subsequent jobs were no better. Between them, he spent months unemployed, wandering the streets, often homeless, always alone. Other Italian immigrants at least had each other's company, but Vanzetti found his fellow *paesani* "in general, rather ignorant." Preferring the solace of books, he spent his time reading, thinking, dreaming. Letters from his father urged him to return to "the paternal home where you will find work and bread for the whole family." Thanking his son for occasional money orders, the grieving Gian Batista Vanzetti wrote that he could not imagine never seeing "*Caro mio Barto*" again.

A year after his arrival, Vanzetti fled New York, "the immense hell pit of the poor and paradise of the rich," and took a steamer up the Connecticut River to Hartford. Following a friend into the rolling countryside, he sought handiwork on farms but found little. Finally, the men headed for cities where they joined Italian workers toiling all day, rollicking all night. In Springfield, Massachusetts, Vanzetti loaded bricks ten hours a day. In a Connecticut quarry, he split stones with a pickaxe. All but broken by hard labor, he finally returned to Manhattan to become an assistant pastry chef, but a year later he was back in Springfield working in a railroad gang. In 1912, Vanzetti moved on to Worcester, Massachusetts, where he lugged stones to build a dam, then sweltered in a foundry. There he also made his first good friends, anarchists who shared his dream of a perfect world, one with no laws, cops, or government to oppress the common man.

Wherever Vanzetti went, he consumed books. He read Tolstoy, Zola, Darwin, Dante, and Marx. He studied American history, the French Revolution, the Bible, and, growing angrier about his life, probed works by the Russian anarchist Kropotkin and his Italian disciples. Reading late into the night, seething at the poverty and misery all around him, the lapsed Catholic formed a new faith: "I came to believe in brotherhood, in universal love. I came to see that whoever helps or hurts a man helps or hurts the species. I found my liberty in the liberty of all, my happiness in the happiness of all."

After five years as a "perambulating philosopher of the main road," Vanzetti finally found a home. Coming to Plymouth in 1913, he settled with the Brini family and came to care for their children, who were charmed by his kindness and his Vandyke beard. At the huge Plymouth Cordage Factory, he hefted heavy coils of rope on a loading dock, earning sixteen cents an hour. He remained at "the Cordage" until 1915, when the company tried to move him to an indoor job. A year later when cordage workers walked out, Vanzetti returned to throw himself into the strike. Many anarchists addressed the strikers, but the pedantic Vanzetti was not a convincing speaker and was sometimes pulled from podiums. Subsequent jobs—gardener, handyman, ice cutter—were less grueling, yet Vanzetti could never forget how his mind had been ignored and his strength abused. His mounting sense of injustice burst out in a letter to his sister, Luigia:

> I have had to suffer injuries and mockery from people that, were I a tenth as fluent in English as I am in Italian, I would have left face down in the dust. Here public justice is based on force and brutality, and woe to the stranger and particularly the Italian who wants to win justice through energetic methods; for him there are the clubs of the police, the prisons and the penal codes.

Growing up shy and humble, struggling with his second language, Ferdinando Sacco judged himself "a dumbling." In contrast to the man to whom his name is forever linked, Sacco did not spend hours "crushing, burning a world" within himself. But then, America was easier on him than on Vanzetti. Had he not met the same end, Sacco might have been just another Italian who crossed the Atlantic, got a job and settled down, then watched his childhood fade into memory, only speaking Italian with his graying wife and long-time friends.

At his trial, Sacco said he had left school at fourteen. Perhaps he was ashamed to admit he had quit third grade to tend his father's vineyards. The grapes grew on a gentle slope near the spur of Italy's boot. Like hundreds of other Italian towns, Torremaggiore produced wine, olives, wool, and wheat. It had an abandoned medieval castle at its center and a cathedral as its spiritual hub. A dirt road led to the town center, where Sacco was born in a small two-story home near the castle. From his home's wrought-iron balcony, he could see the length of his street—the clothes drying in the breeze, the stores with balls of cheese in the windows, the chickens and goats roaming the nearby piazza. Every morning, every noon, every evening, the bells of Torremaggiore rang out above the braying of donkeys bringing home the day's harvest. The Saccos were among the town's most respected citizens. Ferdinando's older brother, Sabino, later became Torremaggiore's mayor. His father, Michele, was a successful vintner who also ran an olive business, making enough to provide for seven children, "Nando" being the fourth. Unlike Vanzetti, Sacco never regretted leaving school. He enjoyed his pastoral work, but mostly he loved machines, the mesh of their gears, the whir of their motors.

In 1904, Sacco became the eldest son at home when one brother married and Sabino was drafted. Upon Sabino's return, he and Nando decided to fulfill a dream common to Italian men in the early 1900s—to go to "La Merica." "I was crazy to come to this country," Sacco testified at his trial, "because I was liked a free country." Landing in Boston in April 1908, Sabino Sacco and his sixteen-year-old brother were taken by a family friend to Milford, thirty miles southwest. Sabino got work at a foundry, where each afternoon he met his brother waiting "like a puppy" at the gates. The younger Sacco found odd jobs in construction, earning $1.75 a day. The brothers fit well within Milford's Italian community. There, on streets named Naples, Genoa, and Columbus, one could buy gelati and speak Italian all day. Yet Sabino soon tired of his dream. Nando Sacco might have gone home with his brother, but having turned eighteen—the draft age in Italy—he decided to stay in America. Weary of menial work, he forked out fifty dollars to apprentice at a shoe factory. With Massachusetts as America's leading shoe producer, Sacco had a trade for life and soon excelled at it. "Sacco was a genius at his work," a friend said. "That machine running so fast, sharp like a razor; you miss a thousandth of an inch and you ruin the shoe. He was quick, precise, a wonderful worker."

In 1912, Sacco met the two loves of his life. That winter, when textile workers stormed out of the mills in Lawrence, Massachusetts, strike fever swept through neighboring Italian communities. Something in the so-called Bread and Roses strike—perhaps the speeches of its Italian leaders Joseph Ettor and Arturo Giovannitti—moved Sacco to raise money for the strikers and later for the Ettor-Giovannitti defense fund. Their murder trial had just ended when, on Thanksgiving Day, wearing a tuxedo and sporting a full head of wavy black hair, Sacco married sixteen-year-old Rosina Zambelli, whom he had met that spring at a dance. Soon the dapper shoe trimmer with the gold front tooth and his red-haired wife were fixtures of Milford's anarchist community. "Nick and Rosie," as they were later remembered, acted in radical dramas, went to anarchist picnics, and charmed the locals. "I don't know anybody in Milford who said anything against Sacco," one longtime resident recalled. "He was a wonderful fellow, a gentleman in every sense of the word. . . . [Rosina] was small and pretty, with a little round face, rather quiet and shy. She was a doll." For the rest of his life, Sacco's two loves—anarchism and family—would compete for his loyalty.

If the political were always personal, Sacco would not have shared Vanzetti's passion for anarchism. Sacco had no personal reason to resent the American industrial system. As an edge trimmer, he was well paid and steadily employed, yet he could not ignore the struggles of fellow workers. The eight years between the Lawrence strike and Sacco's arrest saw a savage war between capital and labor. More than twenty thousand strikes kept America on the brink of violent upheaval. Outside the coal mines of Ludlow, Colorado, militia torched a strikers' tent colony and opened fire. Before the shooting stopped, seventy-four people, including women and children, were dead. The "Ludlow Massacre" was followed by others—the Everett Massacre, the Centralia Massacre—turning labor into a militant army. Workers slugged it out with police and militia, waging gun battles, fleeing vigilantes, sometimes retaliating with dynamite. Sacco marched on picket lines outside factories where he was not even employed, once getting arrested while supporting a miners' strike in Minnesota. (He was sentenced to three months, but the charge was dismissed in a higher court.) Following the IWW slogan he had learned in Lawrence—"An injury to one is an injury to all!"—Sacco took each affront to labor personally. "The nightmares of the lower classes saddened very badly your father's soul," he would write to the daughter born after his arrest. As a balm for his dream deferred, he sought a better future for the working class. He found it in the political system that shuns all systems, one whose followers called it simply "the idea." The rest of the world knew it as the terrorism of its time.

In the mid-nineteenth century, a handful of ultra-radicals turned the ancient Greek word *anarkhos*—"without a ruler"—into a philosophy. Hailing from czarist Russia and royalist France, Mikhail Bakunin and Pierre-Joseph Proudhon scoffed at the notion of a government "of the people, by the people, for the people." Their followers across Europe, where government was embodied by stodgy royal families and club-wielding cops, agreed. No government could possibly serve humanity. Instead, as Proudhon wrote, governments "watched over, inspected, spied on, directed, legislated over, regulated, docketed, indoctrined, preached at, controlled." Though its philosophical tracts were complex, the anarchist "idea" was simple, even childlike: abolish government and men would be free. Over the next fifty years, while unbridled industry divided Western societies into rich and poor, anarchism grew into a dream, a scourge, and a doctrine inspiring all the hope and zealotry of a religion.

German immigrants brought anarchism to America in the 1870s, where it acquired native martyrs. In 1886, eight anarchists were accused of bombing a rally in Chicago's Haymarket Square. On no evidence other than their writings, all were convicted and four were hanged. The legend of the Haymarket martyrs spread anarchism throughout America's grimy shacks and desperate tenements, but the dream took deepest root among Italians, whose own government had always been inefficient, oppressive, or just plain corrupt. By the 1890s, small anarchist circles flourished among Italians in Pennsylvania mining camps, New Jersey silk factories, and Massachusetts mills. In teeming lecture halls, the frock-coated Luigi Galleani and other gentlemanly anarchists spoke and sometimes sang to the disenchanted. Touring America, anarchist Pietro Gori crooned, "Eppur la nostra idea è solo idea d'amor." (And yet our idea is only the idea of love.) Sharing poetry, strumming songs, dodging cops, anarchists cultivated a romantic aura of masculinity that resonated with disillusioned Italians like a Verdi opera.

In the early 1900s, American progressives were backing modest reforms—an income tax, public utilities, a minimum wage, and an eight-hour workday. Anarchists had a more incendiary solution—abolish all laws, police, priests, and other evils Bakunin called "mankind's tormentors." Such extremism led to "what-if" questions. What if there were no government and no laws? Wouldn't chaos erupt? Anarchists answered with an unshakable faith in "the people." Left to their own devices, people would band together in "mutual aid," forming workshops, communes, and cooperatives. To the anarchist, all defects in society and human nature sprang from an oppressive class system protected by government, sanctioned by the church, enforced by militias. Eliminate the system and humanity would rise. In the *Federalist Papers*, James Madison had offered a contrasting view. "If men were angels, no government would be necessary," he wrote. Anarchists, however, claimed that if all government were taken off their backs, free men would become angels someday. Theirs was to be a society run on the honor system. To the boyish Italian cores of Sacco and Vanzetti, the idea that church and state were flawed because people were flawed seemed cynical. To their hard-edged American sides, the hope of a benevolent government seemed naïve.

Until 1901, anarchists in America were frequently harassed but rarely rounded up. Then that September, President William McKinley was gunned down by a drifter who boasted, "I killed President McKinley because I done my duty. . . . I am an anarchist." For the next two decades, anarchists were Public Enemy Number One.

Newspapers branded them "crypto-lunatics" and "wild beasts." President Theodore Roosevelt called anarchism "a crime against the whole human race." In the public mind, the anarchist was, as novelist John Dos Passos noted, a "red-handed, unwashed foreigner whom nobody could understand, sticks of dynamite in his pocket and bomb in the paper parcel under his arm."

Despite public perception, the vast majority of anarchist literature did not advocate violence. Anarchism's gentler philosophers, including Thoreau ("That government is best which governs not at all"), promoted change through long-term enlightenment. But some preferred an instant recipe for revolution, one whose main ingredient was dynamite. Even philosophical anarchists romanticized "the propaganda of the deed"—sporadic violence to shake the certainty of "the ruling class." Along with bombings, recent anarchist "deeds" included the assassinations of an Austrian empress, a Spanish premier, the king of Italy, and the president of France, and firing the bullet in the Balkans that triggered World War I. Overshadowing all the red-and-black pamphlets, all the utopian philosophy, such violence fanned fear of anyone, no matter how meek, who boasted of being an anarchist. Following McKinley's assassination, anarchist groups were outlawed. Admitted anarchists were turned back at Ellis Island, while politicians debated sending the rest to mental institutions, the Philippines, or an international penal colony.

Beneath their kindly exteriors, Sacco and Vanzetti were anarchists to the core. "Oh friend," Vanzetti wrote, "the anarchism is as beauty as a woman for me. . . . Calm, serene, honest, natural, virile, muddy and celestial at once, austere, heroic, fearless, fatal, generous and implacable—all these and more it is." For Sacco, anarchism promised a world of "no government, no police, no judges, no bosses, no authority; autonomous groups of people—the people own everything—work in cooperation—distribute by needs—equality, justice, comradeship—love each other." But how was such a paradise to be forged out of this iron world? Not by trimming edges, Sacco knew. When Luigi Galleani advocated violent overthrow of the American government, Sacco wrote him, "In whatever concerns *Cronaca Sovversiva* I am with you. Yours for the revolution." When Vanzetti wrote of throwing himself into "the grand battle that is about to break out," he was not just waxing metaphoric. Sacco and Vanzetti did not imagine themselves at the barricades, but they longed for those barricades to go up soon. For different men who had taken different paths through America, anarchism was the magnet that drew them together and the quicksand that dragged them down.

Before they met, Sacco had heard of Vanzetti. He was that fiery Plymouth anarchist whose letters to *Cronaca Sovversiva* savaged his critics: "If you don't know any better, or can't do any better, go throw yourselves in an outhouse!" And Vanzetti may have read of a Ferdinando Sacco, whose infant daughter, *Cronaca* lamented, had died suddenly, "as if she did not care for this wretched world dripping in blood and degradation." The two men finally met at an anarchist gathering shortly after America's entry into the Great War triggered their own war on America. Within a week, they were boarding a train taking them toward their dream.

By June 1917, Sacco and Vanzetti had been in America for nearly a decade, yet they had seen little of the nation beyond its grinding labor. Suddenly they found themselves rolling across Pennsylvania, Ohio, Michigan, gawking at America's openness and promise, staring into its heartland, riding deeper into the country where workers would later shout their names. The train took them west through Cleveland and Detroit, then south past St. Louis and San Antonio. They had fled Boston on marching orders from their "master." With America suddenly at war, ten million men were registering for the draft. Few anarchists were among them. Galleani had told his minions not to join ranks with the "soldier who prostitutes himself, the voter who sells out, the servant who adores his chains and kisses the hand that whips him." Failure to register meant a year in jail, so Sacco bid a sad good-bye to Dante and Rosina, Vanzetti left the Brinis and his "spiritual son," and after a long train ride chattering in Italian about anarchy, Italy, and other passions, they reached Laredo, Texas. Crossing the border, they made their way to Monterrey, Mexico, to join sixty other *Galleanisti* living in adobe huts. They did not expect to stay long. The czar of Russia had fallen, and in the power vacuum, anarchism stood a chance of sweeping across war-torn Europe. Sacco, Vanzetti, and their friends expected to head on to Italy to spread their creed. While revolution brewed, however, they had to survive a scorching summer.

"I cannot describe how Mexico punishes a man," Vanzetti wrote home to Villafalletto that July. Working in a bakery, he brought bread to the group, but his new friends, unable to find jobs, lived on dwindling savings. News from America set them to seething at the repression the war had unleashed. Radicals were being rounded up, lynched, run out of town on a rail. Luigi Galleani had been arrested, and the American Sacco and Vanzetti most admired—Socialist Eugene Debs—was just one of hundreds jailed for speaking out against the war. All through the blistering Mexican summer, the future Anarchist Fighters holed up in bungalows, sweating, starving, and swearing allegiance to their cause. Among them were Carlo Valdinoci, whose wavy hair would later be found on a roof in a bombed-out neighborhood in Washington, D.C.; the saboteur Mario Buda, who would be with Sacco and Vanzetti on the night of their arrest; and Amletto Fabbri, who would later serve on the Sacco-Vanzetti Defense Committee. Mexico's miserable July gave way to a torrid August, but still they dared not return to a flag-waving America where being a "slacker" was tantamount to treason.

While Vanzetti was in Mexico, federal agents visited the Brini home in Plymouth. Scouring the house for traces of a draft dodger, they came within seconds of finding a letter with a Mexican return address. Twelve-year-old Lefevre Brini spotted the letter on a kitchen shelf and hid it in her blouse. The exiles remained hidden, their hardships infusing them with a lockstep loyalty. In September, when revolution failed to spread beyond Russia, letters told them they could safely return to America and the group dissolved. One by one, its members crossed the border, going separate ways with a common purpose—revenge. Within months, mysterious bombings—in Milwaukee, in Philadelphia, in a mill town near Boston—targeted police, politicians, and others who had fired, arrested, or deported anarchists.

Returning to the Boston area, Sacco found Dante and Rosina living in Cambridge. "I leave my wife here and my boy," he later testified. "I could not stay no more far away from them." For the next few months he worked under his Mexican alias, Nicola Mosmacotelli, taken from his mother's maiden name. He later reclaimed his original surname but remained "Nicola" in honor of a recently deceased brother. The skilled edge trimmer was now forced to take odd jobs. He wielded a pick and shovel, and worked in a candy factory and briefly at the Rice & Hutchins shoe plant in Braintree. Fired from one job when he refused to buy a Liberty bond, he fled others when draft inspectors came into factories searching for slackers. Finally, he found steady work with the Three-K Shoe Company in Stoughton.

Vanzetti made a more circuitous return. Stopping in Youngstown, Ohio, he worked in a steel mill, "a volcano erupting day and night." He spent his spare time reading, but according to one anarchist, Vanzetti also placed a homemade bomb in a church. Sniffed out by a dog, the bomb was defused, so this lone source claimed. While Vanzetti was in Youngstown, federal agents raided the offices of *Cronaca Sovversiva,* finding a photo of him with Luigi Galleani. Agents also seized subscription lists that landed "Ferdinando Sacco" and "Bartolomeo Vanzetti" on a watch list of radicals. After ten months in Youngstown, Vanzetti returned to Plymouth. He and Sacco had reached the last homes they would have before entering a purgatory of police stations, courtrooms, and jails. But both men had changed since leaving home. Before the war, they had been revolutionaries in their own minds, content to live on the hope of the anarchists' utopia. Mexico was their crucible. Tempered there by heat, hunger, and their comrades' militancy, both men had come home as fierce revolutionaries. Back in Plymouth, Vanzetti vented his rage in a letter to his aunt:

> I have seen human greed and egotism poison every mouthful of food, make the springs sad, darken the glory of the sun, violate natural law, incite delinquency, nurture corruption, plant hatred and condemn a large part of humanity to every kind of calamity, every kind of shame, every kind of misery. All this I have seen and learned, and because of this spectacle . . . I am no longer the smart aleck little boy. I am a taciturn man of iron who sees all the brutality, all the injustice, a man who fights with all his energy against the present society of wolves and lambs, ready to throw himself without any qualms or uncertainty, into the grand battle that is about to break out.

In the pro-patria mood of wartime America, friends warned against any mention of radicalism. "Stop talking, Nick, till this time of anti-radical excitement is passed," Sacco's boss told him. Placing one hand on his chest, Sacco responded, "It is my heart that talks." Their hearts inspired them to more than talk, however. Both men watched as their comrades' bombs blew off a maid's hands, shattered homes, and targeted the icons of American capitalism. Along with their fellow Anarchist Fighters, Sacco and Vanzetti kept a low profile throughout the Palmer Raids, peddling fish and tending a garden, but they had soured on the dream that had sent them to America. That dream had exacted an exorbitant price. Born into a land of vineyards and horse-drawn carts, they now lived in a land of tenements and factories. From a country where workers argued endlessly about politics—Socialism, anarchism, fascism—they had come to a country where workers were expected to shut up and work. Raised in a boisterous culture of shouts and gestures, they were baffled by staid, stiff-upper-lip New England. They still dreamt, but now their dreams were set in some future paradise or back in the land of their birth. Paradise was inaccessible, but they might have made it back to Italy. They might have slipped out of the closing net, booking passage on a steamer. They might have remained "anonymous in the anonymous crowd," but on April 15, 1920, two Italians stood leaning on a fence with guns in their pockets. One of them bore a striking resemblance to Nicola Sacco.

CHAPTER TWO

"A Gunman Job"

*I shall enter on no encomium upon Massachusetts; she
needs none. There she is. Behold her, and judge for yourselves. There is her history; the world knows it by heart.
The past, at least, is secure.*

—Daniel Webster

On April 15, 1920, Braintree, Massachusetts, was still living
with one foot in the nineteenth century. One of a dozen industrial villages stamped into the wooded scenery south of Boston,
Braintree was a place where everyone claimed to know everyone
else, even though the town had thirteen thousand residents. Tracing its heritage to its founding in 1640, Braintree saw itself in sepia
tones—a hometown, a quiet town, a town far removed from the
mayhem of modernity. The smokestacks of shoe factories dominated a low skyline. Six mornings a week, start-up whistles sent
throngs marching along gravel streets and into faded four-story
brick buildings in South Braintree. At 5:00 p.m. each weekday, at
noon each Saturday, whistles reversed the parade. Downtown on
Washington Street, Model Ts rattled past three-story façades, but
only merchants, doctors, and the men who owned or ran the factories drove them. Most people walked or took trolleys. Quaint and
quiet, Braintree still had a horse-drawn carriage pick up factory

payrolls each Thursday morning when the 9:18 train arrived from Boston. And although there had been a rash of recent robberies, Braintree was still innocent enough to have that $30,000 payroll delivered in cash.

Hefting a steel strongbox from the train to his wagon, American Express clerk Shelley Neal was the first to spot the two strangers. Languishing in a doorway, one was slim, with light hair and pale blue eyes, which he averted as Neal approached. The stranger wore a gray felt hat and a dark overcoat buttoned to the collar. With sunken cheeks and sallow complexion, the man struck Neal as "a tubercular patient." The other stranger, behind the wheel of a sleek car idling near the station, sat with his back to Neal. The clerk, toting $30,000 in cash, sensed trouble. Passing the men, he entered an office to deliver one shoe company's payroll, then came back onto Railroad Avenue. For the first time, Neal noticed a second car across the street, dusty and not so elegant. Suddenly its driver called out, "All right!" No one moved. Neal patted the .38 in his overcoat and walked on, taking the rest of the payroll to the second-floor office of the Slater & Morrill Shoe Company. "Some funny looking people round here today," he said to the woman at the desk. And in a town where everyone claimed to know everyone else, others soon noticed the funny-looking people and their fancy car.

The car was dark blue and shiny, as if just washed and waxed. Boxy yet stylish, with a powerful six-cylinder engine and huge, owlish headlights, it was known on the street as a "Buick Baby Six." The car's elegance—spoke wheels, abundant chrome, a canopy draped by curtains—stood out in a neighborhood of factories and vacant lots, with its rickety water tower propped on wooden legs. Though the Buick looked brand-new, several times throughout the morning its hood was up and one man was seen tinkering with the engine. The other man just stood, glancing down the street as if someone were watching. The two were watched all over the sleepy town that day. Just before the noon whistle, they were seen downtown in front of Torrey's Drugstore. After lunch, they were spotted at the train station, smoking and speaking "a foreign language" that identified them as "Dagos." At 2:15 p.m., they frightened tellers at the Braintree National Bank while changing a ten-dollar bill. "They had that character you could pick out in a thousand," a teller remembered. Back on the street, they stared down one worker until he shouted, "I don't think I owe you fellows anything!" The strangers moved on.

By midafternoon, all was quiet in South Braintree. At 2:45, paymaster Frederick Parmenter, and his guard, Alessandro Berardelli, entered the Slater & Morrill office on Railroad Avenue to pick up five hundred pay envelopes containing $15,776.51. Around the corner on Pearl Street, the two strangers leaned against a fence. Across the street, near a team of laborers digging a foundation, a third man holding a rifle crouched by a pile of bricks. Seventy-five yards down the block in the shadows of the Rice & Hutchins factory, the Buick stood idling. Inside, hundreds worked at their machines. It was a clear, crisp April day. That much everyone later agreed on. The rest was soon refracted through the looking glass of memory.

Parmenter and Berardelli had just finished flirting with "the girls" in the Slater & Morrill office. On most Thursday afternoons, the guards drove the payroll from the office to the factory, but Mr. Slater's car was still being gassed up. "Go ahead, never mind the car," Slater told Parmenter, and the two men set out on foot. Walking down creaking stairs, they reached Railroad Avenue at about 3:00 p.m. Each carried a heavy steel box, shifting it from one arm to the other. They passed the Muriel Cigar sign on the corner and turned left onto Pearl Street. Many eyes followed them from factory windows. The weekly pay, known as "the roll," was on the way, watched, tracked, anticipated step by step. At the foot of the wooden water tower, Parmenter and Berardelli stopped to relay a message to mechanic Jimmy Bostock as he approached.

"Bostock, when you go up by," the short, sturdy Parmenter said, "you go into the other factory and fix the pulley on the motor." Telling the paymaster he'd get to it later, the mechanic turned toward the tracks, leaving Parmenter and Berardelli heading east on Pearl. The afternoon sun was warm. Lilacs bloomed on a triangle of grass near the strangers leaning on the fence up ahead.

Parmenter, slightly in front of his guard, walked out of the factory's shade toward the men. Then, just as Berardelli came into the light, one of the strangers uncoiled like a snake. Seconds suddenly slowed into what seemed like minutes. Down the block a woman looked out her front window. In the excavation across the street, men turned and dropped their shovels. Jimmy Bostock whirled. It took a moment for the danger to register. One man thought a gang of boys was scuffling in the street. Then the afternoon was shattered. To some the shots suggested a car backfiring, to others a string of firecrackers. Pigeons erupted from sills overhead. Factory windows flew open. Sharp cracks echoed off brick walls, doubling the number of shots people heard. Berardelli, his white shirt now a spreading scarlet, staggered into the street. Parmenter wheeled. Hit in the chest, the paymaster stumbled, struggling to hold the cashbox. He tried to run but, shot again, slowly sank to the street. Jimmy Bostock started toward Parmenter, but two shots sent him scrambling for cover.

For an instant, both cashboxes lay on the street. Then the man in the felt hat grabbed one. Berardelli flailed in the gutter, trying to reach the other. The man in the cap got it first, then stood and waved his pistol overhead. From down the street, kicking up dust, came the big, boxy Buick. Its engine misfiring, the car picked up speed as it emerged from the shadows and into the diamond glint of the sun. Berardelli struggled to his knees, but a gunman hovered over him, pumping bullets into his body. Sprawled on his side, the guard teetered for a few seconds, then flopped on his back in the gravel. The Buick slowed. The gunmen piled in. One hung out the passenger side, firing at random. In upper factory windows, workers ducked. Several women fainted.

With its engine still misfiring, the Buick headed up the slight slope leading to the railroad tracks. At the crossing, a dapper teenager in a derby and dark coat was leaning on crutches and washing the windows of his gatekeeper's shed. When a bell signaled the arrival of the 3:15 train, he hobbled on his one leg to the crank and lowered the gates, blocking the street. Just then, the Buick reached the crossing.

"Put them up!" the gunman shouted, taking dead aim at the gate-keeper. "Put them up or we will put a hole through you!" The gates rose, but the bandit fired anyway. The bullet whistled past the shed and the Buick rumbled across the tracks, its curtains flapping and a gun barrel protruding from the rear window.

At the corner of Railroad Avenue, the car passed a traveling salesman, his sample case in hand. "Get out of the way, you son of a bitch!" the gunman shouted, firing again. The Buick raced down Pearl Street, past a cobbler shop, a poolroom, and a barber's slowly spiraling pole. Making a left turn so tight it almost flipped, the car righted itself and sputtered on. A scattering of tacks came flying out the back, landing points up on the gravel as the Buick disappeared. Seconds later a crowd rushed onto Pearl Street.

It had all been over in a minute. One crime had been committed. One car had picked up the bandits. One bandit had fired from its passenger seat. But as the crowd began to babble, a kaleidoscope of impressions swirled around the scene. More than fifty people had witnessed the robbery and murder. A handful now swore they had seen everything—the men, their faces, their clothes, the guns, the shooting. "I seen a glance of the whole thing," one man later said. Others shook their heads and said they had seen nothing, at least not enough to identify anyone. The crowd mingled, mixing certainty and doubt until there were as many versions of the one-minute crime as there were people who had seen everything. And nothing.

A circle of faces huddled around each victim. Beneath a pastel blue sky, dozens looked on as Alessandro Berardelli, his lips bubbling with blood, died in Jimmy Bostock's arms. A few yards away, Frederick Parmenter lay in his own crush of anxious onlookers. A blanket was placed under the paymaster's head and another over his body as he was lugged to a house down the street. By the time an ambulance took Parmenter away, police were arriving to investigate the most horrifying crime ever perpetrated in their quaint city.

Braintree had just one full-time policeman and no police station. Chief Jeremiah Gallivan and three part-time officers worked out of the chief's home. On most spring afternoons, the chief could be found on the steps of town hall chewing tobacco and spitting juice on the sidewalk. Gallivan had repeatedly requested full-time officers; repeatedly he had been refused. Instead, some four hundred citizens had been deputized with officers' badges. At about 3:15 p.m., American Express clerk Shelley Neal came striding onto the scene with his badge pinned on his coat. Neal was elbowing through the crowd when Chief Gallivan pulled up in the city's only patrol car.

The chief found witnesses of little use. There had been two gunmen. No, three. They had been light-haired. No, they were dark, swarthy men. They wore caps. Hats. Their heads were bare. They wore blue suits. Gray suits. Dark suits. The car had been shiny. No, it was dusty. One thing everyone agreed on, pointing west down Pearl Street. Within minutes, the city's red fire engine, its bell clanging, set out in pursuit. Chief Gallivan and fire chief Fred Tenny turned left onto Washington Street, stopped to whisk away tacks, then raced through downtown. Pausing to ask onlookers if they had seen a dark Buick race by, they continued south to the one-steeple town of Holbrook. There a soldier said he had seen the car ten minutes earlier. The chiefs sped on but soon entered New England's labyrinth of wooded two-lane roads where they lost all trace of the bandits. Back in Braintree, Chief Gallivan could only gather the tacks off Washington Street. He kept them for a while, then gave them away as souvenirs.

The Buick, meanwhile, had taken a sharp turn just south of Braintree, then made several harelike evasions. While the fire engine headed southeast, the gunmen barreled due south through Stoughton, passing less than a mile from Sacco's bungalow, tearing along at forty miles per hour and kicking up dust. Several people—a farmer and his wife, a road crew, a high school girl, two men driving a horse-drawn wagon—saw the Buick race past. One witness heard men in the car "laughing and talking some foreign gibberish."

The car was last seen at a railroad crossing seventeen miles south of the crime scene. At 4:15, crossing guard Austin Reed spotted the Buick headed his way. As it approached, a locomotive came down the tracks carved through the woods. Seeing the huge black steam engine belching smoke, Reed lifted his hand-held stop sign, but the oncoming car did not slow. Alarmed, Reed stepped into the middle of the road, frantically waving. The car shuddered to a halt. From across the tracks, the man in the shotgun seat shouted, "What the hell are you holding us up for?" After the train roared by, the car rumbled over the tracks. Again the man barked, "What the hell are you holding us up for?" As the car passed, Reed memorized the face of "a dark complected man, kind of hollow cheeks, with high cheekbones, [and] a stubbed mustache." A few minutes later, the car came back down a parallel fork, passing Reed one final time. Then with its curtains flapping, the Buick grew smaller on the horizon but larger in local lore as it disappeared toward the Rhode Island line. With it went the last vestiges of New England's innocence.

In 1920, a New Englander did not have to be especially old to recall the gentle ease of the nineteenth century. Parents often waxed nostalgic about horse-drawn buggies, bicycles built for two, and lazy lemonade afternoons. Grandparents spoke from memory of the Civil War, and some remembered their own grandparents telling of childhoods back when one could still see crusty old John Adams on the streets of Quincy. Evoked with what Abraham Lincoln called "the mystic chords of memory," America seemed so ingenuous then. The only bombs exploded on battlefields; the only shoot-outs were out West. By contrast, this delinquent twentieth century— already host to history's worst war and deadliest plague—seemed headed for trouble. Perhaps the future promised more leisure, yet if men could be gunned down in a small town just south of Boston, who knew what chaos was to come? Was this still (ahem!) the Commonwealth?

From the beige dunes of its shoreline to the white steeples of its postcard villages, Massachusetts in 1920 was suffused with its own significance. Massachusetts was where America had begun, home to Bunker Hill, the Boston Tea Party, and the Puritans whose blue laws still kept every store locked tight on Sundays. While the rest of America faced forward, Massachusetts lived on in the past tense, venerating its antiquity. Here one could visit the Old North Church, Old Ironsides, the Old State House, the Old South Meeting House, and Old North Bridge. Scattered across Massachusetts were old graveyards whose tilted black gravestones dated to the 1600s. Known as "the Bay State," Massachusetts was no mere state. It was a *Commonwealth,* the very name suggesting concern for the "common welfare."

At the heart of the "Old Commonwealth" sat its capital. Often called "the cradle of liberty," Boston had other nicknames. Its magnificent colonial architecture made it "the Athens of America," while Bostonians, as if they lived at the center of the universe and not the commercial center of a small state, called their city "the Hub." Yet in 1920, neither Boston nor Massachusetts was as small as it seemed. Boston was America's fifth largest city, while Massachusetts had more people than Florida, Michigan, even California. The old Commonwealth also contained more self-importance than any region on earth.

Massachusetts industries led the nation, their "Yankee ingenuity" pumping out a sizable portion of America's shoes, textiles, and machinery. But the Commonwealth's chief product was pride. Pride was served with tea on Paul Revere silver sets in Beacon Hill manors. Pride shone from Boston's State House, its gold dome visible all over the Hub. Pride powered Yankee farmers plowing the same land their grandfathers and great-grandfathers had plowed. Pride poured forth each Patriots' Day, when citizens reenacted the battles of Lexington and Concord, and each June 17, when a hundred thousand commemorated the battle of Bunker Hill. Throughout the year, pride saturated Boston's "First Families"—the Adamses, the Lowells, the Cabots, the Forbeses. And with pride came a ramrod-stiff morality. "We are moral over the breakfast table and moral the last thing at night and moral all the hours between," wrote one Cabot in her diary.

Pride and morality gave Boston another nickname—"Cold Roast Boston"—a city the journalist Walter Lippmann called "the most homogeneous, self-centered, and self-complacent community in the United States." Citizens of Massachusetts might be convinced of a fault or two in their Commonwealth, but such convincing had to be done by other citizens of Massachusetts. The slightest critique from "outsiders" aroused a fierce backlash and the highest of dudgeon. As one Harvard historian noted, "Nothing is clearer in Massachusetts history than the sense, which has not entirely disappeared, that the descendants of the original Massachusetts stock were the Lord's anointed."

Industry bankrolled Massachusetts, and the men who bankrolled the industries powered state politics. These men championed a "stand pat" Republicanism. Between the Civil War and World War I, the Commonwealth never elected a single Democratic senator nor gave a majority of votes to a Democratic presidential candidate. Secure in the bedrock of their Republican politics, citizens of Massachusetts agreed with Daniel Webster: "The past, at least, is secure." But the future?

If the Commonwealth in 1920 could have been reduced in microcosm to its most familiar tableau—the Thanksgiving dinner—the majority of the guests would have been unwelcome. The faces had begun changing in the 1850s when Irish immigrants poured into Boston, followed by Germans, French Canadians, Italians, and a human tide of others. Nearly two million immigrants came to Massachusetts between 1880 and World War I. Throughout the influx, embattled Yankees kept a tight hold on their WASP heritage through a network of exclusive private schools, private colleges, and private clubs. But by 1920, the Commonwealth surrounding these islands was not white, Anglo-Saxon, or Protestant. Instead, it was the most ethnically diverse region of America. Seated at the Thanksgiving table were Greeks, Poles, Russians, Syrians, Armenians, Portuguese. Each group had its own enclave teeming with the language and customs of the land left behind. Few ventured out of these neighborhoods without being stamped as Micks, Kikes, Huns, Polacks, and so on. The Thanksgiving feast still had enough turkey, but guests were bickering and hosts were rescinding their invitations. "We are vanishing into provincial obscurity," another Harvard historian wrote of his Yankee peers. "America has swept from our grasp. The future is behind us."

The tension at the table was most visible in Boston's North End. Once an Irish haven, by 1910 the district teemed with Italians. To "Cold Roast Boston," the Italians, a.k.a. "Guineas," "Wops," and "Dagos," seemed strangely passionate people. They drank odd beverages like Chianti and dined not on meat and potatoes but on an utterly alien dish called "spaghetti." "The Italian experiences no difficulty whatever in eating this slippery food," one observer noted, "for he merely sucks it into his mouth from his fork in a very unconventional if not elegant manner." But worse than their drink or diet was the Italian propensity for crime.

The twentieth century was brand-new when many Americans learned their first word in Italian—"Mafia." In big cities, granite quarries, mining camps, wherever Italians toiled, stories circulated about a criminal society known as "the Black Hand." "This aggregation of assassins, blackmailers, and thieves have piled up a record of crime in the United States unparalleled in the history of a civilized country," wrote the *Outlook* in 1909. The stereotype was not without roots. Hundreds of unsolved murders, with most victims being Italian immigrants, marred police blotters in cities along the eastern seaboard. Most Italians worked too hard to have time for criminal activity, yet the Mafia stereotype penetrated American society.

With the Italian influx, the Commonwealth that had pioneered abolitionism jump-started another nationwide movement—anti-immigration. The Immigration Restriction League was founded in "the Athens of America" in 1894. Its staunchest ally was Massachusetts senator Henry Cabot Lodge. As a young congressman, Lodge had been appalled when eleven Italians, acquitted of murdering New Orleans's police chief, were lynched. Many blamed the lynch mob or the Italians, but Lodge had a different take. "The underlying cause . . . is to be found in the utter carelessness with which we treat immigration in this country. If we permit the classes which furnish material for these [secret] societies to come freely to this country, we shall have these outrages to deal with." On into the 1920s, Lodge would lobby Congress to close America's doors to "inferior stocks."

Clinging to its embattled pride and its venerated past, Massachusetts festered throughout the 1900s and 1910s. Wary of change, immune to criticism, longing for its genteel Victorian or even colonial heyday, the old Commonwealth feared that modern morals would lead to further outrages such as the murders in Braintree. In the wake of the crime, the entire state shared the sentiments of the *Braintree Observer*—America had to "stand firm and stamp out lawlessness and terrorism." Pride demanded that the murderers be held up as an example, and once two men were, pride would play as big a role as any prosecutor in sealing their fate. But first they had to be caught.

Sacco did not work on April 15. He had asked his boss for the morning off to go to Boston and get his passport. Back on the job the next day, he read about the Braintree murders in the *Boston Post*. He had a vague familiarity with Braintree, having worked briefly at Rice & Hutchins, the factory that shadowed the murder scene. He might have known some of the workers who poured onto Pearl Street after the shootings. His face might have looked familiar to them. On April 16, he discussed the crime with his fellow workers. All the next week, he worked his regular hours. One day that week, he came home from work to find another mournful letter from his father.

> Dear Son,
> I know very well that because of the receipt of news of your mother's death you are very grieved. But I pray you not to forget to come back, as you have promised that you will be back by May. We are desirous to see you. Just think how anxious we are of seeing you, after

having a son away 11 years. What you must do is to embark the moment you receive this letter. . . . A thousand kisses from me to you and your wife and son.

Your father,
Michele Sacco

Vanzetti peddled fish on April 15, at least according to his later testimony. It was his last day on his route. The spring catch out of Boston was slight, and fish prices had soared, eating up his profits. The day after the crime, he dug for clams, but this too yielded little profit. He looked for construction work, only to be thwarted by a cement shortage. Idled by the economy, he read more than usual and spent entire days with friends. If either Sacco or Vanzetti had any reason to flee the area, neither made any moves to do so. And neither was aware of the trap that was being set for them.

On the evening of the murders, police released descriptions of five suspects. The driver was said to be twenty-five to twenty-eight years old, of medium complexion, with a smooth face, deep dimples, and light hair. A second suspect was about twenty-two, five feet five, 120 pounds, clean-shaven with light hair and a pale, soft hat. Two more were listed as twenty-nine, five feet nine, of medium build. The gang's leader was described as a young foreigner, about twenty.

While this bulletin went out, doctors struggled to save Frederick Parmenter. Cutting through the paymaster's abdomen, a surgeon removed a .32 slug. Another bullet was found on the operating room floor. Toward midnight, Parmenter awoke from the ether. Asked about the gunmen, the paymaster weakly said he had not seen them. It had all happened so quickly. Five hours later, Parmenter died, leaving a wife, a ten-year-old son, and a four-year-old daughter. That Sunday, his death claimed one more casualty when, hours before the funeral, Parmenter's father died of what doctors called "a broken heart." Berardelli's body, meanwhile, had been removed to a local funeral home. Sarah Berardelli, who had been stitching shoe linings in the Slater & Morrill factory when her husband was gunned down outside, was haunted by his actions in the days before his death. "About a week before the shooting, my husband became very nervous and talked a great deal about some bad men around the factory," she told police. "He said they looked bad and he didn't like their actions."

By the time Parmenter died, police were patrolling crossroads throughout Norfolk County. No fancy Buicks were seen, no suspects apprehended. Aside from a handful of shells found on Pearl Street and six bullets extracted from the victims, all that remained of the crime were rumors. Parmenter must have known the bandits; that explained why they were so determined to finish him off! Berardelli had actually gotten off several shots! There were two getaway cars! At the Slater & Morrill factory, bookkeeper Mary Splaine gossiped that a clerk in the order department had masterminded the murder to get rid of Parmenter, whom he feared would take his job. But Pinkerton detectives, learning that Splaine's boss considered her "one of the most irresponsible persons he ever came in contact with," looked elsewhere. All that Friday, volunteers combed nearby woods searching for the car or other clues. That evening, a flop-eared cap was found on Pearl Street. It was given to Chief Gallivan, who, thinking it unimportant, kept it in the back of his car for two weeks.

On Saturday, April 17, a stream of out-of-towners came to Braintree, drawn by front-page news of the crime. Cars and pedestrians toured the scene of the "cold blooded shootings." They stopped at the spot where "Berardelli fell at the first shot," then eyed the gravel where bandits had "closed in on Parmenter." Some stared at factory walls pockmarked by the "fusillade of bullets." Many walked to the railroad shed to hear the gatekeeper boast of how he had narrowly dodged the gunman's bullet.

That same morning, a police inquest was held in Quincy. Twenty-six witnesses described the driver, the car, and the man firing from the passenger seat. A dozen miles south in the big city of Brockton, witnesses at the police station flipped through mug shots of possible suspects. Four people singled out Anthony Palmisano, a.k.a. "Baby Tony" or "Tony the Wop." All four were sure the notorious bank robber had been one of the gunmen. Searching for Palmisano, state

police sent a detective to New York, but his telegram soon halted
the investigation: PALMISANO NOW IN AUBURN PRISON SERVING
SEVEN TO TEN YEARS—HAVE VERIFIED BY TELEPHONE WITH
PRISON.

Despite this false lead, descriptions at the inquest were more
helpful than those at the scene of the crime. One gunman was described as "a short stout fellow," "terribly white," "about my build,
medium." The driver was "a pale fellow, sickly looking," with "a
dark complexion, dark brown mustache," who "may have been
American, may have been Swedish." A few were certain they could
identify the men if they saw them again. "The way they looked at
me was enough," said one man. But most were not so sure. The
shootings had happened like lightning—"only three or four seconds and it was all done." Besides, the sun had glinted through
dirty factory windows, the car was shrouded in curtains, and recognizing the killers based on a glance was "a pretty hard thing to
do." "I don't think I could," one man told police. "Two minutes
after, I was talking with another fellow out there . . . that was in
the window, and he says one thing and I another." Almost everyone agreed on the car, however. Several had gotten the Buick's license number—49783—but the "murder car" was still missing.
Then that Saturday afternoon, two men on horseback set out for a
ride in the woods just down the road from Braintree.

Through a tangle of budding branches, the men spotted the an-
gular outline of an automobile. They rode off to call police, who
came on the run. Everything about the vehicle checked out. A dark
blue Buick touring car. Dusty. Flapping curtain on the passenger
side. Missing rear window, but wait—here was the plate glass torn
from the leather canopy and tossed on the floor. And where the license plate should have been was a dark rectangle, free of dust. The
license had been removed, undoubtedly when the gang switched to
another car, one that made those thinner tire tracks on the forest
floor leading back to the highway. Inside the Buick, police found a
tattered coat, a fur robe, and sixty-two cents in change. Speculation
ran rampant. The bandits had planned the whole job perfectly, cops
said. Taking back routes to avoid being seen, they had ditched the

Buick in the woods, hopped into the second car seen in Braintree the morning of the crime, then gone on toward Rhode Island. Back on Pearl Street, a man found shards of a bottle thought to have contained "dope," leading state police to suspect the getaway driver was "a drug fiend." Bridgewater police chief Michael Stewart said, "The men who did this job knew no God."

When the murder car was driven to Boston, police checked the engine number, learning that the vehicle had been stolen the previous Thanksgiving. State police remained in Providence asking questions about "Ritzy" cars and lavish sums of money spent suddenly. Then on Patriots' Day, word leaked out that one police chief was pursuing a lead closer to home.

Tough, righteous, and self-confident, Michael Stewart was the very model of a small-town Massachusetts police chief. A former amateur boxer with a ruddy complexion and wild shock of dark hair, Stewart was the son of an Irish immigrant who had toiled in shoe factories. Growing up in the Boston area, he had absorbed all its pride and many of its stereotypes. Bridgewater's chief was a fundamentally fair man, not inclined to act on prejudice, yet neither was he immune to the fact that recent immigrants—Russians, Poles, Italians—committed a majority of the crimes on his beat. In his nine years in law enforcement, the middle-aged, cigar-chomping cop had seen plenty of robbery and assault, but the slaying of two men in broad daylight was something new. Even if the murders had not been in his town, the chief was both appalled and fascinated. Stewart did not bring a degree in criminology or in anything else to his job, but he was proud of helping federal agents round up six actual Reds in Bridgewater during the Palmer Raids. He knew he had not been hired to let gangs of thugs shake the certainty of the Commonwealth. The men "who knew no God" had to be found. Fortunately for the chief, the Braintree murders resembled another shocking holdup in his own town.

The previous Christmas Eve, a payroll had been bound for the L. Q. White Shoe Company in Bridgewater. In the crisp sunlight shortly after dawn, three men jumped out of a car and jogged toward the delivery truck. Toting a shotgun, the leader opened fire.

The truck careened out of control and smashed into a telephone pole. Before the bandits could pounce on it, a passing streetcar cut them off. In the confusion, they fled in a car witnesses identified as a Hudson. No one was hurt, and the payroll—more than $33,000—was untouched. Pinkerton detectives hired that morning heard from witnesses that the holdup men were Polish, Russian, or any of several other nationalities. The man with the shotgun was described as "5'8", 150 pounds, dark complexion, 40 years of age . . . [with] a closely cropped mustache which might have been slightly gray."

While the Pinkertons did their work, Bridgewater's chief conducted his own investigation. At first, Stewart suspected a roving gang of "Reds and Bolsheviks," but now he steered the case in a direction he would be forced to defend for the rest of his life. Learning that a Buick touring car had been stolen a month earlier, Stewart began searching for it and not a Hudson. A tip soon sent the chief looking for a house in the woods occupied by Italian anarchists said to be tied to the holdup. After a few frustrating weeks, finding no car, no house in the woods, no anarchists, Stewart tabled his investigation. Months passed. On the day after the Braintree murders, a phone call set the chief to thinking.

The call had come unexpectedly. The Bureau of Immigration in Boston wanted Stewart to find Ferruccio Coacci. The name sounded familiar. Back in 1918, the chief had arrested Coacci following a raid on *Cronaca Sovversiva*. Stewart assumed the anarchist had since been deported, yet Coacci, released on bail, had quietly moved back to Bridgewater, where he had since worked at both L. Q. White in Bridgewater *and* at Slater & Morrill in Braintree. He had recently quit the latter job. Scheduled to surrender himself for deportation on April 15, Coacci had not appeared. The following day he had called the Bureau of Immigration, explaining that his wife was sick. At the bureau's request, Stewart sent his lone officer along with a federal inspector to find Coacci. They traced him to a ramshackle two-story shack beneath a twisted old maple tree in West Bridgewater. Everyone in that part of town called the shack Puffer's Place. A bunch of Italians lived there,

though no one knew what any of them did for a living. Since Prohibition, bootlegging had been suspected.

On Friday evening, April 16, police found Coacci packing his
bags for Italy. His wife did not seem sick. "There is nothing the
matter with her," Stewart's deputy told him. "She was sitting in
the kitchen talking to Coacci." Stranger still was the Italian's response when told his deportation could be postponed. Coacci insisted on leaving right away, the deputy said. That evening. He was
led down the steps of Puffer's Place while his wife and children
stood in the doorway crying. Back at the Bridgewater station,
Chief Stewart pondered the sudden twist. "Something hit me," he
said years later. "The dates involved, the fifteenth deadline for
Coacci's bond, the holdup and the phony illness." Stewart spent
the weekend connecting the dots. Bridgewater. Braintree. Another
"Ritzy" getaway car, this one abandoned not a mile from Puffer's
Place. An anarchist working at both targeted factories, failing to
show in Boston on the day of the second heist, now suddenly in a
hurry to leave the country. By Monday, Stewart was certain the
Braintree bandits were not spending their loot in Providence. They
were right in his small town. Announcing this new twist, the *Boston Globe* predicted, "It would not be surprising if an arrest were
made within a very short time."

The following Tuesday, April 20, Stewart and a state inspector
headed for Puffer's Place. Dressed in plain clothes, they knocked at
the shack in the shade of the maple. Opening the door was a short,
balding man with a trim mustache, greenish eyes, and a bulbous
nose that made him look like a clown without makeup. Mysterious,
elusive, and as deadly as dynamite, this was Mario Buda. At least,
that had been his name when he was with Sacco and Vanzetti in
Mexico. He now gave his name as Mike Boda. The chief introduced
himself as a Bureau of Immigration agent. He and his partner had
come to get a photo of Coacci. Buda, or Boda, was a seasoned dy-
namiter with plenty to hide, but he let the visitors in and talked
freely. Coacci's friends, he said, were "bad people, what you call
anarchists." He didn't have much to do with them. Yes, Coacci
owned a gun, kept right there in the kitchen drawer. Stewart found

no gun, just a diagram of a Savage automatic, but Boda eagerly showed the men his own revolver. After wandering the cluttered house, the trio went out back to a shed where Boda kept his car. The vehicle was in the shop, the little man said. When Stewart asked to look inside the shed, Boda opened a sliding door to reveal something even more suspicious. Boda said his "machine" was a 1914 Overland, a five-passenger touring car with a crank starter and skinny spoke wheels. Yet beside the planks where the Overland had been parked were wide tire tracks about the thickness of a Buick's Royal Cord tires. The floor had been "carefully raked over, having the appearance of a newly made lawn," Stewart remembered. Asked about the second set of tracks, Boda said he sometimes drove his car in straight, sometimes at an angle. After final words, the chief left.

Stewart later regretted not arresting the small man with the big nose. He would not get another chance. The next morning, when the chief returned to Puffer's Place, Boda saw him coming and hustled out the back door, leaving his breakfast on the table. On Thursday evening, Stewart paid one last visit. Through the window, his flashlight beam fell on empty tin cans littering empty rooms. Puffer's Place had been cleared out. The chief then drove to the Elm Square Garage, where the shifty Italian said his Overland had been towed. Finding the car still there, Stewart told the mechanic, Simon Johnson, to stall anyone who might come for it until police could get there. The trapdoor that would send Sacco and Vanzetti into their long, spiraling descent had been rigged. Each day would bring them closer to it.

Eleven days after the Braintree murders, Vanzetti again found himself on a train heading west, this time on an errand. Broke and unable to find work, he had been the only member of Gruppo Autonomo able to go on a crucial mission. Nearly two months had passed since federal agents had nabbed Roberto Elia and Andrea Salsedo in their Brooklyn print shop. Suspected of aiding the 1919 bomb plots, the two men remained in federal custody. Vanzetti knew Salsedo had steered agents toward Gruppo Autonomo, but he did not know his friend was buckling under the pressure of house arrest. Groaning in his sleep, refusing to eat, Salsedo told Elia they were being constantly watched. Even their playing cards were tampered with. Elia later insisted agents had beaten Salsedo during repeated interrogations: "He had red spots and scratches on his cheeks and temples and his eyes were vacant." Federal officials denied any mistreatment. Salsedo's latest letter to Vanzetti asked only for a legal defense fund, and at their weekly Sunday meeting on April 18, Gruppo Autonomo voted to raise the money. All the next week, as Chief Stewart set his trap, Vanzetti roamed the North End collecting dimes and quarters. Sacco, with his large savings account, contributed forty dollars. The following Sunday, with no further word from Salsedo and Elia, Gruppo Autonomo sent Vanzetti to New York to see what could be done to keep the men quiet, perhaps even free them. It would be the first time in several years that Vanzetti had visited what he called the "immense hell pit." He dreaded the journey but had one locale he hoped to visit—the Statue of Liberty. Owing to fog on the morning of his arrival from Italy, he had never seen it.

Arriving in Manhattan on Monday, April 26, Vanzetti set out to meet with lawyers and friends. Each shared disturbing news. Salsedo and Elia were in legal limbo. Given the choice of going to prison or remaining on the fourteenth floor of the Department of Justice building, they had chosen the latter. No one knew what they might reveal next. Then Vanzetti heard more ominous reports. Nearly four months had passed since federal agents last stormed homes and meeting halls, rounding up thousands of radicals, but the raids Palmer called "the mopping up" were not finished. With the attorney general warning of more May Day bombings, new raids were expected soon. After a few days in New York, disappointed at not having seen the Statue of Liberty, Vanzetti returned to Plymouth.

On Sunday, May 2, Gruppo Autonomo heard Vanzetti's report. If raids were imminent, all radical literature—and any last sticks of dynamite—had to be rounded up. To make a wide sweep of friends' homes, they would need a car. "The best way to take by automobile," Sacco later testified. "Could run more fast, could get more fast, could hide more fast." Because Mario Buda had a car, Gruppo Autonomo decided Sacco, Vanzetti, and another friend from their summer in Mexico would help him gather all incriminating evidence. Yet despite their fears about imminent raids, neither Sacco nor Vanzetti hid the many anarchist pamphlets in their own homes. This itself would later incriminate them.

As the anarchists scrambled for cover, their friend in custody high above Manhattan was losing his race with insanity. That Sunday night, Roberto Elia went to sleep to the sound of his friend's groans. At dawn, federal agents burst into his room.

"Is it not early?" a drowsy Elia asked.

"Your comrade is dead," he was told. "He has jumped from the window."

Federal agents tried to cover up the importance of the broken body on the sidewalk. Only when the dead man's lawyer blabbed about Salsedo's inside information did newspapers announce that the 1919 bomb plots had finally been cracked. They had been the work of Boston anarchists known as the *Galleanisti*. Any day, the feds were expected to round up group members. On May 4, learning of Salsedo's death and seeing *Galleanisti* linked to the bombings, Sacco and Vanzetti were terrified. "I was afraid," Vanzetti recalled, "for I know that my friends there in New York have jumped down from the jail in the street and killed himself. The papers say that he jump down, but we don't know." Sacco and Vanzetti made plans to go to Bridgewater the following evening to pick up the Overland at the garage. Then with Sacco bound for Italy, he and Vanzetti would bid each other good-bye. Vanzetti spent the night at Sacco's home in Stoughton, where both men awoke on their last day of freedom.

On the morning of May 5, Sacco and Vanzetti chatted over breakfast. While Rosina packed for her family's return to Italy, the two men went out to cut wood. Leaving the kitchen, Vanzetti noticed some shotgun shells on Sacco's kitchen shelf near the big wood-burning stove and put them in his pocket to sell to friends, hoping to get money for "propaganda." Or so he later claimed. That afternoon, Mario Buda and another friend, Ricardo Orciani, arrived on a red motorcycle with a sidecar. The four men sat talking in Sacco's kitchen. Rosina Sacco remembered them discussing deportation, "that it was terrible to be deported, you know, many different things they would do to you if they caught you." Buda and Orciani stayed for dinner, after which the men stood. Then the "poor fish peddler" stuffed a fully loaded .38 in his left hip pocket. The "good shoemaker" put a loaded .32 Colt under his belt. And for reasons no one will ever be sure of—to round up radical literature? to prepare for another Thursday payroll robbery? to hide dynamite?—they went out for the evening.

The night was black and moonless. The darkness was broken only by a few streetlights scattered like small candles across the wooded suburbs south of Boston. The motorcycle with sidecar held only two, so the men split up, agreeing to meet in Bridgewater at 9:00 p.m. Buda and Orciani took the motorcycle; Sacco and Vanzetti rode streetcars. Arriving in Bridgewater, they sat in a lonely café drafting a speech Vanzetti planned to give that coming Sunday to workers who had "fought all the wars." Then as 9:00 p.m. approached, they walked up a gloomy dirt road toward the home of mechanic Simon Johnson. Arriving, they saw the motorcycle, and beyond it, Buda knocking on the door. Johnson had already gone to bed, but his wife called out, asking who was there. Buda answered that he had come for his car. Ruth Johnson opened the door and was blinded by the motorcycle headlight. Squinting into the glare, she made out a short silhouette. In the distance, two men stood in the blackness and another sat in the sidecar. A voice said, "His wife." Ruth Johnson was just twenty-one and frightened, yet she knew what Chief Stewart had asked her husband. Stalling, she assured Buda that Simon would be right with him. She had to go next door. Walking toward her neighbor's, she thought she heard two men trailing her. She reached the adjacent house and called out, "I've come for the milk!" Inside, she picked up the phone and whispered through its black cone, telling the operator to get her the police. Ten minutes later she stepped back into the night carrying a milk can. On her way home, she thought she heard the word "telephone" muttered behind her.

Back at the house, Simon Johnson was telling Buda he had repaired the Overland's magneto. Still, the car could not be driven that night. It had no license plates. Buda said he'd take the chance, but when Ruth Johnson returned, he suddenly changed his mind. It was too late in the evening, he said. He'd come back the next day. The Johnsons watched as the motorcycle sped away. The two men on foot, one crowned by a derby, the other sporting a floppy felt hat above a drooping mustache, disappeared into the darkness. Sacco and Vanzetti walked along the trolley line for about a mile. At 9:40 p.m., a streetcar rumbled to a halt.

Alone at the rear of the trolley, Sacco and Vanzetti rode in silence. Shortly after ten, Brockton policeman Michael Connolly boarded at a stop next to a vaudeville theater. Ambling down the car's narrow corridor, Connolly came to the men. He asked where they had been that night. "Bridgewater," both answered. Connolly then told them they were under arrest as "suspicious characters." A plainclothes cop boarding the car was told to "fish" the man with the mustache. The officer found Vanzetti's .38. Connolly gave Sacco "a slight going over" but did not find the Colt tucked in his belt. Taken off the trolley, the suspicious characters were hustled into a patrol car that had pulled across the tracks. What happened next is another mystery. Testifying at an inquest that fall, Connolly would swear he rode with Sacco and Vanzetti in silence all the way to the station, but at the trial the officer would recall a more sinister scenario.

At the station, officers searched Sacco, finding his gun with eight cartridges in its clip and one in the chamber. Police also found twenty-three cartridges in Sacco's pocket. The Colt was set beside Vanzetti's .38 and the shotgun shells found on him. Police puzzled over a note in Sacco's pocket, written in Italian. Later translated, it read:

Proletarians, you have fought all the wars. You have worked for all the owners. You have wandered over all the countries. Have you harvested the fruits of your labors, the price of your victories? Does the past comfort you? . . . On these questions, on this argument, and on this theme, the struggle for existence, Bartolomeo Vanzetti will speak. Hour—— Day—— Hall—— Admission free. Freedom of discussion to all. Take the ladies with you.

By midnight, police were descending on the Brockton station. Thinking they had captured the masterminds of a brutal holdup, they did not know they had arrested men with inside information on the biggest assassination plot in American history. Sacco and Vanzetti, given their devotion to anarchism, might have preferred being implicated in the larger crime. Later, the less articulate of the two better expressed their despair.

"If I was arrested because of 'the Idea,' I am glad to suffer," Sacco said. "If I must I will die for it. But they have arrested me for a gunman job."

CHAPTER THREE

"Yeggs"

There's no story in it. . . . Just a couple of wops in a jam.
—city editor of the *New York Call*

One photograph stands out from the rest. The most famous photo of Sacco and Vanzetti, taken in 1923, shows them handcuffed, hats in hand. Seated on the viewer's right, Sacco is numb, dull-eyed, and deathly thin, the result of a hunger strike in its twenty-fifth day. Beside him sits Vanzetti, his mustache seeming to droop with the weight of the world's sorrow. Vanzetti's expansive forehead is unfurrowed, his head unbowed, his eyes tinged with suffering. A guard, often cropped out of the picture, sits with the two men. Behind them, blurred courtroom walls suggest that their guilt or innocence will forever be in the eyes of the beholder. Sad and poignant, this is the photo their supporters have long cherished, but it is not the photo that introduced Sacco and Vanzetti to Massachusetts.

Because the Brockton Police Department had no camera for mug shots, both men were taken to a photographer's studio on May 6, the day after their arrest. Beyond being "suspicious characters," they had not been told why they were in custody. One after the other, each stared into the camera, whose blinding flash captured their bewilderment and rage. The following morning, when the mug shots made the front page of several Boston papers, "Mike

Saco" and "Bert Venzetti" looked like dangerous thugs. Above his dapper suit, Sacco wore a derby and a diffident air. Vanzetti, his fedora pulled low, the outlaw cut of his mustache giving him a menacing look, glared at each newspaper reader. Reporters pinned a slang term on the suspects, one commonly used to describe bandits in the 1920s—"yeggs." Headlines were equally indicting—FEELS HE HAS BRAINTREE BAND, PROSECUTOR KANE SO DECLARES, read the *Boston Globe*—and anyone stared down by the mug shots could be forgiven for shuddering and feeling the same.

In its first few days, the case against Sacco and Vanzetti resembled a new touring car struggling up a rise, its engine misfiring. Just two of five suspects were in custody. Ferruccio Coacci had been deported. No one knew the whereabouts of the slippery "Mike Boda," and the fifth suspect, Ricardo Orciani, was being hunted throughout the Boston area. Police hoped fingerprints would rev up the case, but although a state inspector dusted the Buick, his conclusions were never announced. Had others handled the car before it was impounded, invalidating all prints? Did the car reveal only smudges? Or were the fingerprints, failing to match the suspects', buried? No one will ever know, but fingerprints would never be mentioned again. The defense lawyers' many requests for this evidence were ignored. The sputtering case rolled on.

Within an hour of his arrest, alone, terrified, and in police custody for the first time, Vanzetti found himself in a shadowed room facing Chief Michael Stewart. Beside the ruddy chief stood four officers, all staring bullets at the dark-eyed Italian they suspected of murder. Chief Stewart began with routine questions—name, nationality, business. Vanzetti answered truthfully—at first. "Am fish peddler," he said. What was he doing in Bridgewater that night? He and Sacco were on their way to see "my good friend," a man everyone called Pappi. When had he left Plymouth? "Sunday morning," Vanzetti said. Where had he stayed Sunday night? "I don't remember," he lied. Then, as if this fib gave him license, Vanzetti began lying routinely, covering up facts that would not have implicated him in anything. He explained his route that evening, but denied everything else. He had not seen a motorcycle. He did not know

"Boda." He was not even sure when he had come to Sacco's house. "I don't remember," he said. "That is the difficulty."

Questioned separately, Sacco lied with equal aplomb. He admitted they had gone to Bridgewater to see Vanzetti's friend but did not know the man's name. He remembered walking a long way, but as to a motorcycle, "I no see any motorcycle." He did not know Boda. He had a gun "to protect myself. Lots of bad men." He was carrying twenty-three cartridges because "we go into the woods and fire them." During their trial, Sacco and Vanzetti would be forced to acknowledge these lies. They would explain that they had been afraid—afraid of being branded as radicals, afraid of deportation, afraid of ending up like their friend Salsedo. They could not mention bomb plots nor explain the tight code binding them to their *fratelli* in anarchist circles. It took six years and imminent execution before Vanzetti would explain his lies in a letter to his "Mexican comrades":

> To give a name, an address or information, would have meant to cause homes to be raided, finding of libertarian literature and private correspondence, hence terrorized divided families, arrests, indictments, deportations, and so on. Why should we turn spies? We are not men to betray friends and comrades for self-liberation; never.

Chief Stewart did not tell either man why he had been arrested. As a veteran of the Palmer Raids, however, the chief fed their fears about roundups of radicals.

"Are you a Communist?" the chief asked Sacco.

"No."

"Anarchist?"

"No."

"Do you believe in this government of ours?"

"Yes. Some things I like different."

Vanzetti echoed his friend's evasions.

"Are you an anarchist?"

"Well, I don't know what you call him. I am a little different."

"Do you like this government?"

"Well, I like things a little different."

"Do you believe in changing the government by force, if necessary?"

"No."

"Do you subscribe for literature or papers of the Anarchistic Party?

"Sometimes I read them."

When Stewart finished, the two men spent a restless night in separate cells. Why were they there? "I don't know myself," Sacco later claimed. "I been hear so many times, they say, 'You know, you know,' that is all. . . . I never think anything else than radical." Midway through Vanzetti's first night in jail, a cop spat at him through the bars, then carefully loaded a gun, aimed, and pretended to shoot. When Vanzetti asked for a blanket, the officer told him he would be warm soon enough and that come morning he would be lined up and shot.

On May 6, shortly after the mug shots were taken, the suspects met the district attorney, who would be known for the rest of his life as the man who "got Sacco and Vanzetti." Canny and tenacious, with a gentlemanly demeanor and the chiseled head of a football quarterback, Frederick Katzmann did not harbor illusions about his job. A district attorney was the *public's* prosecutor, and he owed it to the public to put men like Sacco and Vanzetti in jail or in their graves. Norfolk County expected no less of a Harvard man.

Climbing from working-class Boston to the halls of Harvard, Katzmann had worked his way through college by tending furnaces, graduated without distinction in 1896, and became assistant superintendent for a local power company. After taking night classes at Boston University Law School, he was admitted to the bar in 1902. He worked for a firm in Boston's elite Pemberton Square, where he developed a taste for fine cigars and natty suits, then left to set up his own practice in his native Hyde Park, an industrial neighborhood eight miles south of downtown Boston. For two years, Katzmann alternated law with the state legislature, where he served one term. In 1910, he became assistant district attorney of Norfolk County. Seven years later, his boss retired and Katzmann assumed the office. When elected in his own right—with the largest number of votes in county history—Katzmann earned praise for his "shrewdness and cleverness." He became known as a hard-hitting DA, merciless in questioning witnesses. His tenacity quickened when trying sex offenders, leading to speculation that one had victimized his own family, yet he was equally obstinate with any witness who dared to doubt his authority. At forty-five, with silvered hair and thick jowls, Katzmann was well into his first full term when given this front-page case no ambitious prosecutor could afford to lose.

As he strode into the Brockton police station on Thursday, May 6, Katzmann carried all the pomp and circumstance of the Gilded Age that had nurtured him. Beneath his straw boater and impeccable Burberry coat, he bristled with certitude. An intensely private man in what was about to become a very public position, Katzmann walled himself off from the press. Throughout his seven-year crusade to convict and execute Sacco and Vanzetti, he gave no interviews, no press conferences, no public statements. And for the rest of his life, he refused all public comment on the world-famous case. A staunch Republican, like nearly every prominent Massachusetts man in 1920, Katzmann had his eye on a judgeship or perhaps the state attorney general's office. Neither goal, however, fueled his relentless pursuit of Sacco and Vanzetti. He would argue his case, clamping onto it like a pit bull to a stick, for a simpler reason. He *knew* Sacco was guilty; he was not yet sure about Vanzetti. And from the moment Frederick Katzmann entered the police station, the case took on the momentum of a new touring car topping a rise and gathering speed on the downhill.

That Thursday afternoon, Katzmann questioned the accused about their guns, their friends, their actions the previous night. Then he floated the first hint of a crime worse than radicalism.

"Do you know Berardelli?"

"No," Sacco replied. "Who is this Berardelli?"

"Do you read the newspapers?"

"*Boston Post* every day."

"Did you ever look for work in Braintree?"

"Never," Sacco lied.

"You know a Buick car when you see it?"

"No, I do not think so. I never saw it. I do not understand any make of cars."

After further questioning, Katzmann asked Sacco point-blank, "Did you ever hear about anything happening in Braintree last month?"

"I read in the *Boston Post* there was bandit—robbing money over near Rice and Hutchins," Sacco said. He and fellow edge trimmers had discussed the crime on April 16. When Katzmann asked if he had worked the day before, Sacco lied again: "I think I was working the day before I read it in the paper. I don't remember for sure if I stayed out half a day. I think I worked Thursday." Katzmann was more direct with Vanzetti, but the fish peddler still found the truth elusive. Pressed about his answers to Chief Stewart, he admitted lying about his whereabouts the previous Sunday. "I am ashamed. I am sure I slept in Boston but I had a woman with me—that is why I did not want to tell you. A woman I met in Boston . . . a woman who goes with everybody." Katzmann cared little about that. Where was Vanzetti on Patriots' Day, April 19? And the Thursday before it? Vanzetti could not remember. That was the difficulty.

Following this second round of questioning, Sacco and Vanzetti were booked for carrying concealed weapons. They pled guilty and were held without bail. Later that day, they faced some two dozen witnesses brought to Brockton from the smaller towns of Bridgewater and Braintree. For an hour, each man stood alone, not in a police lineup. Sacco was told to kneel, to take off his hat, to assume a shooting pose. Vanzetti was simply studied. Witnesses' answers were all over the map. The one-legged gatekeeper from Pearl Street, Michael Levangie, fingered Vanzetti as "the man who was driving the machine. He looks just like him. . . . No doubt whatever." Three witnesses from Bridgewater identified Vanzetti, but nine others from Braintree gazed on him with bewilderment.

"I never saw that man before."

"That is not the man I saw."

"It does not even have a resemblance to him—age, features or anything."

Sacco's identifications were more positive. "That looks like the man who killed Berardelli," shoemaker Lewis Wade said. "I would pick him for the man." Bookkeeper Mary Splaine studied Sacco. "I am almost sure that is the man that was standing in the machine as it was making its escape," she said. After a second look, the prim woman added, "He is as close to the man as could be." But a dozen others flatly stated that Sacco was not one of the Braintree bandits. While witnesses studied the men, police searched their homes—without warrants. In Sacco's bungalow they found a gray cap, a rifle, and stacks of radical literature. Vanzetti's cluttered room offered up shelves of subversive books and letters from the notorious anarchist Carlo Tresca. The new evidence left Chief Stewart even more certain. Sacco had been one of the Braintree gunmen, Vanzetti the driver. "Mike Boda" had been somewhere on the scene, along with Ferruccio Coacci and Ricardo Orciani. Coacci had taken the stolen money to Italy, where the rest had been ready to follow. Stewart's scenario gained more speed that afternoon when Orciani was pulled over for having no taillight on his motorcycle. In custody, the tight-lipped man with a pencil-thin mustache impressed Stewart as being "not like Sacco or Vanzetti—a real tough." Orciani also lied, saying, "That man Sacco might know me but I don't know him," and "I never heard of Bartolomeo Vanzetti." Officers from Brockton soon found the small-town chief "obsessed with the desire to get somebody."

On Saturday, May 8, a large crowd filled Pearl Street in South Braintree. As factory workers watched, an open police car containing Orciani passed, trailing glares and whispers. The car drove through the factory shadows where the Buick had waited. It reached the spots where Parmenter and Berardelli had fallen, passed the water tower, then slowed at the railroad crossing. At each telltale point, the suspect's expression was eyed for hints of guilt. At each point, Orciani displayed what one newspaper called "the unemotional exterior of an American Indian." When the test was over, the patrol car sped to Brockton, where Sacco and Vanzetti were entering the courthouse past a mean, muttering crowd. Fearing the men might be lynched, the judge ordered an extra police guard. Inside, a preliminary hearing ended with the granting of a week's continuance. The prosecution needed more time—time to link Sacco and Vanzetti to the Christmas Eve Bridgewater holdup, time to chase down "Mike Boda," time to wire Italy and have Coacci's luggage searched for the stolen payroll. The case kept rolling. A final push came on May 14 when a state police officer visited the Boston office of the federal Bureau of Investigation (not yet known as the FBI). Digging through files on *Cronaca Sovversiva*, he found the names "Ferdinando Sacco" and "Bartolomeo Vanzetti." Now state police knew what the feds knew—that as *Galleanisti*, the suspects in the Braintree murders may have conspired in the 1919 bombings.

The trial was still a year away, but testimony was already piling up in the court of public opinion. Following the headline arrest, the Boston press presented little doubt that Sacco and Vanzetti were key members of the gang that "shot up the peaceful town of South Braintree." Sacco had not worked on the day of the crime, newspapers reported. When arrested, he carried a passport, proof he was planning to "take it on the lam" following one last robbery. As for Vanzetti, the press reported that "alleged Bolshevik literature" had been found in his room, that he had dodged the draft, and that a shell found on him matched a shell found in Bridgewater. A known labor agitator who "admits to being a radical of the most pronounced form," Vanzetti was "versed in English classics of the economic nature" and "speaks English perfectly." William Randolph Hearst's *Boston American*, the most widely read paper in New England, quoted prosecutors' predictions—convicting Sacco and Vanzetti would be "comparatively easy."

The nation of Italians clustered throughout the Boston area feared as much. As word spread of *due Italiani arrestati,* fear gradually gave way to anger. On May 6, shortly after officers searched her home, Rosina Sacco gathered anarchist pamphlets they had missed. Terrified of what might happen next, she burned the tracts in the nearby woods. Off in Plymouth, Vanzetti's friends were in shock. His customers were especially surprised by accusations that he had driven the getaway car. They did not know their local fish peddler could drive. But then, they had never known him to carry a gun either. The reaction at the Brini household was recalled by fifteen-year-old Lefevre: "We couldn't believe that the man did what they said he did. He was so gentle, so good. He helped people, not hurt them. Never! Besides, he was in Plymouth. We knew he didn't do it. I said to Mother, 'It can't be. There's a mistake.' But we didn't get alarmed. We thought it would be rectified." Older Italians knew the "mistake" would not be rectified without a vigorous legal defense. At the Gruppo Autonomo meeting on Sunday, May 9, the Sacco-Vanzetti Defense Committee was formed. Some present had been with Sacco and Vanzetti in Mexico. Fearing publicity, they put the committee into the hands of Vanzetti's friend Aldino Felicani.

During the next seven years, nearly $300,000, the modern equivalent of $3.4 million, would be raised for Sacco and Vanzetti. Every penny would be charted by a tall, goateed gentleman with a deep baritone. Aldino Felicani had come to America in 1914 with the Italian police on his heels. Only twenty-three, he had been arrested two dozen times for publishing firebrand articles denouncing Italy's rising militarism. Among his many cellmates had been another young rebel—Benito Mussolini. Arriving in America, Felicani wrote for Italian anarchist papers in Cleveland and New York. He had come to Boston during the flu epidemic, and when the disease claimed the editor of the Socialist paper *La Notizia,* he had taken the job. A year later, he befriended Vanzetti. Whenever he was in Boston buying fish, Vanzetti would drop by Felicani's office in the North End, where the two would discuss anarchism till the early-morning hours. Felicani knew of Sacco but did not know him well, yet he recognized the profound differences between the two men. "Sacco was a man of action, more of a violent anarchist," Felicani recalled. "He was capable of throwing a bomb. I would say yes to that without any hesitation. But not Vanzetti." So it was more to defend the latter than the former that Felicani assumed control of the Sacco-Vanzetti Defense Committee. "Due to the relationship we had established I had to do something," he remembered. "Friendship for me is something sacred. That is my religion—friendship."

Starting with little more than outrage, Felicani rented two cramped rooms above his newspaper office in the North End. In the years to come, committee headquarters would become a colorful scene of frenzy and disorder. Strewn with typewriters, yesterday's newspapers, old rolltop desks, and a portable fan, the office would be perpetually crammed with journalists, poets, Socialists, and socialites laboring to "Save Sacco and Vanzetti!" But at first the office was quiet. By mid-May, a few local anarchists were typing letters to alert the network of Italian immigrants across America. One early letter proclaimed, "THIS IS A BATTLE WHICH ALL MEN OF HEART MUST FIGHT. . . . We must win to save the honor of men and of anarchists; we must win to vindicate this infamous insult to our community; we must win to save two innocents from the electric chair." To win, each letter stressed, the committee needed money. Initial contributions, almost all from Italians, were small—seventy-five cents from Liborio Russo, a dollar from Giuseppe Tamburello, an occasional ten dollars from a Dante Alighieri Lodge—but they gave hope to Felicani and other "men of heart" who were as certain of their friends' innocence as the district attorney was of their guilt.

As Italians entrenched, Katzmann and Chief Stewart held tightly to their suspicions even when their case veered into oncoming traffic. First, police searched Coacci's trunk, held up in Boston, and his luggage arriving in Italy. Neither contained any money, though the trunk had stolen shoe parts. Next, Sacco was cleared of the Bridgewater robbery when factory records proved he had worked the previous Christmas Eve. Finally, Orciani was released after time cards showed him at work in a foundry on both Christmas Eve and April 15. (Stewart later insisted someone else must have punched Orciani's time card on the days of both crimes.) That left Vanzetti, who punched no clock while peddling fish, hanging out in the wind. On May 18, witnesses at another inquest singled him out as the shotgun-toting leader of the Bridgewater burglary.

Fingered as a common bandit, Vanzetti marshaled his own defense. Friends advised him to dismiss his court-appointed attorney and hire a portly white-haired lawyer named John Vahey. If the trouble continued, friends said, Vahey's brother, a powerful Boston lawyer, would come to his aid. Trusting and naïve, Vanzetti did as he was told. It was a mistake, as Vanzetti realized during the May 18 inquest when Vahey stood and said, "The defendant has nothing to offer." With not a word said or a witness called in his defense, Vanzetti was sent back to jail. Behind bars, his mind reeled with arguments for his innocence.

For more than a dozen years, Vanzetti had thrived on intellectual discussion in cafés and kitchens. Now he began crafting a defense based on discussions with himself. With his books still in his room, he wrote Felicani in early June asking about injustices throughout history. From his "more cultured" friend, Vanzetti sought "the following information—How many regicides had provoked the Jesuits? What was the place, the date? . . . When had [President] Wilson defined the Italians as the 'Chinese of Europe'? . . . What were the names of the martyrs of Chicago, the old ones?" Intending to testify at his trial, Vanzetti searched his memory for patriotic stories that might stir an American jury. "It was not a tentative insurrection, that first one captained by Washington," he wrote. "What were the places and the dates, the names of the fallen?" He had read American history but could not remember who had said, "When the people are not satisfied with the government, they have the right to rise up in arms and overthrow it." Could Felicani please find the quote? With even more fever of knowledge than had consumed him as a young man, Vanzetti mailed his letter and waited. He was still waiting on June 11, his thirty-second birthday, when he was indicted for attempted robbery and murder in Bridgewater. His trial would begin in eleven days.

The rush to judgment in the Bridgewater case was fueled by a new fear gripping the nation. By June 1920, the Red Scare had faded into allegations and denials. With the nation's most notorious radicals in jail or deported, concern had shifted to a spreading lawlessness. Across New England and the nation, gangs of armed robbers were attacking in broad daylight. Dressed in fine suits, sporting snap brim hats, and driving shiny spoke-wheeled Buicks and Hudsons, gangs gagged or killed guards, grabbed sacks of cash, and made their getaways. In the month leading up to the Braintree murders, the news had brought one shocking report after another.

March 7—robbers tie up a guard in Cambridge, blow a safe, and steal $2,500.

March 10—Gunmen in Baltimore steal $80,000 worth of whiskey.

March 12—Three men in Philadelphia stun a guard with chloroform and make off with $368,250, while in Manhattan, "armed yeggs" smash a jewelry store window on Broadway, hold a crowd at gunpoint, and help themselves to handfuls of diamonds.

March 24—Gunmen near Worcester hold up an express messenger carrying $10,000.

April 15—Bandits rob a jewelry store in Newark and a truck carrying $4,000 in gold in Providence, while gunmen in Braintree kill two guards and make off with $15,776.71.

Well after the arrest of Sacco and Vanzetti, the lawlessness continued. Bandits in Manhattan stole a $5,400 payroll. Twenty grand was taken at gunpoint in St. Louis. Not even the dead were safe. At Boston's Mt. Hope Cemetery, a guard reported, "There is hardly a burial in that cemetery where the grave is not robbed. . . . They steal even the flowers."

It was "an age of lawlessness," it was the dawn of the "crime

wave." Arguments raged about who was to blame. Was it the deepening recession? Prohibition? Barbarity left over from the war?
Social critics pointed to the movies as "a training-school for anti-
Americanism, immorality, and disregard for law." Some singled out
the automobile, which enabled robbers to take the money and run
long before police wagons ambled to the scene. The small weekly in
Dedham, Massachusetts, where Sacco and Vanzetti would be tried,
recommended posses to hunt down criminals, "giving them no
quarter when captured." Given the number of crimes, the criminals'
daring, and the speed of their escapes, few suspects were apprehended. With no one sure where a gang might strike next, the cap-
ture of Sacco and Vanzetti stood out as a bellwether, offering hope
that the "age of lawlessness" might soon end. Against this backdrop,
Vanzetti's first trial began.

On Tuesday morning, June 22, Chief Stewart drove Vanzetti to
court. The chief knew the defendant as a hard-boiled anarchist and
alleged murderer. He did not know that the Italian he called "Bertie" was an amateur singer. As the patrol car rattled over two-lane
roads, Vanzetti entertained the chief, whom he called "Mickey,"
with old Italian songs. "He had quite a voice," Stewart remembered.
Vanzetti's lyrical mood sobered as he approached the colonial courthouse in Plymouth. There in a barren courtroom whose arched
windows let in the smell of salt air, he faced a jury who knew only
that Bartolomeo Vanzetti was an Italian charged with armed robbery and attempted murder on the previous Christmas Eve.

One by one, witnesses re-created the crime on that icy morning—
the car stopping, the men leaping out, the shotgun blasts, the swerv-
ing truck, the frantic escape. One by one they identified "the man
in the dock" as the shotgun-toting leader. "I feel sure that he is the
same man," one witness said. Another added, "I have seen him
since in Brockton. I have seen him in Plymouth. . . . I see him this
morning in the dock. . . . I am positive." The same man who had
first told the Pinkertons, "I did not get much of a look at his face,"
now said Vanzetti was definitely the man with the shotgun. Witnesses detailed the gunman's coat, his hat, but above all, they remembered his mustache. It was "a short, well trimmed mustache,"

one witness told the court. Another added, "The ends had been cut off, anyway. It was not what you would call a flowing mustache." One man added that the mustache was slightly larger than Charlie Chaplin's. Through each accusation, Vanzetti sat in silence, his walrus mustache not fitting the testimony. Yet the witnesses were not through.

In a commonwealth subdivided by immigrant nationalities, the gunman stood out as anything but American. "He struck me immediately as being a foreigner," one witness said. Another added, "He was some kind of foreigner" who spoke a language that "was foreign." A fourteen-year-old boy testified, "I was just getting a fleeting glance at his face, but the way he ran I could tell he was a foreigner."

How did foreigners run, Vanzetti's lawyer wanted to know. "Does an Italian or a Russian run differently from a Swede or a Norwegian?"

"Yes," the boy said.

"What is the difference?"

"Unsteady."

"Both the Italians and the Russians run unsteadily?"

"As far as that goes, I don't know . . ."

"You don't want to have this jury think, do you, that you can tell what the nationality of this man was by the way he ran?"

"Yes, I do."

Moving beyond identification, the prosecution outlined a larger case—that five men, including one named Sacco, had stolen a Buick and used it for robberies. One witness testified to seeing a "Mike Boda" driving the Buick through Bridgewater. Material evidence included the cap found in Vanzetti's room—witnesses singled it out among six others as the one worn by the gunman—and a spent shotgun shell from the crime scene, said to be identical to one found on Vanzetti when arrested. Over objections, Judge Webster Thayer left it to the jury "whether finding a shell within three or four months after the alleged crime is important."

On Friday, June 25, Chief Stewart testified all afternoon, recounting the evening of May 5, the men on the motorcycle coming to claim the Overland, their suspicious activity, and Vanzetti's lies. The following morning when the chief picked up "Bertie," Vanzetti did not speak. He did not sing. He just glared. "The thing I remember most about him is his eyes," the chief recalled. "He had terrible eyes, like fire when he looked at you."

Following the chief's testimony, the prosecution rested. Vanzetti, despite his bitter distrust of governments, courts, and police, could not believe what was happening to him. During the trial he wrote again to Felicani, denouncing the "political and racial vendetta" and recapping testimony—the boy who recognized foreigners by the way they ran, the woman who identified him but under cross-examination "began to tremble, change color and lower her eyes." "You know me and you know that I can bear this misfortune," he wrote. "But nevertheless, it swells my heart. With a fierce brutality, that gang of men ruins my life and that of my father."

On June 28, John Vahey took up Vanzetti's defense. If he had known of the Pinkerton report on the Bridgewater case, the lawyer might have called the jury's attention to several inconsistencies. Had the getaway car been a Buick or, as several had told the Pinkertons, a Hudson? Was the gang leader an Italian or, as reported on Christmas Eve, a Russian? A Pole? A Portuguese? An Austrian? Since December, some witnesses had changed their descriptions of the mustache in question, letting it grow ragged until it vaguely resembled Vanzetti's. But the Pinkerton report was still in the agency's files, so Vahey based his defense on an alibi. Vanzetti would later wonder "if in the whole judiciary history of this State, there has been a defendant with a more convincing, coherent, consequent, powerful . . . truthful alibi than mine." The alibi was based on an Italian delicacy.

Vanzetti insisted he had been selling eels on Christmas Eve. A barrel of them had been shipped from Boston. He claimed to have spent the night of December 23 cleaning the slippery catch and wrapping orders in newspaper. Italians devoured eels, sometimes with spaghetti, on the day before their Christmas fast. As the jury was to learn, eels tasted better when left in salt for a day or two. While Vanzetti listened from the dock, sixteen witnesses speaking in broken English or interpreted Italian testified to buying eels from him on Christmas Eve for twenty cents a pound. Carlo Balboni bought two pounds of *anguille*. John DiCarli took home a pound and a half. Margaretta Fiochi purchased a pound. Testimony traced Vanzetti as he made his rounds with his cart. He was seen: in the early morning at his landlady's house, an hour later at a bakery, selling eels on Cherry Street, on Court Street, on Suosso's Lane, calling a woman from the kitchen where she was making polenta, taking eels into a tenement where an old woman was cleaning. Wherever he went, Vanzetti was spotted with Beltrando Brini. Finally, Vanzetti's surrogate son, proud of his English and certain of his testimony, was called to the stand to save his idol. But in the unassuming words of a young boy, Frederick Katzmann saw his chance to demolish the alibi.

Only once before had Vanzetti asked Beltrando to help him make his rounds, and the boy considered the job an unforgettable treat. Now he remembered as if Christmas Eve had been only a week ago. From 7:30 a.m. until early afternoon, Beltrando testified, he had traipsed along, handing out orders, making change, chatting. He remembered talking to Vanzetti about a horse. He described the sloppy streets, the factory whistles, the exact change given to certain customers. When he finished, Beltrando felt he had told his story well, but to Katzmann it was just that—a story.

Approaching the boy, the DA asked whether he could repeat his testimony "word for word." Beltrando did so, omitting few details.

"That is just the same story, isn't it?"

"Sure."

"How many times did you tell that story?" When Beltrando said he had told it just a few times, Katzmann went on the attack. Hadn't he told it more often? "Maybe ten times?"

No.

"Maybe nine times?"

"Maybe five."

"Perhaps six?" Katzmann prodded. And when the boy had told the story to his parents, hadn't they reminded him when something was left out?

"Sure, at first."

"And your papa would say 'be sure and put that in'?"

"Yes sir, sure."

"And your mother would say it?"

"Sure."

Didn't such coaching remind the boy of school when he had "a little poem or piece of history to recite"? And hadn't he learned this long, detailed story of eels and muddy streets and exact change "just like a piece at school"? Unaware of Katzmann's purpose, Beltrando responded brightly.

"Sure."

Katzmann then displayed the stabbing persistence Sacco and Vanzetti would later see at their joint trial. A barrage of questions followed, bewildering the boy with precise days of the week before Christmas.

"What day of the week was the twenty-second?"

"Tuesday—no Monday."

"Are you sure of that?"

"The twenty-second was Tuesday . . ."

"So you say the twenty-second of last December was Tuesday, don't you?" Katzmann continued, showing the boy a calendar. "Now do you want to change your answer?"

"Monday."

"You thought the twenty-second came on Tuesday, didn't you? You said Tuesday twice, did you not? You got it wrong twice, didn't you?"

Exactly how many packages of eels had he carried at once? That many? Was he sure? Precisely how many hours had they spent delivering eels? What time had they finished?

"One fifteen, was it?"

"I can't say. I don't know."

"Was it one twenty?"

"I don't know."

"Ten minutes past one?"

"I ain't got no idea."

Katzmann then turned to the friendship between Vanzetti and

Beltrando's father, a well-known anarchist. Had Vicenzo Brini collected funds for Vanzetti's defense? Beltrando supposed so. Had the boy heard the two men talking in the kitchen? "Did you hear them talk about our government?" Vanzetti's lawyer objected, but Judge Thayer allowed the question. "What society do your papa and the baker and Vanzetti belong to, do you know?" This time, the judge disallowed Katzmann's attempt to inject anarchy into the trial. Had Beltrando ever seen a man named Sacco in Plymouth? He had not. Had he ever heard Vanzetti talk about Mike Boda? No. Finally, with the boy just wanting out of the witness box, Katzmann asked Beltrando why Vanzetti had been arrested. "It had nothing to do with the day before Christmas, did it?" And Beltrando softly answered, "No."

To the jury, the alibi of the eels was shaping up like a story rehearsed throughout the cohesive Italian community. Aside from several overlapping incidents, there was no evidence—no receipt, no bill of sale—proving Vanzetti had bought or sold any eels. And there were disturbing doubts. If Italians liked to salt eels a day before eating them, why would they buy them on December 24, the day of their feast? Might customers have seen Vanzetti and his helper on December 23? Doubts were also cast by Katzmann's relentless "Where were you on the date of?" questions.

"Of course you know where you were on the twenty-third but where were you on the twenty-ninth at 7:30?"

"Where were you at 9:30 on the twenty-ninth of January?"

"Where were you on the twenty-second of December?"

Witness after witness could not recall, so how could they remember the exact time, the exact location they had seen a fish peddler six months before? Sensing his fate, Vanzetti protested. What about the mustache? he asked Vahey. Was his a slightly larger version of Chaplin's? Several witnesses had sworn Vanzetti's mustache had always been long and shaggy, but all were Italians. Wouldn't the jury dismiss their testimony because "The Dagos stand together"? Why not go to the Plymouth community, to barbers, businessmen, former employers who knew the mustache better than they knew the man behind it? When his lawyer balked, Vanzetti was outraged. "I told him that if he would not provide a stronger defense I would stand in the dock, protest my rights and denounce him in open court," he recalled. Vahey agreed, and so the trial returned to where it had begun—a mustache. Two Plymouth cops, Vanzetti's barber, a hotel owner, and a businessman testified that the notorious mustache had always been as ragged as it now appeared. But under Katzmann's cross-examination, none could swear the mustache had not been cropped on the day of the crime. With this last-ditch effort, the defense rested. Customers, friends, and acquaintances had testified, but the crucial witness, the one who had summoned history to prove his innocence, had sat silently in the defendant's dock. As with other mysteries, conflicting stories explain Vanzetti's silence.

"I was willing to take the stand," Vanzetti recalled, "but Mr. Vahey opposed it. . . . He asked me how I would explain from the stand the meaning of Socialism or Communism, or Bolshevism. . . . I would begin an explanation on those subjects and Mr. Vahey would cut it off at its very beginning. 'Hush, if you tell such things to the ignorant, conservative jurors, they will send you to state prison right away.' " But Vahey's assistant told a different story. According to James Graham, he and Vahey had mentioned the dangers if anarchism surfaced but also warned Vanzetti that a defendant who did not testify was usually convicted. Uncertain, Vanzetti sent Graham to consult with Sacco. The two prisoners finally agreed that the eels alibi would have to be enough. Vanzetti's decision not to testify, Graham insisted, was his own.

On July 1, the case went to the jury. Disregarding sixteen Italians claiming to have bought eels, jurors quickly agreed on a guilty verdict for attempted robbery and turned to the charge of attempted murder. Some then became curious about the shotgun shells on the jury table. Captain William Proctor of the Massachusetts State Police had testified that such shells were often used for hunting birds. Could a man be convicted for attempted murder if his gun was loaded for quail? To answer the question, the foreman decided to open one or two shells. Yanking out cotton wadding, he found buckshot—capable of killing a man. Several jurors later said this discovery swung their second guilty vote, and some kept buckshot pellets as souvenirs.

After five hours of deliberation, the jury returned late that afternoon. When the verdict echoed through the courtroom, a wail rose from several Italian women at the back. Judge Thayer thanked the jury: "You may go to your homes with the feeling that you did respond as the soldier responded to his service when he went across the seas to the call of the Commonwealth." As guards led Vanzetti away, he raised shackled wrists and shouted, "Coraggio!" (Courage!) The following day, learning that the jury had tampered with the shells, Judge Thayer ordered the pellets returned to the district attorney. Katzmann told one juror to keep quiet about the incident. "He did not want it known," the man said. That week another juror learned a lesson about identification. Throughout the trial, Arthur Nickerson had assumed "the man in the dock" was the same mustachioed man he saw daily at the Plymouth Cordage Factory where Vanzetti had not worked since 1915. When the juror returned to "the Cordage" following the trial, he was startled to see the lookalike still on the job. "If I had known that Vanzetti wasn't Tony, knowing that they did look alike," Nickerson remembered, "then I would have had a doubt. I don't know how I would have decided."

Back in Italy, Vanzetti's father received a letter from the Brinis sharing the sad news and predicting appeals all the way to the Supreme Court. But the swift and sudden conviction stilled Vanzetti's prolific pen. From the weeks following the verdict, there are no surviving letters, no reminiscences, no way to measure the blackness of his anguish. If he had committed the Bridgewater robbery, then he could expect no mercy at his next trial. And if he was innocent, then the wolves circling him were even more vicious than he had suspected. When Vanzetti finally wrote about his first trial, years behind bars had case-hardened his rage. The trial was "a legal lynching," his lawyer "a Judas" who had done nothing but smoke "big cigars bought for him by the poor Italian people." The witnesses were all "perjurers" who "mocked and glared cynically at me and at the Italians who were in the court."

Six weeks after the verdict, Vanzetti was back in the Plymouth courtroom, now guarded by police with riot guns. Judge Thayer, dodging the attempted-murder conviction tainted by the jury's tampering with the evidence, sentenced Vanzetti solely for armed robbery, giving him twelve to fifteen years, the maximum for a first offense in which no one was hurt and no money stolen. Within hours, Vanzetti was gazing up at the imposing iron gates of the Massachusetts State Prison at Charlestown.

If ever a place deserved a sign warning, "Abandon hope, all ye who enter here," it was this gloomy granite fortress. Looming over the gritty maze of factories across the Charles River from Boston's North End, Charlestown State Prison had housed the Commonwealth's hardest criminals—murderers and thieves, rapists and saboteurs. Surrounded by smokestacks, the prison reeked with their fumes. Its windowless cells were sweatboxes in summer, iceboxes in winter. Prisoners were regularly sent to solitary confinement, sometimes for refusing to smile at a guard. Thrown into the pitch-black, they lived on bread and water. Since 1901, when it added the newest technology in capital punishment—the electric chair—the prison had executed twenty-two men. Each electrocution began with the eerie hum of high voltage crackling through jail corridors. Each ended at midnight with flickering lights. A few years after Vanzetti arrived, an independent board would declare the prison "barbaric and antiquated," but on August 19, 1920, Charlestown's gates opened for the man who would become world famous within its walls.

As he passed through the gates, Vanzetti could glimpse the gray obelisk of the Bunker Hill monument and the tall masts of "Old Ironsides" moored in the Charlestown Naval Yard. Swept into the admitting room, he spoke with a psychologist, who found convict #16102 calm and articulate except for an edgy rage when discussing his life of labor. Noting him as "a man of much greater intelligence than one would infer from the kind of work that he has followed in this country," the psychologist concluded that the new prisoner was "a pretty deep fellow." Then, as Vanzetti recalled, "I heard the iron door of this prison closing itself at my shoulder; a few minutes after that I was in a dark cell."

The case was moving at top speed now. The day after the verdict, Katzmann hired a new investigator. Replacing Captain William Proctor, who was beginning to have doubts, was Michael Stewart. The chief quit his Bridgewater job to throw himself into the investigation. Come September, Vanzetti found himself in a different court, this time alongside his friend. On Saturday, September 11, 1920, Nicola Sacco and Bartolomeo Vanzetti were indicted for first-degree murder. Faced with a crime wave, the old Commonwealth was standing firm. The yeggs were in custody, headed for trial and probably "the chair." But the old Commonwealth had not caught the most dangerous man Sacco and Vanzetti knew. For Mario Buda, it was again time to "plant the poof."

After fleeing Puffer's Place, Buda had moved to East Boston, where he read about the arrest of the men he had befriended in Mexico. In July, he moved to Portsmouth, New Hampshire, but when Sacco and Vanzetti were indicted, he left in a fury. The clownish, deadly man went to Manhattan, where he got a horse and wagon. In the back of the wagon, he packed enough dynamite to send one last message to America. Carefully assembling a street-sized version of the mail bombs of 1919, he surrounded the dynamite with five hundred pounds of iron sash weights, then wired a clock and set it for noon. The device worked perfectly, although the clock was a minute slow.

Across lower Manhattan, the bells of Trinity Church echoed down Wall Street and up Broadway. Both hands of the clock on the U.S. Assay Office were straight up. With the lunch hour beginning, brokers and bankers, clerks and messengers streamed onto the street. It was a sunny September day. Nothing unusual or ominous stirred the crowd. In 1920, no one thought twice about a horse-drawn wagon parked near the House of Morgan. Then the minute hand on the clock moved. A second was frozen in time, and a blinding blue-white flash lit up the street. The flash was followed by a deafening roar. Model Ts were tossed like toys. Trolley cars two blocks away were blown off their tracks. Windows rained shards of glass, while awnings twelve stories above the street burst into flames. Iron sash weights blasted into buildings and tore people in half. Then came a lull and the tinkling of glass. Just after noon on September 16, 1920, five days after the indictment of Sacco and Vanzetti, Wall Street had become the last major battlefield of the Anarchist Fighters.

Inside the Stock Exchange, President William H. Remick heard the blast, the silence, the shouts and screams outside. "I think we had better stop trading for the day," he said. Emerging onto the street, brokers saw what looked like the aftermath of a siege. Bodies lay strewn on the pavement. People scurried in all directions, shrieking, crying, bleeding. Windows were left sawtoothed and gaping. A massive yellowish mushroom cloud rose above the street, while white-faced men and women staggered onward, dumbstruck or hysterical.

Within minutes, clanging ambulance bells filled the financial district. Ex-servicemen cordoned off the area, locking arms, driving back onlookers. Up and down Wall Street, people tended to each other, nursing wounds, offering water, or just leading survivors away. Policemen struggled to pacify sobbing women looking for husbands, children, relatives. Hundreds soon crowded the nearest morgue. By midafternoon, the scene had settled into a numbed stillness. Thirty-eight people were dead or dying and more than three hundred were hospitalized. Soldiers patrolled the streets, while high above Wall Street, plate-glass companies were already replacing shattered windows. Throughout Manhattan, federal agents checked explosives stores and construction sites, finding no unusual sales or theft of dynamite. Once accident had been ruled out, suspicion was cast on the usual suspects—Reds, Bolsheviks, and Wobblies like "Big Bill" Haywood, whose arrest was ordered in Chicago. Then after a full day of speculation, the Bureau of Investigation announced it had found flyers.

A few minutes before noon, the flyers had been discovered in a mailbox a short walk from the House of Morgan. A mailman puzzled over them, then after the explosion turned them over to the police. On yellow paper imprinted with hand-stamped red letters, the flyers read:

REMEMBER

WE WILL NOT TOLERATE

ANY LONGER

FREE THE POLITICAL

PRISONERS OR IT WILL BE

SURE DEATH FOR ALL OF YOU.

AMERICAN ANARCHIST FIGHTERS

"The plot was conceived by the same group of terrorists who planned and executed the June 2, 1919, outrages," said Bureau of Investigation director William J. Flynn. Federal agents renewed their search for *Galleanisti*. Within days, an informer named Dominic Carbone was placed in the Norfolk County Jail in Dedham, on the third floor, Cell 13, next to Sacco's. As they paced together through the jail corridors, Sacco told Carbone that he was an anarchist, "against the capitalist," but that he had never killed anyone and would be proven innocent. "They have accused me of having committed a terrible crime, simply because I have been the defender of the workers and also because I am Italian," he wrote in a note to Carbone. "The Italians are despised by the Americans." But Sacco said nothing about the Wall Street bombing, and the informer was soon removed.

The search for the Wall Street bomber continued in print shops, in stationery stores, in stables where a horse might have been rented or stolen. Rewards for information totaled $100,000, but the only lead came from a blacksmith in Manhattan's Little Italy. The day before the explosion, the man had shoed the horse of a Sicilian with a wagon. Two men later confessed to the bombing, but their stories did not add up and police dismissed them. The bomber made a clean getaway, fleeing New York for Providence. Within weeks, Mario Buda, a.k.a. Mike Boda, was on a steamship bound for Italy. He left behind him the rubble of bombings from Milwaukee to the East Coast. Buda also left his "best friends in America," who on September 28, 1920, were arraigned in the Dedham courthouse. Pale, sad-eyed, and already starting to resemble their famous mournful photo more than their sinister mug shots, Sacco and Vanzetti pleaded not guilty.

CHAPTER FOUR

"Shout from the Rooftops"

The vilest deeds like poison weeds
Bloom well in prison-air:
It is only what is good in Man
That wastes and withers there:
Pale Anguish keeps the heavy gate,
And the Warder is Despair.

—Oscar Wilde,
The Ballad of Reading Gaol

By any measure of the human condition—innocent or guilty—
the year between their arrest and trial must have been the longest Sacco and Vanzetti spent in the custody of the Commonwealth.
For a full year and a month, the two men weighed their worst suspicions of America against the hope that had lured them from Italy.
If they were guilty, they hoped the truth could be hidden, and if
they were innocent, they could only hope this nightmare would
end. Not yet numbed by the drudgery of prison life, neither knew
he had begun the seven-year ordeal Sacco would later call "this
long and dolorous Calvary . . . this terrible and iniquitous Bastile."
Instead, each looked forward to a trial that kept receding in time.
No trial date was scheduled until November, when it was fixed for
March 7, 1921. As that date approached, the proceeding was postponed until the last day in May. As weeks and months dragged on,

both men recognized their lives to be in others' hands. "Now they are accusing me of murder," Vanzetti wrote his father, "when I have never killed nor hurt, nor robbed. But if they have another trial like my first one, they would find even Christ guilty." With time as their constant companion, both men waited while the endless march of days brought out the dueling nations inside them.

Vanzetti regressed to his Italian childhood, the bright boy from Villafalletto conquering the embittered immigrant. Ever since his arduous apprenticeship, he had feared being confined indoors. Now he took to it like a monk cloistered with his books. He had not chosen this life, but it seemed to have chosen him, bringing his idealized Italian upbringing to the fore, casting off the hard American shell formed by his toil.

Sacco took the opposite road. In jail, his boyish Italian demeanor toughened and the frenetic, industrial energy he had acquired in America ran circles inside him. Only a few months earlier he had been tending his garden, hugging his son, loving his wife. Now he sat alone in Cell 14, a six-by-eight-foot box with a wooden water bucket, a tin mug, a barred window, and an enameled chamber pot. Caged, pacing, unable to vent his fury, he counted the hours as if toiling under a time clock in an endless shift. The self-described "dumbling" plowed through *Les Misérables,* perhaps identifying with the persecuted Jean Valjean, but each time he closed the book, there were the mug, the bucket, the chamber pot, the bars. His mind was free to wander from his Italian hill town to his factory machine, from his anarchist faith to his memories of Mexico, but his hands, his idle hands made his days feverish and his nights eternal. Sacco was not in jail long before he began to have the delusions—that something was being put in his food—that would eventually land him in a mental hospital.

Because their names were now linked as if by handcuffs, many assumed Sacco and Vanzetti must be together behind bars. Yet between their arrest and trial, the two saw each other only twice, at their arraignment and indictment. The rest of the year Vanzetti remained in the dismal Charlestown State Prison while Sacco was a dozen miles to the southwest in Dedham's Norfolk County Jail.

The jail was a cross-shaped building of New England granite, its four wings extending outward from a broad central rotunda, its three-tiered cellblock painted white with green bars on each cell. Draped by ivy, surrounded by a brick wall topped with concrete and barbed wire, the jail sat two blocks from downtown Dedham, across the street from an old graveyard where the town's founders were buried in the 1600s. Most prisoners stayed in the jail a few months. Sacco would spend seven years there.

Separated yet united in their ordeal, Sacco and Vanzetti did not write each other during this year, sending greetings solely through visitors. These were many at first, but most were lawyers or police. Vanzetti had no family in America, and Rosina Sacco, about to have another child and unable to bear the sight of her husband in prison, did not visit him for months. Until the fall of 1920, almost no one came to greet Sacco as a person rather than as a prisoner. Then, in mid-October, he learned he had visitors.

Led through the echoing cellblock, he emerged into the tidy visitors' area lined with books and oak paneling. There he saw his new lawyer, Fred Moore, and two women, one plump and middle-aged, the other younger with dark hair and piercing blue eyes. When the women introduced themselves as Mary Heaton Vorse and Elizabeth Gurley Flynn, Sacco suddenly remembered the latter. "Elizabetta, I know you," he said. "I heard you speak for Lawrence strikers." Sacco was gladdened by the passable Italian spoken by Vorse, a socialite turned Socialist writer. Moore shared the latest legal developments, then the visitors listened as the prisoner, in his uniform of gray pants and striped shirt, poured out his story.

After sharing his faith in anarchy, Sacco told how he had worked all his life, that his hands were those of an edge trimmer, not a murderer. "To steal money, to kill a poor man for money! This is insult to me," he protested. "I am innocent! I no do this thing! I swear it on the head of my newborn child!" The outcry convinced Flynn, who had been rallying Socialists and Wobblies since her teen years. It had a different effect on Vorse. Like several older women who would later serve as surrogate mothers to Sacco and Vanzetti, she took a maternal view. Where others saw Sacco's intensity, she noted "a friendly way with him almost like that of a child who had never known anything but affection."

"What have I worked for in my life?" Sacco asked. "I have worked for educate myself, my comrades. Only so we go on—by learning. Do I want to go back to gorilla days, shooting men in the back?" He asked for poetry books in Italian. "Scientific books and history, too," he said. "It's a great time for me to learn." But what stayed with both women was Sacco's plea for work. "I have never loafed one day in my life," he said, holding out his hands. "If they won't let me work, better they kill me right off, for anyhow I die." After a few more minutes, the visitors left and Sacco trudged back to his cell.

Vorse, Flynn, and Moore later visited Vanzetti, finding him "calm and controlled." This second visit was shorter, the monkish Vanzetti having less to say. His chief concern was a separate trial for Sacco lest his friend be linked to the Bridgewater verdict. "Wouldn't that go against Nick?" he asked Moore. Back in his cell, Vanzetti continued his prison routine. Up with a bell at sunrise, he reached for his latest book chosen from the prison library, where he was pleased to find "the masterpieces of art and science." Another bell signaled breakfast, which, like all meals, prisoners ate in their cells. At 8:00 a.m., each prisoner, holding his nose and his stomach, lined up to dump his stinking chamber pot into a walled-in cesspool. A whistle then started the day's work. For the first time in his laboring life Vanzetti enjoyed an eight-hour day—making license plates. A second whistle meant lunch—the best he could hope for was hot dogs and baked beans, which he supplemented with olive oil or fruit bought with small sums sent by the defense committee. Another whistle sent him back to work before a final shriek gave him a half hour in the prison yard. Mingling on the asphalt, he found his fellow prisoners—about a quarter of them Italians—to be "wretches, except for a few victims of circumstances more disgraced than guilty."

Vanzetti's cell had no window, and when winter grayed the diffused light, his mood was too bleak for reading. On dreary Sundays, he often went to the prison chapel to enjoy liturgical music.

Each evening, after mail call, he sat at his table answering letters or reading while standing, leaning against a wall. Lights in the cellblock went out at nine, leaving him no choice but to sleep—or try to—then wake to another bell. Somehow in this hellhole—where "wolves" meant sodomists, where men suffering "prison stupor" stared blankly for hours—he kept his spirit alive. Gradually the dueling "I's" within him came to be a starry-eyed monk calming the angry anarchist with an ever-darkening view of America.

As word of his first trial spread, mail brought letters from strangers. The Italian Workers' Defense League offered help. Textile workers in Lawrence telegrammed their support, and news from New York told of a petition for his release signed by two hundred thousand. Such backing convinced Vanzetti that salvation lay in telling his story. "Do not keep my arrest hidden," he wrote his father. "I am innocent and you should not be ashamed. Do not be silent but shout from the rooftops that a crime has been plotted for a fistful of dollars to restore, through my sacrifice, the reputation of police lost in a hundred scandals and a hundred failures." Publicity may have offered salvation, but in a nation determined to move beyond the Great War and its lawless aftermath, where Wobblies were in jail, Socialism had peaked, and caring about causes seemed quaint, who cared about "a couple of wops in a jam"? One radical lawyer had an answer.

Fred Moore had come to Boston a few weeks after Vanzetti's conviction. He came merely to report on the case; he stayed four years. Before he left, Moore would be accused of blackmail, coercing witnesses, and entrenching the opposition with his careless manners and morals. Yet no one ever doubted that he shouted the plight of Sacco and Vanzetti from the rooftops, and few doubted his dedication. "He lived cases twenty-four hours a day until he collapsed," a friend remembered. As an attorney, Moore's career had taken a curious left turn. Admitted to the bar in 1906, he had begun practice as a Seattle railroad lawyer. Moving to Los Angeles, he kept rising through the ranks until he got a call from an old friend who had joined the Industrial Workers of the World. It was the 1910s, and throughout the West, Wobblies waging "free speech" campaigns were being jailed just for speaking on street corners in Spokane, Fresno, San Diego. . . . For reasons he never stated, Moore took his hat and revolver, walked out of his Los Angeles law office, and began defending them. For the next ten years, he, like his clients, dodged vigilantes and corporate thugs, and was sometimes run out of town on a rail. But he persisted, acquiring a bitter view of America, capitalism, and cops. Between 1910 and 1920, Moore participated in every celebrated IWW trial, yet his role was rarely as celebrated as he claimed.

In 1911, Moore liked to tell everyone, he worked with Clarence Darrow on the infamous McNamara bombing case in Los Angeles. Moore did not like to admit that he had been little more than an errand boy, once going to Oregon to see whether a witness would help destroy evidence. The following year, he was in Lawrence defending Joseph Ettor and Arturo Giovannitti on a murder charge following the great textile strike. Five years later, he had another high-profile case in Everett, Washington, where a Wobbly was charged with murder following a gun battle that killed two sheriff's deputies and a dozen union men. During the war, Moore helped defend more than one hundred "IWWs" charged with sedition in Chicago. But although Moore boasted of his headline trials, he rarely detailed his role in each. While he did much to prepare the famous cases, he was not the lead attorney in any of them. When he assumed such responsibility, the results were not always so successful.

A year before taking up the cause of Sacco and Vanzetti, Moore tried simultaneous midwestern cases. In Wichita, Kansas, he represented twenty-six Wobblies charged with sedition and draft dodging. While that case dragged toward trial, he was in Tulsa, Oklahoma, defending a man charged with dynamiting a Standard Oil executive's home. He proved the Tulsa case a frame-up, resulting in a hung jury, but winning a second trial there left him little time for the Wichita case. He desperately sought a postponement but had to face the Kansas court half prepared. His inept cross-examination drew out numerous examples of IWW sabotage, and all twenty-six defendants were found guilty. Then he fumbled again. Granted ninety days to appeal, he failed to file in time. Enraged, "Big Bill" Haywood called Moore to Chicago early in 1920, blasted him for his error, cited other "delinquencies," and forced him to resign as an IWW attorney. The following summer, Moore arrived in Boston with a reputation that exceeded his ability and a career in decline.

Recommended by Flynn and Tresca, who remembered him from Lawrence, Moore was a James Cagney lookalike in his late thirties. Slim and of average height, he had a feisty manner more suggestive of a bootlegger than a lawyer. He peppered his letters with clichés ("keep your eye on the ball and hit it hard") and laced his speech with ethnic stereotypes ("Talk to me on white man's basis!"). Photos of him reveal a cynic so steeled by courtroom tussles that his eyes seem to shift even in print. His decade with the IWW had made him intensely suspicious of every boss and stockholder, every DA and judge. With his passionate hatred of capitalists, Moore saw in Sacco and Vanzetti the makings of more than a murder case. He envisioned the men as poster boys for an embattled labor movement. Even if he could not free them, he could make them into a cause célèbre, exposing what he called "the frame-up system" and perhaps even rekindling his career.

Both in and out of court, Moore's style mirrored that of the IWW. Like the Wobblies he had defended, he was alternately noble, reckless, inspiring, disorganized, and scornful of decorum. To a commonwealth suffused with puritanical propriety, his life seemed even more scandalous than his politics. He was not just an "outsider," he was an uncouth outsider. Boston Brahmins, whose idea of "the West" was the Berkshires, saw this California lawyer as beyond the pale. None were accustomed to a man with longish hair slicked back over his head and coming almost to his collar. Few knew what to make of a lawyer strolling outside the courtroom in sandals and a Stetson. These quirks, in addition to Moore's habit of discarding a wife in favor of a secretary, marrying the latter, then moving on to the next secretary, made him the embodiment of the loose modernity the old Commonwealth feared. Moore was rumored to take drugs—morphine or cocaine. He also had the habit of disappearing during trials. Often, seeking respite from the pressure, he wandered into movie houses, where he slept to the tinkling piano of silent pictures. During the Chicago IWW trial, he simply vanished. Some said he had suffered a nervous breakdown. Haywood sent telegrams all over America trying to find his lawyer, but had to leave the case to another single attorney. While defending Sacco and Vanzetti, Moore never strayed far, yet he remained indifferent to the hostility he caused simply by entering certain rooms, and he refused to rein in his brashness, even with allies.

From the start, Aldino Felicani was skeptical of Moore but, convinced that Vanzetti's lawyer had botched the Bridgewater case, had little choice but to hire him. "We didn't know what to do . . . we were just in despair," Felicani remembered. Sweeping in with his whirlwind energy, Moore soon found himself "busy as the devil chasing after a saint." He promised only to prepare the case and let local lawyers defend it. Late in August 1920, he opened an office with an ironic phone number—Haymarket 5399—then hired a lovely Lithuanian stenographer and began dictating letters about the plight of the two men he called "the boys."

First Moore wrote Flynn asking her to find an American to join the defense committee, "at least someone with an understanding of the English language and some responsibility to the organized labor movement." Next he sent an investigator to Bridgewater, hoping to reopen the case that had tarred Vanzetti's spotless record. Moore's man turned up two witnesses who claimed the gunman did not resemble Vanzetti but were told "to keep out of this thing." Reaching out to old friends, Moore alerted a who's who of American radicals and labor leaders. He also put out feelers to respected progressives, including Harvard law professor Felix Frankfurter and Roger Baldwin, head of the newly formed American Civil Liberties Union. For Moore, no lead was too small, no contact too remote.

Would the *Nation,* the *New Republic,* or the *New York Call* provide lists of subscribers? Sharing such lists "is directly contrary to our policy," the *Nation* replied, then added, "we have decided to make an exception in this case." Would the Harvard Student Liberal Club devote a meeting to Sacco and Vanzetti? Winter meetings were booked, but a dinner address by Flynn was scheduled for spring. Might garage owner Simon Johnson have been running a stolen car ring with Mario Buda? Had anyone seen Mario Buda? Lead after lead went out; only a few came back. Moore kept dictating. By October 1920, his leads stretched all the way to Italy.

Early that fall, a journalist named Morris Gebelow had gone to Milan to cover what he hoped would be a revolution. Moore soon cabled his friend. Could Gebelow, who preferred his pen name, "Eugene Lyons," find the deported Ferruccio Coacci and convince him to return to America to testify? Could he track down Sacco's father in Torremaggiore? And might "Eugene Lyons" write some articles for the Italian press? Lyons, a small, bookish, romantic revolutionary surviving in Italy on "a mixture of bad Italian and good nerve," cabled back:

> My itinerary has been as follows: Naples, Torremaggiore, (a hell of a way out towards the Adriatic) back to Naples, and Rome. Sabino Sacco is a mighty fine fellow and devoted with all his heart to Nicola. He came to Rome and spent two days helping me get in touch with the proper people. By this time you know what a job it is to pin Italians down to definite arrangements.

When not reaching out to America and Italy, Moore reached out to the defendants, visiting them often in jail. Vanzetti was swayed by Moore—"a man of faith and ability"—and excited by the thought of having the world's workers on his side. Sacco was not so sure. He did not want to be a cause célèbre; he wanted to be home with Rosina and their newborn daughter. But Moore insisted that a favorable courtroom verdict depended on a public outcry. "Do you know what chance a colored boy has down South to get a square deal?" he wrote one journalist. "Well, an Italian in Massachusetts has just about the same kind of a chance to get a square deal on the charge of murder. Please put your shoulder to the wheel."

Money was always an object. Moore earned $150 a week but was perpetually in need of another few dollars or a few hundred. "Money talks more effectively in the courtroom than any other thing that I know," he wrote one union boss. "Its voice is omnipotent." Vanzetti's guilty verdict had increased contributions to the defense committee, and Moore helped himself to the ready cash, tapping the committee for $2,350 in September, $2,710 in October, and $3,485 in November. He allowed himself a few luxuries— fine dinners and a driver, the same Ricardo Orciani once implicated in the murders—but spent the rest of the money hiring assistants to dig up leads and paying publicists to pump out articles and pamphlets. "Moore was . . . an honest person," Felicani remembered, "but there was no limit to Moore's spending money. If Moore came to my office at five o'clock and asked me for $1,000, for some reason or another at ten o'clock in the evening, if he knew I had some money left in the treasury, he would ask for $500 more. . . . Of course this established, from the very beginning, a very difficult business between me and Moore. We were just like cat and dog."

Sensing a worldwide audience, Moore sent solicitations to labor publications in Europe and South America. Closer to home, he enlisted radicals who had survived the recent purge. Carlo Tresca, a volatile anarchist with a penchant for stirring up trouble, now spoke to Italian workers about the fate of Sacco and Vanzetti. The gentlemanly poet Arturo Giovannitti, who had spent several nights with the Saccos during a 1915 strike, lent his eloquent voice to the cause, speaking all over New England. The omnipresent Elizabeth Gurley Flynn threw her Workers Defense Union behind Sacco and Vanzetti. Moore also garnered the support of the ACLU and its New England affiliate. The latter's director was initially skeptical, having been a juror in a trial prosecuted by Frederick Katzmann. Recalling the DA's "ability and fairness," the director demanded to know why Sacco and Vanzetti would not receive impartial treatment. He was shown transcripts from Vanzetti's first trial. The New England Civil Liberties Union soon published *Sacco and Vanzetti: Shall There Be a Mooney Frame-up in New England?* The pamphlet began, "There is grave danger that two men now held in Massachusetts prisons for alleged murder will be sent to the electric chair on evidence no more substantial than the fabricated testimony which put Mooney and Billings behind bars. . . . It will be asked, can such things happen in America?"

In these early days, when few had heard of Sacco and Vanzetti, the names Mooney and Billings framed an ominous scenario. On July 22, 1916, someone threw a bomb at a San Francisco parade rallying Americans to prepare for the war in Europe. Ten were killed and forty wounded. Police arrested Tom Mooney and Warren Billings, each previously accused of dynamiting high-voltage towers. In hasty trials, Billings got life in prison and Mooney was condemned to hang, but the verdicts soon unraveled. Published letters proved the government's chief witness had perjured himself, and a photo showed Mooney a mile from the scene just five minutes before the bombing. As Mooney sat on death row at San Quentin, a clamor arose for his pardon. When it grew to an international outcry, President Wilson urged California's governor to intervene. A federal commission did the same, but California's Supreme Court upheld Mooney's conviction. The hanging was set for December 1918. While labor held rallies, parades, and a nationwide "Mooney Day," still more proof of a frame-up emerged, including Dictaphone recordings of San Francisco's DA (another target of the 1919 mail bombs) proposing devious methods to get "that son-of-a-bitch Mrs. Mooney." Finally, two weeks before the scheduled execution, the governor commuted Mooney's sentence to life in prison for a crime he did not commit.

By the fall of 1920, most of the nation had forgotten Tom Mooney, but to union leaders and radicals his story suggested what might happen to Sacco and Vanzetti. The parallels were already disturbing. In both cases, suspects had been identified without a police lineup. The press had presumed guilt. The accused had been linked to labor unions, anarchism, and a previous crime. Given these similarities, supporters of Sacco and Vanzetti worried. Would their trial, like Mooney's, include witnesses changing their stories? Impassioned appeals to a jury's patriotism? Wholesale denunciations of anarchism? Human life hanging by the thread of a governor's mercy?

As Sacco and Vanzetti endured their first winter in prison, Moore continued to spread their names. In December, a *New Republic* article written by a defense committee publicist charged the prosecution in Vanzetti's first trial with creating "an atmosphere of viciousness and violence around the whole Italian race." A few weeks later, Flynn's Workers Defense Union put out a ten-cent pamphlet entitled *Are They Doomed?* Recapping the recent Red Scare, the arrest and "frame-up," the pamphlet tiptoed around anarchism, calling Sacco and Vanzetti "Italian labor organizers. . . . Looking at them, talking with them, it would be hard for an intelligent person to conceive of their robbing or murdering anyone." All that winter, the defense committee sent weekly updates to labor and Socialist papers across America. As Moore intended, these broadened the case beyond Italian anarchists. Soon money began pouring into the cluttered office in the North End: December—$6,634.85; January 1921—$5,988.54; February—$8,226.33. Although Sacco and Vanzetti were far more radical than any union, their cause was taken up by cement makers in Oklahoma, tailors in Kansas, painters in Florida, and butchers in New York. Vanzetti was thrilled. "The people proclaim my innocence, demand my freedom," he wrote his father, "and if you knew what they have done, are doing, and will do for me, you would feel proud." From his cell, however, he could not see a countercrusade mounting to protect Massachusetts from radicals like Fred Moore and his clients.

With the trial shaping up as a high-profile battle between law and lawlessness, Frederick Katzmann did not want to be known for the rest of his life as "the man who *did not* get Sacco and Vanzetti." His dogged investigation, led by the single-minded Chief Stewart, continued all through the winter of 1920–21. The chief checked material evidence—guns, bullets, shells, a cap—while the DA interviewed more than two hundred witnesses. Several still swore the Italians they had seen in the Brockton police station were the Pearl Street gunmen. Many more, however, insisted Sacco and Vanzetti were not the murderers. A railroad cop who had seen two strangers at the Braintree station on April 15 remembered them smoking. "Sacco does not smoke," prosecution papers noted. (Vanzetti smoked "like a Turk," as he admitted, but only a pipe and an occasional cigar.) A state police report on Sacco reported that "the sight of blood made him sick," and that many who knew him "do not think he would have had the courage to commit such an act as the Braintree murder." With a case to win, Katzmann tallied the incriminating testimony and filed the rest.

Talking to witnesses was easy, however, compared to ferreting out the background of the men in custody. Sacco and Vanzetti came from an alien world, America's subnation of Italians, with its confusing language and tangled web of aunts, uncles, and cousins. The Italian community was impenetrable to an Irish-bred police chief and a Harvard-educated DA. Early investigations contained obvious errors. One report claimed Sacco "could speak good English in 1909." Having heard Sacco, Katzmann realized that only an Italian could infiltrate his world. Aside from court interpreters, the DA did not know any Italians, yet he knew men who knew some. In December, he contacted one of these, a detective with a flop brim hat, a pencil-thin mustache, and an exotic name.

Feri Felix Weiss had infiltrated anarchists for the Bureau of Investigation and raided the offices of *Cronaca Sovversiva*. He knew both Sacco and Vanzetti as members of the "notorious Galleani group . . . who had bomb-outrages on the brain." Still, he was skeptical. "Anarchists do not commit crimes for money but for a principle," Weiss assured Katzmann. Banditry, he added, "was not in their code." This did not deter the DA, who, with a trial three months away, needed inside information. A month after the federal mole, Dominic Carbone, was removed from the cell beside Sacco's, Weiss agreed to find another Italian to go undercover. He sent a letter—marked "Burn this as soon as you read it"—to John Ruzzamenti in Pennsylvania. Ruzzamenti had helped Weiss spy on Italian draft dodgers, and the detective was sure his friend would want more such work.

> My Dear John,
> . . . Would you like to help me out on a case which I may clinch here? It is the case of Saco and Vanzetti, who are in jail awaiting trial for having shot the paymaster of the South Braintree shoe-factory. . . .
> It is a very important case and I need a clever Italian who would mix with the gang, and if necessary even stay in jail for a few days just to find out what they say. . . .
> If we are successful in this venture, we might tackle the big Wall Street affair in New York, as all the other agencies are up against a wall in that matter.

Weiss later swore the plan was Katzmann's. Katzmann swore it was Weiss's. Whoever cooked up the scheme, it brought Ruzzamenti rushing to Boston. Weiss sent him on to Katzmann's office, where the DA greeted him and told him about the scheme. Ruzzamenti was to be arrested breaking into a house, then thrown into a cell beside Sacco's. Somehow he was to get the pacing prisoner to talk, especially about Mike Boda. Ruzzamenti refused, not wanting to acquire an arrest record. Katzmann then lamented that he was "right hard up against it," that he "had no evidence," Ruzzamenti recalled. "I haven't got a case against these fellows unless I can get this fellow Boda," the DA said. Katzmann then suggested Ruzzamenti go to Stoughton to rent a room from Rosina. Ruzzamenti agreed, but the plan went nowhere. Weiss heard no more from Katzmann. Ruzzamenti heard no more from either man and was soon back in Pennsylvania writing Katzmann for expenses. Katzmann later denied being more than an unwitting recipient of a surprise visitor whom he had sent packing, and no stranger speaking Italian ever showed up at Rosina Sacco's bungalow.

All that winter, however, strangers speaking Italian did show up at Sacco-Vanzetti defense rallies throughout Boston. The strangers were undercover federal agents. As Flynn, Tresca, and Giovannitti fired up audiences, agents took notes and, two ex-agents would later charge, placed spies on the defense committee. Agents also intercepted Aldino Felicani's mail. Fred Moore, having learned of the informer placed near Sacco's cell, fired off brisk letters to Katzmann inquiring about federal involvement in the prosecution, but received no replies. No federal activities came to light until 1926 when Bureau of Investigation officials called accusations of their involvement in the case "a figment of imagination."

While snow drifted outside his cell window, Sacco's restless energy merged with despair. As winter wore on, he suffered "this evil inquisition that crushes me every day, this continual exchange of to-day for tomorrow, for next week." He wrote few letters and had few visitors other than the demons beginning to swirl around him. "The poor Nick must have been very sorry for a little visit," Vanzetti noted. "He is so expansive and social. . . . Certainly he suffer the confinement more than I, for I was always a wild bear." Entering their ninth month awaiting trial, neither prisoner suspected that the first of many shady characters was about to tarnish their case.

Just before the new year, the phone rang in the defense committee office. An anarchist named Beniamino Cicchietti volunteered startling news. He could free Sacco and Vanzetti—for a price. Suspicious but interested, Felicani suggested a meeting. On January 2, 1921, Cicchietti burst into the office trailing a frumpy young woman he introduced as Angelina DeFalco. Claiming to be a court interpreter and good friend of Katzmann's, DeFalco explained that a "not guilty" verdict could be guaranteed by hiring Katzmann's brother Percy to defend Sacco and Vanzetti. With his brother heading the defense team, Katzmann would turn over the prosecution to a subordinate. "The district attorney and his assistants and the foreman of the jury will all have to be fixed," DeFalco said. "There will be a mock trial and the men will be acquitted." But there were stipulations. Freedom was guaranteed solely for Sacco. "Vanzetti is a tough case," DeFalco added. "He's been sentenced. It's pretty hard. But you can get Vanzetti out too, provided you are in a position to pay." Pay was the other stumbling block. The scheme would cost "a great deal of money."

Uncertain whether he was staring into a trap, looking at a lunatic, or on the verge of freeing his friends, Felicani turned to his committee. Over the next few days, anarchists met with Cicchietti and DeFalco, bargaining in Italian, fixing details, setting the price at $50,000. When Felicani balked, the fee dropped to $40,000, with just $5,000 up front. And if he did not go through with the deal? Felicani asked. Would the men be convicted? "Of course," DeFalco answered. Fred Moore was not told about DeFalco but somehow got word. Sensing another frame-up, he put a stop to the affair, infuriating anarchists on the committee. Moore talked Felicani out of attending a Friday evening *banquetta* at DeFalco's home with the Katzmann brothers and another well-respected attorney. Late that evening, curious about what he had missed, Felicani drove past DeFalco's house in Dedham. Three cars were parked outside. Felicani noted the license plates and had them checked. The cars belonged to the Katzmanns and the third attorney. Something was clearly afoot.

The next time DeFalco went to committee headquarters, Moore bugged the office, wiring a microphone to the basement where a shivering stenographer sat taking notes. With the conspiracy on paper, Moore then had DeFalco arrested. Two weeks later, the case came to trial. In the witness stand, Felicani quoted DeFalco. "Oh, we have a little society of our own," she had told him. "Fred Katzmann, Mr. Squires and Percy Katzmann and others are in it." A Boston police inspector recalled DeFalco vowing to "fix those anarchists." The defiant woman wept on the witness stand. She claimed to have seen a poster in the defense committee office depicting the beheading of Katzmann. "Don't you know we are Anarchist Bolsheviks?" one Italian allegedly told her. "If those two victims are convicted, the head of Fred Katzmann comes off." Denials flew as thickly as accusations. Moore called the scheme a frame-up engineered by the Katzmann brothers. Katzmann, although his car had been seen at DeFalco's home, swore he had never heard of her before her arrest. Adding to the incendiary atmosphere, one anarchist refused to take an oath on a Bible, while another remained silent when asked if he supported the United States government.

Judge Michael Murray could barely conceal his contempt. Ruling that witnesses' stories were at "hopeless variance," the judge declared, "I have heard all the testimony I care to." DeFalco was found not guilty, and the judge dismissed Moore's attack on Katzmann as "reprehensible to the last degree." Angelina DeFalco returned to her duties as court interpreter and later to her "little society." In 1931, she was convicted of extorting $1,550 in another ploy to free a prisoner.

The DeFalco affair did more than expose a sordid scheme; it made mortal enemies of Moore and Katzmann. Instead of meeting as equal rivals before the bench, the DA and defense attorney had squared off, with Katzmann in the witness stand and Moore asking questions. Had the DA received privileged information about the Sacco-Vanzetti case? In a huff, Katzmann replied, "Neither in this case or any other case, nor in any case pending in my office since I have been District Attorney." The brief clash reverberated from Charlestown Prison to the jail in Dedham. "It was front page stuff in the Boston papers day after day," Felicani remembered. "We tried, and we actually did, put the Massachusetts court on trial in a Massachusetts court. That's the thing that Judge Thayer never forgave us for. We sealed, at that trial, the fate of Sacco and Vanzetti." Reading about the affair, Vanzetti was appalled. "What a pigsty!" he wrote Luigia. "What a prostitution of justice! What scoundrels these honest men!"

On February 13, ten days after the DeFalco verdict, jury summonses went out to five hundred "good men and true" of Norfolk County. For Sacco and Vanzetti, judgment seemed just weeks away, but their attorney was nowhere near ready for a trial. Moore needed additional time, especially to pursue his Italian leads. "Getting started is damned hard," Eugene Lyons cabled Moore. "I do wish

Italians could keep dates." In four months roaming Italy, Lyons had stirred up politicians in Sacco's hometown, placed a few articles in the Italian press, and started a Comitato Pro-Sacco-Vanzetti in Rome. High in an Apennine hill town, he had even tracked down Ferruccio Coacci—"a nice fellow, but he has darn little courage," Lyons wrote to Moore. "I can by no stretch of the imagination imagine him in the role of villain in a plot to rob." (Lyons also relayed Mrs. Coacci's version of Chief Stewart's visit to Puffer's Place—that she had opened the door to find three men with guns drawn, that her husband had not agreed to be deported that evening.) Coacci would not return to America, Lyons told Moore. Another cable soon sent the journalist in search of a more respectable witness who might single-handedly win the case.

Sacco insisted that on the afternoon of the Braintree murders he had visited the Italian consulate. Seeking travel papers, he had presented a five-by-seven photo of himself, Rosina, and Dante. A clerk had told him to return with a smaller snapshot. Sensing an airtight alibi, Moore contacted the consulate but was told that the clerk on duty the previous April 15 had returned to Italy in ill health. Moore wired Lyons, providing the man's name and hometown on the coast south of Rome. In early February, Lyons found Giuseppe Andrower. Told about the murder case, Andrower remembered Sacco, the oversized photo, and how he and fellow clerks had laughed at it. He remembered seeing Sacco on a Thursday. He thought it was the fifteenth. He checked his calendar. "Sure enough the 15th was on a Thursday," Lyons wrote Moore. "As to the hour . . . he has no hesitancy in asserting that it was between two and three in the afternoon because he recalls that Sacco's visit was the last he had in the office that day."

Andrower offered to sign an affidavit, but Moore knew that a government official testifying in person would sway a jury better than any number of the defendants' radical friends. He wired Lyons to bring Andrower back to America—immediately. Because the clerk could not possibly arrive by March 7, Moore filed for a continuance. The trial was postponed until May 31. Sacco and

Vanzetti sat in jail, their patience stretched to the breaking point, while Moore frantically pursued the man whose willingness to cross the Atlantic might save them.

Come March, Moore and his comely stenographer whipped out cables and letters, but each took its time getting to Italy. Letters needed weeks to make the crossing; even cables, entangled in the Italian bureaucracy, were far from rapid. Moore would not be deterred. Lyons suggested that strong letters, especially one from Sacco, might persuade Andrower, so Moore returned to the Norfolk County Jail to get Sacco busy writing, then dictated his own plea. "The boy is as innocent of the crime of April 15th as are you or I," he wrote Andrower. "But powerful forces are arrayed against him and only the truth can save him." Moore recognized the hardship of a transatlantic journey but added:

> The jury who will be Americans of limited experience and narrow social vision will question why you are not here. There will be apparently reputable persons who will say that they saw Sacco at Braintree at the hour of 3 o'clock, but you know that he was not there. You know that he was in your office at that hour. We must have the power of your personality in front of the jury.

Weeks passed while this letter steamed across the Atlantic. In the meantime, Lyons met Andrower in Rome and treated him like "a potentate." In early April, Moore finally received a reply. "The fellow is mighty agreeable until the money question is touched," Lyons wrote. "The only way to keep him friendly is to act liberally with him." In other words, if Andrower were to go to America, he would need to be reimbursed. Money, of course, was no problem for Moore. He immediately wired $300, assuring Lyons, "We will take care of whatever he may be losing by reason of his coming here. This is simply an advance payment." He also enclosed a letter from Sacco. But just as Moore was budgeting a round trip from Italy, an urgent cable came from Rome. The Italian police, cracking

down on radicals after an anarchist bombing in Milan, had arrested Lyons. Released after a day in custody, he found himself
trailed, hounded, and on the verge of losing his crucial witness.
Andrower's health was rapidly deteriorating, Lyons cabled Moore.
He now claimed he would only go to America if fully compensated
for his losses, "and he mentioned the modest figure of $5,000!!"
Even for a lawyer who believed money's voice "omnipotent," this
was an outrage. "He cannot get $5,000 or indeed, any part of that
sum," Moore fired back. "If he cannot come in the name of common ordinary decency, he had better stay away. . . . We are not going to purchase his testimony."

As the April 15 anniversary of the Braintree murders passed,
the anguished cat-and-mouse game continued. Moving cautiously
between Rome and the clerk's coastal town, Lyons managed to
dodge police, but Andrower held out for his "modest figure." Then
on April 29, Lyons was arrested again and ordered to leave Italy.
"The chief charge against me is I was doing propaganda for the
case," he wrote. Like a radio signal beamed over the Atlantic,
Moore's Italian connection was breaking up. The attorney wired
back, telling Lyons to make one last plea.

A few days before leaving the country, Lyons made a final trip
to Rome. He found Andrower in the American embassy looking
"more like a cadaver than a man." The clerk would not change his
mind. On May 13, Andrower completed his affidavit, swearing he
had seen Sacco in Boston on the afternoon of April 15: "I have
done my duty and I hope that an American Jury will do theirs, saving an innocent man," Andrower wrote Moore. "If I were a millionaire, I would come at my own expenses as Justice demands,
but I am still sick and have a big family to support. I am not able to
come in States without getting a-nough money." If the trial could
be postponed until June 15, the clerk suggested, and if he could get
$3,000, he might still make the trip. Moore, who had taken a few
days off to marry another secretary, did not respond. On May 17,
Lyons left for Paris, taking with him advice from a police commissioner: "Stop bothering with the Saccos and Vanzettis and the
socialist dogs, and take care of your own interests."

After dozens of letters and cables, Moore had nothing to show from Italy except affidavits from the clerk and Ferruccio Coacci. The latter's proved useless. Coacci swore he did not know Sacco and Vanzetti, a lie Moore knew would drag the rest of his statement down with it. Moore discarded Coacci's affidavit, submitted Andrower's—filed late but accepted by the court—and made final preparations. By late May, when the leaves were Celtic green outside Charlestown Prison and the Norfolk County Jail, Sacco and Vanzetti finally ended their thirteen-month wait for their day in court. May 31 dawned clear and warm in the Boston area. At 9:30 a.m., police wagons began to pull up outside the courthouse in the peaceful little town of Dedham.

CHAPTER FIVE

"I Seen This Fellow Shoot This Fellow"

Law, says the judge as he looks down his nose,
Speaking clearly and most severely,
Law is as I've told you before,
Law is as you know I suppose,
Law is but let me explain it once more,
Law is The Law.

Yet law-abiding scholars write:
Law is neither wrong nor right,
Law is only crimes
Punished by places and by times.

—W. H. Auden, "Law Like Love"

Listed as just another trial—docket numbers 5545 and 5546—*Commonwealth of Massachusetts v. Nicola Sacco and Bartolomeo Vanzetti* unfolded as a variety of genres. It was a whodunit, a seminar on ballistics, an inquisition, a perpetual puzzle. But as it dragged on and on, the trial came to resemble that venerable Boston institution—the marathon.

The trial lasted six and a half weeks. Its transcript filled 2,266 pages. It featured 167 witnesses. Among these were four doctors in total agreement, dozens of eyewitnesses completely at odds, and four ballistics experts who seemed to be speaking about different guns, different bullets. The jury was asked to keep 167 testimonies straight without taking notes. Useful evidence was mired in swamps of jargon—about automobile accessories, the precise locations of dead bodies, and exhaustive statistics on bullets and shells. Some witnesses spoke Spanish, others Italian or fractured English. And after sitting through thirty-seven days of numbing testimony, the jury rendered its verdict, one proper Boston saw as just but the world regarded as blind or bigoted.

Like the stage plays that would later re-create it, the trial began with an entrance. But the entrance seemed farcical—as if two Italian anarchists had stumbled onto the set of a play about the American Revolution. Just after 9:30 a.m. on May 31, 1921, escorted up the courthouse steps by a circle of police, came first Sacco, and, a few minutes later, Vanzetti. Though gaunt and pale, each was nattily dressed, Sacco in a dark suit and a derby, his friend wearing a long coat and sporty cap. Hustled toward the courtroom, neither man had much chance to survey the scene, yet each was dwarfed by the power and tradition emanating from downtown Dedham.

One of the oldest towns in the old Commonwealth, Dedham was among its most picturesque. The scene surrounding the courthouse could have come from Currier and Ives. Rising above oaks and elms on the adjacent common stood the gleaming white, triple-decked steeple of the First Church of Dedham, host to the village's initial town meeting in 1644. The church was flanked by the white façades and black shutters of stately colonial homes. Crowning the stage set was the amber dome of the Norfolk County Courthouse, topped by the Stars and Stripes hanging limp on this bright spring morning. What Sacco and Vanzetti failed to notice of Dedham on May 31 they would have ample time to absorb later. Twice a day—each morning and after lunch—the defendants would be marched out of jail, past the old graveyard, up a shady street alongside white picket fences, and finally into the courthouse.

On this first morning, Sacco and Vanzetti were led to an open cage with wrought-iron rails. Meeting for the first time since the previous fall, they kissed each other on both cheeks and took seats in the cage. As lawyers conferred in the judge's chambers, they chatted until a sheriff stepped before the court. "Hear ye! Hear ye!" he began, reeling off a long peroration that ended with "God save the Commonwealth of Massachusetts." A moment later, a robed, white-haired man emerged from a door beside the bench and took his seat before tall walnut bookshelves. A pale moon of a clock hung high above him. Against this backdrop, the judge seemed a specter, his dark, penetrating eyes shrouded in leathery skin, his white mustache a whisk broom beneath his prominent nose. He was a head shorter than any guard or bailiff near him, yet his imperial manner left no doubt of his authority. Vanzetti knew him all too well, but this was Sacco's first look at Judge Webster Thayer.

In a voice encrusted by time, the judge addressed potential jurors who filled the courtroom. Jury duty might be "painful, confining, and distressing," the judge cautioned, but "you must remember the American soldier had other duties he would rather have performed than those that resulted in his giving up his life upon the battlefields of France." The judge asked jurors to "perform with the same spirit of patriotism, courage, and devotion to duty." Then the first name was called and the shirking began.

The trial, the *Boston Globe* predicted, would be "more closely watched than any trial in the history of the State." Jurors would be sequestered for weeks. The DA had received death threats, the judge had his own bodyguard, and the defendants were *anarchists*. The word kindled its own brand of fear. An anarchist had assassinated President McKinley. Anarchists had bombed a Bronx courthouse. The Anarchist Fighters, their midnight bombs, and the Wall Street carnage all remained fresh in public memory. With two anarchists now come to disturb its peace, Dedham was clearly terrified. The dignified courtroom, with its high ceiling, ornate wooden benches, and white terra-cotta walls, had been turned into a fortress. Inside and out, twenty-two armed guards stood watch. Two Bureau of Investigation agents and a member of the New York City bomb squad circulated through the building. Police flanked the men in their cage. Cast-iron shutters and sliding steel doors protected courtroom walls. But who would protect the jurors once the trial was over?

For the next twelve hours, the good men of Norfolk County came up with imaginative reasons why they could not sit on this jury. One was excused as a Christian Scientist, another by claiming union membership. Scores were opposed to capital punishment. Sending a man to the electric chair, one said, would upset his nerves.

"Not lack of courage, is it?" Judge Thayer asked.

"No."

"Excused."

Those few willing to serve came under intense scrutiny. Prosecution and defense had carefully screened the jury pool. Now, Fred Moore, with his black suit and gangster face, and the sturdy, gray-suited Frederick Katzmann, sporting a sunburn from weekend golf, made their challenges. Each was scribbled on typed notes prepared by the defense:

> Gelotte, Otto, stone-cutter, Quincy: Age about 52. Not a religious man. No church affiliations. He has voted for a Socialist candidate. . . . A union man— liberal minded and reads extensively. . . . —Challenge State.

> Chamberlain, Percy A., conductor, Dedham: The father and brothers of this man have been friends and clients of District Attorney Katzmann. This particular man is described as being narrow-minded and ignorant. Is the chairman of local "American Society."—Challenge Sacco.

Assisting Moore were Thomas and J. J. McAnarney. Moore had hired the longtime Quincy fixtures—J. J. a railroad lawyer and Thomas an associate district court judge—to represent Vanzetti. A third McAnarney, John, well respected in Boston legal circles, would offer advice. Before taking the case, the brothers interviewed Sacco and Vanzetti, whose sincerity convinced them to lend the prestigious McAnarney name to the defense. Short, meticulous, and anything but radical, the McAnarneys added roots to Moore's fly-by-night style. Moore had promised to take a backseat at the trial, but needing a victory to restore his reputation, he had no such intention. Arguments about potential jurors showed him to be in charge. The McAnarneys would have preferred at least one banker or businessman on the jury, but Moore would have no "capitalists."

> Carter, Roscoe A., manufacturer, Needham: Age 40; member of the well known Wm. A. Carter knitting goods manufacturers of Needham. . . . He and his brothers are prominent in state and national politics. Protestant—Free Mason and rich.—Challenge Sacco.

The parade continued all afternoon and into the night. By 10:00 p.m., 175 candidates had been screened. The next day, another 175 were vetted. Finally on June 2, the last of 500 potential jurors was excused. The jury numbered seven. Throughout the process, Judge Thayer was livid, angrily lecturing about civic duty. Now, faced with a four-day delay to summon new prospects, he fell back on an old law allowing the court to round up "bystanders." Late that Thursday evening, sheriffs and deputies roamed Norfolk County grabbing any voting-aged man who had not fled the streets when word of the juror search spread. Men were taken off streetcars, from isolated farmhouses, from smoke-filled social clubs. A groom was brought from his wedding dinner. On Friday morning when Sacco and Vanzetti entered their cage, 175 men sat staring at them. Another twelve-hour session featured more excuses. One man claimed to be deaf, then blithely answered the judge's questions. Sacco and Vanzetti laughed until tears ran down their cheeks. Toward midnight, the twelfth juror was chosen. The trial could begin, but not before Moore protested. The law, he told Judge Thayer, called for soliciting "bystanders" *in and around* the courtroom.

"When we adjourned there were no bystanders here as I understand it," the judge snapped. "Don't say there were. You prove it!"

Claiming sheriff's deputies had grabbed men they knew would favor conviction, Moore formally challenged the jury selection.

Thayer overruled, and at 1:35 a.m., while guards yawned, while Sacco and Vanzetti struggled to stay awake, the judge called for the jury to be sworn in. "The jury is in bed," he was told, but Thayer had the men brought from makeshift quarters down the hall. Some with shirts open, others wearing slippers, the twelve were empaneled. The trial was adjourned until Monday.

A grocer. A mason. Two machinists. A retired police chief. Two factory workers. A photographer. A farmer. Two real estate brokers. A clerk at Filene's. The jurors all had Anglo or Irish surnames— Ripley, McHardy, McNamara, King, Hersey. Only one was close to the age of either Sacco or Vanzetti. The rest were bald or balding, white-haired, with faces the color of library paste. Each was given a comb, a brush, and a whisk broom, then assigned a cot in the grand jury room and told to bide his time. All that weekend, the strangers trapped in the echoing courthouse got to know one another. They read dog-eared *National Geographic*s and thumbed through doily-like newspapers with trial news snipped out. The papers listed vaudeville revues and movies starring Fatty Arbuckle and Jackie Coogan. Front pages reported a riot in Tulsa, Oklahoma, where rampaging whites had torn through the city's "Negro Wall Street," torching buildings and killing dozens. Jurors read about the ongoing crime wave—an Italian gangster had robbed a jewelry store in Times Square—and lamented the Red Sox, who were staggering again. By Sunday afternoon, weary of reading and playing cards, jurors listened to scratchy 78s on a hand-cranked Victrola. Finally, the long weekend ended.

The grueling trial opened with a grueling trip. On Monday morning, eight cars set out from the courthouse carrying jurors, attorneys, reporters, and Judge Thayer. Their first destination: the scene of the crime. Arriving on Pearl Street, jurors were shown the fence where the gunmen had waited and the places where Parmenter and Berardelli had fallen. From inside shoe factories, they peered out windows through which witnesses had seen everything and nothing. Then they sped on, following the getaway route. After lunch at a diner, the convoy drove through choking dust to the woods where the Buick had been found. There they startled two lovers on a blanket, sending a woman fleeing while her beau shrugged and wondered. On the procession went, visiting Puffer's Place, the Johnson home where Sacco and Vanzetti had stopped on the night of their arrest, and the garage where Boda, or Buda, had left his car. At sunset, after ninety-five bouncing, backbreaking miles, the jury returned to the courthouse. Each man had dust in his hair, dust in his eyes, dust coating his skin, but each also had vivid images to match the mountain of words about to bury him. Jurors desperately wanted baths, but bathing would have required them to separate, something court officials would not allow during sequestration. Grimy and gritty, the twelve men crawled onto their cots.

The following morning, the prosecution began laying out its case. A simple detective story, it began with bullets and blood. Dr. George McGrath told of extracting four bullets from Berardelli and scratching the base of each with a needle marking I, II, III, and IIII. One bullet was singled out. Bullet III had torn through lung, aorta, kidney, and stomach, killing Berardelli. Passing a magnifying glass, jurors examined the flattened hunk of lead. Then the courtroom was stunned by the sight of bloody clothes, overcoats with ragged holes, and undergarments more blood-red than white. Gasps came from the gallery. Sacco and Vanzetti sat stone-faced.

Next came eyewitnesses. While Katzmann looked on and Chief Stewart whispered advice, questioning was conducted by Assistant DA Harold Williams. An affable, bespectacled man with a quiet intensity, Williams asked Shelley Neal about first spotting the bandits. The American Express clerk had seen only one face—sallow, blue-eyed, and sunken. Neal did not claim either "funny looking" stranger was Sacco or Vanzetti, but he remembered the Buick. Under cross-examination, he described the "murder car" in exhausting detail, but admitted that having seen it more than fifteen times since the crime, it was "pretty well burned into [my] system." He said nothing about seeing the second car he had mentioned at the inquest. The prosecution called its next witness.

From his third-floor window, shoe cutter Mark Carrigan had heard shots, then watched the Buick drive by with a man firing from the passenger seat. But the car had passed quickly; Carrigan had not gotten a good look. Nor had mechanic Jimmy Bostock, who had spoken to Parmenter seconds before he was gunned down. Bostock remembered the men leaning on the fence—"I thought they was Italian fruit peddlers." He had just turned away when the shooting began. "As I looked down there, this Berardelli was on his knees in a crouched position . . ." Williams invited Bostock to imitate the guard's pose. Crouching before the jury, Bostock said the gunman "shot, I should say, he shot at Berardelli probably four or five times. He stood guard over him." But despite his proximity, Bostock could not identify anyone. Lewis Wade was next.

He had been gassing up Mr. Slater's car on Pearl Street. In Brockton after the arrest, he had singled out Sacco as "the man who killed Berardelli." He had said the same to the grand jury. The prosecution was counting on his testimony, but Wade was no longer certain. He described the gunman as "probably twenty-six or twenty-seven," with a gray shirt and brown hair. "And he needed a shave." But after indicating "the man on my left in that cage," Wade hesitated. "Well, I ain't sure now," he said. "I have a little doubt." Wade explained that he had recently seen a man in a barber shop who resembled Sacco. Further questioning deepened his doubts until he could only repeat, "I do not know, it is so long ago." As he left the stand, a policeman said, "We're not through with you yet." Wade, who had worked at Slater & Morrill for sixteen years, was soon fired.

For the next three days, witness after witness described the shooting, yet none identified Sacco or Vanzetti as a murderer. Then late Thursday afternoon, a prim woman in a stiff floral hat took the stand. Mary Splaine worked upstairs around the corner from Pearl Street. Forty-three, unmarried, and living with her brother, Splaine was the gossip—"one of the most irresponsible persons he ever came in contact with," her boss had told the Pinkertons—who had been spreading rumors linking one Slater & Morrill employee or another to the murders. On April 15, she had chatted with Parmenter and

Berardelli as they picked up the payroll. From her second-story window, she then watched them heft the strongboxes across the railroad tracks. They had just disappeared down Pearl Street when she heard what sounded like an auto backfiring. "There is shooting!" someone yelled. Splaine looked up and saw the Buick pass. A man was hanging out the passenger side nearest her. From eighty feet away, she took a mental snapshot that made one juror wonder whether Mary Splaine had a photographic memory. But a bookkeeper is paid to be precise.

"He was a man that I should say was slightly taller that I am," Splaine testified. "He weighed possibly from 140 to 145 pounds. He was muscular—he was an active looking man. I noticed particularly the left hand was a good sized hand, a hand that denoted strength. . . . He had a gray, what I thought was a shirt—had a grayish, like navy color. . . . The forehead was high. The hair was brushed back and it was between, I should think, two inches and two and one-half inches in length and had dark eyebrows, but the complexion was a white, peculiar white that looked greenish."

And had Miss Splaine seen the man since?

"I saw him at the police station in Brockton . . . three weeks after the murder."

And did Miss Splaine see him now?

"Yes sir, the man sitting nearest to me on this side of . . . what do you call it, a cage?"

"The man with the mustache, or the man without the mustache?"

"No, sir. The man without the mustache."

"Is that the same man you saw at Brockton?"

"It is."

"Are you sure?"

"Positive."

Rising to cross-examine, Moore had Splaine recap what she had seen. Soon her memory seemed more telescopic than photographic. Splaine had seen Sacco but nothing else—no one running, no gatekeeper raising the gate, nothing but a strong hand. A left hand.

"His left hand was on the same side—on the side of the driver of the car, wasn't it?" Moore asked.

"It ought to be."

"Yes, it naturally would, wouldn't it? . . . So that his body should have been between him and his left hand, shouldn't it?"

"Yes."

"Yes. How was it you saw his left hand and could not see anything of the right hand?"

"Because I saw his face, and I watched that, and I did not look for the right hand."

Moore then turned to the transcript in his own hand. He read Splaine's testimony at the inquest where, pressed to identify the gunman, she had answered, "I don't think my opportunity afforded me the right to say he is the man." Moore thought he had won this lawyer's game of "Gotcha," but Splaine had an explanation. The transcript was wrong. She had never said any such thing. No matter how Moore rephrased it, Splaine remained certain. Sacco was the gunman, and she had never said he wasn't.

After a brief recess, J. J. McAnarney took over. The staid Commonwealth lawyer was more blunt than the ex-IWW attorney. "Miss Splaine, you really did not have sufficient opportunity to observe that man to enable you now to say that you recognize him, did you?"

"Yes sir, I think I did. . . . I felt that it was possible to make a mistake, but I never admitted I ever made a mistake or do make a mistake."

Yet she had made a mistake, McAnarney said. In Brockton, Splaine had picked out a photo of Anthony Palmisano, fingering him as a Braintree bandit even as he sat in a New York prison. Chastened, Splaine gave little ground during a cross-examination that lasted the afternoon. The following morning, however, she admitted her doubts at the inquest. Yet as if erasing an "accounts receivable" error and filling in the correct entry, she went on. Under questioning that would have wilted previous witnesses, the tidy woman in the floral hat remained certain. Sacco was the gunman. As she spoke, Sacco leaned forward, his face set in a grim

smile. Splaine would not be shaken, leaving McAnarney to wonder. Had she seen Sacco since the inquest?

"Not since I saw him in Quincy."

"In other words, you changed your mind as to whether he was
the man without making any further examination of him, didn't
you?"

"Yes, sir."

"That is all."

Following Splaine, doubt and indecision returned. Witnesses
provided other angles on the crime—from houses down the street,
from the excavation site opposite the shooting, from another factory window. But each had seen little, remembered less, and none
pointed a finger at Sacco or Vanzetti.

"The best I can remember is close-shaven, clean-shaven," said
one man. "I never seen any mustache."

"Well," said another, "I can't say that they are the men or they
are not the men, because I ain't sure."

Then just when it looked as if an ambiguous crime story was
the best the prosecution had to offer, Louis Pelser was called.
Pelser, a pudgy young man in a dark suit, had been cutting leather
in the Rice & Hutchins factory when the shooting began. Timid
by nature, he had not gone to Brockton to identify suspects. When
the prosecution found him in January, Pelser insisted he could not
identify anyone. In March, he told the defense the same. But shortly
after the trial began, he spoke to his foreman about what he had
seen. The foreman told a sheriff, and the prosecution subpoenaed
Pelser. After a brief interview with Harold Williams, he was told
to enter the courtroom and study Sacco. Pelser did. A half hour
later, he was on the witness stand. Again the shots of April 15 rang
out, but this time the witness had not been somewhere down the
street. Louis Pelser had been on the factory's ground floor just a
sidewalk's width from the gunman.

"I seen this fellow shoot this fellow," he told the hushed courtroom. "It was the last shot. He put four bullets into him." The
gunman "had a dark green pair of pants and an army shirt tucked
up. He had wavy hair pushed back, very strong hair, wiry hair,

very dark . . . dark complexion." Staring at Sacco, Pelser added, "I wouldn't say he is the man, but he is the dead image of the man I seen." Pelser had also scrawled the Buick's license number on a shoe-cutting board. Moore was unprepared for this surprise witness, but he knew Pearl Street and what could and could not be seen from its factory windows.

"Now, those windows in that building on that floor are opaque, are they not?" he asked Pelser. "That is, you can't see through the window?"

"Yes, sir. You can't see through the window."

"So that the windows have to be opened to see anything, is that correct?"

"Yes, sir."

"At the time this affair started, what was the condition of that window or those windows where you were?"

"Well, there was a little window open about that much," Pelser said, holding his hands slightly apart.

"About three to four inches?"

"Yes."

Pelser said he had opened the window, but how long had he stayed there a few feet from a man with a gun? About a minute, he replied. "I seen everything happen about that time, about in a minute." Though it was not especially warm in the courtroom, sweat poured down Pelser's temples as Moore couched his next question. On March 26, hadn't Pelser told a member of the defense team—a Mr. Reid—that he had seen *nothing* of the shooting, just a body on the sidewalk? Pelser admitted he had, "because I didn't want to tell my story . . . because I didn't like to go to court."

"In other words," Moore said, "you think so lightly of your word that in order to avoid being called as a witness, you deliberately told a falsehood?"

"Yes sir."

Moore kept at Pelser. Hadn't he told Mr. Reid he had ducked under a bench at the first shot? Pelser denied it. Yes, he had briefly ducked when the gunman aimed at him, but otherwise he had stood in the window watching. Moore, despite his profound respect for workingmen, could not let the leather cutter off so easily. His words echoed through the courtroom—"falsehood!" "all false!" "utterly and completely false!" Pelser could only perspire and say, "Yes, sir." Moore tied further testimony in knots until Pelser finally said, "If you want me to tell my story, I will tell it. That is the only way I can fix it up."

Fixed up, the story remained firm. Pelser had seen the shooting, seen Berardelli's body, seen Sacco standing over it, firing. He had told no one until telling the assistant DA that morning. Moore was incredulous: "And what peculiar quality of Mr. Williams' personality or points of persuasive power were there that enabled him to wring from your lips the story that Mr. Reid was not able to wring?" The prosecution let Pelser tell his story again, but doubt hung in the air until court adjourned.

Saturday, June 11, was Vanzetti's thirty-third birthday. Marching to the courtroom that morning, he must have been pleased with the trial so far. No one had identified him in Braintree. Only Mary Splaine and Louis Pelser had placed Sacco there, and Moore had raised doubts about each. "Things seem to be going well," Vanzetti had written his father. "However this trial ends, my innocence remains, and the error, we know from sweet experience, cannot endure forever. Time is a gentleman; the people are with me." Sacco, however, was more despairing than ever. Racked by chronic stomach pains, he remained convinced that someone was poisoning his meals. A doctor had recently examined him and a chemist had analyzed his food. Both blamed his stomach trouble on stress. In court, Sacco only relaxed during recesses when Rosina brought their children to the edge of the cage, where he lifted his baby daughter in his arms. But if Sacco was calmed by his children and Vanzetti by the trial itself, nothing could dispel the McAnarneys' despair. From the trial's opening day, they had been following a separate case, one that might have been called *Thayer v. Moore*.

Whenever Moore addressed the judge, Thomas McAnarney recalled, "It was quite similar to waving a red flag in the face of a wolf. . . . Mr. Moore would make an objection or make some remark and it would be perfectly clear that it got under Judge Thayer's skin." With each confrontation, the judge summoned his propriety, informing "*Mis*-ter Moore" that such tactics might work "in the West or in California, but not in Massachusetts." Attorney William Thompson, who would later take the case, also saw the tension. Summoned by the McAnarneys on the trial's second day, Thompson had arrived in court to find Rosina shouting at Moore, asking him by what right he represented her husband. When the trial resumed, "Katzmann would say something and Moore would object to it," Thompson recalled. "He was jumping up all the time. He would make objection after objection. Judge Thayer would sit there and look at Moore with the fiercest expression on his face, moving his head a little . . . and say 'Objection overruled.' It wasn't what he said, it was his manner of saying it. It looked perfectly straight in the record; he was too clever to do otherwise." The McAnarneys had hoped the highly respected Thompson might agree to replace Moore, but after noting the judge's every "sneer," Thompson sidled up to them. "Your goose is cooked," he said, and walked out.

The McAnarneys were not accustomed to losing cases, but this one seemed a long shot. A sheriff had already whispered to Thomas, "I hope to heaven you will lose this case, that these men will be convicted. They are no good." Desperate to defuse the tension, the McAnarneys offered to return their fee—$2,000—if Moore would leave the case. Moore refused. Back in court, he went right on with outlaw style, sometimes pacing before the judge without his coat— "For God's sake, keep that coat on in the courtroom!" Thomas McAnarney whispered—other times even taking off his shoes. On the bench, Judge Thayer's leathery face tightened, but he reined in his anger until court recessed. Striding back from lunch one day, Thayer met a reporter. "I'll show them that no long-haired 'arnuchist' from California can run this court!" the judge huffed. Two lunches later, the judge confronted reporters at the Dedham Inn. "Did you ever see a case in which so many leaflets and circulars have been spread . . . saying that people couldn't get a fair trial in the State of Massachusetts?" he asked. Turning to leave, the judge shook his fist. "You wait till I give my charge to the jury," he said. "I'll show 'em!" Amazed reporters talked it over and agreed not to write about the outburst.

Webster Thayer had been showing people a thing or two all his life. Born in 1857 to a middle-class family—his father was a meat wholesaler—Thayer had eschewed Horatio Alger's rags-to-riches dream, choosing a life of public service instead. If one word should have been chiseled on the judge's gravestone, that word was "duty." After attending the Worcester Academy, "Web" Thayer went to Dartmouth, where, despite his small stature, he captained the football and baseball teams. Back in 1880, a bright young man did not need law school to become a lawyer; he only needed to "read the law" under the tutelage of an attorney. Thayer was admitted to the Massachusetts bar in 1882. He specialized in civil cases but, like Frederick Katzmann, saw law as a stepping-stone to politics. Elected as a Democratic alderman in Worcester, he ran for mayor in 1894. After losing, he became a Republican, trying cases in the same city where Vanzetti would build a dam and work in a foundry. In 1917, the governor of Massachusetts, a Dartmouth classmate, appointed Thayer to the bench, where he worked mostly on divorce cases. Making his presence strongly felt in any courtroom, the judge rephrased attorneys' questions, endlessly cited legal precedent, and punctuated his remarks with nineteenth-century locutions such as "Mark you" and "What say?" Despite his Ivy League education, the judge also made occasional mispronunciations. The anarchists he loathed were always "arnuchists." Throughout the trial, he referred to the slain guard Berardelli as "Bernadelli."

In the decade to come, Judge Thayer's name would become synonymous around the world with rank injustice. Vanzetti would call him "a self-conceited, narrow-minded little tyrant" and "part tiger and part ass." His mere presence would move Sacco to rage. H. G. Wells would coin a word—Thayerism: "the self-righteous unrighteousness of established people." Upton Sinclair would portray him as an arriviste from the "hardware" town of Worcester—"a Thayer but not one of the 'right' Thayers." There was a Thayer Academy in Braintree and a Thayer Hall at Harvard, but "Web" Thayer was not from *those* Thayers, Sinclair noted, and status envy led him to court the approval of Boston bluebloods. But for millions of others, the diminutive judge with the cragged face would stand as a pillar of righteousness in a lawless decade. And for all the courtroom bias perceived by the McAnarneys, jurors noticed none of it. Decades after the judge had made more notorious comments, jurors still remembered him as "a sincere, honest, absolutely fair and impartial man" and "the fairest judge I ever saw or heard of."

Kindly father of two, loyal Mason, upstanding member of the best country clubs in Worcester, Judge Thayer was compromised by his devotion to duty. Having given his life to public service, he could not imagine anyone answering duty's call, whether soldier, juror, or DA, as anything less than upright and honest. Any such suggestion hinted that barbarians were at the gates. In 1919, Thayer had watched in horror as "arnuchists" blew up judges' homes and mailed bombs to politicians, tycoons, and upstanding members of the judiciary. The shocking mayhem led the judge to lament the rise of "a new propaganda . . . the propaganda of force, of might and revolution. . . . Oh, how unfortunate that any such a doctrine, so destructive in its character and so revolutionary in all its tendencies should ever have reached the sacred shores of these United States."

Thayer would later tell a Dartmouth classmate how deeply his sense of duty ran. If the "Reds" lurked outside a door, he said, and he could save America by passing through that door and being gunned down, he would gladly do it. Despite his reputation for fairness, the aging judge could not keep such self-righteousness off his bench. As the Red Scare moved from midnight raids to trials, America's enemies were no longer at the gates—they were in his courtroom. On April 15, 1920, the judge was presiding over the trial of a man charged with advocating anarchy. When Segris

Zagroff was found not guilty, Thayer confronted the jury. "Gentlemen," he asked in full view of the court. "How did you arrive at such a verdict? Did you consider the information that the defendant gave to the police officers . . . that he was a Bolshevist and that there should be a revolution in this country?"

Two months later, Judge Thayer handled the case of another anarchist named Vanzetti. After meting out the harshest possible sentence, he wrote to Massachusetts's Supreme Court chief justice, another Dartmouth alumnus, asking to handle the trial in Dedham. The stage had its colonial set and its villains. Now it had its self-styled hero. As Judge Thayer strode into the courtroom on Saturday morning, June 11, he was again called to duty by the familiar "Hear ye! Hear ye! . . . God save the Commonwealth of Massachusetts."

During the trial's first two weeks, newspaper interest waned. This trial was not nearly as exciting as those with female defendants, the *Brockton Evening Enterprise* wrote. The *Boston Transcript,* a stodgy paper read by Boston's upper crust, had yet to cover the proceeding. Hearst's *Boston American* had cut daily coverage to a mere ten column inches. Over lunch one day, Judge Thayer had remarked to his bodyguard that the prosecution's case had been weak and he did not think the men would be convicted. Reporters also considered a conviction unlikely. Then on June 11, Lola Andrews awakened the courtroom "like a clap of thunder" (*Boston Post*).

A short, saucy woman in her mid-thirties, Andrews wore a black straw hat and frilly polka-dot dress. Standing in the witness box, she told of being in South Braintree on the morning of April 15. She and an elderly friend had just applied for work at Slater & Morrill and were headed for Rice & Hutchins. Not knowing the way, she had asked the man tinkering with the shiny Buick. The conversation had lasted barely a moment. Andrews had not thought twice about it until lawyers began dropping by her room in Quincy. Moore came first, showing her a mug shot of Sacco mixed with a rogue's gallery. Leafing through the photos, Andrews had assured Moore that none showed the man she had talked to in Braintree. Moore had asked her to be a defense witness, but now here she was for the prosecution describing the man who had given her directions that April morning.

"Do you see him in the court room now?"

"I think I do, yes sir . . . In the cage, I should say." Pointing to Sacco, Andrews said, "That man there."

"Do you mean—" But before his name could be uttered, Sacco jumped to his feet. "I am the man?" he shouted. "Do you mean me? Take a good look!" Shock waves ran through the courtroom. A guard shoved Sacco back in his seat. He glanced at Vanzetti, then glared at Andrews while the gallery continued to buzz. Andrews was cross-examined for the rest of the Saturday session. Moore was in no mood to be polite to a witness who had betrayed him. Had he not talked with her in January? Had she not told him the man she had spoken to looked Greek or French? That none of the photos depicted the man she had seen? Andrews initially denied her statements, but as the grilling intensified—"Did you so state?" "Did you so state?"—she softly replied that she no longer remembered what she had said in January.

Moore asked Andrews to recall the February afternoon when she had gone to the Norfolk County Jail to identify suspects. The petite woman told the court of peering through a window into a lower room. There she had seen a man pacing. Glancing up at her, the man had looked very much like the man she had spoken to in Braintree. Moore tried to recover from this surprise. How far had she stood from the man? Was she certain there were no other men present? But as in his final IWW trial, Moore had brought out testimony tarring his client. Sacco was the man, Andrews insisted. She had talked to him on Pearl Street. She had seen him in jail. She saw him now.

When court adjourned, Moore, outfoxed and infuriated, sent an assistant to Quincy to learn more about Lola Andrews. "Miss Andrews," the man reported back, was known in Quincy as "a common woman, a woman of the town" whose "reputation for truth and veracity is nil." She was known to be living with a sailor in a boardinghouse. Divorced, estranged from her son and husband back in Maine, she worked odd jobs—waiting tables, cleaning hotel rooms. Some also hinted that she was a woman who, for a few bucks, could show a guy "a swell time." On Monday morning, Moore returned to court, determined to reveal Lola Andrews as a liar, a "floozie," a slut. It might have worked in some IWW trial out West, but in a commonwealth where ladies were presumed innocent, it backfired. Lola Andrews, as street-smart as Fred Moore, also knew how to play tough.

As if questioning a mining foreman, Moore again lit into Andrews. He mocked her "hopeless confusion," drawing a swift rebuke. "The time for criticism of that kind is when you reach your argument, not now," Judge Thayer warned. Moore challenged Andrews's testimony about the location of the Buick on Pearl Street. He tried to pinpoint her exact words to him in January. Andrews stood her ground, then fought back, accusing Moore of offering her a "vacation" to see her friend in Maine and a new job if the trip resulted in her dismissal. Moore struggled to portray this as an innocent suggestion. He had merely advised Andrews to go to Maine and ask her friend about that morning in Braintree, but the witness stuck to this story as well. Then Moore turned to the dirt his assistant had just dug up. Where had Andrews worked? When? For how long? The innuendos brought the woman to tears. As one juror remembered, "It was obvious that Mr. Moore was trying to turn up something but as far as I could see the only thing he turned up was the fact that Mrs. Andrews was a lady who worked hard for her living."

J. J. McAnarney was no more successful. Finally, when Andrews had been on the stand nearly eight hours, the defense cast its last aspersion on her—for the moment. Returning from the jail in February, hadn't she met a tailor in Quincy? Hadn't he told her she looked exhausted? And had she not replied, "I am tired of this thing. They wanted me to say that that is the man and I said, 'How can I? I cannot recognize him' "? Andrews denied ever talking to the tailor. The questioning dragged on. The witness grew pale. Judge Thayer offered to let Andrews sit, but she remained standing. A moment later she said, "I feel faint."

"She feels faint," Katzmann echoed, starting out of his seat.

"I think she should have a rest," Judge Thayer said. The defense agreed, but before she could step down, Andrews swooned and fainted dead away. Katzmann caught her in his arms. Gasps filled the room. Above them, a single word—"gun"—came from the rear of the gallery. Judge Thayer ordered the court locked down. While deputies were slamming doors and locking deadbolts, the pretty woman in the polka-dot dress was carried out of court.

Along with sudden dramatics and a flustered defense, the prosecution now had three positive placements of Sacco in Braintree. With momentum shifting, attention turned to Vanzetti. Others had claimed the Buick's driver was light-haired and sickly, but gatekeeper Michael Levangie now swore the driver had been a "dark complected man, with cheek bones sticking out, black hair, heavy brown mustache, slouch hat, and army coat." That man now sat in the cage on the left, Levangie said. No doubt. Next came woodworker John Faulkner. Riding the train into Braintree on the morning of April 15, Faulkner had seen "a foreigner with a black mustache." The foreigner had asked Faulkner whether a certain stop was East Braintree. It wasn't. When notified of the correct stop, the man got off toting an old leather bag. Again, no question. Vanzetti. Rising to cross-examine, J. J. McAnarney asked Faulkner if he knew the saying "all coons look alike to me." And might all Italians look alike?

"There is a difference," Faulkner responded. "Some are big and some are small."

Harry Dolbeare, a piano repairman, had been called as a potential juror but, recognizing Vanzetti in the cage, became a witness instead. Dolbeare had seen a dusty car downtown that morning with five men in it. "That carload was a tough looking bunch, if you will excuse my language," he told the court. One man in back stood out. "He looked like a foreigner, and he had a very heavy mustache, quite dark." Any doubt that it was Vanzetti? "Not a particle."

On the morning of Dolbeare's testimony, Judge Thayer ordered deputies to search spectators entering the courtroom. Police found three suspicious items in one man's pocket. At first thought to be bombs, they were found to be hard-boiled eggs. The trial resumed, with evidence rising to meet each reasonable doubt. A friend of Mary Splaine's, another bookkeeper, gave a final identification of Sacco at the scene. Resembling a nurse in her matronly dress and white cap, Frances Devlin said the man she had seen from Splaine's window was Sacco. As Devlin spoke, Sacco smiled strangely at her, his gold tooth showing. Three more witnesses pinpointed Sacco and Vanzetti around Braintree—in the back of the Buick that morning, leaning against Torrey's Drugstore toward noon, at the railroad station acting "kind of funny . . . nervous." Talking. Smoking. All three witnesses had later seen the men in jail. None had the slightest hesitation. The prosecution moved on to the chase.

From a poolroom on Pearl Street to the railroad crossing where the car was last seen, eight witnesses described the getaway. Only one identified Sacco. Stepping out of the poolroom, Carlos Goodridge had seen the Buick go by with "the gentleman on the right, in the cage" hanging out the passenger side firing at random. The defense tried to impugn Goodridge. The middle-aged, balding man was not just a Victrola salesman, as he claimed, but someone who needed his own attorney—for something. Judge Thayer would not allow the jury to hear more, and Goodridge left the stand unscathed. Other witnesses fleshed out a crime scenario familiar to anyone who read a newspaper. The Buick barreling down the highway at fifty miles per hour. A rifle or shotgun aimed out the back window. The car kicking up dust, its curtains flapping. Moore and McAnarney tried to sow suspicion. Had Alta Baker ever driven fifty miles per hour in order to know what such a speed looked like? "Well, no." Did Francis Clark have any reason for asserting the Buick he later saw in Brockton was the one that passed his horse-drawn wagon? "No, not positively, no." And crossing guard Austin

Reed, who heard the man with the "stubbed mustache" shout, "What the hell are you holding us up for?"—had he noted the man's English? Was it "unmistakable and clear"? It was, yet the defense never mentioned this again.

The plot now needed little thickening. Once there had been doubt—witnesses hesitating, doubling back on their stories. But such testimony had faded so many long, dull days ago. Three decades later, one juror recalled his first impressions. Raised on "the wrong side of the tracks," young Filene's clerk John Dever considered himself a champion of the underdog. Selected for the jury, he "was already marshalling my force for the defendants." Now he was all but convinced of their guilt. To Dever, Mary Splaine had come across as a "good witness. Damaging to defense. Not impeached." Lola Andrews was "a lady." Dever suspected Carlos Goodridge might have a criminal record, but "he placed the defendant Sacco in the same part of the car and in very much the same position as both Miss Devlin and Miss Splaine." These witnesses were the jurors' peers, workingmen and -women much like them. Sacco, however, had shown his fiery Italian temper. Vanzetti would soon show his. So the detective story took root, flowering at last with the motive.

For the next two days, jurors learned of a five-man plot to steal payrolls. A policeman had spotted the Buick the evening it had been stolen, with a mustachioed man driving it. Ruth Johnson told the jury about the night of May 5—the motorcycle with sidecar, the blinding headlight flashing on the road as if giving some sort of signal, the two men following her to her neighbors to "get milk," and Mike Boda's sudden decision to leave without the car. Tracing Sacco and Vanzetti to their arrest, the prosecution called the streetcar conductor. Austin Cole said the men had also boarded his car on April 14 or 15. Next came the officers who had arrested the men, fully armed. Stepping into the stand, Officer Michael Connolly told a different story from the one he had given at the inquest. There Connolly had sworn that he and his suspects had ridden to the station in silence. Now he accused Vanzetti of reaching for his hip pocket. "I says, 'Keep your hands out on your lap, or you will be sorry.'"

Before the officer could say another word, Vanzetti blurted out, "You are a liar!" The courtroom slowly quieted and the officer continued.

"I put Sacco and Vanzetti in the back seat of our light machine, and Officer Snow got in the back seat with them. . . . I told them when we started that the first false move I would put a bullet in them. On the way up to the station Sacco reached his hand to put under his overcoat and I told him to keep his hands outside of his clothes and on his lap. . . . I says to him, 'Have you got a gun there?' He says, 'No.' He says, 'I ain't got no gun.' 'Well,' I says, 'keep your hands outside of your clothes.' We went along a little further and he done the same thing. . . . I says, 'Mister, if you put your hand in there again you are going to get into trouble.' He says, 'I don't want no trouble.' We reached the station, brought them up to the office, searched them."

Connolly's testimony brought Moore leaping to his feet again and again. Overruled. Overruled. Overruled. Judge Thayer was growing testy. "You try to cooperate, Mr. Moore, with the court," he said. "The court is trying to assist you." But Moore would not cooperate, not when the Buick, now revealed to have a bullet hole in the door that no one had seen when it was found in the woods, was admitted as evidence.

"Did you read *Commonwealth v. Snell* in Massachusetts?" Thayer asked.

"I have not, Your Honor."

"That was the same as the case of *State v. Mollineaux*. That is one of the leading cases . . ."

Like two vines, *Thayer v. Moore* entangled around *Commonwealth v. Sacco and Vanzetti*. Addressing Moore, the judge often commented on how law was practiced "in our State." The jury, excused for one legal dispute after another, traipsed in and out of court. Lawyers wrangled in long conferences at the bench. When a stenographer came up to record one conference, Thayer glared and whispered, "You get the hell out of here!" And the days and hours and onslaught of witnesses wore on, taking spring into summer and the trial into a fourth week. Finally the prosecution closed with material evidence.

Throughout the thirteen-month buildup to the trial, Katzmann had assured Moore he would not link any bullet with Sacco's gun. Having consulted experts, the DA felt ballistics evidence was unlikely to stand up in court. But Moore needed to clear his clients in every way possible, so he asked Sacco's permission to test his gun. Sacco did not hesitate. He had nothing to hide, he said. An expert could examine whatever he wanted. During the trial's opening week, Moore asked Judge Thayer for permission to hold ballistics tests. Twelve days later at a firing range in Lowell, fourteen bullets were fired through Sacco's Colt into a box of sawdust. On June 21, "in light of the results of the experiments," Katzmann withdrew his earlier promise. While experts compared test bullets with those marked I, II, III, and IIII, the prosecution offered other material evidence.

Following the shooting, Fred Loring had come outside Slater & Morrill to find his friend Berardelli dead on the ground.

"Now, when you arrived on the scene, was there anything which you noticed on the street near the body of Berardelli?"

"A cap."

"Where was the cap?"

"It was about eighteen inches from Berardelli's body, towards the street."

"Did you do anything in regard to that cap?"

"Yes, I picked it up."

Taken by surprise, the defense could only ask Loring whether anyone in the crowd might have lost the cap. Loring couldn't be sure. Further witnesses then traced the cap, black and fur-lined with earflaps, to Sacco. The guards' sad-eyed widows, Sarah Berardelli and Hattie Parmenter, swore the cap had not belonged to their husbands. Sacco's boss, George Kelley, testified that his edge trimmer often wore a cap to work, hanging it near his machine. Examining the cap, Kelley found its lining torn as if by a hook. He refused to say the cap was Sacco's, only that it was the same color, but his testimony and the tear were enough to overrule Moore's objections. Judge Thayer admitted the cap. With test results from Sacco's Colt still pending, the prosecution turned to Vanzetti's gun.

Eleven days had passed since Jimmy Bostock had told of seeing Berardelli with a gun five days before his death. Now a silver snubnosed .38 was held up for all to see. Berardelli's gun, the prosecution maintained, had been stolen from the dying guard. It was the gun found on Vanzetti. But no witnesses had seen either gunman take the guard's revolver. How did anyone know this was the same .38? Three weeks before the murder, Berardelli had taken the gun to Iver Johnson Sporting Goods in downtown Boston. A store employee now testified to admitting the gun—here was the receipt dated March 20, 1920, "property of Alex Berardelli." A repairman had replaced the hammer—here was the repair slip. Examining the gun, the repairman noted the new hammer and a firing pin that "does not show of ever being struck." Berardelli, though toting thousands in cash, had no gun on him when he died. Like a photo in a darkroom, material evidence was emerging, but under cross-examination, it soon blurred.

Vanzetti's gun was a .38. The Iver Johnson repair slip listed Berardelli's gun as a .32. The prosecution scrambled to show there was little visible difference, that the repairman had made a common mistake. Still, was this the gun? Although the shop had receipts for accepting and repairing the revolver, there was no proof Berardelli had ever claimed it. Iver Johnson sold unclaimed guns at the end of the year but had no record of such a sale. The .38 must have been picked up, the shop owner testified, "because the gun is not in our place of business now." But that was for the jury to decide.

On Tuesday, June 21, the prosecution's case drew to a close. That morning, a portly white-haired man wearing policeman's blue swore to tell the whole truth and nothing but. State Police captain William Proctor had been Katzmann's chief investigator until the day after Vanzetti's Bridgewater trial ended. Doubting the case, he had been replaced by Chief Stewart. Now, as one of three experts who had test-fired Sacco's Colt, he took the stand. Proctor described the bullets found in the guards' bodies. Five of six were remarkably similar, each a .32 caliber, each with grooves measuring .035 inch, each marked with nicks twisted to the right. Each had been fired by the same gun, the captain said. A Savage automatic. But the last bullet—the fatal bullet—was different. Bullet III had wider grooves—.060 inch, twisted to the *left*. Such a slant came only from a .32 Colt, Proctor told the court.

The captain's testimony was laden with technical terms— "lands," "rifling," "knurl"—and precise details about each bullet, each shell. As jurors passed around bullets and a magnifying glass, he described the shells found on Pearl Street. Again, all except one had been fired by the same gun. But the one—labeled Shell W— displayed a similarity to shells ejected by Sacco's Colt during its test firing. The jury was allowed to examine the shells under a microscope. Proctor then gave an answer that would haunt him for the rest of his life.

"Have you an opinion as to whether Bullet III was fired from the Colt automatic which is in evidence?"

"I have."

"And what is your opinion?"

"My opinion is that it is consistent with being fired by that pistol."

Consistent with. The delicate phrasing could be read different ways. J. J. McAnarney considered seeking a definite answer but feared a trap that would allow Proctor to hammer home the fatal bullet's path through Sacco's gun. McAnarney settled for suggesting that a Bayard automatic also gave bullets a left twist. Captain Proctor, unfamiliar with Bayard models, was unsure. He gave way to another expert.

Touting a decade of experience with the Springfield Armory, the U.S. Army, and various gun makers, Captain Charles Van Amburgh continued the ballistics lesson. He explained the firing procedure of a .32 Colt. He defined "jacketed bullets," "rifling," and "land cut" and sketched each cartridge. Finally, after twenty numbing minutes, the captain offered the only expertise the jury needed:

"I am inclined to believe that it was fired, number III bullet was fired, from this Colt automatic pistol." Van Amburgh pointed out a rough, rusted groove in the barrel of Sacco's Colt and a corresponding cut on Bullet III. Stepping from the witness stand, he took jurors to the window overlooking the leafy town square to show them the cut and groove under better light. To discredit Van Amburgh, McAnarney led him through "a wilderness of lands and grooves," one reporter noted. The captain would not be dissuaded. The following morning, the prosecution rested.

The narrative was complete. From the dusty road trip through the crime scene to the bloody clothes of the victims, from the eyewitnesses on Pearl Street to those detailing a sinister plot on a dark night, Frederick Katzmann had presented a simple scenario of heartless murder. Embellishing the argument with a cap, a gun, and bullets the jury had held in its hands, the prosecution's case—dramatic, detailed, and perfectly plausible—charged that Nicola Sacco and Bartolomeo Vanzetti, whose sinister mug shots jurors had seen in newspapers, whose rage they had witnessed themselves, were guilty. Now let the "long-haired" lawyer prove otherwise.

CHAPTER SIX

"I Do Not Think I Ever Saw Them Men in the World"

Where all the facts are out of sight a true report and a plausible error read alike, sound alike, feel alike. Except on a few subjects where our own knowledge is great, we cannot choose between true and false accounts. So we choose between trustworthy and untrustworthy reporters.

—Walter Lippmann, *Public Opinion*

On the Saturday afternoon before the prosecution rested, jurors were whiling away another dull day cooped up inside the empty courthouse. Since being sequestered, they had exited the building only for meals, escorted evening walks, and chauffeured Sunday drives. Still dusty from the opening road trip, the twelve men had not bathed in more than two weeks. Then sometime that afternoon a sheriff stuck his head in the grand jury room.

"Would anyone like a bath?" he asked.

Jurors thought the sheriff was kidding but were told to fetch combs and brushes. Marching to the Norfolk County Jail, they descended beneath the tiers that held Sacco and Vanzetti. In the basement they found, side by side, a dozen bathtubs. For the next hour, twelve men splashed in dirty water, joking and playing catch with bars of soap. Toweling off, they dressed again and walked back to what juror John Dever called their "Bastille without bars."

From here on in, they would share the camaraderie of a baseball team rather than the rancor of twelve strangers called to disagreeable duty. The following Wednesday, June 22, as a muggy heat wave turned the courtroom into a sauna, the defense of Sacco and Vanzetti began.

Prosecution and defense are at loggerheads in any trial, but the cases presented by Frederick Katzmann and Fred Moore contrasted in style as well as substance. The prosecution had been as focused as Katzmann; the defense would be as scattered as Moore. The prosecution had presented a detective story; the defense would offer a Cubist painting of overlapping scenarios and shifting points of view. And while jurors had toured the scenes of the crime from Pearl Street to Puffer's Place, none ever visited Plymouth, where Vanzetti had peddled fish, or the North End, where Sacco had allegedly spent April 15, 1920.

Under Katzmann's strategy, the jury heard sixty-two witnesses in fourteen days. Some had testified for three, five, eight hours, etching their names into jurors' memories. Moore preferred quantity to quality. During his opening six days he called seventy-five witnesses. Like small-time sinners stepping into a confessional, they came and went, came and went. Fidgeting in the broiling courtroom, jurors listened to the first dozen describe the crime from different perspectives. Each recalled the murders, the getaway. Each said Sacco and Vanzetti did not resemble the gunmen. Yet unlike Mary Splaine or Louis Pelser, Moore's witnesses were neither precise nor certain. Sacco and Vanzetti were not the gunmen, they said, but "I am not positive, but I don't think so." "It may or it may not have been. I don't know positively." Few could state specifically where the guards had fallen or how many shots they heard, and each seemed a little hesitant, making them ideal targets for a DA eager to pounce.

Since May 31, Katzmann had let his easygoing assistant, Harold Williams, guide witnesses through their testimony. Now the DA stormed the trial with the full force of his will. Determined that ten, fifty, a hundred witnesses would never derail his case, Katzmann strode before the jury, commanding attention, firing off questions, showing his mastery of the most minute details. The Harvard gentleman was unfailingly polite, yet if anyone dared to undercut his authority, he'd turn into the tough kid from the streets of Hyde Park. When Frank Burke, at whom the gunman had fired a shot, added that the gun was an automatic like one his son had brought home from the war, Katzmann's comeback chilled a steamy courtroom.

"Did you think I asked you about that, Mr. Burke?"

"What, sir?"

"Did you think I asked about your boy bringing one home? . . . You thought you would tuck that in, did you? You thought you would tuck that answer in, did you?"

Katzmann had a handful of sharp rhetorical tools, yet he used them like blunt instruments. The first was a volley of questions that flustered witnesses.

"Which man did you notice first?" he asked Burke.

"The man that was driving the car. I seen the man driving the car."

"How long did you watch him?"

"I didn't watch him any length of time at all."

"How long did you watch him?"

"I couldn't say."

"Give us your best judgment."

"It was less than a minute."

"How much less than a minute?"

"I don't know. I cannot be pinned down to things of that kind, because I don't know, Mr. Katzmann. I am going to try to do the best I can but I want you to be as fair with me as I want to be with you. I am here to tell the story as I saw it."

When Katzmann's needle dulled, he tried other tools. In questions as carefully clipped as his own graying hair, he probed eyewitnesses for details. Precisely how fast was the Buick traveling? *How* fast? *That* fast? How far would it have traveled in so many seconds? *That* far? Witnesses who volunteered specifics were pumped for more.

"All right," Katzmann said, leading a witness to a map of Pearl

Street. "Show me on the sidewalk as shown there where it was the body lay?"

"About there."

"You have it out in the gutter, haven't you?"

"Right there."

"What caused you to change its position from the original position you showed?"

"Well, I can't just exactly put it on the map for you."

"Is there any object on the ground there? You know the stump down there?"

"No sir."

"Do you know where the pole is?"

"No sir."

"Is there a pole in front of it?"

"I couldn't say."

"Do you remember a pole down there?"

"No sir."

"Do you remember two poles there?"

Bombarded by questions, Moore's witnesses appeared uncertain or forgetful. When a few gave careful responses, Katzmann repeated them with slight distortions, hoping to catch them changing their stories. Any witness hesitating about a fact was asked if his memory was adequate. Anyone uncertain of a visual detail had his eyesight questioned. Moore played "Gotcha" with words; Katzmann used pawns. When Albert Frantello testified that he had seen one gunman for a full second—"he had no mustache; he needed a shave"—Katzmann had him stand with his back to the jury. Frantello was told to turn and stare at two jurors for a full second, then turn away and describe them. The witness failed the test, adding a mustache and watch chain to a juror who had neither. When Katzmann's tools were used up, he simply repeated questions—once asking the same question eight times in a row—until most witnesses had to admit they hadn't been certain, weren't so sure, couldn't say now.

A wiser defense attorney would have coached witnesses to handle such tactics, but Moore sent his like soldiers going over the top of a trench. Among the first dozen, many were mowed down for having bad eyesight, selective memories, or insufficient time to identify anyone. Moore lined up another dozen. Realizing that certain prosecution witnesses lingered in jurors' minds, Moore tried to impeach them. He began with Louis Pelser, who had "seen this fellow shoot this fellow." Three coworkers had been in the first-floor cutting room with Pelser. All three recalled the scene—another man opening the window, spotting the gunmen, closing the window as fast as he had ever done anything in his life. Then the three—and Pelser—had ducked under a bench. After the Buick passed, the men had opened the window to see Berardelli lying in the street. Pelser had told the others, "I did not see any of the men but I got the number of the car."

Pelser's credibility lay in tatters until Katzmann took out the tool he had polished during Vanzetti's first trial. These men claimed to know where Louis Pelser had been during the shooting, but "where was he at four o'clock on the afternoon of April 18, 1920?" "Where was he at three o'clock on the afternoon of April 16th?" "Where was he . . . ?" Finally one witness blurted out, "I can't keep track of a man, and I think you think I am a fortune teller." Still, the uncertainty lingered. What else didn't these witnesses know? Didn't one claim a shot was fired *before* the window was closed while another said *after*? Badgered and belittled, the three ended up tangled in their own testimony. Moore's march continued.

From her factory window, Barbara Lipscomb had looked straight down at one gunman. She would "always remember his face." Neither Sacco nor Vanzetti was that man. But Lipscomb admitted to Katzmann that she had fainted during the shooting—"sort of fainted, about half the way." Nurse Jennie Novelli had walked alongside the Buick just before the crime, eyeing the men inside. None were now in the cage. Katzmann then revealed what Novelli had told a Pinkerton detective—that a photo of Sacco resembled one man she had seen—and another witness stepped down trailing whispers of doubt.

On Monday, June 27, the start of the trial's fifth week, sixteen

more witnesses testified. In a single hour, Moore sent six Italians
to the stand. All six had been digging the excavation. All six swore
the defendants were not the men they had seen on Pearl Street. All
spoke through an interpreter, telling the familiar story—*un uomo
che sparava, due uomini a terra,* and *una macchina nera sparire
lungo Via Pearl.* And all received Katzmann's dressing-down. Next
came men impeaching John Faulkner, the woodcutter who swore
he saw Vanzetti get off the train in Braintree that morning. A conductor told the court he had sold no tickets to Braintree on April
15. But Henry McNaught did not know whether a passenger might
have bought a ticket to Boston and gotten off early.

"You don't say a man wearing a black mustache with a grip
didn't get off at East Braintree that morning?"

"I wouldn't say he did or didn't."

Two station agents then swore that no man with a shaggy mustache had boarded the train in Plymouth on April 15, yet each admitted Vanzetti might have taken a train from anywhere else in the
greater Boston area. And as Moore's scattergun strategy dragged
on, it was beginning to look as if he would call all of greater Boston to the stand.

The press found this chorus of naysayers not worth the trouble.
Hearst's *Boston American* had cut daily coverage to four inches on
page three. The *Boston Post*'s caricaturist, who had sketched prosecution witnesses, was now at the shore drawing bathers seeking
relief from the heat. Judicial authorities were equally impatient.
The chief justice who had assigned Judge Thayer to the trial warned
him the marathon had to end within a week. Jurors asked for night
sessions, but Thayer refused, saying twelve-hour days would tax
their attention, infringing on the defendants' rights. Instead, the
judge extended sessions from 9:00 a.m. to 6:00 p.m., hoping two
extra hours a day would get jurors home before the Fourth of July.
But Thayer had not seen Moore's witness list. Dozens had yet to
testify.

Still angry at Lola Andrews, Moore called five witnesses to de-
fame her. First, the woman who had been with Andrews applying
for work that morning came from central Maine. Along with her

younger friend, grandmotherly Julia Campbell had seen the two men near their shiny car. But her story differed from her friend's. Lola Andrews, Campbell said, had never spoken to the man tinkering with the car. She had only briefly asked the other man how to get into the factory. Katzmann tried to be polite, but his staccato questions quickly had the old woman in tears.

"I told the same story, dear man, every time," Campbell sobbed, "and I don't want to get into this trouble."

"I don't want you to."

"Just as true as you live. It ain't my good will I am here."

"That is all right," Katzmann said. "You and I are still friends, are we? So far, I mean?"

Once the old woman recovered, Katzmann resumed. She had cataracts, didn't she? Yes. What had she done that day after seeing the men? And where had she been last Tuesday? "I was in the washtub last Tuesday." And the week before that? Finally the exasperated woman blurted out, "Oh, chestnuts!"

Katzmann's one-hour grilling shook Julia Campbell but not her certainty that Lola Andrews had lied. And Sacco and Vanzetti? "I do not think I ever saw them men in the world." Nor could Katzmann refute the truck driver who had overheard Chief Stewart at the Brockton police station. "We haven't got the right men," the trucker heard the chief say. "They have got away." The defense was gathering its own impetus, quickened by aspersions cast on Carlos Goodridge, the "Victrola salesman" with the hint of a criminal record. Goodridge may have stepped from the poolroom to see a man firing from the Buick, but witnesses now claimed he had come back in saying, "This job wasn't pulled by any foreign people." Goodridge had also told a barber, "I saw a man in the car but if I have got to say who the man was, I can't say."

By the defense's second week, reasonable doubt had spread through the courtroom, where a small crowd watched and listened. Moore, however, was neither watching nor listening. He had moved to the defense counsel room, where he would stay for the next two weeks lining up witnesses. And because he was not following the trial firsthand, his witnesses soon wandered all over the case as if called by some lazy lawyer randomly flipping through a stack of depositions. There seemed no sense to his sequence. Two more witnesses swore Sacco and Vanzetti had not been in the Buick. They were followed by a railroad clerk impeaching gatekeeper Michael Levangie. Just after the shooting, Levangie had said, "it would be hard to identify these men." Next came three more impugning Lola Andrews. Andrews had told a cop, a journalist, and a neighbor that she "had not seen the faces of the Braintree men." The medley continued, with witnesses stepping into the box for two minutes, four, five. Three more saw the getaway. One said Carlos Goodridge's "reputation for truth and veracity" was "bad." Then came still another getaway witness. And another impeacher. What did it all add up to? In a muggy, airless courtroom, where sheriffs and deputies were nodding off, where only a small portable fan cooled the jurors, what would they remember from the eightieth defense witness? The ninetieth? The hundredth?

By June 28, a shelf near the witness stand was piled high with evidence. Pistols, bullets, sulfur casts of gun barrels, photographs, maps, shells, the cap—each sat tagged with a string and small label. When another piece of evidence was requested, sheriffs dug through desk drawers to find the item. They were still digging shortly after the noon recess when Moore sent his own ballistics experts to the stand.

James Burns, a bald Daddy Warbucks lookalike in a coal black suit, worked for the United States Cartridge Company in Lowell. Ten days earlier he had helped test-fire Sacco's Colt. Stepping into the stand, Burns, like the prosecution's experts, felt he had to prove his expertise. For twenty minutes, he spewed statistics about the weight of the test-fired bullets—70.6 grains—the width of the lands—.040 inch—and their diameter—.305 to .302 inch. Finally he was asked, "Was Bullet III fired from the Sacco gun?" Burns did not hesitate. "Not in my opinion, no." The test-fired bullets, Burns told the court, did not show the slightest similarity to Bullet III. The fatal bullet might have been fired by someone else's .32 Colt, he said, but could just as easily have been fired by a Bayard, the Belgian gun "becoming common since the war." Then Burns turned to Vanzetti's gun. Prosecution witnesses had seen a new hammer in it, suggesting it was the same gun Berardelli had taken for repairs. Burns said the opposite. He took the jury to the window, letting each man look inside the .38 to see the hammer he swore was as old as the gun that housed it.

Katzmann leapt to the attack. First he tested Burns on the minutiae of guns and bullets. Then he asked why Burns had not test-fired any bullets exactly like Bullet III—an obsolete Winchester .32. Burns said he had looked for a duplicate but couldn't find one. Instead, he had tested his own company's .32s, nearly identical to the Winchester. Asked to pinpoint differences between the two, Burns refused.

"It isn't an honest question . . . It is a misleading question. If you will allow me—"

"What did you say that question was before you termed it misleading?"

"I take that back. I withdraw it."

"You want to withdraw that, don't you?"

"Yes, I do. It is a misleading question, your question is."

"Have you any personal feeling about this case, Mr. Burns?"

"Not a bit, not a particle, no." Katzmann and Burns bickered all that afternoon. Before they could resume the next morning, however, bullets entered the trial in a more sinister manner. At 8:30 a.m. on June 29, a train was approaching the Dedham station when a bullet struck one window, narrowly missing one of Moore's investigators. No one was hurt. Police investigated but made no arrests.

Back on the stand that morning, James Burns was even more feisty. Recalling the previous day when Katzmann had showed him the cast of a barrel from "the wrong end," Burns said, "You fooled me yesterday and I don't want you to do it again." He and Katzmann tangled for another hour. Burns's testimony was then backed by J. Henry Fitzgerald of the Colt Firearms Company. Bullet III had not been fired by Sacco's Colt, Fitzgerald told the court. And Vanzetti's .38 did not have a new hammer. The ballistics battle finally ended in a draw. One expert had said Bullet III was "consistent with" being fired by Sacco's gun, one said he was "inclined to believe" it had been, and two more swore it had not. The same ratio applied to Vanzetti's gun. The jury was then led out of the "wilderness of lands and grooves" and into navigable waters.

"Alibi" is Latin for "elsewhere," but where else had Sacco and Vanzetti been on April 15 if not in Braintree? Six witnesses now testified that Vanzetti had been selling fish in Plymouth. Joseph Rosen had seen the mustachioed man and his big-wheeled cart on Cherry Street that morning. Rosen, an itinerant cloth peddler, had shown Vanzetti a ragged swatch of blue wool. Vanzetti considered the cloth ideal for a new suit but wanted a second opinion, so he and Rosen had gone to the Brinis. On the way, Vanzetti had sold a cod to Angelo Guidobone. Once in the Brini house, Alfonsine Brini testified, Vanzetti had shown her the cloth. Later that afternoon, Vanzetti had chatted with a fisherman painting his boat. To Katzmann, this must have seemed like déjà vu. A bunch of Italians from Plymouth telling where their local fish peddler had been on a certain day long ago? The DA knew what to do with such stories.

Along with his tools, Katzmann enjoyed a fundamental advantage based on the whims of memory. No one needed to ask Mary Splaine how she remembered April 15. One did not witness murders every day, so each memory of the crime was well grounded in time. But those who claimed to have seen Sacco or Vanzetti far from Braintree on April 15 had some explaining to do. How could they be sure a certain lunch, a certain conversation had taken place on *that* day? The same question had dominated Vanzetti's first trial, when his alibi had taken place on Christmas Eve; yet April 15, 1920, was no holiday, just another Thursday long since buried by more than a year of Thursdays. Any prosecutor would have taken a shot at this caprice of memory. Katzmann riddled it with holes.

Joseph Rosen might have remembered Vanzetti and the cloth, but he remembered nothing else. Nothing. "I got to get straight here," Rosen said early in his cross-examination. He never did.

More than fifty times in as many minutes, Rosen answered, "I can't recollect," "I couldn't say," "I don't know." Befuddled by nature, the peddler did not even know the day's date—June 29. He thought it was a day or two earlier. The witness was asked so much and knew so little that Judge Thayer finally asked Katzmann, "Haven't you tested him on recollection sufficiently?" Before stepping down, Rosen presented a receipt proving he'd paid his taxes on April 15, but little else. Katzmann moved on to the Brinis.

Vanzetti was an old friend of the Brini family, wasn't he? Alfonsine Brini, a middle-aged, bespectacled factory worker who spoke almost no English, acknowledged that Vanzetti had lived in her house. How long? Until "he went away from Plymouth." The answer seemed innocent, yet it led to a question that hovered over the courtroom like the summer afternoon thunderheads gathering above Dedham. "Was he away from there June 5, 1917?" Katzmann asked. Even before Mrs. Brini could answer, Sacco and Vanzetti realized—Katzmann *knew*. June 5, 1917, had been the day they had not registered for the draft. Katzmann knew they were slackers. The only question was how he would let the jury know. Wrapping up, Katzmann was polite to Mrs. Brini but not to her teenage daughter.

The night before testifying, Lefevre Brini had a fever. She was sure it was caused by her hatred of the district attorney who had embarrassed and belittled her brother Beltrando during Vanzetti's first trial. Now in court wearing a long dress and feathered hat, the fresh-faced girl recalled seeing Vanzetti and the blue cloth. She remembered April 15, 1920, because her father had called a nurse for her mother, just home from the hospital. Katzmann suspected the jury might find the association tepid. "On the day when you saw the cloth," he asked, "did you say, 'I will remember this day because it is the day my father is telephoning to the Cordage nurse?'" Katzmann insisted he was "seeking to be gentle with the child," but soon had her weeping. Exactly as he had undermined her brother, the DA asked Lefevre how many times she had told her story. Ten times? Twenty times? So many times she couldn't count them? The girl was terrified, but Katzmann had to finish her off. Where had she been on March 18, 1920?

"Does that date mean anything to you, March 18, 1920?"

"Why should it?"

"Is that your answer to me? Do you love your mother, Miss Brini?"

"Yes."

"Don't you know that was the day that she says she went to the hospital?"

Katzmann was gentler with other alibi witnesses. Perhaps they had talked with Vanzetti in April, but on the fifteenth? Fisherman Melvin Corl pinpointed the date because he had finished painting his boat while talking to Vanzetti and had put the boat in the water two days later, on his wife's birthday. Katzmann asked every detail one could ask a fisherman. Corl recited his schedule, his daily catch, but could not recall whether his wife's most recent birthday fell on a Sunday or a Monday. That was all Katzmann needed—some hint of uncertainty to make a jury wonder. John Dever, and perhaps other jurors, was already wondering how witnesses uncertain of simple dates could be so sure about April 15.

Angelo Guidobone knew he had bought a cod from Vanzetti on April 15 because four days later he had an appendectomy. Katzmann sauntered up to him. "I take it, Mr. Guidobone, that the fact you were operated on on April nineteenth makes you remember you bought some fish on the fifteenth, is that it?" Couldn't he have bought fish on the thirteenth? "Do you think I keep a fish in the house for a week?" Guidobone asked. Pressed for the possibility of another purchase date, the Italian could only say, "Perché non era così. Perché non era così." (Because it was not so. Because it was not so.) By the time Katzmann finished with Vanzetti's alibi, it was as tattered as the blue cloth the fish peddler had allegedly considered that day. And the cloth was set beside the guns and bullets on the shelf overloaded with evidence.

Following Vanzetti's alibi, it would have been logical to bring up Sacco's, but Moore, still holed up in the defense counsel room, had his own peculiar logic. Instead he sent character witnesses to the stand. Sacco's boss, Michael Kelley, told the court, "I never saw a man that was more attentive to his family." Sacco's reputation at the Three-K shoe factory was "the best." As night watchman, Sacco had keys to the factory and carried a revolver. "The whole thing was in his hands." Kelley's son, George, vouched for Sacco's reputation, and the company paymistress, also a Kelley, revealed Sacco's respectable weekly wage—$52.22 on average. Two Plymouth policemen told of Vanzetti's good reputation, but when the trial resumed on July 1, Moore did an about-face.

Standing before the jury, Katzmann announced that both sides had agreed to strike all evidence that Sacco and Vanzetti "bore the reputation of being peaceful and law-abiding citizens." Why? Why would Moore renounce his clients' good reputations? Some historians speculate that Katzmann, alerted by federal authorities that Sacco and Vanzetti were *Galleanisti,* may have threatened to question their involvement in the 1919 bombings. Katzmann later swore the deal had been made to keep him from cross-examining the Plymouth police who had testified to Vanzetti's character at the Bridgewater trial. Judge Thayer, Thomas McAnarney said, insisted the Bridgewater trial not be mentioned. It was only fair to Vanzetti. For whatever reason, Moore agreed. All testimony painting Sacco as a trusted night watchman and loving father and Vanzetti as a fish peddler well respected by police was stricken from the record. No one knows how this affected the jury.

With character no longer an issue, Moore attacked the notion that Vanzetti's gun had been stolen from the dying guard. Luigi Falzini told of buying the gun in October 1919. Rexford Slater had also owned it—he had once used it to shoot a cat. But neither could be positive this shiny silver .38 was the same one he had owned. Falzini told the court the gun had six chambers. Opening it, he discovered it had five. And when Slater clung to his testimony that the gun "looks exactly like it," Katzmann asked him to search for telltale marks. Slater found a nick near the trigger guard; Katzmann pounced again.

"Why didn't you answer without looking at the gun that there was a mark there if you knew it was there?"

"You told me to look at the gun."

"Couldn't you have answered that question without looking at the gun? . . . Did you intend to try to deceive this jury?"

As jurors began to doubt their own doubts, Sacco's alibi finally came into court. It began with the consulate clerk Moore had courted long-distance in Italy—Giuseppe Andrower. But instead of a respected government official testifying in person, jurors now heard a six-page deposition bogged down by repetitive legalese. Andrower's statement told how Sacco had come to the consulate on April 15, presented the oversized photo, and was told to return with a smaller one. The clerk remembered April 15 as a quiet day. While laughing at the photo with other clerks, Andrower had noticed the date on a desk calendar. Sacco had spent just six or seven minutes at the consulate. Thirty or forty others had visited that afternoon, but the clerk had "no doubt or uncertainty in my mind as to the date." Reading the deposition took fifteen minutes. Perhaps Moore wished he had spent $5,000 to bring Andrower from Italy after all, for he never mentioned the clerk again, not even in his summation.

Additional witnesses claimed Sacco had done more than visit the consulate on April 15. Shortly before lunch, he had spoken with a friend in the North End, telling the man he was on his way to get his travel papers. An hour later he had dined at Boni's Restaurant across the street from the Paul Revere House. At the same table had been a newspaper ad salesman, a professor, and the editor of the Italian daily *La Notizia*. Each diner now offered details—the professor smoking, the quality of the chef, the time it took the meal to arrive. But how did men remember a lunch fifteen months earlier? The ad salesman said he always made his rounds through the North End on Thursday and offered a sales book from that day to prove it. In addition, on April 15 his doctor had treated him for asthma. The doctor then told the court of treating the salesman that day. And the editor remembered meeting Sacco over coffee at 2:45 p.m. after attending a noon banquet for an editor of the *Boston Transcript*.

Jurors must have known what to expect next, yet the DA had a surprise in store. With his familiar tools a little worn, Katzmann turned to another—guilt by association. That professor? Wasn't he a member of the Sacco-Vanzetti Defense Committee? He was. And so was Aldino Felicani, whose name, as printer of *La Notizia*, now surfaced. The jury learned that the defense committee's office was directly above the newspaper's, and that Felicani had reminded all these witnesses of the April 15 lunch. Some of these men had met with Moore, and others were constantly leaving *La Notizia* to work upstairs for the defense committee.

Sacco's alibi closed with a carpenter who had seen him on the train platform in Stoughton. According to Dominick Ricci, Sacco had mentioned going to get his travel papers that day. Ricci received Katzmann's best "Gotcha" of the trial. So the carpenter remembered the date because he was finishing work on a ceiling, did he? What other days had he worked that week?

"April nineteenth, eighteenth, seventeenth, eighteenth, and going right along."

"Did you work on the eighteenth, too?" Katzmann asked.

"Yes I did."

The DA then took Ricci through the rest of the year, simply adding seven to each date. If he had worked on April 18, had he also worked on April 25? May 2? May 9? May 16? Katzmann continued all the way to Christmas. Ricci agreed he had worked on all the offered dates.

"I have got to the end of my calendar," Katzmann said. "You worked every Sunday, didn't you, from then on. That is all."

The trial had now stretched from Memorial Day to the Fourth of July. For two Italians jailed in a colonial town, the long holiday weekend promised to be as relentless as any other. As they had every Sunday throughout the trial, Sacco and Vanzetti enjoyed soup and pasta brought by local anarchists. Vanzetti read; no one knows what Sacco did. The jury, however, was unusually busy. On Saturday, July 2, jurors enjoyed a second bath in the basement of the jail. The following day, they were taken for a drive through the posh towns of Newton and Wellesley. Jurors were getting along fine now. Despite weeks of confinement, they had not had a single argument. Each night the twelve reclined in adjacent cots, told a few final jokes, and went to sleep. One evening, they snuck into the sheriff's room and loosened the screws on his cot so that it crashed to the floor when he lay down.

That Monday was the Fourth of July. Judge Thayer had hoped the jury would be back home with their families, but they remained in the grand jury room. Taking pity on the men, the judge arranged an outing. As the temperature again climbed into the nineties, jurors were driven to the shore at North Scituate. Sequestered on an outdoor veranda overlooking the ocean, the men ate lobster and soaked up the salty breeze. While other diners pointed and stared at the "Sacco-Vanzetti jury," the twelve men got to know each other even better. One juror, having brought his camera, joked about taking pictures of the pretty girls on the beach. After lunch, deputies cleared bathers off the rocky end of the shore so jurors could stroll there. Each was given a fishing pole. All posed for a group photo, their dark ties in place, poles in hand. Late that afternoon, tired and sunburned, the jurors returned to the courthouse. After playing cards and talking about their Fourth, twelve weary but contented men rested up for another day in court. The light in their window above the Dedham town square went out at nine.

CHAPTER SEVEN

"I Was Crazy to Come to This Country"

Both Nick and I are anarchists, the radical of the radical, the black cats, the terrors of many, of all the bigots, exploitators, charlatans, fakers and oppressors.

—Bartolomeo Vanzetti

For five weeks, Sacco and Vanzetti had awaited their turn. Aside from each man's outburst, the jury had heard nothing from them. In the cage just eight feet from the jury box, Sacco sat—nervous and distracted—while Vanzetti, penciling notes, riveted his dark eyes on each witness. Often they conferred with lawyers and with each other, comparing details, one translating what the other had not understood. Then, with little warning, their turn came.

July 5 began with no expectations, just another witness—the trial's 145th. Aldeah Florence, Sarah Berardelli's landlady, shared what the guard's widow had said a few days after her husband's funeral: "Oh dear. If he had taken my advice and taken the revolver out of the repair shop, maybe he would not be in the same condition he is today." Despite Katzmann's questions, these words still hung over the courtroom when J. J. McAnarney stood and said, "Will the defendant Vanzetti be brought forward?"

A wave of anticipation ran through the gallery as the cage was unlocked and Vanzetti began his slow amble, the kind fish peddlers soon adopt, toward the stand. More than any other witness, he had prepared for this moment—studying American history, memorizing martyrs' stories, crafting noble explanations of anarchism. Regretting his failure to testify at his first trial, Vanzetti had since worked to improve his English, perhaps imagining how each new word might impress a jury. Now, like some middle-aged Italian waiter in his dark coat, white shirt, and bow tie, he raised his right hand and swore to tell the truth. But how much truth about anarchism did Fred Moore want a jury "of limited experience and narrow social vision" to hear?

In each of Moore's major trials, his defendants had been tied to the notorious IWW, but here in Dedham, his clients were far more radical. The common association of anarchism with crime presented Moore with a dilemma. When arrested, Sacco and Vanzetti had acted guilty. If not of murder, then what? The jury had to know what an edge trimmer and a fish peddler were doing out on a dark night, fully armed. Why had their mysterious friend suddenly decided not to claim his car? And why had Sacco and Vanzetti lied? Fear of being arrested, detained, and deported might explain their lies, but could Moore trust either man to testify without preaching a sermon on anarchism? And what would the strident Katzmann do once the defendants' politics were open for assault?

Before the trial, Judge Thayer had told lawyers he saw no reason politics should enter into the proceeding. Sacco and Vanzetti were on trial for murder, not advocating anarchy. When the judge learned Moore intended to broach the subject, he warned him in private. If this fuse was lit, the prosecution would be free to blow the defendants' radicalism wide open. On Thayer's advice, Moore had consulted the third McAnarney brother. "I realized it was liable to prejudice the jury as citizens and men," John McAnarney recalled, "but I did not suppose it would prejudice the jury in regard to the innocence or guilt of the men. . . . It was the only thing, the only sensible thing to do, tell the facts why they were there." Seeing no alternative, Moore sent Vanzetti to the stand.

Beginning softly, Vanzetti was told to speak up. He recounted his backbreaking years in industrial America, telling of working "for a quarry—stone," of building a reservoir and later quitting "the Cordage [to] make the water breaker up near the Pilgrim place in Plymouth." Proud of his labors, Vanzetti stood erect in the witness stand, hands on the railing, fingers spread. The man the public knew solely through his sinister mug shot impressed reporters with his composure. His English was broken and notably weak on the past tense, but one word had been ground into him—"worked." "In Plymouth I worked for every contractor, almost every contractor, and I worked every day. Everybody know that." He told of becoming a fish peddler, making his daily rounds, and finally of selling fish on April 15, 1920. Late that morning, he said, "I met this man that go around with cloths." Then he told of taking Joseph Rosen's blue swatch to Mrs. Brini and, on her advice, buying enough material for a suit, spending "$12.75 or something like that." Vanzetti spoke without hesitation until questions led to how he used to spend his Sunday afternoons. Then, unwilling to identify his anarchist circle, he left jurors wondering what a weekly meeting at the Italian Naturalization Club in East Boston had to do with murder.

"How is that involved in this matter at all, Mr. McAnarney?" Judge Thayer asked.

Uncertain if this was the time, McAnarney steered his questions from the abyss. Asked about his gun, Vanzetti said he bought it because he often carried more than a hundred dollars when selling fish. "It was a very bad time and I like to have a revolver for self-defense." He recapped the evening of May 5—the trip to Bridgewater, he and Sacco getting coffee, then walking toward the Johnson house. But why had they gone? As if on cue, Vanzetti plunged in. "We were going to take the automobile for to carry books and newspapers. . . . Three, five, or six people have plenty of literature, and we want—we intend to take that out and put that in the proper place."

"What do you mean by a 'proper place'?"

". . . A place not subject to policemen go in and call for, see the literature, see the papers, see the books, as in that time they went through in the house of many men who were active in the radical movement and Socialist and labor movement, and go there and take letters and take books and take newspapers, and put men in jail and deported many."

Katzmann leapt to his feet.

"I say that in that time—"

"Wait one moment," the DA said.

"And deported many many many have been misused in jail and so on."

As Vanzetti continued, as the words "radical movement" washed over the jury, Judge Thayer saw what they signified—the turning point. He said nothing, but John McAnarney, just then leaving the courtroom, never forgot the judge's look. "Judge Thayer looked over to me, well, in his peculiar way of laughing or smiling, sort of threw back his head as much as to say, 'Well, you see Mr. McAnarney, it is coming out.'" And out it came.

First Vanzetti spoke of rounding up "literature," but for all the description he offered, the literature might have been *Moby-Dick* instead of manuals on making bombs. Then after recounting his arrest and how he did not—"no, absolutely"—did *not* reach for his gun, Vanzetti told of the officer aiming a gun at him in his cell that first night. He detailed plans to find his friend Pappi to see whether he might hide literature. He explained his lies to Chief Stewart. "In that time there was the deportation and the reaction was more vivid than now and more mad than now. . . . There were exceptional times." Next Vanzetti mentioned going to Mexico in 1917—"not to make a soldier, not to go to the war."

Katzmann objected to each detail yet secretly he must have reveled in his good fortune. With the Great War and its 126,000 American dead still fresh in memory, with the 1919 bombings capping anarchism's notorious career, could any prosecutor have asked for a better bull's-eye than two defendants willing to brand themselves anarchists and draft dodgers? Here was a chance to go beyond bullets, caps, and guns, into the dark heart of anarchy itself. When allowed to cross-examine, Katzmann wasted no time with formalities.

"So you left Plymouth, Mr. Vanzetti, in May 1917 to dodge the draft, did you?"

"Yes, sir."

". . . When this country was at war, you ran away so you would not have to fight as a soldier?"

"Yes."

Vanzetti's answers were polite, but his eyes blazed. He was as proud of his beliefs as he was of his work and he would not be belittled. Katzmann asked if he had ever worked in Springfield, Massachusetts. Yes, he had worked nearby "in a shanty, you know, the little house where the Italian work and live like a beast."

"Did you think I asked you what kind of a building the Italian workingman lived in? . . . Did you think if you put in your answer that it was a shanty where the Italian lived like a beast then I would know where that shanty was? Did you think that part of your answer would tell me?"

"No, not exactly."

"What did you put it in for, then?"

"I put it for to tell you if I refused to go to war, I don't refuse because I don't like this country or I don't like the people of this country. I will refuse even if I was in Italy. And you tell me it is a long time I am in this country and I tell you that in this country as long time I am, that I found plenty good people and some bad people, but that I was always working hard as a man can work and I have always lived very humble and—"

"I ask that answer be stricken out, if your Honor please, and the witness required to answer my question."

Launching rather than asking his questions, the DA maintained tight control. He abruptly blocked Vanzetti's carefully considered answers—"I am not asking you that, sir!"—and insisted he stick to the point—"Pardon me, sir, will you answer my question?" Taking umbrage at Vanzetti's politics, Katzmann also resented his audacity in asserting a policeman had aimed a gun at him. What was the officer's name? How old was he? What color was his hair? Vanzetti did not know.

Letting this doubt drift, Katzmann challenged Vanzetti about his supposed roundup of radical literature. Couldn't he have done the job in the motorcycle? No. Huge quantities of books and pamphlets had to be rounded up from several cities. Why had four men gone to get one car? To help each other look for the homes of friends with literature. Why hadn't they gone during the day? Because Boda and Orciani had not come to Sacco's until late afternoon. Katzmann then forced Vanzetti to admit every lie he had told under initial questioning. As the DA hammered away, the flickering candle of Vanzetti's English began to melt in the midday heat.

"Yes, I say in the Italian Boston hall that it is better to clean up the house of the literature, to clean up the house of the more active friends. We speak about the means, about how to do, and if you remember well, maybe you don't carry it. It is enough—"

"Well, one moment, if your Honor please."

"Let him answer," McAnarney said.

"I submit his answer is irresponsive and argumentative. I ask that it be stricken out."

Twisting in the wind, Vanzetti struggled to explain his lies.

"Even if you ask me one hundred times I answer one hundred times, 'No,' because I have some purpose."

"You intended to deceive myself and the officers who were present, did you not?"

"I intend to not mention the name and the house of my friends."

After revealing more lies, Katzmann asked why so many had been necessary. Had lying about the price of his gun protected his friends? Had he been asked about any friends besides Boda and Orciani? And were they really rounding up literature? Standing before the court, Vanzetti's feet burned as if he were still a baker's apprentice working eighteen-hour days. He asked for a glass of water, drank it, wiped his mustache, and faced more questions. How could he have directed Mike Boda to Pappi's house if he admitted he did not know the address? Vanzetti could only answer vaguely: "I don't tell he want to go directly to Bridgewater. Maybe go to Brockton, maybe go take Nick." Why did he freely tell Katzmann the date he was to address proletarians who had "fought all the wars," but he would not admit knowing Boda? "If I have to tell you the truth I must give you the name of plenty of my friends," Vanzetti explained.

The 6:00 p.m. adjournment let Vanzetti leave, but the following morning he and Katzmann were back at each other. Vanzetti asked for an interpreter, but after one question fell back on his English. Mumbling, he was again told to speak up.

"You have a good strong voice, haven't you, Mr. Vanzetti?"

"Not very much now. It is more than one year I am in jail."

"Was your voice weak the day Michael J. Connolly was on the stand and you called him a liar when he said how you made a move to your hip pocket?"

All morning, the two men locked horns. The Ivy League DA bestrode the courtroom, firing questions. The self-educated Italian fumbled with his English, backtracked, hesitated, then fired back. Katzmann spoke so fast Vanzetti could not keep up. When Vanzetti sought to explain himself, Katzmann fumed: "Will you answer my question?" "Answer that directly!" What had he been up to that night? He had *not* been gathering radical literature, had he? If so, why could he not name a single friend whose house they had planned to visit? Vanzetti danced around the questions, repeating his story, infuriating Katzmann further.

"Do you tell this jury that while you can't remember the day when you first knew that you were charged with this murder, yet you can remember where you were more than twenty days before that date? Do you say that to this jury?"

"Yes, yes, yes, sure!" Vanzetti shouted, shaking a finger at Katzmann. "And you can be sure that I can remember that I never kill a man on the fifteenth, because I never kill a man in my life!"

"I ask that be stricken from this record."

"*Mis*-ter Vanzetti," Judge Thayer cautioned. "You are again making a talk to the jury which isn't responsive. That may be stricken out."

"Please," Vanzetti protested. "I like to have explanation to explain." But Katzmann did not give him a chance. Soon Vanzetti was as confused as any other defense witness, not certain whom he had seen when, when he had gone where, where he had said what to whom. He managed to deny significant details at the Johnson house. He had not seen overhead phone wires suggesting Ruth Johnson had called the cops. He had not heard conversation about a sudden departure. But then he blurted out that Sacco had fled with him to Mexico.

"Oh, did Sacco go with you too? For the same purpose, Mr. Vanzetti?"

Katzmann read from the flyer of Vanzetti's address to workers who had "fought all the wars." "Are you the man, sir, that was going to address the returned soldiers? . . . Are you that man?"

Vanzetti drew himself up to his full height, still several inches shorter than the DA. "Yes, sir, I am that man! Not the man you want me, but I am that man!"

The two squared off until almost noon. When Katzmann played "Gotcha" with dates and times, Vanzetti protested. "I make a mistake, not meant for a liar, but a mistake that I don't remember exactly the particulars, and the number of minutes, the number of the steps I made." Katzmann dug deeper. If Vanzetti had bought his gun a few years back, why didn't he know how many bullets it fired? Why didn't he recognize the gun when it was handed to him in the witness stand? "I cannot recognize," Vanzetti said. "I do not know the name, I do not know the number, I do not know nothing, see." If he recalled April 15 with perfect clarity, why could he not name a single person who had bought fish from him on April 14? On the night of his arrest, how could he and friends have rounded up literature from Plymouth all the way to Salem, fifty miles north? Vanzetti now changed his story—the four men had gone out that night to find someone who could *later* hide the literature. But why had he lied about so many facts that had nothing to do with his politics? "When I say the first thing false I have to say everything false," Vanzetti admitted.

When Katzmann finished, McAnarney's follow-up allowed Vanzetti to explain his fears. He told the court of Salsedo's suicide—or had it been murder? "He was killed before my arrest and I hear that the day before my arrest." He explained that fear of another raid on radicals—"most probably for the May first"—had "operated very bad" on his mind. He estimated that five hundred pounds of radical literature needed to be gathered, and he assured the jury that neither Chief Stewart nor Katzmann had told him in Brockton that he was suspected of murder. That was all Vanzetti said about radicalism, but was it enough? Too much? For all his studies, he had not explained what anarchism meant to him. Would Sacco try?

During the two weeks since the defense had taken up its arguments, a thick blanket had smothered greater Boston. Ninety-degree heat and ninety percent humidity made walking feel like swimming. Seventeen people were hospitalized with heat prostration. Fleeing stifling tenements, people dragged chairs into shady streets, slept on fire escapes, and camped out on the Boston Common. Each morning the sun rose blood-red, burning through a haze darkened by forest fires in Canada. Each noon it bore down from a white-hot sky. Each afternoon it kept up its assault. In the uncooled courtroom, walls and furniture were beaded with condensation. Judge Thayer told jurors they could take off their coats, but only a few did. The rest sat stewing in their own juices. On Wednesday, July 6, the judge set an electric fan on his bench and sat in its cool breeze. Then just after calling the court to order, he gazed down at the short man in the witness box. The judge informed Sacco that an interpreter was available if needed, then said, "You may proceed, Mr. Moore."

With Moore again before the bench, the courtroom bristled with tension. Sacco's nervous demeanor, restrained by arms folded across his chest, set others on edge. Katzmann objected frequently. Thayer again became prickly, and Moore was as unfocused as ever. The trial was not going well, and his hopes hinged on Sacco. Standing before an overflowing courtroom—onlookers lined up at the rear, jurors fanning themselves in the box—the slight, jittery, soft-spoken man began answering in English that barely surpassed a beginner's. Asked why he had come to America, Sacco said, "I was crazy to come to this country because I was liked a free country. Call a free country."

After telling of his early jobs, marriage, and flight to Mexico, Sacco detailed his alibi, filling in fine points—how he had lingered in the North End that afternoon, buying groceries, taking the train back to Stoughton, stopping in a drugstore to "buy elixir for physic." Asked about fellow radicals, Sacco cautiously called them "Socialists." His mumbling was often lost to the crowd, yet his story of visiting the Johnson house on May 5 precisely fit Vanzetti's. Then, when Moore asked whether Sacco knew men who had been deported for their beliefs, Judge Thayer noted the deepening theme of radicalism. "We are going a good ways, aren't we, into this matter?" the judge said. "I can't see why now the whole thing is not opened up."

Sacco told of friends deported and of going to round up the literature, taking Boda's automobile "to find where you could put so well some place to hide, see; to learn where nobody could know anything." Sacco's wayward sentences were further obscured by Moore's rambling approach. Once, as if introducing a suggestion for lunch instead of vital evidence, he handed Sacco the flop-eared cap found on Pearl Street.

"By the way, Mr. Sacco . . . is that your cap?"

"I never wear black much," Sacco answered. "Always a gray cap."

Sacco tried on the cap. It sat atop his head, causing chuckles throughout the courtroom.

"Could not go in," he said. "My size is 7⅛."

"Put that on again, please," Thayer said. Sacco obliged and Thayer stared at him, stared for thirty seconds. "That is all," the judge finally said. The next day, sketches in the *Boston Post* and *Boston Herald* showed Sacco with the cap perched like a large yarmulke on his head, revealing the high rise of his brow.

That morning, Moore concluded his questioning. Sacco explained how he had tucked a gun in his belt on May 5 to go hunting, then went out that evening forgetting it was there. He told of his arrest—no, he had not reached for his gun—and of later being forced to duck, turn, and pretend to shoot while witnesses tried to identify him. "They watch pretty carefully, pretty close, and the most of the people I could see the head very sorry, shaken." Then, following a full day of Moore's soft questions, Sacco was thrown to the DA. Face-to-face with a draft dodger and anarchist, Katzmann plunged into his attack.

"Did you say yesterday you love a free country?"

"Yes, sir."

"Did you love this country in the month of May 1917?"

Sacco protested. He could not answer such a question simply. With slight variations, Katzmann asked it seven times. Finally—"Yes."

"And in order to show your love for this United States of America when she was about to call upon you to become a soldier you ran away to Mexico?"

For the next twenty minutes, Katzmann rained questions down on Sacco. Was *that* his idea of showing his love for his country—running away? Would it be his idea of showing love for his wife, to run away from her? Sacco fought to explain, calling the suggestion that he ran away "vulgar. . . . You can say a little intelligent, Mr. Katzmann." Undeterred, Katzmann strutted before Sacco, asking why he hadn't stayed in Mexico.

"Well, first thing, I could not get my trade over there. I had to do any other job."

"Don't they work with a pick and shovel in Mexico? . . . Haven't you worked with a pick and shovel in this country? . . . Why didn't you stay there, down in that free country, and work with a pick and shovel?"

"I don't think I did sacrifice to learn a job to go to pick and shovel in Mexico."

"Is it because—is your love for the United States of America commensurate with the amount of money you can get in this country per week?"

"Better conditions, yes."

"Better country to make money, isn't it?"

"Yes."

"Mr. Sacco, that is the extent of your love for this country, isn't it? Measured in dollars and cents?"

McAnarney stood. "If your Honor please. I object to this particular question."

"You opened up this whole subject," Thayer said. Allowed to go on, Katzmann confined Sacco's "love" for America to food, money, and a job. "Is standing by a country when she needs a soldier evidence of love of country?" he asked. When McAnarney again protested, denying he had "opened it up," Thayer lashed out.

"Are you going to claim much of all the collection of the literature and the books was really in the interest of the United States?" the judge asked. McAnarney claimed only that Sacco and Vanzetti were "Socialists" and that "riot was running a year ago last April, that men were being deported, that twelve to fifteen hundred were seized in Massachusetts." Thayer asked for evidence of such a roundup. McAnarney said he would have to present it later. Allowed to continue, Katzmann let Sacco hang himself with his own words.

"What did you mean when you said yesterday you loved a free country? . . . I am asking you to explain now."

It was time for the sermon Moore had feared. Sacco spoke for five minutes. Seeming small and frail in the expansive courtroom, he gazed out at the jury, the judge he now loathed, and the white handkerchiefs fanning spectators in the gallery. He told of being a boy in Italy and of coming to America for freedom. Working, always working, he had begun dreaming of a broader freedom. "The free idea gives any man a chance to profess his own idea, not the supreme idea, not to give any person—not to be like Spain in position, yes about twenty centuries ago, but to give a chance to print and education, literature, free speech, that I see it was all wrong." Looking at America, Sacco had seen "the best men" in prison. "Debs, one of the great men in his country, he is in prison, still away in prison, because he is a Socialist." He took aim at "D. Rockefeller" and others who stifled the poor so "they won't have no chance to go to Harvard College because men who is getting twenty-one dollars a week or thirty dollars a week, I don't care if he gets eighty dollars a week, if he gets a family of five children he can't live and send his child and go to Harvard College." Sacco told why he had fled America during the war. "The war is not shoots like Abraham Lincoln's and Abe Jefferson, to fight for the free country. . . . They are war for business, million dollars come on the side. What right have we to kill each other? I been work for the Irish, I have been working with the German fellow, with the French, many other peoples. . . . Why should I go kill them men? What he done to me? He never done anything, so I don't believe in no war. I want to destroy those guns." He concluded with a reference to Socialism in "Italy, a long time ago," saying, "That is why I like people who want education and living, building, who is good, just as much as they could. That is all."

Katzmann stood before Sacco, hardly knowing where to begin. "And that is why you love the United States of America?" he finally asked. "She is back more than twenty centuries like Spain, is she?"

It was late Thursday morning, July 7. Judge Thayer was celebrating his sixty-fourth birthday, his bench decorated with red roses sent by the wives of Katzmann, Williams, and a sheriff, but Sacco had little to celebrate. Grappling with questions, groping for words, he would lose everything that day—his English, his dignity, his hope—as Katzmann berated him. At first, Sacco stood his ground. No, he had not meant to condemn Katzmann's alma mater "as being a place for rich men." Yes, he subscribed to anarchist journals, but "a man must read his books to the extreme, the extreme, the foundation of those books, then to know what anarchist means." He admitted having the same beliefs as men who had been deported, but "anarchistic is not criminals." Sacco stuck to his beliefs, however muddled they came across.

"And the books which you intended to collect were books relating to anarchy, weren't they?"

"Not all of them."

"How many of them?"

"Well, all together. We are Socialists, democratic, any other socialistic information, Socialists, Syndicalists, Anarchists, any paper."

"Bolshevist?"

"I do not know what Bolshevism means."

"Soviet?"

"I do not know what Soviet means."

"Communism?"

If he was so frightened of raids, Katzmann asked, why hadn't he hidden his anarchist books in the woods?

"I don't want to destroy because I love those books."

As the sultry afternoon dragged on, as Vanzetti gripped his penciled notes until they were twisted and damp with sweat, Katzmann cornered Sacco again and again. So he and Vanzetti were going out on May 5 to collect radical literature? Didn't he realize Vanzetti had finally admitted that had *not* been their purpose? "Probably I mistake or probably Vanzetti is right," Sacco said.

Katzmann walked to the evidence shelf and found Vanzetti's gun. He held it before Sacco.

"Did you take that revolver off the person of Alessandro Berardelli when he lay down on the sidewalk in front of the Rice & Hutchins building?"

"No, sir."

Katzmann stared at Sacco. Sacco stared back. The courtroom froze as the two men, their faces a foot apart, eyed each other in steely silence, neither man flinching or looking away.

"Do you mean that, Mr. Sacco?"

"Yes sir, I mean it."

Returning to the shelf, Katzmann hefted the cartridges found on Sacco. Where had he bought them? When? The three different brands had not come from a single box as he had said on May 5. Had they? The cartridges led to Sacco's Colt, and the Colt raised the most damning evidence of all—lies. Sacco admitted he had lied about knowing Boda and Orciani. He had lied about not having worked in Braintree. He had lied about working on April 15. He had lied about his passport, lied about Pappi, lied about recognizing the name Berardelli. Most of the lies had nothing to do with covering up radicalism, did they? *Did* they? With each confession,

Sacco's spirit crumpled, until he seemed like a little boy being scolded.

"You told me what was untrue, didn't you?"

"It was not true."

"What?"

"It was not true."

"It was not true. I have asked you why you told me that. Can you answer that question?"

"I don't see the way I could answer."

Katzmann continued, scarring Sacco's testimony with more doubts than he had scratched into Vanzetti's. Why did he and Vanzetti, supposedly fearing a crackdown on radicals, schedule a speech on a radical topic? If Vanzetti returned from New York with warnings of a raid on May 1, why did the men do nothing to hide literature until May 5? Sacco had no good answers. Katzmann asked him to try on the cap again, pulling it down in back this time. Sacco did so.

"Oh, but it is too tight."

To his many tools, Katzmann now added innuendo. "Will you let me see your left hand, Mr. Sacco? Will you just put it down there where the jury can see it please?"

On Friday morning, Katzmann wrapped up ten hours of cross-examination. "Did you shave this morning?"

"Yes, sir," Sacco replied.

"Have you shaved every morning since this trial opened?"

"Yes, sir."

"That is all."

That weekend, with their testimony finished and their day of judgment approaching, Sacco and Vanzetti sat in separate cells frittering away the endless hours. If they believed in omens, one awoke them in the pitch-black of night. At 2:00 a.m. Saturday morning, the heat wave finally broke as a slashing thunderstorm lit up the sky. Torrents of rain fell. Lightning crackled all over the Boston area, toppling trees, striking steeples, casting eerie shadows through the hollow confines of the Norfolk County Jail. But a more portentous storm came the following day.

Judge Thayer spent Sunday, July 10, at the Worcester Golf Club, where he ran into an old friend. Sensing a sympathetic soul, the judge launched into a tirade about "those bastards down there!" He called Sacco and Vanzetti "Bolsheviki" who were trying to intimidate him. He "would get them good and proper!" The same went for that "bunch of parlor radicals [who] were trying to get these guys off!" He "would show them and would get those guys hanged! . . . No Bolsheviki could intimidate Web Thayer!" Emerging from the club, Thayer's friend shared the remarks with another Worcester native, the humorist Robert Benchley. Hearing the biased comments of a sitting judge in an ongoing trial, Benchley was appalled. He did not reveal the remarks, however. The judge's tempest remained a secret as he called court into session for one final Monday morning.

Moore had littered the courtroom with testimony. The naysayers. The impeachers. The alibi witnesses. Now he tried to weave his frazzled case together. Two final days brought two dozen more witnesses. James Hayes told how on April 15 he had seen Sacco on the train. Carlos Affe, a grocer in the North End, had taken a payment from Sacco that day and had a receipt to prove it. Four radicals told of speaking with Sacco or Vanzetti, then hiding their own pamphlets. Katzmann, his voice now hoarse, discredited some witnesses as defense committee members and another as an anarchist who had refused to take an oath on the Bible. To the North End grocer he dictated an order—"N. Sacco, Stoughton—fifteen pounds pasta, six cans salcina, one gallon of olive oil"—then argued that the grocer's handwriting was not the same as on his receipt. Sacco's boss, George Kelley, returned to identify the telltale cap, then shocked the courtroom by admitting what he had told a police officer: "I have my opinion about the cap but I don't want to get a bomb up my ass." Finally, Moore called one last weaver of loose ends.

Rosina had been in the courtroom every day, often with her baby daughter, telling reporters she had "plenty of hope and courage."

Called to the witness stand, her red hair offset by a blue dress, Sacco's wife summoned that courage. She called Sacco "my man," and said the cap found on Pearl Street did not look like his. "My husband never wore caps with anything around for his ears, never, because he never liked it and because besides that, never. He never wore them because he don't look good in them, positively." She had never seen a hole in the back of her husband's caps. Rosina told of police visiting her home on May 6. "I wasn't home but the girl was home that lives with me now." She did not volunteer that the "girl" was Susie Valdinoci, sister of the man who had blown himself up outside the attorney general's home in June 1919.

Rosina began in English, but when Katzmann pinned her to specifics, she asked for an interpreter. The cross-examination was polite, even when Rosina said Sacco had gone to Boston for his passport just two weeks after hearing of his mother's death. With the letter received on March 23, Katzmann did not need a calendar to place Rosina's date a week earlier than in Sacco's alibi. Rosina quickly corrected herself. She was positive April 15 was "the day my man went to the consul. . . . I intend to answer your question, but as to one or two days' difference a person could make a mistake because I have a lot of sorrow."

Late on the afternoon of July 12, Judge Thayer looked over at the jury. "Well, gentlemen," he said, "the book of fate in these cases has been closed." The session ended early to give lawyers time to prepare closing arguments. In that era of Clarence Darrow, lawyers routinely addressed juries for up to eight hours, making impassioned pleas that brought spectators to tears, but Judge Thayer would have none of that. Moore and J. J. McAnarney would each have two hours and Katzmann four to sum up more than a million words of testimony. Before preparing his summation, Moore approached Vanzetti with a proposition.

With testimony complete, the evidence seemed severely slanted toward Sacco. "There was so little evidence against Vanzetti—almost none in fact," Moore recalled. If his summation stressed Vanzetti's innocence, Moore felt he might be acquitted. But Moore also knew that in acquitting one defendant, the jury was likely to find the other guilty. The decision, he felt, should be Vanzetti's. "Save Nick," Vanzetti told Moore. "He has the woman and child."

The following morning, the hands on the pale moon clock above Judge Thayer had just ticked past nine when the shifty-eyed lawyer in the black suit stepped before the courtroom. At ease, moving from the jury rail to the center of the room and back, Moore laid out his case, focusing first on "the primary issue and the only issue here"—identification. Witness by witness, he took apart the prosecution's testimony, calling it "human credulity stretched to the utmost." Why had mechanic Jimmy Bostock, just a few feet from the gunmen, refused to identify them? Why had not a single witness come forth from Rice & Hutchins, where Sacco had once worked, saying, "We saw the man. We know Sacco. It was Sacco"? "Ah, gentlemen," Moore said over and over, raising yet another doubt. Zeroing in on star witnesses, he accused book-keeper Mary Splaine of having "all the positiveness and assurance and definiteness that we are accustomed to find sometimes in the members of the opposite sex." But hadn't Splaine offered "rather infinite detail for eighty feet away of a car running at eighteen miles an hour at least twelve to fourteen feet below"? Splaine's certainty of Sacco's features, Moore said, was "built bone and sinew" from having seen him three times in the police station. "Gentlemen," he asked the men watching him intently, "are you going to use that kind of testimony to take a human life?" Moore said little of Lola Andrews, choosing only to refute her charge that he had offered her a trip to Maine. Andrews "killed herself on the witness stand by her own personality," he said. Later attacks on her character "finished her up."

Summing up identification, Moore pounded on the rail of the jury box. "Gentlemen, there isn't a single witness called by the government who had an unqualified opportunity of observation who gives an identification! Not one! Bostock had the opportunity and wouldn't! McGlone had the opportunity and wouldn't! So on down the line. But it is the Lola Andrews, the Goodridges, the Pelsers that make the identification. Miss Splaine and Miss Devlin I reject, because their testimony is utterly unreasonable. They did not have the opportunity. They could not. You know it and I know it."

Turning to "consciousness of guilt," Moore asked the jury to remember the recent Red Scare. Lies to cover up radicalism did not prove men guilty of murder. Then, after a forceful ninety minutes, Moore's focus began to blur. He spoke briefly of bullets but did not cite his experts, saying only, "If the time has come when a microscope must be used to determine whether a human life is going to continue to function or not and when the users of the microscope themselves cannot agree . . . then I take it that ordinary men such as you and I should well hesitate to take a human life." Reviewing the alibis, Moore said that disbelieving them would mean "the whole Kelley family lied" and that "some twenty odd witnesses . . . are all liars, unequivocal, unmitigated, unfaltering liars." In conclusion, Moore urged the jury to avoid "compromise verdicts" such as second-degree murder. Then, as abruptly as he had started, he thanked the jury. He was done. "You ran over your time twenty minutes, Mr. Moore," Judge Thayer said. Despite taking too long, Moore had neglected to mention the cap, Vanzetti's gun, the unaccented English spoken by the gunman at the railroad crossing, or the Italian consulate clerk. Rising to fill the gaps was the prim Quincy attorney Moore had hired as his assistant.

If Moore's approach had been Cubist, J. J. McAnarney's relied on another modern mode of expression—stream of consciousness. After blaming Katzmann for trying to "confuse the witness on the stand," McAnarney confused the jurors with barely coherent sentences: "I can't think of the district attorney or the court or anybody else but to protect everything which in my mind is the right of that man. So, then, don't think it is any reflection when I say—but to get to what I mean, it is this . . ." McAnarney made a few salient points. He mentioned witnesses Moore had missed—Barbara Lipscomb, who looked right down on the gunman, and Jennie Novelli, who had walked along beside the Buick. He asked the jury to consider what type of man, having saved for years and on the verge of taking his family home to a grieving father, "would be out doing a hold-up job"? And he cautioned the jury against linking murder, draft dodging, and anarchism. "You have got to be very careful that you don't vibrate in unison with those words. They are fearful, they are potent, they are laden to the limit." But when Sacco and Vanzetti most needed a closing argument rounding up all reasonable doubt, McAnarney withered in the heat.

"Well, we are passing along. Sacco and Vanzetti had some gun on them. Conscious guilt again—Connolly. Is it what transpired? Did it happen? Were they getting ready—were they going away? Is that true or is not true? How about Hayes? Of course he is subject to Katzmann . . ." By the time he concluded, without mentioning Vanzetti's alibi, his own ballistics experts, or nearly two dozen eyewitnesses swearing Sacco and Vanzetti were not the gunmen, McAnarney could only tell jurors to "treat these two defendants as if they were your own individual brother."

It was not a tough act to follow. Stepping before the jury, the DA whose questions had made an old woman and a teenage girl cry now became the most mannerly gentleman in the Commonwealth. In his hoarse voice, Katzmann flattered Moore as "a credit to the West from which he comes" and Judge Thayer as having "a kindly heart and an inherent sense of justice." But he saved his most effusive praise for the jury—"twelve good men," "twelve honest men . . . determined to do your duty . . . [whose] countenances bespeak the intelligence which assures us that you will do it well."

Katzmann recapped the crime, recounting testimony with pinpoint precision. He reminded the jury of alibi witnesses who had faltered under his questioning. Waxing metaphorical, he shared an old joke about a farmer lost in a fog near his barn. When anyone doubted a fog could be so thick, the man protested, "If you don't believe me, you walk over there and I will show you the barn." For the next half hour, mocking defense witnesses who swore they remembered April 15 for one trivial reason or another, Katzmann echoed, "If you don't believe me about that fog, come and I will show you the barn."

How could fisherman Melvin Corl—or any man—remember a specific day because it was near his wife's birthday? Katzmann wondered. Weren't women always haranguing husbands with the dates? "I have been married seventeen years, gentlemen of the jury, and I can't tell you my wife's birthday now, and I don't need to tell you. I have a yearly reminder of it in ample season." Ignoring Judge Thayer's insistence that the Bridgewater trial not be mentioned, Katzmann called Mrs. Brini "a convenient witness for this defendant Vanzetti," having testified during his previous trial. And that tattered piece of blue cloth on the evidence table? Such was Vanzetti's alibi "in its full absurdity." As to Sacco's alibi, he reminded jurors that one witness had refreshed his memory by consulting an appointment book while others remembered discussing a banquet they had thought was in the evening but turned out to be at noon.

Katzmann conceded the defense one point. Michael Levangie claimed Vanzetti had driven the getaway car, yet others stated the driver had light hair. In the panic of the moment, Katzmann explained, Levangie must have seen Vanzetti "directly behind the driver." But the DA gave no other ground. He drove home his nagging questions about consciousness of guilt. Why had Sacco and Vanzetti lied? "Nobody had the goods on them." "But," Katzmann said, rising to his full presence, "they had arsenals upon them!" Vanzetti, "this man who ran to Mexico because he did not want to shoot a fellow human being in warfare," carried a loaded .38. Sacco, "another lover of peace, another lover of his adopted country," carried "thirty-two death dealing automatic cartridges." Didn't their attempts to draw guns on the arresting officer prove their guilt? And Vanzetti, confronted in court with "his natural enemy, a police officer," had blurted out, "You are a liar!" "Will you ever forget the uncontrollable outburst of the defendant Vanzetti?" Katzmann asked. And then there was the getaway car, found not in Pittsfield or Fall River but in West Bridgewater where the two men were later arrested "within hailing distance of it. Can you put two and two together, gentlemen?"

Taking up ballistics, Katzmann told the jury to look again at Bullet III, to eyeball its markings and those on the bullets test-fired in Lowell. He told them to examine the sulfur cast of Sacco's barrel for pits mirrored on the bullet. And countering Moore's fear of a microscope deciding a human life, he said, "Heaven speed the day when proof in any important case is dependent upon the magnifying glass and the scientist." Returning to flattery, Katzmann defended his own witnesses. Could jurors imagine that Mary Splaine and Frances Devlin, "two young women presumably endowed with Christian instincts," would perjure themselves? What interest could they have in sending two strangers to the electric chair? Louis Pelser, after lying to avoid testifying, had come forward, "big enough and manly enough now to tell you of his prior falsehoods." And Lola Andrews? In his eleven years in office, Katzmann said, he had never "laid eye or given ear to so convincing a witness as Lola Andrews."

Katzmann's mastery was belied by a few errors, or perhaps "falsehoods." Sacco's alibi witnesses had confused the hour of the April 15 banquet, he said, claiming it was in the evening when it had been at noon. Actually, a witness who had not attended the banquet said it was in the evening, but the witness who had been there testified it had been at noon. Turning to the cap, Katzmann told the jury that it "fits the head of the defendant Sacco exactly." As to why Rice & Hutchins workers did not identify a former employee, Katzmann claimed Sacco had testified to working in a different factory "way up near the track." Sacco had never said that. Later, Katzmann discredited the Italian consulate clerk for citing two different dates when he had left for Italy. Who among the jury remembered that Andrower had noted only one date? Finally, Katzmann claimed that Bostock identified Vanzetti's gun as Berardelli's. As Moore would point out the next morning, Bostock never made such a claim. But Moore did not refute the DA's other falsehoods.

At 6:30 p.m., as a bloated orange sun shone through courtroom windows, Katzmann closed: "Gentlemen of the jury, do your duty. Do it like men. Stand together, you men of Norfolk!"

The following morning, July 14, Judge Thayer had breakfast at the University Club near Boston's Copley Square, where he had stayed throughout the trial. While dining, he badgered a stranger, calling

Sacco and Vanzetti "Reds" and saying America must stand together against them. Then the judge went to court. Head down, reading from a thick green binder, he began as he had begun the trial, comparing a juror's duty to that of "the true soldier [who] responded to that call in the spirit of American loyalty." He made oblique references to anarchism, urging the jury to uphold the rule of law over "the arbitrary rule of men . . . [which] when carried to excess means the impairment, if not the destruction, of the American government." But where Moore might have expected the judge to wave the red flag, Thayer read quasi-biblical passages praising "the beautiful sunshine of truth, of reason and sound judgment. . . . I therefore beseech you not to allow the fact that the defendants are Italians to influence or prejudice you in the least degree. They are entitled, under the law, to the same rights and considerations as though their ancestors came over in the Mayflower."

Turning to evidence, the judge agreed identity was the central issue. Without naming witnesses, he summed up the prosecution's case, reviewing conflicting stories of the arrest and spending fifteen minutes explaining "consciousness of guilt." "The real question is as to the mental state of either and both defendants Vanzetti and Sacco at that time." He did not, however, sum up the defense's case. After reviewing the lies told in Brockton, the judge concluded with a final call to duty. "Gentlemen, be just and fear not. Let all the end thou aimest at be thy country's, thy God's, and truth's."

Vanzetti had hoped to address the jury, but after a long talk with Moore, he agreed not to. At 2:58 that afternoon, twelve weary men filed down the hall to the narrow room whose frosted glass door was labeled JURY. The deputy locked the door behind them and the wait began. At the police station in Brockton, betting on the verdict favored acquittal. Back at the courtroom, reporters expected an overnight deliberation that might go either way. That morning, Rosina Sacco had brought eight-year-old Dante into court for the first time. Sacco and Vanzetti had each tousled the boy's hair. Vanzetti couldn't stop smiling at him, but once deliberations began, friends took Dante home, just in case. All that afternoon, men in straw boaters and shirtsleeves sat fanning themselves on the shaded courthouse steps. As Model Ts puttered past the town square, they talked—about what? How President Harding was doing? Whether that Italian crook Charles Ponzi would be convicted for his financial racket? The heat? Occasionally, someone glanced up to the high window where the jury was deliberating.

Seated in leather chairs around a long table, jurors began with a straw poll. The vote was 10 to 2 in favor of conviction. One juror had voted "not guilty" only to open up discussion. Then after weeks of avoiding all talk of the trial, the men opened their floodgates and it came pouring out. Names were tossed around. Splaine. Goodridge. Andrews. Pelser. The men discussed the cap, the guns, the lies. They did not, however, discuss anarchy. "That had nothing whatsoever to do with it," one juror later told a reporter. "Absolutely nothing. The question never came up. I think every juror will tell you that." Years later, every surviving juror agreed.

Late that afternoon, the jury asked for a magnifying glass. Over Moore's objections, one was taken to the jury room, where the men examined the bullets. No one knows what lands or grooves they noticed, but ballistics proved key to the verdict. Some jurors even noted facts no lawyer had stressed—that the three makes of shells picked up on Pearl Street were the same as those found on Sacco and that the same type of obsolete Winchester bullet had been found both in Berardelli's body and in Sacco's pocket. "You can't depend on the witnesses," one juror recalled. "But the bullets—there was no getting around that evidence." Jurors talked on toward dinner. One was impressed by Splaine and Bostock. Several thought the defense had used radicalism as a smokescreen. Jurors agreed on almost everything. During six weeks of sequestration, they had slept in the same room, bathed together, fished together, played pranks together. They now found themselves "of the same mind, the same opinion." They reached a verdict in three hours but decided it would look hasty if announced so soon. Adjourning for dinner, they returned to the jury room at 7:30. Out on the courthouse steps, lawyers were enjoying the cool of the evening, expecting deliberation to drag on. Then at 7:55 p.m. word raced through the square.

Within minutes, the courtroom was sealed off. Armed guards took their posts inside and out. Sacco and Vanzetti were hurried out of their cells, down the street, and through a side entrance, arriving in the lighted courtroom just ten minutes after the news had been announced. Sacco looked deathly pale. Vanzetti's broad forehead was creased, his brow furrowed. Moore and Katzmann waited at their tables, Moore tapping a pencil and shifting his gaze. Finally, the jury entered, each man averting his eyes. Judge Thayer told the clerk, "You will please take the verdict."

"Gentlemen of the jury, have you agreed upon your verdict?"

"We have."

"Nicola Sacco," the clerk called.

Sacco stood and raised his right hand. "Present," he said.

"What say you, Mr. Foreman? Is the prisoner at the bar guilty or not guilty?"

The verdict was met with no gasps, no expressions of surprise. Sacco remained silent as his friend rose and raised one hand. When the same verdict was announced, Vanzetti stood stunned, his right hand remaining raised for several seconds. The packed courtroom remained quiet.

"Gentlemen of the jury," Judge Thayer began, "I again offer you thanks for the services you have rendered." But seconds after the judge's gavel cracked down, Sacco's voice rang out.

"Sono innocente!" he cried. The jurors were already filing out, but Sacco pointed at them. "Two innocent men!" he shouted. "You kill two innocent men!" As the words lingered, a streak of red hair surged from behind the cage. Bursting past startled guards, Rosina flung herself at her husband. Her hat falling to the floor, she leaned over the iron rail and threw her arms around Sacco. "You bet your life!" she cried. "What am I going to do? I've got two children! Oh, Nick! They kill my man!"

Vanzetti watched, his eyes melting as Rosina buried her face in her husband's shoulder, crying and crying. Moore came over and gently tried to separate the two. Sacco stood, holding his wife, caressing her hair, whispering to her. Guards hesitated. Judge Thayer stood and walked out. "Don't forget!" Sacco shouted at him. "Two innocent men they kill!" Finally a guard pried Rosina loose and led her away, sobbing and calling for her son.

When the courtroom cleared, Katzmann retired to the DA's quarters, refusing to talk to the press. Thomas McAnarney stepped over to the prosecution table to congratulate Harold Williams on "a brilliant victory." "For God's sake, don't rub it in!" the assistant DA blurted out as tears streamed down his cheeks. "This is the saddest thing that ever happened to me in my life!" He then walked briskly from the courtroom. Fred Moore strolled alone along the town square to a diner. At the counter, a Brockton lieutenant greeted him.

"Tough luck, Mr. Moore."

"What could you expect with the case I had?" Moore said as he sipped his coffee.

As the last rays of light faded from the summer sky, Sacco and Vanzetti made one more march. Hemmed in by police, handcuffed to deputies, they walked again past the tall white steeple of the First Church, beside the black-shuttered colonial homes, beneath the rustling trees. More than a hundred people had gathered along the common to stare. Once when the crowd got too close, a policeman threatened to draw his revolver, driving onlookers back. Passing the white picket fences, the two Italians walked in a daze dulled by a single word—"Guilty!"—that made this warm July twilight seem nightmarish, surreal, and final. Turning the corner, they saw the jail looming ahead, its ivy blackened by twilight, its granite a dull dun color. Marching toward it, not knowing when they would again see this side of its walls, the condemned men took one last look at Dedham's colonial stage set. The last thing they saw before entering the jail was the graveyard.

Book Two

> . . . do not weep,
> not yet, that is, for you shall have to weep
> from yet another wound. Do not weep yet.
>
> —Dante, *Purgatorio*

CHAPTER EIGHT

"Coraggio"

Man is never honestly the fatalist, nor even the stoic. He fights his fate, often desperately. He is forever entering bold exceptions to the rulings of the bench of gods.

—H. L. Mencken

When the Commonwealth of Massachusetts found them guilty of murder, Sacco was thirty, Vanzetti thirty-three. Neither was sure how much longer he might live, but the time seemed tallied in months, not years. In the 1920s, capital punishment was a swift one-way road. Death row did not host dozens awaiting appeals, and no convict expected to linger there. As avowed anarchists, Sacco and Vanzetti were in the fast lane to execution. Four Haymarket anarchists, convicted in 1886, were publicly hanged in 1887. The anarchist who assassinated William McKinley went to the gallows seven weeks after his deed. First-degree murder brought a mandatory death sentence in Massachusetts, and having affirmed their creed before a judge who despised it, Sacco and Vanzetti could expect to go to the electric chair without the slightest delay.

Yet even as their temperaments diverged—Sacco careening into depression and dementia, Vanzetti rising to face down his fate—the men shared a fragile faith. If neither would live to see a forthcoming revolution, nor would he surrender to fears that this small cot would be his last bed, this cramped cell his last home. Tom Mooney's sentence had been commuted to life; three Haymarket martyrs had even been pardoned. On better days, Sacco and Vanzetti could envision freedom, but never in their most utopian dreams could they imagine that their names would soon be shouted from London to Buenos Aires. Nor could they foresee how their lives would be twisted and tormented for six more years, turning what now seemed the final act into a mere prologue. Championed by workers around the world, backed by famous authors and statesmen, they would find powerful voices within themselves. But first they had to descend through desolation, thoughts of suicide, and appeals sullied by the most ordinary people their times had to offer.

On the Monday following the verdict, Fred Moore filed an appeal. Judge Thayer set no date for the hearing, but it was expected before autumn leaves fell. Sometime that week, Vanzetti sat alone in his cell on a starry night, unable to sleep. He would soon urge his sister in Villafalletto to have "coraggio," yet as the stars crept past his cell bars, misery drowned his courage. "With the face in my hands I began to look at the stars," he wrote a friend. "I feel that my soul want goes away from my body and I have had to make an effort to keep it in my chest. So, I am the son of Nature, and I am so rich that I do not need any money. And for this they say I am a murderer and condemned me to death." Nearby on that same night, Sacco lay, with no desire to call for courage, to reach out to nature, to see anyone other than his family. It would be months before he could even muster the will to write a letter.

The verdict pleased the Commonwealth. Thayer and Katzmann received letters of commendation, Katzmann from the state attorney general, Thayer from the chief justice of Massachusetts's Supreme Judicial Court. Supporters of Sacco and Vanzetti, however, were as stunned as the men themselves. A cadre of Boston activists—most of them former suffragettes—had attended the entire trial. One described the verdict "as a crushing and wholly unexpected blow. . . . It is unbelievable that twelve men could so deceive themselves as to believe these two defendants guilty." Moore, despite his offhand comment to the cop at the diner, was equally shocked. "The worst part of it was, that it was a complete surprise," he wrote. "No one expected a conviction."

The press offered little comment. The *Dedham Transcript,* noting that Sacco's denunciation of Harvard and Rockefeller had not portrayed the defendants as "good and law-abiding citizens," judged the verdict "a fair, just one." Hearst's *Boston American* was not so sure. Calling the evidence "most unconvincing," the *American* added, "nearly all of the reporters from the Boston papers who covered this trial agreed that the verdict of guilty was not justified." One reporter took the unusual step of writing to Massachusetts's attorney general. *Boston Globe* veteran Frank Sibley had covered dozens of trials, but none had angered him like this one. He singled out the "obviously coached and perjured policeman" who had accused Sacco and Vanzetti of reaching for their guns. He cited the jury selection among "bystanders," the judge's opening patriotic appeal, and his off-the-record attacks on Moore and those "lunkheads" assisting him. "From the start," Sibley told the attorney general, "Judge Thayer was forming the atmosphere of a conviction." The reporter received no reply.

The verdict incensed Italian papers from New England to California. San Francisco's *L'Italia* saw Sacco and Vanzetti as "two unfortunates . . . condemned because they are Italians and radicals." The conservative *Gazzetta della Massachusetts* called the verdict "macabre." In New York, Carlo Tresca's radical *Il Martello* romanticized the new martyrs. "And all of us are proud of you, Sacco and Vanzetti . . . of you who have known how to hold aloft, so pure and so immaculate, the flag of the ideal, in the midst of the enemy's field, where you are kept prisoners." Beyond Boston, Americans who did not read Italian would have to wait until fall to hear of Sacco and Vanzetti, and by then, much of the Western world would be chanting the names. But first, once his shock subsided, Fred Moore began "working like the Devil."

It did not take an astute lawyer to realize Judge Thayer was unlikely to overrule the jury and grant a new trial based on existing evidence. Moore's only hope was "that we may be able to unearth new facts. This means endless investigations. . . . As you know this means money." Moore's strategy was three-pronged. First, through a blitz of pamphlets, press releases, and speeches, he would tell the world of this injustice. Within days of the verdict, he mounted an appeal for funds to be signed by a pantheon of labor martyrs from Mooney to Debs to Mother Jones. In August, he wrote Rena Mooney asking for the names of her husband's supporters. She sent expansive lists of private contributors, union locals, and labor publications. Next Moore made plans to investigate key prosecution witnesses, digging into their past to discredit them and perhaps prove perjury. Finally—though who knew how or where—he vowed to track down the real Braintree murderers. Summoning his stenographer and the resolve that had brought him through so many battles, the radical lawyer from California took up one final fight to save "the boys."

Sacco was indifferent to Moore's efforts. "They are keeping this thing on, but it is only a money scheme," he told a doctor. Silenced by the verdict and starting to loathe his lawyer, Sacco focused on his health. He was doing daily calisthenics in his cell, but his early delusions were blossoming into full-blown paranoia. He reported seeing faces at his cell window. Along with a burning stomach, he now suffered headaches and chest pains. He refused to eat fruit Moore brought him, claiming, "They can put something under the skin." Depending on the day, Sacco's "They" included "officers," "authorities," "the State," "bankers," and "capitalists." Convinced his guards were pouring something in his ear while he slept, he had moved his cot to a corner of his cell. He reported hearing knocking overhead. "They have a couple of spies," he told the doctor. "They do it to make me nervous. I have got a charge of dynamite." Sizing up his patient, the doctor told Felicani, "You better get an alienist because I think this man has a case of dementia."

Vanzetti, however, was inspired by Moore's outreach. "Our innocence was clearly demonstrated at the trial," he wrote his sister. "We will never be abandoned. The revolutionary press in Italy will begin a campaign and the workers of Italy will have our lives and our liberty in their hands. They have the power to make tyrants shake, even across the ocean." Boasting of vital health, Vanzetti saw his ordeal as a challenge to his manhood. "Well, dear Tresca, we have been found guilty," he wrote his friend. "Why, it would be a great wonder if we had been absolved. . . . The American juries condemn by pre-concerted action, in spite of everything. After all they did not have the satisfaction of seeing us tremble, nor will they ever have."

While Sacco turned inward and Vanzetti outward, anarchists on the defense committee huddled around clattering typewriters in the North End, turning out incendiary pamphlets—*Fangs at Labor's Throat, Doomed to Die*—and sending them to labor and anarchist journals in the United States, Europe, and South America. Some pamphlets included a grisly description of death in the electric chair. Felicani sought another lawyer, an Italian in Providence, who insisted on a $5,000 retainer and an equal sum if a new trial was granted. The cash-strapped defense committee let the lawyer's offer linger. Moore continued his running feud with Felicani, once writing to Elizabeth Gurley Flynn, "I love the anarchists, but God deliver me from having to live with them." The radical Italian press blasted Moore's conduct of the case and undermined his efforts to broaden it, assuring readers that the bourgeois *assassinati* of Massachusetts had singled out Sacco and Vanzetti solely as anarchists. Fighting, arguing, trading insults, Moore and the committee worked long hours, raking in and doling out $10,000 a month. Yet no matter how fierce their conflicts, the serene faces of Sacco and Vanzetti staring from the committee's letterhead kept them true to their cause. Come fall, letters from strangers—neither Italian nor radical—also lifted spirits. From a Minneapolis man: "Good God! America has no conscience! . . . If these 2 men are executed it will be judicial murder. . . . I hope a crime so deeply damning may not be fastened on this country to cause the blush of shame to appear on the face of every decent American for 1000 years to come."

In the fall of 1921, the world beyond Boston got its first warning of how volatile the names Sacco and Vanzetti would become. Across postwar Europe, where Communists, Socialists, and labor unions were jousting for workers' support, word spread of "a new judicial crime." An American jury had rendered "an odious verdict of class," condemning two *militants libertaires* to *la peine de morte.* On September 25, a Communist paper in Basel, Switzerland, put out an urgent call to save "Sachi und Vanzetti." A week later in Italy, workers called on their government to intervene. "The United States government is perfectly aware that it can with impunity lynch Italians like Negroes without the majority of the public arousing itself," wrote the anarchist *Umanita Nuova.* On October 6, the Paris-based *L'Humanité* urged Communists to rise on behalf of Sacco and Vanzetti and "tear them away from the executioner." In remote French provinces, peasants gathered around as the Paris papers were read aloud. While Judge Thayer's patriotic appeals were quoted and alibi testimony reviewed, one reporter noted how "the peasants listened, interested, with their mouths a little opened."

Most European uprisings were stirred by Communists, yet they had not gotten the news from anyone affiliated with Sacco and Vanzetti. Moore, like many in the IWW, was suspicious of Communists and had not included them in his outreach. Felicani, an anarchist wary of Lenin's all-encroaching government, was screening each article the "Communistic" Eugene Lyons, back from Italy, wrote for him. Reading labor journals, however, Communists had learned of the two radical workingmen in an American jail. Sensing a class war, they turned "Sacco and Vanzetti" into fighting words. By mid-October, the fight was on. In Italy, workers marched in sixty cities. In Paris, the American embassy was deluged with letters. Most asked only for a reprieve from an execution thought to be set for November, but some threatened vengeance. The American ambassador put the letters in his "crank box." Then, on October 19, the ambassador's mail included a pocket-sized package.

In his bomb manual *La Salute è in voi!* Luigi Galleani had written, "Redemption springs from audacious revolt!" The audacious

At midnight on June 2, 1919, bombs destroyed homes, including the U.S. attorney general's, in eight East Coast cities. The Anarchist Fighters, including several friends of Sacco and Vanzetti, took responsibility. The Red Scare and its crackdown against radicals began.

On April 15, 1920, two brutal murders on Pearl Street in South Braintree, Massachusetts, set off the case that would reverberate around the world. The Rice & Hutchins Shoe Factory, shadowing the murders, is to the left.

Of four bullets found in the slain guard, Alessandro Berardelli, three had grooves with rightward slants. The fatal bullet (third from the left) had grooves slanting leftward. In ballistics tests made during the trial and after, Bullet III was linked to Sacco's gun, but defense lawyers came to suspect it had been substituted.

SACCO FLAYS CAPITALISTS IN FIERY SPEECH IN COURT

Holds Courtroom Spellbound by Address---Went to Mexico to Escape War Service, He States--- Proud of Having Been a Slacker

A *Boston Post* cartoon published during the 1921 trial shows Sacco (circled in center) trying on the cap found at the scene of the crime. Though the prosecution claimed the cap was his, the cartoon (and one in the *Boston Herald*) showed it as too small for him.

The twelve jurors, chosen from 675 men screened, were sequestered for almost seven weeks. Here they are shown on a July 4 outing, with fishing poles.

Known for the rest of his life as "the man who got Sacco and Vanzetti," District Attorney Frederick Katzmann pursued the case with dogged determination. His politically charged grilling of Sacco drew criticism from many corners.

Jurors considered him eminently fair, but Judge Webster Thayer's post-trial comments about "anarchistic bastards" made his name synonymous with injustice.

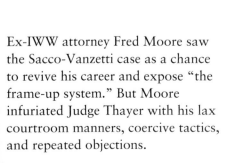

Ex-IWW attorney Fred Moore saw the Sacco-Vanzetti case as a chance to revive his career and expose "the frame-up system." But Moore infuriated Judge Thayer with his lax courtroom manners, coercive tactics, and repeated objections.

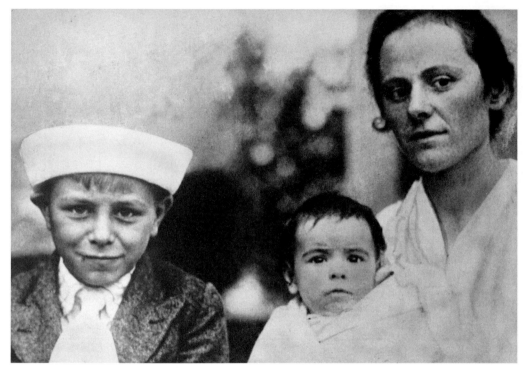

For seven years, whenever her husband was in court, Rosina Sacco was there, often with her children, Dante and Ines.

Within months of the guilty verdict, the names "Sacco and Vanzetti" were shouted by outraged workers across Europe and Latin America. Here, workers in Belgium take up the cause.

On September 16, 1920, five days after Sacco and Vanzetti were indicted, a bomb planted by one of their anarchist comrades killed thirty-eight people on Wall Street. Later, behind bars, Vanzetti was enraged to see his and Sacco's mug shots juxtaposed with the Wall Street carnage in a *Boston Herald* exposé.

Long cherished by their supporters, this most famous photo of Sacco and Vanzetti shows them in 1923. Sacco is in the twenty-fifth day of a hunger strike.

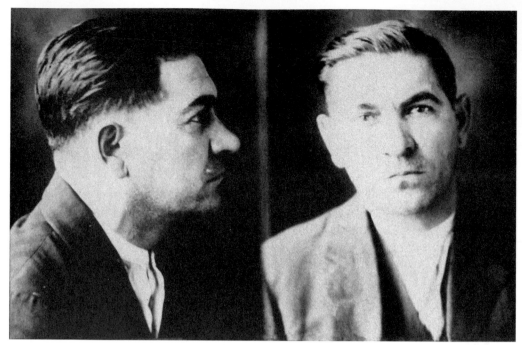

Late in 1925, when a convicted murderer confessed to the Braintree crime, clues steered the defense toward Providence mobster Joe Morelli and his gang. Defense lawyers were soon showing Morelli's mug shot (above) to witnesses, who often mistook it for Sacco's (below).

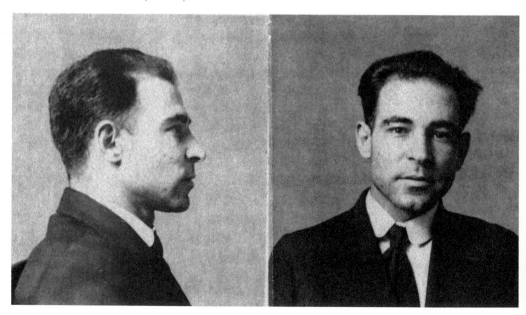

On April 9, 1927, Nicola Sacco and Bartolomeo Vanzetti were sentenced to die in the electric chair. World famous by then, they posed for banks of photographers just before the sentencing.

The pending execution, set for July 10, sparked a storm of protest that grew into the greatest cause célèbre in world history.

While the whole world watched, Harvard University's esteemed president, Abbott Lawrence Lowell, headed a three-man commission investigating the case.

As execution approached, the poet Edna St. Vincent Millay was among hundreds arrested while picketing the Massachusetts State House.

Vanzetti's sister, Luigia, made a last-minute journey across the Atlantic to plead for the life of her brother. Here she walks from the prison with Rosina Sacco (left).

Under a gray drizzle, the funeral procession of Sacco and Vanzetti drew two hundred thousand mourners.

Thousands of mourners wore red armbands reading
"Remember—Justice Crucified—August 22, 1927."

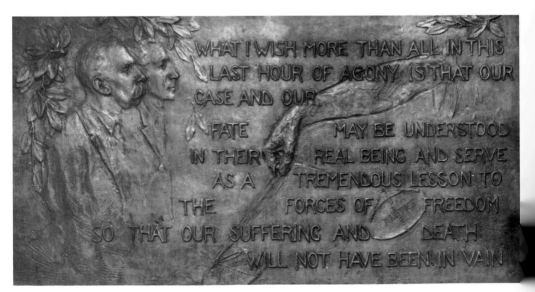

WHAT I WISH MORE THAN ALL IN THIS LAST HOUR OF AGONY IS THAT OUR CASE AND OUR FATE MAY BE UNDERSTOOD IN THEIR REAL BEING AND SERVE AS A TREMENDOUS LESSON TO THE FORCES OF FREEDOM SO THAT OUR SUFFERING AND DEATH WILL NOT HAVE BEEN IN VAIN

Mount Rushmore sculptor Gutzon Borglum offered a bronze plaque of Sacco and
Vanzetti to the city of Boston several times. It was finally accepted in 1997 but has yet
to be put on public display.

parcel delivered to Ambassador Myron T. Herrick was marked
"Perfume." Thinking it a gift, an aide took the box to the ambassador's home and put it on a table. There it sat until evening. When
a valet peeled off the wrapping, a sudden *click!* reminded him of a
chilling sound he had heard in the trenches of the Great War. He
hurled the box into an adjacent bathroom. The grenade exploded,
lodging shrapnel in the man's back. Two days later, marches rocked
cities across France. At a demonstration in Marseilles, a grenade
thrown into a crowd failed to go off. Consulates heard threats that
the verdict would be revenged by attacks on American tourists. A
mob broke into the American consulate in Brest. In Paris, ten
thousand workers near the Arc de Triomphe shouted, "Liberté à
Sacco et Vanzetti!" Mounted police charged, swinging clubs. Shots
rang out, someone lobbed a bomb, and twenty people were killed.
Soon threats were arriving at the American embassy in London:

> Dear Sir:
> Our committee wish to warn you that if poor Sacco and
> Vanzetti get Electricuted in that dirty country of yours
> shotlr after yuo and several dear ones of yours will fol-
> low them same way west.
> —Dinamite and Bombs

Audacious revolt was not part of Moore's plan. His speakers'
bureau—Elizabeth Gurley Flynn, Arturo Giovannitti, Tresca, and
Moore himself—had been assuring small crowds that Sacco and
Vanzetti were convicted by "atmosphere." More clearly than any
evidence, they argued, Dedham's palpable fear of anarchists—the
courtroom guards, the weapons searches, the daily police escort—
had branded the defendants as dangerous criminals. And, Moore
felt, it had all been a gross overreaction. But Europe's violent protests made Sacco and Vanzetti seem sinister after all and made
Moore furious. "This affair is a challenge to the spirit of fair play
in America," he told the press, "and I believe the authorities will be
big enough to disregard what has happened in considering the
guilt or innocence of these two men." Moore could not imagine

anyone thinking violence would help his clients, but in Washington, D.C., the logic of bombs and dynamite seemed all too reminiscent. Remembering the Anarchist Fighters, federal agents did not regard any threat as the work of a crank. With protests now raging from London to Bern, from Brussels to Rome, they braced for a wave of bombings across America.

Judge Thayer had set the appeal hearing for October 29. With barely a year having passed since the Wall Street explosion, all the familiar terror—of Reds, of midnight bombs, of homes reduced to rubble—surfaced again. Threats were not long in coming. On October 23, a Philadelphia mailman found a postcard depicting a dagger dripping in blood. "Unless the two Italians of Braintree are released," the card warned, "there will be slaughtering of high officials of this Imperialistic Government." In Cleveland, an informant revealed plots to kill American diplomats in Europe—German Communists and anarchists had drawn lots to do the deed, and "one of the most violent anarchists in Europe" was headed for Paris. On October 27, newspapers in Boston and New York warned of a three-day "reign of terror over the whole United States." "The conspirators," the *New York Times* reported, "planned to dynamite buildings all over the country." The following day, the Bureau of Investigation cabled agents in forty-five cities from Alaska to Puerto Rico, alerting them to possible "disturbances by the followers of Sacco and Vanzetti." Another warning went out to police chiefs in Granite City, Illinois; Centreville, Iowa; and a hundred other small towns. Chiefs were told that subscribers to *L'Agitazione*, the Sacco-Vanzetti Defense Committee publication chock-full of articles about anarchism, lived in their jurisdictions. Local police were encouraged to investigate.

The twenty deaths in Paris, the grenade in Marseilles, the uprisings from Belgium to Italy, introduced Americans at large to Sacco and Vanzetti. Headlines and brief recaps of the trial quickly parted the waters of public opinion. The parting, however, was not down the middle. The few thousand readers of the *New Republic* and the *Nation* learned of doubts about the trial—the dozens of skeptical witnesses, the antiradical overtones, the strange testimony of Mary Splaine. But the vastly larger readership of the mainstream press was given no cause for concern. "The men had a perfectly fair trial and there remained practically no doubt of their guilt," wrote the *Washington Star*. The *New York Tribune* cited Judge Thayer's speech to the jury about treating the defendants "as though their ancestors came over in the Mayflower." The *Baltimore Sun* warned, "Sacco and Vanzetti belong to a school of thought which makes them potential, if not actual, assassins. . . . We will concede everything to reason but nothing to force." With the names now familiar, with America choosing sides, with all of Boston on a hair trigger, Moore returned to the Dedham courtroom to fight for a second trial.

On Saturday, October 29, Dedham's bucolic town square resembled a military bivouac. A battalion in blue—ten mounted police, Boston's twenty-man "riot squad," and a hundred armed guards—stood shoulder to shoulder before the magisterial pillars of the old courthouse. Suddenly, from down the street came the two men whose names were now plastered across American front pages and reverberating through Europe. A large crowd was on hand to watch them approach. All that week, the rumor mill had been grinding. Italians in the North End spread the word that Frederick Katzmann had champagne ready to toast the execution. Radical papers from New York to Switzerland claimed each juror had received a $25,000 reward for the verdict. Boston papers reported that a mob of Italians—or was it "a Communist band"?—dressed in army uniforms and carrying automatic pistols, was headed from Manhattan to storm the courthouse. Given the incendiary climate, those seeing Sacco and Vanzetti approach might have expected them to shout or raise clenched fists. Instead, onlookers saw Sacco bowing to the crowd while his mustachioed friend, thrilled at being outside prison walls, gazed at the multicolored leaves, the blue sky, the charming colonial houses.

That morning Vanzetti had been driven from Charlestown through the streets of Boston. Though shackled to a deputy, he found the trip delightful. All along the route, he noticed nature, people, life. In his letter describing the trip, dewdrops reminded him of pearls, houses of home: "O, funny, humble, old, little houses that I love; little house always big enough for the greatest loves, and most saint affections. Here I see two girls of the people going to work. They look like to be sisters. . . . Poor plebian girls, where are the roses of your springtime?" But Vanzetti's mood sobered when he and Sacco climbed the courthouse steps and entered a grimly familiar scene. Though the jury box was now filled with police, the rest of the set—from the DA's chiseled forehead to the cage the defendants knew too well—was still in place beneath the same pale moon clock and the same judge's ghostly gaze.

Arguments for the defense took the entire Saturday session. J. J. McAnarney began by attacking the case against Vanzetti. McAnarney questioned the testimony of John Faulkner that he had seen Vanzetti on the train into Braintree. Would an armed robber "have advertised himself by jumping up at four stations asking if this were East Braintree?" McAnarney accused gatekeeper Michael Levangie of "the rankest perjury." He noted how Rosina Sacco, learning of the arrest, had mirrored her husband's "consciousness of guilt," burning radical literature although knowing nothing of the murder charge. And he reviewed the conflicting testimony of those who repaired Berardelli's gun before it allegedly fell into Vanzetti's hands.

Judge Thayer listened intently, asking occasional questions. Then after lunch, he and Moore renewed their personal vendettas. First Moore angered the judge by refusing all conferences at the bench, claiming his clients "want to know in detail and in full what their counsel are doing at each and every step in the proceedings." When Moore explained the dilemma that had forced him to bring radicalism into the case, Thayer remained polite: "Mr. Moore, I am afraid you do not recall the facts. . . . At my request you came to the bench—all counsel. I said, 'Gentlemen, you have opened up a matter which I agreed to keep out and if you are going to open up these things you cannot criticize the court if they get in.' "

Moore protested. Dodging the defendants' politics had been futile, he argued. "Every juror in the box knew the character of issues involved, and if he did not then something was wrong, because we had an atmosphere here by reason of the large—"

Growing edgy, Thayer interrupted. "May I ask one question?"

"How is that, your Honor?"

"May I ask you this question, on what you now say, that it was always your intention to bring in this question of Radicalism? Assuming I should give you a new trial, how are you going to keep it out?"

"I am frank to your Honor," Moore answered. "I do not think it can be kept out, but . . . is that a reason why if because it is in and these defendants have been injured thereby that they shall be debarred from a new trial?"

All afternoon, Moore reviewed testimony. He noted how few prosecution witnesses had placed either Sacco or Vanzetti at the crime scene, and how many had refused to do so. He contrasted the character of his witnesses with that of Lola Andrews and Louis Pelser. Asking the judge to "apply Yankee, ordinary horse sense to the testimony," he was coming to "consciousness of guilt" when the session ended. Closing the long day, Judge Thayer took issue with the case's growing notoriety. A statement published overseas had quoted him telling the jury Sacco and Vanzetti "should be convicted because they were Italians and were Radicals." "This statement was absolutely false," Thayer said. "It was the result of either ignorance or malice." Recounting his efforts to keep radicalism out of the trial, Thayer read from his charge to the jury, highlighting his "Mayflower" remark. Then he adjourned the hearing until the following Saturday.

In the interim week, the names Sacco and Vanzetti spread from Europe to Latin America. Demonstrations broke out in Cuba, Panama, Argentina, Brazil, Chile. In Veracruz, Mexico, which U.S. Marines had recently shelled and occupied, a poster fanned the embers of rage:

SACCO AND VANZETTI will be electrocuted by the Yanqui inquisition but we are standing here in order to continue the work of their redemption!

THE PROLETARIAT OF THE WORLD spits on your criminal action! . . .

Free Sacco and Vanzetti or the world proletariat will rip out your entrails!

From Europe, Anatole France, just awarded the Nobel Prize for Literature, sent an "Appeal to the American People." Having worked to free Alfred Dreyfus from Devil's Island, the author knew how a court case could tear a nation in two. Now he offered an "appeal of an old man of the old world." Sacco and Vanzetti had been "convicted for a crime of opinion," France cautioned. "Don't let this most iniquitous sentence be carried out. The death of Sacco and Vanzetti will make martyrs of them and cover you with shame. You are a great people. You ought to be a just people. . . . Save Sacco and Vanzetti." In Italy, Mussolini proposed a resolution to his new Fascist National Party denouncing the conviction of two men "merely because they belong to the Italian race and the Italian nation."

Back in court on November 5, Moore wrapped up his argument. Nine witnesses had testified that Sacco was in Boston on April 15, he reminded the judge. Eight had sworn Vanzetti was in Plymouth. Yet the jury had ignored all alibi evidence. And what proof had the prosecution offered besides consciousness of guilt? Moore closed by warning that "the administration of justice in Massachusetts is on trial here."

Throughout the defense arguments, Sacco and Vanzetti had appeared as mild-mannered as when entering the courtroom, but when Katzmann took over they could not contain their rage. Sacco erupted first. When the DA said the prisoners had been identified by witnesses in Brockton, Sacco shouted out, "Yes, that man he said, 'There's Sacco!' That's the way he know!"

A guard reached over the rail but Sacco yanked his elbow away. "Go easy!" he snapped.

Katzmann tried to continue, but Vanzetti blurted out, "You bring every crook in Massachusetts to testify against us! You and every man of sense know it!"

Judge Thayer remained calm. "The defendants ought not to interrupt," he said, but Vanzetti continued shouting until a policeman neared him. Finally, Katzmann resumed. He cited long passages of testimony. He again flattered the jury—"as good a jury as ever handled a case in this county." He asked the judge why his witnesses, honest, fair-minded citizens of Norfolk County, would perjure themselves to convict total strangers. Moving beyond identification, he claimed Bullet III alone would have been enough to convict. Sacco and Vanzetti remained silent, but the afternoon was stormy. Bristling over Moore's frequent interruptions, Katzmann whirled on one heel to shout at the defense attorney, who shouted back. The DA concluded by calling the verdict "intelligent and righteous" and asking the judge to let it stand. Then, with a final gavel, Sacco and Vanzetti were returned to their respective prisons not knowing when they would see each other again, nor whether it would be at another hearing, at a new trial, or to face the electric chair.

If a second trial was denied, electrocution could be expected within months. The specter of death gave Moore a deeper purpose— keeping his clients alive. As winter approached, he began inundating the court with requests for additional time to prepare his bill of exceptions detailing each objection overruled during the trial. Even if Judge Thayer remained rock firm, he could not sentence the men until he had plowed through the hundreds of pages Moore began compiling. But this was not the only paper blanket shielding Sacco and Vanzetti. Three days after the hearing, Moore filed the first of five supplementary motions for a second trial. Each would be named for its protagonist. The first was the Ripley motion.

Walter Ripley, former police chief of Quincy, had been the jury foreman. A big-shouldered man with a white handlebar mustache, Ripley liked to tell people he was descended from Plymouth Colony founder Miles Standish. During the trial, he had often saluted the flag when coming into the courtroom. The *Boston Herald* had praised the jury foreman as "the kind of man who is the backbone of the country today." When pronouncing the verdict, Ripley's voice had quivered, yet a few days later he was calmly chatting with J. J. McAnarney on a Quincy street corner. In the course of conversation, Ripley mentioned that he owned a .38 like the one found on Vanzetti. The day before the trial, he had taken the gun, with three bullets tucked into his vest pocket, to a Memorial Day gathering of firemen. The next day he had worn the same vest to court. Chosen for the jury, Ripley found he still had the bullets with him. McAnarney sensed an appeal in the making but dawdled until October, when he bumped into Ripley again and was shown one of the bullets. Three days later, Ripley was found on the floor of Quincy's Department of Water building—dead. Though he was seventy and in poor health, the foreman's role in the case led to suspicion of murder. By the time investigators concluded the old man had died of a heart attack, McAnarney was visiting jurors house by house. On November 8, the Ripley motion asked for a new trial on the grounds that seeing the bullets in the courthouse had biased two jurors. It was not the strongest motion Moore would file, but it bought time for another.

Two days after filing the Ripley motion, Moore visited Sacco, bringing a new witness. Even before the trial, Moore had heard others mention Roy Gould. A traveling salesman of "razor strop dressing," his own concoction to smooth the burn of a straight razor, Gould was seen on Pearl Street on April 15, yet he had not testified. Who was this Gould? What had he witnessed? Where was he? No one knew. In early November, defense witness Frank Burke, an itinerant glassblower who knew Gould from the carnival circuit, checked into a hotel in Portland, Maine. Eyeing the register, Burke saw the name "Roy E. Gould." That evening, Burke dropped in on Gould and asked him about Braintree, then wrote to Moore, who hurried to Portland to gather some of the "new facts" he desperately needed.

On April 15, 1920, Roy Gould had arrived in Braintree on the 2:59 p.m. train to sell his razor paste to workers flush with the week's salary. Stepping onto Railroad Street, he had asked a taxi driver where and when shoe workers were paid. "There goes the paymaster now," the driver said. "Follow him." Toting his sales case, Gould hurried to catch up with Parmenter and Berardelli. From fifty yards behind, he saw them turn onto Pearl Street. Approaching the tracks, he watched them walk toward two men leaning on the fence. He saw the gunmen pounce, the guards stagger and fall, the Buick sputter to the scene. As the car sped past him, the gunman had fired at Gould; the bullet passed through the lapel of the salesman's coat. Unlike bookkeeper Mary Splaine, Gould had a point-blank view of the man firing from the passenger seat. He had worn a cap, Gould now told Moore. He had a mustache and squinty eyes. After the shooting Gould had given Braintree police chief Gallivan his address, then moved on, following the carnival circuit to Canada. After listening to Gould, Moore paid his way to Boston and took him to see Sacco. Moore had Sacco walk up and down in his cell, then turn and face Gould. The salesman was certain—Sacco was not the gunman. His eyebrows were not as heavy, his eyes not so piercing, and he did not have a mustache. For the next few months, Gould roamed the East Coast, cabling Moore asking for small sums and promising to return whenever he might be needed.

While Moore pondered his next motion, a still jittery nation struggled with fears of his clients and their volatile supporters. Hearing that huge sums were pouring into the defense committee, Massachusetts governor Channing Cox urged a federal investigation to determine whether "grafters" led by Fred Moore might be fleecing wealthy Bostonians who were "cranks on the subject of anarchy and militant socialism." Katzmann urged federal agents to deport Felicani and other defense committee anarchists. And J. Edgar Hoover continued picking up tips on what he called "the Sacco-Vanzetti crowd." No bombs had gone off in America, but threats continued. Shortly before Thanksgiving, Manhattan police searched for bombs in St. Patrick's Cathedral. Plainclothes cops accompanied "G-men" to Sacco-Vanzetti rallies in New York, Cleveland, Pittsburgh, and Chicago. Small-town chiefs proved as vigilant as their big-city counterparts. "Thair is about five hundred of these Italians here and a bad bunch at that," the chief in Virdon, Illinois, wrote the Bureau of Investigation. "I will still be on the lookout."

No matter where they looked, however, agents and officers saw little agitation. American embassies remained on alert—a bomb on the steps of the ambassador's house in Lisbon was kicked away before it exploded—yet the protests that had swept Europe and Latin America never started in the United States. Hoover's men kept rolling back the date of anticipated violence—November 6, November 22, sometime in December. Infiltrating rallies, agents heard incendiary accusations. That all enemies of capitalism were "sent to prison to rot, like Debs and Mooney, or sent to the electric chair like Sacco and Vanzetti!" That "the judge wanted them shot, too!" That the execution would finish the plot against radicals begun when "the daily prostituted capitalist press" planted stories about bombings in 1919, "to poison the minds of the people [so] the Department of *In*justice might carry on its dirty work." But despite the rhetoric, supporters were not calling for assassinations or attacks on federal buildings. They were merely passing out red Sacco and Vanzetti buttons, selling ten-cent pamphlets, and demanding a new trial. Police broke up meetings in Philadelphia and Newark, the latter when the police commissioner said, "This was not a proper sort of meeting for Newark." In late November, agents intercepted a message from Moscow calling on the workers of the world to rise up on behalf of "Sacco and Vangetta." But the workers of the world were settling down, while those in America had never risen.

On December 24, 1921, Judge Thayer ruled on Moore's appeal for a second trial. The judge cited a dozen legal precedents, selectively reviewed evidence—Sacco's cap and Vanzetti's gun, Sacco's alibi but not Vanzetti's—and minutely detailed "consciousness of guilt." But it was duty that swayed the decision. Thayer concluded, "I cannot—as I must if I disturb these verdicts—announce to the world that these twelve jurors violated the sanctity of their oaths, threw to the four winds of bias and prejudice their honor, judgment, reason and conscience, and thereby abused the solemn trust reposed in them by the law as well as by the Court." The motion was denied.

The following day was Christmas. Sacco spent it alone in his cell. He remained skeptical of Moore, but workers' cries for his freedom had lightened his despair. "The echo of shouts of thousands and thousands of proletarians reaches my ears and revives me with a Herculean courage," he had written a friend. Reading his name linked to the Haymarket martyrs, he could even romanticize death. "It would be glorious to die for this grand faith and for the oppressed and for the redemption of humanity." But as he spent his second Christmas in jail, with only the flimsiest of motions standing between him and the electric chair, his anguish deepened and his paranoia seemed more logical than clinical. Did death still seem "glorious"?

In the gray prison a dozen miles north, Vanzetti fondly remembered holidays in Villafalletto. "If Christmas means peace of mind and of heart, for me every day is Christmas," he wrote his sister. Noting another Christmas in prison, he added, "This time I find myself weakened in neither body nor spirit. Our cause is going well. New witnesses have been found on our side. . . . I comfort you with the hope of a well-earned compensation that will return me to those I love and to freedom." Then after a long letter touting his good health, he concluded, "Coraggio, coraggio, coraggio. It comes with strength, the strength of the universe. Don't forget it."

CHAPTER NINE

"Nice People and Good Killers"

"So who is this guy Sacco Vanzetti anyhow?"
"I think he's a Frenchman who robbed a bank and we are going to war about it."

—overheard on a Manhattan street corner

At twenty-four, Louis Pelser was already a tired man. A factory job cutting shoe leather had worn him down, hardening his hands but softening his will. Life in a cramped Roxbury apartment with his elderly parents and another couple had made him eager to say whatever would get people off his back. With his widow's peak and pudgy face, Pelser looked older than his years, but when confronted by authority, he spoke like a child desperate to fit in. His deep well of fear explained why, although he had stood just a sidewalk's width from the gunmen on Pearl Street, he told no one what he had seen until summoned by the prosecution. Then, as sweat trickled down his temple, he had told the court, "I seen this fellow shoot this fellow." Louis Pelser was neither a bad man nor a notably good one. He was just an ordinary man whom chance placed at the scene of a brutal crime. When the prosecution needed identification, he provided it, and when the defense needed a retraction, he emerged again to prove that factory work could make an ordinary man as pliable as leather itself.

Shortly after testifying, Pelser announced his engagement, but when recession led to his layoff, his life began to unravel. On a frigid Saturday afternoon in February 1922, one of Moore's investigators tracked him to a South Boston flophouse. Drunk on moonshine, Pelser had barely eaten for days. Moore's assistant bought him a meal and took him to the lawyer's office. When Pelser entered, Moore strode past two assistants to greet him. "You look like a white man," the slick-haired attorney said. Then he handed Pelser a cigar, sat him down, and began firing off questions.

Just what had happened that June morning during the trial when he had been called to the courthouse? Pelser hesitated, then recalled Harold Williams showing him photos. The assistant DA had asked if any were of the gunman Pelser had seen on Pearl Street.

"I said, 'No, I don't think that's the man I seen . . .' I told him I just got a glance of everything, that's all I seen. I said I could not identify if you brought me a hundred pictures here."

"Did you tell him that?" Moore shot back. "That you could not identify the picture of the man himself if he brought a hundred men?"

"Yes, I did. He said something like, 'You know right well that's the man.' "

As cigar smoke filled the room, Moore said he wanted to be fair to Williams. "Now *how* did he say that was the man? . . . What was the tone of his voice and the manner in which he said it?" Moore hardened his voice in imitation. " 'You *know* that's the fellow!' or did he say it like a gentleman?"

"He said, 'You know right well that's the man.' "

"And when you say that, you screw up your face—'You know right well that's the fellow'? He said it in a way that impressed you that you had to come through?"

"Well, he did not really force me . . ."

"Did you think you were being forced?"

"Well, I did in a way—yes."

Pelser recalled being sent into the courtroom to look at Sacco. He remembered Sacco wearing a derby. Pelser had then taken a walk through the busy courthouse before going back to Williams.

"I didn't say much," Pelser recalled. "I think I said, 'I don't think that is the man.' Something of that sort." Moore could barely believe it. Then "why in God's world," he asked, had Pelser stepped into the witness stand a half hour later to swear that Sacco was "the dead image of the man I seen"? As Moore hovered over him, Pelser seemed confused, drunk, weary of the whole affair.

"Are those the kind of words you would ever use?" Moore asked. "That a man is the 'dead image' of another man? Did you ever use them?"

"I don't know how I was forced to say them words," Pelser said. "I don't know how 'dead image' stuff came up. I couldn't tell you."

Under staccato questioning, Pelser admitted he had seen almost nothing through his factory window. Precisely as fellow workers had testified, the first shots had sent him scurrying under a bench. All he remembered was the gunman's army shirt and his hair—wavy and black.

"Black hair like a buck nigger?" Moore asked.

Pelser agreed. Floundering now, pausing before each answer, he could only say, "I thought I had to tell that story."

"Why did you think you had to?"

"I don't know."

"You had some idea what was going to happen to you if you did not tell that story?"

"Fear, that's all I know."

"Fear of what?"

"I couldn't tell you. I don't know."

Amazed, vindicated, exasperated at Pelser's weakness, Moore wanted to be certain. "You can tell anything that is the truth," he barked. "If it's not true that he is the dead image, then you owe it to yourself and your conscience to tell it. If it is the truth, for God's sake stick to your story!" Pelser sat in silence. He had begged not "to go on the stand anymore," but when Moore asked whether he had "the stuff to come through if it is necessary," Pelser said he did. Then, after signing an affidavit, the sad, scared, ordinary man stepped back into the winter, leaving Moore and his men to light more cigars celebrating their good fortune. With salesman Roy Gould as a new witness and now an admission of perjury, they had their first big breakthrough in the case. But . . .

The day after talking with Moore, a sobered Louis Pelser went home and told his parents about the meeting. They suggested he contact the DA right away. Pelser could not reach Katzmann by phone, so he sent a letter. "One word led to another . . . ," Pelser wrote. "He asked me one question & another and finaly had my whole story contradicted what I had said at the Dedham court." Pelser was "worried at the way they have framed me up & got me into trouble." He asked Katzmann to "favor me with an early reply," then added, "P.S. I forgot to mention that I also signed two papers of some kind." The following Sunday, eight days after speaking with Moore, Pelser was again summoned to the Dedham courthouse, where he bent in a different direction.

Harold Williams began by reminding Pelser of their meeting during the trial: "And I said, 'Is Sacco the man?' And you were standing there and the sweat was pouring off your forehead, and you said, 'By George! If Sacco isn't the man, he is a dead ringer for him.' And then I said, 'It is your duty to go into court and testify to the truth.'"

"Yes, I remember that."

"Then you went on the stand and testified."

"Yes."

"I never urged you to say it was Sacco, did I?"

"No, I don't think you did."

After twenty minutes, Pelser signed another affidavit contradicting the one he had signed a week earlier. Then, emerging into Dedham's town square, he achieved his lifelong goal—he blended into the crowd. Four years later when the defense was showing old witnesses new mug shots, several signed affidavits, but Louis Pelser was nowhere to be found.

Unaware of Pelser's retraction, Moore was rejuvenated by this and other leads. From Boston's theater district came word that a blond Italian fitting the description of the pale "Swede" many had seen driving the Buick was running a crap game. From Charlestown

Prison came a tip from a convict. Jimmy "Big Chief" Mede had run a North End cigar store where some said the Bridgewater burglary had been planned. Moore visited Mede, who refused to talk until paroled. And with the new year, a tired but resonant voice was poised to join the fight. The previous Christmas Eve, with the wartime crackdown on radicals now a fading memory, President Harding had pardoned Eugene Debs. Upon his release, the embattled Socialist had sent the five dollars given to parolees straight to the Sacco-Vanzetti Defense Committee. Hearing the news, Sacco and Vanzetti were eager to enlist their hero's help, but thirty months in prison had left the elderly Debs broken and exhausted. Until he recovered, Moore would have to settle for a declaration the defense committee quickly stamped on its letterhead—*"Sacco and Vanzetti are innocent men; they shall not be murdered!—Eugene V. Debs."* Beneath this epigram, volunteers typed the good news—the new witness, the surprise retraction—and asked for more money. Across America, Socialists, union organizers, Italians, anarchists, and activists of all stripes opened their mail and read, "Rarely have death-dealing lies been wrung from unwilling lips by over-zealous officials more unscrupulously than in this instance . . . we are at a critical stage . . . if funds are not forthcoming . . . if they go to the chair there will be no one to blame but ourselves. Please act now."

The winter of 1921–22 was a dreary, hard-bitten season of strikes and recession that saw unemployment approach twelve percent. For ten weeks, Elizabeth Gurley Flynn toured industrial America, speaking about Sacco and Vanzetti in dingy union halls. But workers on strike or bracing for layoffs had little interest in two Italian anarchists doing time for murder. Flynn's February 4 meeting in St. Paul, Minnesota, took in just $18.65. Her widely publicized appearance in Manhattan played to a half-empty hall. Other efforts charted the mounting indifference. The defense committee had distributed fifty thousand copies of one pamphlet and would soon send out a hundred thousand of another. Its mailing list was swelling toward sixty-five thousand names. Felicani had sent two anarchists on a speaking tour throughout the eastern United States, rallying Italian workers in mining camps and factory towns. Still, donations were dropping fast. That February, a *New York Times* reporter interviewed many of the case's principles, including Judge Thayer. "I hope the *New York Times* is not going to take the side of these anarchists," Thayer said off the record. Despite the *Times*'s long and impartial article, the trial, headlines, and massive rallies overseas continued to fade from public memory. From Washington, D.C., to Washington State, federal agents found "not a great deal of interest taken in this case." Vanzetti was still boasting to his sister, "When they arrested us, when they prepared the barefaced plot, neither the cops nor the prosecutor nor the judge thought our defense would be taken up by the entire civil world. . . . The people will not forget us, you can rest assured." But the people had forgotten. Throughout 1922, other than a few rallies in Rome and a small demonstration in Buenos Aires, not a single Sacco-Vanzetti protest was held in Europe or Latin America. And in the United States?

Bathtub gin. Hip flasks filled with the local hooch. Tin Lizzies puttering down Main Street. A happy-go-lucky president urging a return to "normalcy." "Yes, We Have No Bananas." The Bambino circling the bases on bandy legs. A scratchy voice crooning through a megaphone. The click of a stock ticker. General Motors—80. RCA—96. A girl with bobbed hair flapping her arms to a bright melody. "Night or day time, it's all play time, ain't we got fun." A raccoon coat and a rumble seat. Packs of short-haired women smoking in earnest. Modernity putting an entire nation through birth pangs.

The 1920s are routinely seen as one long spree. Unfortunately for Sacco and Vanzetti, the spree—briefly delayed by recession— began in 1922. For the next several years the revelry accelerated, as if the entire nation had shifted into high gear. There was frenetic dancing—the Charleston and the Black Bottom. There was gaudy music by Louis Armstrong, George Gershwin, and a juke joint full of bluesmen. Despite Prohibition, there was plenty to drink if one knew where to look. The timing of the spree was even more intoxicating than the gin. Bursting forth from an era of turmoil—slugfest strikes, war and plague, the Red Scare and recession—the Twenties found Americans eager for escape that would last all weekend, all year, all decade.

But the years Sacco and Vanzetti spent in jail were not so much one wild party—millions were still working too hard to play—as one long Sunday at the park, an amusement park. Though politically conservative, with Republican presidents, Republican Congresses, and a Victorian Supreme Court, the Twenties were liberal in the doling out of the decade's chief commodity—fun. Americans had had fun prior to the 1920s, but never in such numbers, never so publicly, never to the tune of so much money clinking through cash registers. Nearly every amusement that would dominate the twentieth century—radio, TV, sporting spectacles, pop psychology, home appliances, youth culture, crazy fads, "talking pictures," Madison Avenue, Mickey Mouse—got its start during this frantic decade. Some distractions had been kicking around for years as playthings of the rich, but suddenly, like the Ford it seemed *everyone* was driving, like the RCA that piped a ball game or ballroom music into *every* living room, like the frank talk of booze and sex, fun was had en masse. And the masses were larger than anyone could remember: five thousand at a new "motion picture palace," sixty-five thousand at Yankee Stadium, ninety thousand watching a Dempsey fight, a hundred and ten thousand at the Army-Navy game, a half million at Coney Island.

"The world broke in two in 1922 or thereabouts," the novelist Willa Cather recalled. The widest chasm was the newest. America had always been divided by color and class, but 1922 opened another divide—leisure. Farmers and factory hands still found leisure scarce, but a burgeoning middle class and a playful nouveau riche suddenly had hours to kill. How they killed them would define Americans for decades to come. Cather's year of schism saw the dawn of "Masscult," the critic Dwight MacDonald's term for frivolous pop culture. The nation's magazine racks overflowed with new titles: *Reader's Digest* (1922); *True Confessions* (1922); *Better Homes and Gardens* (1922); *Time* (1923). Upstart newspaper chains began turning long-winded news into a boilerplate of factoids, photos, and short clips a hurried nation could digest at a single sitting. New tabloids found a readership hungry for shock headlines, celebrity gossip, and photos of pretty flappers. New pulp fiction, from the detective *Black Mask* to the sci-fi *Weird Tales,* kept readers turning pages, while fan magazines shared gossip from fame's hottest incubator—Hollywood.

The rise of celebrity culture opened a divide between those who tuned in and those who tuned out. The masses who tuned in created a cult of the new. It was much more fun to talk about the newest craze (mah-jongg or knee-length skirts), the freshest faces (Buster Keaton and Clara Bow), or the latest celebrity scandal (the Fatty Arbuckle murder trial) than to rehash the usual strikes and scandals. Those who harped on such depressing topics became party poopers, holed up in the kitchen (or the Hotel Algonquin) venting their disgust with modern America—the blatant commercialism, the mindless fun, the worship of business and the business of worship.

When the world broke in two, shards littered the floor. Not everyone was happy to see Victorian morals trampled. Efforts to revive them sparked a culture war that would last until the lights of the Twenties went out. During the trial of Sacco and Vanzetti, a Connecticut town banned one-piece bathing suits, requiring all beach bathers be covered from neck to ankles. The ban did not last long. A New Jersey court ruled that kissing and "spooning" in public were acceptable—if the couple in question was married. And a Massachusetts town debated banning whips, straps, and hoses to punish schoolchildren. "A light rattan applied to the palm of the hands should suffice," the superintendent decided. As the culture war spread, it would lead to the resurgence of the Ku Klux Klan, the Scopes "Monkey Trial," and dirges for a society increasingly based on buying. But of all the decade's casualties, the least lamented was the death of compassion.

Fred Moore and Elizabeth Gurley Flynn did not know it yet, but they would never rally the American masses to their cause. An amusement park is a poor place to gather marchers. Radicals had been shouting for decades—about the McNamaras, Tom Mooney, the "capitalist" war, and now Sacco and Vanzetti—and what good had their carping done? Labor unions were shrinking, the war had whipped patriotism to an all-time high, and the flu's staggering toll suggested how unforgiving this world could be. In the midst of frivolity, the idea of risking one's reputation for two down-and-out anarchists seemed quaint. Just before the trial, H. L. Mencken had donated twenty dollars to the Sacco-Vanzetti Defense Committee. After the verdict, he had called the case "one of the most amazing scandals in the whole history of American jurisprudence." But by 1925, the legendary cynic was writing, "If I am convinced of any-thing, it is that doing Good is in bad taste." Only a scheduled date of execution would give Sacco and Vanzetti a large American audi-ence. "Presently we began to have our slices of the national cake," F. Scott Fitzgerald remembered, "and our idealism only flared up when the newspapers made melodrama out of such stories as Har-ding and the Ohio Gang or Sacco and Vanzetti." Had they been condemned during a sober decade, they might have tapped a col-lective sense of justice. Yet Sacco and Vanzetti were men of their times, and their times were too hurried to care about immigrants, radicals, or so-called frame-ups. Besides, hadn't the papers said they were guilty?

Entering his third year behind bars, Vanzetti remained as rooted as the spearmint plant he kept in his cell. He was no longer writing his father, who had begun telling him he should never have gone to America. Back in Villafalletto, Gian Batista Vanzetti, now sport-ing a white walrus mustache, was in despair. Several years earlier, he had confessed to his *Caro Barto,* "I am old and before you re-turn I will have passed on; I am crying as I write this." Now that his worst fears had come true, the old man flailed for help. In Feb-ruary 1922, he wrote a defense committee member asking for an American contact, "some more influential authority, some minis-ter, some head of state of minor importance that no one could re-fuse." Lamenting the fate of "il mio disgraziato figlio," the elder

Vanzetti hoped his "disgraced son" would pray for deliverance. Turning away from his father, Vanzetti wrote loyally to the only sibling he really knew—his sister. And thirty-one-year-old Luigia, with the brother and sister she had raised now fully grown, turned her affections to the family's wayward son. She wrote Mussolini demanding her brother's vindication. She prayed her Barto would renounce anarchism and revive his Catholic faith, and she sent him two or more letters a month, arguing religion, updating him on aunts, uncles, cousins, and sadly telling him of how the Italian press had lost interest in his fate.

When not reading or writing letters, Vanzetti devoured newspapers. Each morning over breakfast, while the clatter of the prison echoed through his cellblock, he sat at his small table keeping up with world events in both American and Italian papers. Often, as when reading of the rise of Mussolini, the news tested his conviction that "sadness is weakness." But on March 5, 1922, his resignation gave way to a white-hot rage.

In a full-page article, "My Ten Biggest Manhunts," William J. Flynn, former chief of the Secret Service, told *Boston Herald* readers about the Wall Street bombing and the career of Luigi Galleani. Flynn accused Galleani, Vanzetti's "master," of planning the Wall Street blast. Reading further, Vanzetti's eyes must have flashed fire when Flynn dismissed anarchists as "far from intellectual." But what leapt from the page were the photos. A montage showed the wreckage of Wall Street—overturned cars and corpses in the rubble. Above these stark images were the dark mug shots, taken the day after their arrest, of Sacco and Vanzetti. Flynn's article only mentioned the men once. After blaming the Wall Street and 1919 bombings on Galleani's followers, Flynn noted, "Sacco and Vanzetti, the New England radicals, studied in the Galleani school." But the sight of his own face above the carnage threw Vanzetti into a fury.

What could he do but write? He did not know many English synonyms for "liar" or "bastard," so he sat at his table pouring out nineteen pages in his native tongue under the heading WILLIAM J. FLYNN, *AL SERVICIO DEL BOIA* (aiding the executioner). In prose that seemed to singe his writing paper, Vanzetti began with precise details of Italians arrested for the Wall Street bombing but later released. He accused the federal government of playing "a double game. If they didn't succeed in proving some innocent people guilty, they succeeded beautifully, with their accomplices in the prostituted press, in fostering the political hatred of the race . . . and exciting the mentality of the public which then compromised the jury of our trial." He railed at the nerve of linking "us or any other person to the deeds arbitrarily attributed to foreigners and anarchists." To each accusation he asked, "The proof, where is the proof?" By implicating him in the bombing, Flynn was "giving a hand to the executioner." But the game would not work. "We are still alive, and cost what it costs, we will shout the truth in the brutal and ignoble faces of our jailers."

Vanzetti mailed his polemic to a friend in New Jersey with instructions to submit it to Italian anarchist papers. It is not known whether the tirade ever appeared in print, but Vanzetti need not have worried. Few seemed to have noticed his mug shot above the photos of a ravaged Wall Street. The *Herald* received no letters about it, and Flynn's article, also published (without the mug shots) in the *Los Angeles Times, New York Herald,* and *Washington Post,* remained the only public link the federal government ever made between Sacco and Vanzetti and the Wall Street bombing. Americans at large did not care. It was the Twenties.

Come the spring of 1922, Dedham residents living near the jail noticed an unusual baseball game in their neighborhood. On certain afternoons, a small, dark-haired boy stood outside the jail, his arms outstretched, waiting. After a few moments, a ball came looping over the wall. Sometimes the boy caught it and sometimes it landed at his feet. Then Dante Sacco picked up the ball and tossed it back over the wall to his father.

Though diverting himself with exercise, Sacco could not transcend the tragedy he now saw as his life. Still not allowed to work, he sat, idle, restless, preoccupied with his family. The previous fall,

Rosina had had an operation of some kind. She was receiving twenty-five dollars a week from the defense committee, and with each monthly visit had gained weight and added color to her freckled face. She often broke down in tears when Sacco told her about prison life, but gradually the woman he called "this beloved brittle soul" was acquiring a steely resolve to see her through the coming years. Sacco's daughter, Ines, was toddling and saying her first words. Dante was nine now, able to ask awkward questions. Why did kids at school say bad things about his "Papa"? Why could he only see him in jail, only play ball over a prison wall? Each family visit lifted Sacco's spirits to the sky. "You can imagine how happy I felt to see them so joyful and so gay and in the best of health," he wrote Vanzetti. "If only you could see little Ines. She got so fat, she is really a dolly. Dante also looks very good. He writes to me every week." But each visit's abrupt end plunged Sacco into a swamp of depression. As the months wore on, he saw no end other than execution. In April 1922, he envisioned a bleak timetable: "Look," he wrote a friend. "In June Judge Thayer will be able to definitively refuse a new trial. . . . In October the Supreme Court will be able to reject the petition. That same month the executioner will do his work."

While the men took forking paths, efforts to save them began to sputter. After beginning the year blessed with leads, Moore had watched them go nowhere. He gave up on his widespread workers' campaign—only Debs and Mother Jones had signed on—and concentrated instead on finding the gangsters who had committed the crimes in Braintree and Bridgewater. In answer to his inquiries, police from Ohio to Texas had written him about their local gangs. Now Moore sent a detective to scour the Midwest in search of a "Western mob" that had done one or both burglaries. The detective sent back long letters describing men who held up jewelry stores at noon, men capable of killing paymasters, men with nicknames like "Slim," "Pencils," and "Dutch." "They're all nice people," the detective wrote. "And good killers." With the "Western mob" under investigation, Moore headed south on his own search.

On a warm April day, Moore marched up the circular walkway

leading to the enormous granite façade of the federal penitentiary in Atlanta. He had gone south on the advice of his Charlestown connection, Jimmy "Big Chief" Mede. Finally paroled, "Big Chief" had told Moore all he knew about the Bridgewater burglary. Vanzetti had nothing to do with it, he said. Moore should talk to Frank Silva, alias "Paul Martini," and Jacob "Jake" Luban, both doing time for armed robbery in Atlanta. Inside the prison, Moore met the two convicts. Unfortunately, this was one of the few crucial conversations Moore held without a stenographer. Luban's account, later told to the Bureau of Investigation, is the only record.

A fast-talking swindler who, federal agents said, was "especially noted as a perjurer," Luban said Moore offered him a deal in exchange for his confession to the Bridgewater burglary. Moore knew he and Martini had not committed the burglary, Luban claimed, so he coached them on details, using a map. For their confession, Moore promised them $5,000 each once Sacco and Vanzetti got a second trial and an equal sum when it was over. Moore then scrawled a note Martini signed taking full responsibility for the Christmas Eve crime. Addressed to Martini's accomplices, the note concluded, "The conviction of Vanzetti on the Bridgewater case was a miscarriage of justice. Tell what you know freely to Mr. Moore." Despite the note, no alleged Bridgewater accomplice told Moore anything, and his visit to Atlanta only earned him suspicion. When Luban later told the Bureau of Investigation about Moore's attempt to suborn perjury, the bureau informed the Norfolk County DA's office. Katzmann and Williams were "extremely interested."

After five days in Atlanta, Moore headed north thinking he was about to break open the Bridgewater case. Back in Boston, however, he was scared off the trail. Outraged anarchists on the defense committee thought Moore was acting like a cop. "To us, playing the part of police is impossible," one told Vanzetti. He and Sacco agreed. It was the state's job—not their lawyer's—to track down criminals. One anarchist even threatened to kill Moore if he pursued his Atlanta lead. Whether frightened, frustrated, or just deciding he needed to find someone more reliable than Martini and Luban, Moore dropped them from his list of suspects. The lead vanished, not to surface again until it was too late.

On May 4, 1922, Moore filed his second supplementary motion for a new trial. The Gould-Pelser motion was based on Roy Gould's close-up of the gunmen and Louis Pelser's retraction of testimony made "in response to some sort of force, either physical or psychological." Then as summer began, Moore's life began to fall apart. Quarreling with his new wife—his lovely stenographer was said to be the cause—he was also arguing with Felicani over tactics, organization, and, of course, money. Average monthly contributions had dropped from $12,000 to $4,000. The squeeze caused Moore to close his office and work at home or in defense committee headquarters. An anarchist kept him current on how much money had come in, so he knew how much he could ask for but also how desperate the situation had become. "We are at the 'zero hour,'" Moore wrote a union organizer. "The Committee is literally penniless—flat broke—at a time when money, *cash,* is the only thing between the defense and a brilliant victory." To add to his troubles, Moore was hearing talk that his clients were guilty. So strong were the rumors that one anarchist confronted Sacco at the close of a visit. With tears in his eyes, Sacco grasped the man's hand. "I am as innocent of this crime as my Ines and my Dante could be," he said. During these despondent months, Moore managed only minor victories—the American Federation of Labor endorsed a new trial, and Tom Mooney, in the magazine he wrote from his San Quentin cell, compared his own case with that of Sacco and Vanzetti. With such meager results, Moore could no longer pay investigators; he would have to do more legwork himself. Deterred from tracking down criminals, he began digging up dirt on witnesses.

Early in July, Moore left his angry wife in Boston and headed for Maine on a fishing trip. He was not out to catch trout or bass. He was fishing for people, two by name: Lola Andrews and Carlos Goodridge—if those were, in fact, their names. He went after Goodridge first.

Carlos Goodridge had stepped out of a poolroom to see the Buick speed down Pearl Street. He had seen the gunman leaning out of the car, wearing a dark suit, holding a "dark colored revolver, shining barrel to it." The man was Sacco, he had told the court. Cross-examination established that the middle-aged, beady-eyed man had been arraigned for some crime on the same day as Sacco and Vanzetti, but Judge Thayer had not let the jury hear more. Moore had spent months finding out what jurors had not been told. By the time he left for Maine, he knew more about Goodridge than any court of law. This prime witness for the prosecution turned out to be, Moore noted, "a nice bird to swear a man's life away!"

"Carlos Goodridge" had been born Erastus Corning Whitney. Over the years he had also been known as Edward C. Willis, Edward C. Whitney, and C. E. Willis. More con man than hardened criminal, Whitney had roamed the Northeast acquiring wives, inventing identities, and cheating gullible small-towners. Under various names he had been convicted for grand larceny (of two gold watches), insurance fraud, assault, forgery, armed robbery (of forty-two dollars), bigamy, and stealing a horse.

Before going to Maine, Moore gathered prison records, divorce papers, marriage licenses, checks, indictments, photos, even fawning letters to wives in which Whitney claimed to be "happy in Jesus, my Jesus tonight." Moore's one-hundred-plus pages of affidavits depicted Erastus C. Whitney as a pathological liar, a cunning grifter who "plays the religious game to perfection," and a bigot who often said "all Italians coming over on the ships to America ought to be sunk in the harbors." Moore was ready to file one of judicial history's juiciest motions, but first he wanted to meet this "bird" and learn what Katzmann had offered him for his testimony.

On the evening of July 12, Moore caught up with Whitney in a white clapboard church in the woods of Vassalboro, Maine, a dozen miles up the Kennebec River from Augusta. Approaching a pew, the gruff-faced attorney stopped the balding con man in the middle of a hymn and asked him to step outside. Without identifying himself, Moore took Whitney into his car, where a deputy sheriff sat in the back transcribing their conversation. Shown photographs of his dewy-eyed wives—Minnie, Grace, Hattie—"Goodridge" admitted to being Erastus C. Whitney. Moore then showed him other incriminating evidence, including an outstanding indictment for grand larceny in Livingston County, New York, in 1911.

"You have never served under this last and pending indictment?" Moore asked.

"No sir," Whitney said with a wry smile. "Hoped I never would but guess I will, all right. I know how this come out. It was a woman."

"I might tell you that I know your history fairly well," Moore responded. "I want to say that this history has nothing to do with a lady in this state." He went on, asking about other crimes.

"Whitney, you have been at times rather careless with reference to the truth," Moore understated.

"Don't know but I have," the con man replied. "Quite a lot . . ."

"You have been lying for so many years," Moore suggested, "you could not tell the truth from the false now."

"Oh, well, no. I don't think that."

Running down his long list of crimes, Moore learned that a knife fight in Buffalo had left Whitney deathly afraid of Italians. But when Moore asked whether Katzmann had offered him any plea bargain, Whitney repeatedly denied it. Harold Williams, he said, "chased me all that fall and winter," but, reluctant to get involved, Whitney had refused to identify Sacco. Like Louis Pelser, he could not say why he had finally testified for the prosecution, but he still thought Sacco might be guilty. Seeing Sacco's mug shot in the papers, he had told one wife that the man in the derby was "the fellow that was in the gang down there."

With the sun setting and Whitney trying to slip through his tattered web, Moore got mad. "Talk to me on a white man's basis!" he said. "Now start to put something over that is logical!" Suddenly Whitney recognized the face.

"Haven't I met you before?" he asked. "Isn't your name Moore?" Moore admitted it was and Whitney stuck out his hand. "Glad to

meet you," he said. "I've heard of you from San Francisco to
Maine."

Recognized and flattered, Moore grilled Whitney further, but
the con man would not disavow his testimony. He was positive he
had seen Sacco. Sort of. Then Moore asked whether a husband
"with two babies and a wife" should be sent to the electric chair
on the word of a man with a long criminal record. For once, Whitney considered the weight of his actions. "I didn't calculate to be in
that matter," he said, beginning to cry. "But afterwards, a good
many times since, I have thought that I am not positive. I am not
positive that if I would have to swear that that man was the one, I
could positively identify him as the man." Perhaps there had been
some pressure, he admitted. Harold Williams "talked to me so
much I was just about dead, I guess."

Moore, Whitney, and the deputy sheriff sat in the car for twenty
minutes. Finally, when Whitney still refused to recant, Moore
drove him to Augusta to have him arrested as a fugitive. Following
a 1:30 a.m. call to a furious judge, Whitney was held overnight.
The next morning, a telegram went off to Livingston County asking whether "Erastus C. Whitney" was still wanted there for grand
larceny. While Moore awaited a reply, a judge assured Whitney his
crime was too old for anyone to bother with. "Unless I hear from
them tonight I will let you go in the morning," the judge said. "I do
not intend to have this office used by any lawyer to build up any
cases for the State of Massachusetts." When no answer came, Whitney was released, leaving Moore with equivocations and a stack of
lurid affidavits. He had chased loose leads from Georgia to Maine,
coming up empty. Before returning to Boston, he decided to cast for
one final catch.

Since the day Lola Andrews had accused him of offering her a
"vacation," then upstaged him by fainting in court, Moore had
wanted to get even. The day after watching Erastus C. Whitney slip
away, he was in Andrews's hometown of Gardiner, Maine, speaking
to her teenage son, John. The rawboned, rough-hewn young man
had no love, affection, or any other feeling for the mother he had not
seen in eight years. She might be "Lola Andrews" in Massachusetts,

her son said, but in Gardiner she was Rachel Hassam. And she used to beat him regularly, with a stick, a poker, "anything she could get her hands on. She was never very particular." His mother had not been a good wife either, the young man said. "She never stayed home and kept house like any other woman. She was running up and down the road all the time." Then Moore played a hunch. Had John ever known his mother to faint?

"I have known of lots of times she has fainted. Anybody that faints dead away don't know what's going on around them, do they? If I fainted away on this floor, could I get up and tell you what you had said? She always could get up and tell everything that had gone on." There followed several stories of Lola/Rachel, when cornered by unpleasant truths, fainting or pretending to be poisoned. John Hassam shook his head. "I don't know her," he said. "I don't know any such thing as a mother except I suppose I got one."

Moore spent five days snooping around the little town. Almost everyone he met remembered Rachel Hassam. Pert, pretty, and coquettish, she had been a wayward foster child before turning into a wanton woman who had lived with several men. Later, folks said, she had become a whore who "serviced" whole barracks of soldiers. "The consensus of opinion is that the lady was a person difficult to satisfy," Moore wrote to friends. "To say the least, her pursuit of the Holy Grail was a consistent one. But apart from this, they all agree that she is the most fluent and most consistent liar that county has produced." One woman confirmed Lola's fainting behavior—"I have seen her 'die' a good many times, and after she thought I had gone, she raised up in bed." Mayhew Hassam, asked about his former wife, snapped his fingers and said, "Her word is not worth *that*!" Moore left Gardiner with 373 pages of depositions detailing every sordid aspect of Andrews's life, but he had to go back upriver to Augusta to learn the secret that had made Rachel Hassam change her name. In 1913, a judge had found her unfit to care for her nine-year-old son. Noting her cohabitation with "various and sundry male persons to whom she was not united in wedlock," the judge had made John Hassam a ward of the state. And "the said Rachel A. Hassam did not contest the taking" of her son. With his briefcase now stuffed with dirt, Moore headed home.

By the end of summer, no "Western mob" had been tied to Braintree. With Prohibition rapidly turning America into a bootlegger's paradise, Moore's investigator found too many gangs to track down. Combing the Midwest for months, he had sent back mug shots and a sizable expense account but little else. Closer to home, Moore had secured another affidavit tarring a juror. Just after Sacco and Vanzetti were arrested, Alderic J. Richard swore, he had been discussing the case with John Ganley, his landlord. If Sacco and Vanzetti had not done the Braintree job, the future juror had said, they were at least involved somehow. Then Ganley added, "They ought to hang every damn one of those Italians by the balls." For reasons never explained, Moore did not file this affidavit. Instead, he went forward with his third motion for a new trial, the "Goodridge motion." Then, with the defense committee still strapped for cash, the lawyer had to start paying his own bills. Moore agreed to take a new case that fall, defending a member of the United Mine Workers on a murder charge in Ohio. Before leaving, he hoped one more motion might be enough to clog the courts until his return. It was time to confront Lola. Or Rachel. Or whatever her name was.

Early in September, Moore's investigators summoned Andrews to the seedy Hotel Essex near Boston's South Station. Entering a flea-ridden room, Andrews was startled to see her son. Swept from his sleepy town into an exciting murder case, John Hassam had been hanging around the defense committee office telling volunteers about the mother he never had. Now he watched Moore's men grill his mother—for four hours. Lola Andrews listened as they called her a liar. She hung her head and cried. She denied many accusations but volunteered new information. She had toured the Dedham jail before the trial but had not just happened to spot Sacco pacing on a lower floor. He had been pointed out as "the man she had come to see." Emerging from the jail, Andrews had told Chief Stewart she was still unsure. And Stewart had replied,

"Well now, you *know* that is the man." When she later confessed her uncertainty to Harold Williams, he had shaken a finger in her face, shouting, "You can put it stronger than that! I know you can!" And when, after Moore's cross-examination, Andrews had begged not to return to the witness stand, Stewart had told her, "You do not think we put you on the stand without looking up your history, do you? You have got to go back onto the stand."

Recovering her composure, Andrews demanded to know what Moore had learned about her in Maine. Toward midnight, she was taken to his home, where he read her the affidavit from the Augusta judge. That was enough to forge a deal. Moore would not go public with anything he had dug up about "Rachel Hassam," and Lola Andrews would sign an affidavit recanting her testimony and accusing Chief Stewart and Harold Williams of coercion. A judge might call such a deal blackmail, but Moore merely boasted, "We have melted her." Some weeks later, Andrews was waitressing at a diner when two stout men entered. When she asked for their order, they told her she ought to be in Hollywood, with all the nerve she had. "You told a lie to help the Italians," one man said, "and probably you will be in prison before you get through." The men asked if she had seen Katzmann lately. She refused to reply and the men left.

On September 11, 1922, Moore filed a motion charging that Lola Andrews was "an utterly and hopelessly unreliable and untrustworthy person." With four motions now pending, he then wrote to Katzmann. The letter was firm but polite. During his trial summation, Moore recalled, Katzmann had told the jury a DA should think long and hard before giving any witness "the stamp of approval of the Commonwealth of Massachusetts." Moore then shared what he had dug up on Carlos Goodridge—"as thoroughgoing a scoundrel as ever imposed upon the credulity of a District Attorney and jury"—and Lola Andrews—"a person of such unsavory and reprehensible character that those who know her closest and longest, including her own son, call her untruthful, untrustworthy, and immoral." Given these witnesses, Moore called upon Katzmann to "do the big-minded, public-spirited, courageous

thing . . . to recommend in emphatic terms a new trial for Nicola
Sacco and Bartolomeo Vanzetti." Katzmann never responded to
the letter; he was busy gathering his own affidavits. And Moore,
having exhausted another year of time and energy, turned to the
task of holding his life together. That fall, his father died, his wife
left him, he lost his murder case in Ohio, and he was left alone in a
puritanical city he could not begin to comprehend, clinging to his
career and the innocence of his clients.

By the close of 1922, Americans had rendered judgment on
Sacco and Vanzetti. The verdict: who cared? Other than the dwindling cadre of radicals, only a few intellectuals, men like the Harvard historian Samuel Eliot Morison and the novelist Sinclair Lewis,
each a contributor to the defense committee, were following the
case. As stories shifted and leads evaporated, the only constants for
Sacco and Vanzetti were iron bars, drudgery, and whatever fleeting
interests condemned men can muster. Vanzetti, to the delight of the
surrogate mothers who were writing him weekly, had taken to poetry. His first effort was an ode.

> *Dazzling of light, highly in the skies*
> *Amongst sidereal harmonies vibrated in a flight*
> *Springtime advance; and since thou ardently desire for her.*
> *Faithful among the shadows, by flight thou followest her,*
>   *O nightingale.*

Sacco's constant companion was despondency. He was now calling himself "the sad recluse." Late that fall, he had finally been allowed to work in the jail's shoe factory. At last occupied, he enjoyed
rare moments of contentment "because I am joy whin I am work,"
but then another prisoner threw a shoe heel at him. When Sacco
complained, his work permit was revoked. Confined to his cell, his
mind festered. Suspecting he had contracted tuberculosis, he no
longer trusted anyone, not even Rosina. Once when she brought
him Italian food, he confronted her: "When I was home I never
grudged you anything! I gave you everything money would buy, but
now you bring me poisoned food!" The beleaguered Rosina calmly

explained that the food had come from a store, but Sacco insisted it was contaminated.

At the close of the year the world broke in two, Sacco wrote to friends: "Above all, I have to tell you that I am tired of this life. I have survived months under each modern inquisition. . . . Now enough, I tell you." To guards, he was more circumspect. "Mr. Barrett," he asked, "don't you think my case looks bad for me?" When told not to think about it, Sacco replied, "I am losing my courage." By late December, he had begun a hunger strike, warning, "No Christ can convince me to stop it."

CHAPTER TEN

"Free or Die"

He got into a restless habit of strolling about when the cause was on, or expected, talking to the little shopkeepers and telling 'em to keep out of Chancery, whatever they did. "For," says he, "it's being ground to bits in a slow mill; it's being roasted in a slow fire; it's being stung to death by single bees; it's being drowned by drops; it's going mad by grains."

—Charles Dickens, *Bleak House*

The future mayor of New York, Fiorello La Guardia, was running for Congress in 1922 when Fred Moore wrote to ask for his help. La Guardia set the letter aside, then, after winning the election, finally responded. He had followed the Sacco-Vanzetti case since the trial, he wrote. Friends had urged him to get involved. Now he assured Moore, "I feel so keenly as to the fate of these two defendants that you can count upon my services entirely free." But when he came to Boston to consult with Moore, La Guardia decided to visit the prisoners.

La Guardia was the first politician who cared enough to visit Sacco and Vanzetti. Anarchists, however, cared nothing for politicians, a class of men Mikhail Bakunin had listed among "mankind's tormentors." In Charlestown Prison, La Guardia found Vanzetti pacing his cell, ranting about "the class war," refusing to talk. Visiting Sacco, La Guardia met a more solid stone wall. While the congressman watched, Sacco gripped his cell bars, muttering over and over, "The world will be cleansed by my blood!" Emerging into the public eye, La Guardia managed a statement to the press—"I am absolutely convinced of the innocence of these two men"—but after advising Moore on another motion, he left for Washington and did not concern himself with Sacco and Vanzetti until 1927. He had better things to do than work for two men he judged to be "demented."

Whether demented or just desperate to end his ordeal, Sacco was determined that 1923 would be his last year in prison. He did not know how his "long and dolorous Calvary" would close; he only knew that he could not stand it anymore. Starvation was his means to an end, but he did not find hunger a willing executioner. His first fast lasted eight hours; his second ended after eight days. But by mid-February 1923, when he again pushed away the meager prison fare, he had built up the fury to endure starvation. Three times in the previous month, a date had been set for a hearing on the latest motions. Three times the hearing had been postponed. Furious at Moore, enraged at his fate, Sacco sent a blistering letter to the defense committee.

"Thirty-four months of this long martyrdom in this tomb has exhausted me and broken my limbs and my energy," he wrote. "The hunger strike will decide the life of Sacco and Vanzetti and I will continue it." Urging his "dear friends" to "join us in one last shout," he let each metal tray heaped with food sit in the corner of his cell until a guard removed it, untouched. Three more meals sat throughout an eighth day. A ninth. A tenth. Guards urged Sacco to eat. He refused. Rosina pleaded with him. He turned away. He still drank water, but as the hollow stone of his stomach gnawed at him, he steeled himself against his own emptiness, welcoming its savage purpose. A twelfth day. A fourteenth. On into a third week. Now even the thought of eating made him swoon. As ravenous days dragged on, Sacco's body began to consume itself. His cheeks caved in. His ribs protruded and a dull numbness gripped his limbs. On March 2, a seventeenth day without food, a doctor told

Sacco he was killing himself. "I don't care if I die," he replied. Five days later, shaking and trembling, he was bathed and helped to his feet. Told that the postponed hearing was finally near, that he should eat so he could attend it, he declined. It would not make any difference, he said. Nothing would. Judge Thayer would never grant a new trial. "On the forty-fourth day of my hunger strike," he predicted, "I shall be carried out of here in a box." Hunger, he said, was bringing him closer to his goal—"free or die."

On March 9, wobbly, skeletal, and as white as the winter sky, Sacco was driven to the courthouse. As he walked feebly up the steps, his dark double-breasted coat hung on him like the robes of the Grim Reaper. His bow tie seemed to be a garrote around his neck. Alone in the courtroom cage, he waited while deputies searched entering spectators. The usual group of maternal women took seats. Cops came and went. Then, as she had on that warm July evening when she had cried out for his freedom, Rosina came striding from the rear. Rushing to the cage, she kissed her man. He put an arm around her, pinched her cheek, and smiled, his gold tooth glinting. For a moment, the courtroom fell away and they became "Nick and Rosie" again, talking with their heads together. Then Vanzetti was led in. Seeing his friend for the first time in sixteen months, Sacco's eyes filled with tears. The two men embraced and kissed both cheeks. "Come stai?" Sacco asked. Vanzetti mumbled something in Italian and they sat and chatted. Vanzetti may have told Sacco how he had come from Charlestown on the train, sitting across the aisle from Judge Thayer. He may have urged Sacco to eat. Or perhaps they just spoke about Italy.

At 10:00 a.m., when Judge Thayer entered, the familiar scene was complete. But new elements were about to enter the case. The first was sheer bulk. The full trial transcript—two books each two inches thick—now sat on the judge's bench. Affidavits were piling up like autumn leaves. *Commonwealth v. Nicola Sacco and Bartolomeo Vanzetti* now filled five thousand pages. But despite all the paperwork, a crucial package of affidavits was missing. Earlier that week, the prosecution had left the package at a drugstore for defense lawyers to pick up. When J. J. McAnarney went to get it, the store was closed. Not having reviewed these latest papers, the defense asked for another postponement. Sacco was furious, fuming in the cage until Vanzetti calmed him. The men were handcuffed to a guard and taken into a foyer. There, sad-eyed and staring into eternity, they posed for their most famous photo before returning to separate prisons. They would not see each other again until October. When they did, Sacco would wear the bereaved look of a survivor. Starvation. Suicide attempts. Insanity. What more could affidavits do to him?

The affidavits left in the drugstore were written in the usual legalese—"I, Frederick G. Katzmann, being first duly sworn on oath depose and say . . ." But bitterness saturated the dry prose as surely as if it had been written in bile. Moore's motions had accused the prosecution of suborning perjury, coercing some witnesses and concealing others. Katzmann had retired to private practice, yet under a special appointment from his successor, Harold Williams, he was still handling the appeals and he would let neither his honor nor the signature prosecution of his career be impugned by the radical lawyer who had been insulting him since the DeFalco affair. Until the spring of 1923, *Commonwealth v. Sacco and Vanzetti* had been based on law and evidence. Now Katzmann added another new element—righteous indignation. Since September, his investigators had followed in Moore's tracks, interviewing the same small-towners in the same small towns. Days before the March 9 hearing, Katzmann had filed twenty-nine affidavits. When Moore finally fetched them from the drugstore, he learned that DAs do not appreciate attacks on their conduct and that ordinary people, when hounded and blackmailed, rarely stick to their stories. Louis Pelser, Carlos Goodridge, Lola Andrews—all had, as Moore put it, "flopped."

With his temper rising, Moore read Pelser's retraction of all he had confessed in the smoke-filled office the previous winter. He read Harold Williams's affidavit swearing he had never coerced Pelser to identify Sacco. Then, leafing through the stack, Moore came to the affidavit of Erastus C. Whitney. The erstwhile "Carlos Goodridge" recounted how Moore had tracked him down in

Maine, grilled him, then had him arrested and jailed overnight. After laying out a clear case of blackmail, Whitney countered every one of Moore's charges against him, even his fear and hatred of Italians. "Some of my best friends in former and recent years have been of Italian nationality," he swore. Moving on to the Ripley motion, Moore found affidavits from all eleven surviving jurors swearing that the foreman's .38 cartridges had not played any part in their deliberations. Finally, and perhaps with a wince, Moore began leafing through a transcript entitled *Examination of Mrs. Lola R. Andrews, made at the Court House, Dedham, Mass. January 9, 1923.* The questions were asked by "Mr. Katzmann."

"Mrs. Andrews, I think you know who I am," Katzmann began. "Yes."

"I want to talk to you about the affidavit which they say you signed on September eleventh last in connection with the Sacco case. Do you remember what you signed?"

Calm and composed before the gentleman who had caught her fainting in his arms, Andrews remembered signing "some kind of a paper." Yet she had been in "such a condition at the time," she was not certain what it said. "Why, I was frightened and I was nervous, and I cannot tell you what I wasn't," the diminutive woman said. Had anyone read the paper to her? Katzmann asked. Andrews insisted no one had, but Moore and his men had certainly pressured her to sign it. Why, they had even brought her son from Maine. "The knowledge that my son should be brought into it and seemed to be used as a weapon against me, why, it almost stunned me." She had resisted hours of badgering, saying if she signed, "it meant a terrible disgrace for me." But Moore's men had told her she was "doing the grandest thing a woman could do," that her boy would no longer be ashamed of her, that her past would not be revealed. She then told Katzmann how Moore had led her, weeping, to a small desk, set the paper in front of her, and ordered her to sign it. When she still refused, one of the men had dipped a pen in ink and put it in her hand. Her son had begged her, saying, "Mother, sign this paper and have an end to all this trouble, for you did not recognize these men." Finally, sometime after midnight, she had signed.

In recounting her side of the story, Andrews did not cry. She did not faint. Instead, she assumed the cagey manner displayed in the witness stand. "I should call it a trap—that is the only way I can call it. I was simply, as a man would say, framed, that is all. See, to have the men burst into the room on you and all this business, and I began to realize then, you know, it was more or less of a trap they had sprung on me and they were using the boy, see." The whole business had made her so worried she could hardly work. "A mental strain is a terrible thing, Mr. Katzmann, to be under," she said. Katzmann asked whether her courtroom testimony had been truthful. "Why, as truthful as I can say," she answered. No one had coerced her to identify Sacco at the jail and no one had singled him out as "the man you are here to see." Harold Williams had not shaken a finger in her face, shouting, "You can put it stronger than that!" And Chief Stewart had not warned her that he knew her history.

"Is there anything about your past, Mrs. Andrews, that you are disturbed about?" Katzmann asked. "Is there really anything?"

"Why, I cannot see what I have ever done that is so disturbing."

"None of us know," Katzmann said, "and I wondered what it was."

As the interview drew to a close, Andrews said, "Why, you would think I had committed some unpardonable sin or something. Or I was a fugitive or something."

Before a notary public, Andrews swore to everything she had just recounted. And it was the notary's short affidavit—not the longer ones by Katzmann, Williams, and Chief Stewart, each swearing he had never coerced Lola Andrews—that made Moore's eyes shift and his fists clench. Yet by that afternoon, Moore saw the changing stories in a more favorable light. It was simple, he wrote to Elizabeth Gurley Flynn. With Andrews and Pelser refusing to identify Sacco prior to the trial, then fingering him in court, then retracting their testimony, now retracting their retractions, "We have them telling four stories each. . . . Now as I see it the Court can do nothing properly other than to say that they have completely discredited themselves. . . . They are not the caliber of human beings whose stories would warrant the taking of the life of a yellow dog to say nothing of two human beings." The ground had shifted, Moore realized. His own conduct was on trial now. And "by trying me, we may succeed in saving the two boys. At any rate we are not worrying over here. Sit tight!"

Sacco had begun his hunger strike on February 15. Four weeks later, he had eaten nothing. So weak he could barely struggle out of his cot, he lay shivering in his cell, wasting away. Hunger possessed him now, numbering his days, teasing him with the hope of martyrdom. For the first time since his arrest, "the sad reclus" was where he wanted to be—almost free. His teeth chattering, his body a crumpled mass of sheer will, Sacco summoned thirty-four months of pent-up rage. He would prove to them—the capitalists, the state, the police, the judge—prove they could not cage his spirit or kill his beloved "idea." To make "one last shout," he only had to suffer a little longer. He had predicted his death on the forty-fourth day, but doctors now said it might come sooner—within a week. Day by day, the agony consumed him, yet he preferred it to the alternative—waiting to be killed the way *they* wanted to kill him. So he pushed food away and turned his back to the pleas of friends and family.

When news of the hunger strike reached the press, Sacco and Vanzetti, forgotten in the revelry of their times, again made front-page news. WIFE CAN'T MAKE SACCO TAKE FOOD. SACCO ENDS 27TH DAY OF HUNGER STRIKE. SACCO DOOMED IN TWO DAYS. Boston papers charted Sacco's every move and detailed his every uneaten meal. Would the Commonwealth result to force-feeding, sticking a tube down Sacco's nose and pouring in a liquid gruel? Would Judge Thayer intervene? Could anyone convince Sacco to eat? Picking up on the sensation, the tabloid *Boston Daily Advertiser* offered "exclusive" updates beneath the byline "Rose M. Sacco." No one knows whether "Nicola's loyal little wife" actually wrote the first-person articles, but Rosina soon saw her photo on the *Advertiser*'s front page alongside black-and-whites of pretty flappers and accused murderesses. Rosina's story, if it was hers, gave readers an inside scoop on the man the tabloid called "convicted murderer, Nicola Sacco." "Today I saw Nick," Rose M. Sacco wrote on March 5. "Will I ever get over the chill that goes through me at the sight of those jail doors? Will he ever come out of those doors alive? I wonder."

As the deathwatch continued, rallies around Boston touted Sacco's strike as proof of his innocence. "Did anyone ever hear of a common thief or a murderer fasting twenty-four days in protest against injustice?" one speaker asked. The defense committee eulogized Sacco's "revolutionary spirit and courage," while another solicitation said simply, "Nicola Sacco is dying!" The news of Sacco's strike even reached Italy, where Mussolini wired the Italian ambassador in Washington, D.C., urging federal intervention. The hunger continued through a twenty-eighth day, then a twenty-ninth. Too weak to shave, sporting a full beard and ratty hair, Sacco continued to starve. Vanzetti could only follow his friend's fate in the papers. "Nicola's tragic determination has shaken the public conscience and fevered the unrest," he advised Luigia. "There is excitement in men's souls and electricity in the air."

On March 16, the hearing postponed by missing affidavits resumed, but hunger had changed everything. Beginning his thirtieth day without food, Sacco was too weak to travel two blocks to the courtroom. Instead, he lay in his cot while columns of protesters, deathly silent, marched around the courthouse in a cold rain. Inside, Vanzetti sat alone in the cage reading the morning paper. After a long conference in the judge's chambers, the hearing finally began. Aided by two new lawyers, William Thompson and Arthur D. Hill, Moore presented a grave picture of Sacco's starvation. "This man's life is at stake," Moore told the court. "It is only a question of days at best." A somber Judge Thayer listened as the case threatened to slip out of his control. The law limited the judge's options. Sacco could not legally be force-fed unless committed to a mental hospital, yet the defense was bitterly divided over such a move. Moore wanted Sacco sent to Boston Psychopathic Hospital, but the defense committee, with the full backing of Rosina, "flatly refused" any suggestion that Sacco was insane. After two hours of argument, the judge ordered three "alienists" to examine Sacco. Their findings were to be reported in court the following morning.

That evening, psychiatrists clattered through the jail until they reached Cell 14 on the third floor. There they listened as Sacco described months of suffering. He told of burning sensations throughout his body and an electrical tingling around his heart. He confessed his certainty that he was being watched, poisoned, persecuted. Asked about a new trial, he dismissed the possibility. His only feeling, a psychiatrist testified the following day, was that "he must be set free by the court or die where he was." Listening to the alienists, Judge Thayer was etched with his own weariness, the result of a recent gallstone operation. "I have been through a good deal myself," he told the court. Plainly uncomfortable presiding over insanity hearings, he called for more witnesses. Thayer wanted to know whether Sacco, if sent to Boston Psychopathic, might try to escape. Were the hospital windows barred? Yes. Could a guard be placed outside his door? Day and night. Would all doors be locked? If the judge insisted on it. The judge insisted. William Thompson thanked Thayer for making certain "this poor, half-starved man won't run away." Then Vanzetti weighed in.

As Judge Thayer spoke about following the letter of the law, Vanzetti did not seem to be paying attention. "The time ought never to come when we should depend upon the arbitrary rule of the individual," Thayer said. "When that time comes—"

"It has already come!" Vanzetti blurted out, his eyes flashing, his face red. Thayer continued without comment. The hearing lasted the entire day. Heeding the psychiatrists, the judge finally remanded Sacco to Boston Psychopathic for a two-week observation period. Three hours later, accompanied by a downcast Rosina, Sacco was seen staggering down the steps of the jail. Resembling a bearded hobo, he was helped into a wheelchair, then driven to Boston. As he was wheeled toward the hospital entrance, he finally agreed to end his fast.

"I know that if they wish they can force me," he said to Rosina, walking beside him. "I cannot help myself."

"Then show some sense, Nick!" Rosina cried.

Sacco paused. Rosina pleaded again, perhaps reminding him of what Dante had told him—that if his "Papa" could go on a hunger strike, so could he.

"I'll eat tomorrow," Sacco said.

"He will have to eat tonight," a doctor noted. Rosina kept begging her husband until he said, "All right, sure I'll eat." She kissed him and left him at the hospital door. Within an hour, weak gruel was being spooned into Sacco's gaping mouth. The following day, newspapers began listing his pulse, temperature, and daily weight gain. The hospital's spaghetti was "almost as good as Italian spaghetti," he said. The infamous convicted murderer impressed nurses as friendly, conversant, and remarkably interested in books and flowers. "Tell my comrades that I am still in the fight," he announced, "and that I will stay in the fight till the world knows I am innocent."

During Sacco's first days at Boston Psychopathic, doctors found him an ordinary hospital patient. But a guarded room was neither freedom nor death. Certain that the same bleak cell awaited him once he recovered, Sacco again took matters into his own hands. Early on the morning of March 21, he jumped out of bed, sprinted to a metal chair, and began smashing his head against it. Blood streamed down his face. As attendants wrestled with him, Sacco cried out, "I am innocent! There is no justice!" His forehead required seven stitches. The following day, he was calm again, telling doctors he was ashamed of his outburst, but to a visitor he confessed, "I did not smash my head hard enough. The next time I will dash my brains out."

On March 30, the observation period ended. Back in court, Judge Thayer perused the hospital report. Despite the suicide attempt, doctors found "no evidence of insanity." Moore, however, argued against a return to the jail. Sacco had promised suicide if sent back to his cell, and Moore feared the Norfolk County sheriff

"would furnish Sacco the weapon with which to kill himself."
Thayer agreed to keep the prisoner in the hospital. During this second observation period Sacco lost the last shreds of his sanity.
While Rosina's newspaper column assured readers, "My Nick is
not insane," Sacco veered between serenity and madness. Impress-
ing doctors with his clarity one day, he screamed or cried out
"Rosie!" the next. Shortly after Rosina ended one visit, Sacco bolted
for the door and rammed his head into it. He was put in "dry
pack"—sheets wrapping him like a mummy—while he ranted that
Rosina was still upstairs, that there were roses for him in the lobby,
that he wanted to go to his "Mamma." After two more weeks,
Judge Thayer opened a final hearing, without Vanzetti, on what to
do with Sacco.

The hearing threatened to become *Thayer v. Moore* all over
again. When doctors related Sacco's history of delusions pre-dating
the trial, Thayer lashed out at Moore. So Sacco had been mentally
unstable during his trial? Why hadn't Mr. Moore informed the
court? Moore blamed Rosina, saying she had not wanted her man
considered insane. Next, Sacco's guards testified that he had never
spoken of delusions, that he was a sane, model prisoner. This led
Thayer to suspect Sacco of "simulating" his symptoms. If Sacco was
so determined to starve himself to death, the judge asked, why did
he drink water? If he wanted to commit suicide, why did he take
such a slow method? His suspicions rising, Thayer asked a psychiatrist, "Haven't you known in this Commonwealth where not only
alienists have been deceived, but men have, even after they have
been convicted by a jury, have escaped from the state institutions?"
The psychiatrist did not know of such cases, so the judge cited them.
The new DA, Harold Williams, also suspected Sacco of "concoct-
ing" his delusions. Thayer asked one alienist after another whether
Sacco might be faking. None agreed. All said Sacco suffered from
"prison psychosis," paranoid symptoms eased by moving a patient
to a hospital but likely to recur upon a return to jail. As the hearing
stretched into a second day, Sacco's own words, repeated by friends
on the witness stand, hung over the courtroom: "The police did
this"; "It is a dirty mean trick they played me"; and "free or die."

Sacco's hunger and will had backed Judge Thayer into a corner. If the judge ruled Sacco insane, the defense might suggest he had been insane during the trial, offering clear grounds for a second proceeding. But if Sacco was ruled sane, then his ranting suggested his innocence. Would a sane man develop a persecution complex if he was, in fact, guilty? As the second day of hearings drew to a close, Thayer backed away from suggestions that Sacco was "simulating." The prisoner, the judge stated, "is a man who has been really upset by too much reading and talk about these great big ideas like Socialism." Being judged guilty in a capital case, Thayer added, "is liable to not only impair the brain, the mind, but in some cases it would be not surprising if it wrecked it." Soon the judge was talking about committing Sacco to the state mental hospital in Bridgewater, Chief Stewart's town. Moore objected. Bridgewater, known as the "State Farm," was for mentally unstable *criminals*, he argued. Sacco had not been sentenced. But Thayer ruled that having been found guilty, Sacco qualified as a criminal. A final gavel sent Sacco to Bridgewater. Moore signed the commitment papers, shredding any lingering trust Rosina and the defense committee had in him. On April 24, two days after his thirty-second birthday, Sacco suddenly found himself in another circle of hell, neither free nor dead, alone in a strange hospital where his paranoia was mirrored in leering faces all around him.

As their ongoing ordeal made Sacco and Vanzetti seem less like murderers and more like victims, their most loyal supporters gathered more tightly around them. Unlike Moore or the Italian anarchists, these allies had no political motives. They were instead driven by conscience and a tradition of social service begun even before Sacco and Vanzetti came to America.

For more than forty years, while industrial riches poured into the penthouses of Back Bay, a handful of wealthy women had chafed at society's corsets and questioned its inequalities. While their husbands controlled the purse strings of an expanding economy, these wives gave Proper Boston lessons in empathy. Though only a few dozen in number, they were always in the news. Dressed in floral hats and floor-length skirts, they taught immigrants at South End House, modeled after Chicago's Hull House. They marched for suffrage, temperance, or peace. To the outrage of many a husband, some wives even joined the Socialist Party, but most found politics a poor outlet for their compassion. Childless or having grown children, they saw the poor as family. These were the women who came to Lawrence, Massachusetts, during its 1912 strike, doling out aid from a dingy storefront. They were the women who bailed out men rounded up during the Palmer Raids. And now, upon reading of two Italian immigrants facing the electric chair, these were the women who all but adopted Sacco and Vanzetti. No children could have asked for more devoted mothers.

Sacco and Vanzetti had been young men when their mothers died. For each, the loss had been especially tragic, Vanzetti holding his groaning mother in his arms, Sacco feeling the sudden stab of a black-bordered letter bringing a distant son the worst possible news. So it is not surprising that when reduced to a childlike dependency, each still-grieving son welcomed surrogates. Sweeping into the prisoners' lives like angels on a mission, a half dozen women embraced Sacco, Vanzetti, and their families. Cerise Carmen Jack hosted Rosina and her children on her farm near Stoughton. The middle-aged wife of a Harvard professor, sporting squeaky, high-buttoned shoes, Mrs. Jack became Sacco's most frequent correspondent. At first he called her "my friend," then "my dear friend." Finally, after she had visited him monthly, reading with him, teaching him English, showering him with gifts—flowers, cookies, fruit, poetry—he called her "honey." "You are always surprise me with something or other," Sacco wrote to Mrs. Jack, "that for this kind and generous attitude that you used always to have for me, I am going to call you—honey! Well honey, [how] are you feeling?"

Vanzetti's new female friends fulfilled a variety of roles. Some kept his cell wall decorated with postcards—of beaches, farms, maples in the fall. Others he regarded as teachers, comrades, and in the case of one woman, a would-be lover. The rough-hewn Italian anarchist could never get over this sudden embrace by socialites.

"A player of golf and of tennis, friend of mine!" he wrote one woman. "It is as a reconciliation of the *diavolo* with the holy water! Indeed, I never thought such a thing possible—but it is." Vanzetti's most devoted correspondent was Alice Stone Blackwell, daughter of the pioneering suffragette Lucy Stone. Blackwell sent him valentines, Christmas cards, and long letters discussing politics and history. Vanzetti responded like an eager boy, writing "Comrade Blackwell" ten-page letters, immersing himself in thought until he "almost forgot to be in prison, very near to the electric chair." As if explaining himself to his own mother, he confessed his love of nature and anarchism, shared his poems, described his changing moods: "Ah, my passion for the truth! What a cross. Yet, I am glad of it, and I carry it with a strong heart. I adore freedom, it is my divinity, and the truth is its archangel of liberation." Amazed by his eloquence, Blackwell tried to get "The Nightingale" published, but no magazine would take Vanzetti's ode. She shared his letters with friends, but mostly she just wrote and visited again and again.

Other women found their own ways of helping. Margaret Shurtleff gave Dante swimming lessons and knitted sweaters for Ines. Katy Codman drove Rosina wherever she needed to go. Virginia MacMechan braved the bleak corridors of Charlestown Prison to teach Vanzetti English, praising his progress as he vowed to become "a nightingale of the English Language." MacMechan and a friend even traveled to Villafalletto and Torremaggiore to bring worried families a little cheer. "Treat them as sisters," Vanzetti wrote his own sister, advising her to show them the lush family garden and to ask before putting garlic in their food. To men whose only American acquaintances had been hard-edged bosses and factory foremen, these surrogate mothers were optimism itself. "How many good souls are working in our behalf and suffering for our pains and sorrows who we do not know," Vanzetti wrote to Blackwell. "Human nature is good. I would assert it even I burned a hundred times." All these women gave of themselves, yet none matched the devotion of "Auntie Bee."

Before meeting Sacco and Vanzetti, Elizabeth Glendower Evans had spent three decades at the upper echelons of Boston's social

services. By the 1920s, this grandmotherly woman was the conscience of Boston. As shrewd as she was sympathetic, Evans understood power and saw compassion as its antidote. She had come by
her bottomless empathy in the usual way—through sorrow. Raised
as "poor relations of a very aristocratic family," suffocated by puritanical religion and strict schooling, young Elizabeth Gardiner
considered herself homely and stupid. Hence she was enchanted
when a charming Harvard man, Glendower Evans, fell in love
with her. During long walks and canoe rides, "Glen" opened her
eyes with poetry, social concerns, and the ideas of his friend, the
philosopher William James. Amidst all the opulence of the Gilded
Age, the couple had married in 1882. Four years later, Glen died,
leaving his young widow with plenty of money and "all the time
there is." On a doctor's advice, she took up social causes, first as a
trustee to Massachusetts's reform schools, and then, after studying
Socialism in England, in the trenches of American activism.

As she aged, Evans became a familiar sight on picket lines and at
podiums. During the winter of 1912, the fifty-five-year-old woman
was a regular in Lawrence. She went just to observe, but soon began marching and bailing out arrested strikers, using dividends
from her stock in the American Woolen Company. The strikers'
stirring victory left her feeling "as if a new 'world' were opened, so
vital does one feel that pulse of the common human heart." After
the strike, Evans helped write Massachusetts's groundbreaking
minimum-wage law, and later accompanied Jane Addams to a
women's peace conference in The Hague. Other wealthy women
resented her incessant harping about the poor, but Evans preferred
to think of herself as "one of those old-fashioned Americans who
still believe in the fundaments of our institutions as laid down by
our fathers."

In the summer of 1920, reading of Vanzetti's Bridgewater trial,
Evans sensed an outrage in the making. The following May 31,
when the Dedham trial began, the white-haired woman, with her
frilly flowered hat, wire-rimmed spectacles, and perpetual frown,
was in the gallery. For six weeks she made the daily trip to Dedham, sometimes bringing Mrs. William James. Evans followed the

trial as if it were her own sons in the cage. She took elaborate notes and once viewed judge and jury through opera glasses until ordered to put them in her purse. In early July, she bailed out the bankrupt defense with a gift of nearly $3,000. From the jury selection to the verdict, the trial appalled her. "I could scarcely credit my senses," she recalled. "All along it had perplexed me why the judge saw fit to continue what seemed to me like a solemn farce."

The day after the verdict, Evans swung into action. She had already lifted Rosina from her misery, arranging her stay throughout the trial at the Dedham home of Supreme Court justice Louis Brandeis, an old friend of Glen's. Now she began working with the defense committee. Sitting in on meetings, the dour old matron argued with anarchists about strategy and fund-raising. She wrote articles for the *New Republic* and *LaFollette's,* while authoring her own pamphlet, *Outstanding Features of the Sacco-Vanzetti Case.* And she visited the men so often that she usurped all other surrogate mothers. Opponents of Sacco and Vanzetti found it easy to ridicule Evans and other "sob sisters." An undercover federal agent, watching Evans "flit" around a rally, concluded, "Her actions were childish and indications point to paresis and senile decay." But to condemned men desperate for compassion, she was little less than a saint.

"Since the day that I have meet you," Sacco wrote, "you been occupied in my heart my mother her place, and so I been respect you and I been loved you." Like the Brandeis children, Sacco began calling Evans "Auntie Bee," but sometimes he addressed her as "my dear mother." Vanzetti saw her as "a gentle motherly figure" who encouraged his poetry and his studies. Writing to his other surrogates, he explained anarchism or his hope for vindication. For Mrs. Evans, he saved his most eloquent letters.

December 1924   Charlestown Prison

Dear Mrs. Evans:
    For the water in liquid state, freedom is, to flow from a relative up to a relative down; or vice versa when the

water is in vapor state. For the fire, freedom is, to ex-
pand and to arise. In short, freedom is, for each and
all the things of the universe, to follows their natural
tendencies. . . .

Please permit me to prove you the trueness of this
true conception of freedom by applying it to Nick and
myself. Am I without a lover? Yes, but I would like to
have a lover. . . . Has Nick a wife? Yes, and a good one;
but not being free, he must either thinks that she is con-
soling herself with somebody else, or that she is suffering the unspeakable agony of a loving woman compelled
to mourn a living lover.

Have I no children? Well—I would like to have or to
generate some children. Have Nick some children—yes,
and what his heart experiences when he thinks of them—
is a thing known by him alone.

O the blessing green of the wilderness and of the
open land—O the blue vastness of the oceans—the fra-
grances of the flowers and the sweetness of the fruits—
The sky reflecting lakes—the singing torrents—the
telling brooks—O the valleys, the hills. . . . Yes, Yes, all
this is real actuallity but not to us, not to us chained—
and just and simply because we, being chained, have not
the freedom to use our natural faculty of locomotion to
carry us from our cells to the open horizon—under the
sun at daytime—under the visible stars at night.

Sharing such letters at their own Sacco-Vanzetti dinners, knowing nothing of the men's involvement with the *Galleanisti*, Evans
and her friends could not imagine such sweet souls guilty of murder. And as the case ground into its fourth year, these women
doubled their efforts. Most merely wrote more letters or sent more
cookies, but Evans visited Sacco five times a week at Bridgewater.
There she saw him living in a snake pit of wild-eyed criminals and
muttering schizophrenics.

To anyone else, the "State Farm" would have been a Goyaesque horror. Along with insane criminals, Bridgewater housed "paupers," "drug addicts," and "defective delinquents." The lockdown institution featured barred windows, walls of shiny, painted brick, and eight-by-eight cells whose solid doors had peepholes opening onto long, claustrophobic hallways. Of nearly nine hundred inmates listed as insane in 1923, just twenty-eight recovered and were released. Thirty-three died. Yet for Sacco, Bridgewater was a vast improvement over the jail where he considered his food poisoned and guards capable of pouring something in his ear as he slept. Assigned a bed on an open ward, he began chatting with doctors and nurses. Soon he was given what he knew he needed for stability—work. His first job was polishing floors. Later he tended a garden in the enormous open yard where inmates stood singing, preaching, shouting at no one. Freedom lay just beyond the hospital's huge Victorian headquarters, but contrary to Judge Thayer's concern, Sacco never tried to escape, nor did he have another outburst. Wandering the spacious grounds, enjoying frequent family visits, he gained twenty-six pounds and regained his sanity. Asked whether he might be insane, he answered, "My mind is clear. I am not crazy."

Learning of Sacco's recovery, Judge Thayer scheduled an October 1 hearing on the motions Moore had filed more than a year earlier. Much had happened during the five months Sacco spent at Bridgewater. Monthly contributions to the defense had sunk to less than $1,000, causing Moore to suspect the committee's mail was being intercepted. Scrambling for contributors, he asked a former law partner in Los Angeles for "the name and address of every progressive, liberal and radical Jew in the United States." Felicani raised funds through dances, plays, and selling Vanzetti's autobiography, A Proletarian Life. Touted by Upton Sinclair's syndicated column in the Hearst papers—Sinclair called Vanzetti "one of the world's gentlest spirits"—A Proletarian Life sold throughout North America, but the fifteen-cent price barely bolstered the defense. The funding crisis widened the schism between Moore and Felicani. In late August, Moore toyed with the idea of quitting but stayed on, meeting with doddering American Federation of Labor head Samuel Gompers and pleading with workers not to forget Sacco and Vanzetti. But he was suffering severe doubts about how he had conducted the case. Once he even broke down and cried that Angelina DeFalco "could have saved them."

That summer, as the defense struggled, *Galleanisti* in Springfield, Massachusetts, weighed a plan to break Sacco and Vanzetti out of jail. An anarchist who had pulled off robberies in three states offered to free the men, stealing them away the next time they were led toward the courthouse. His price: $5,000. The *Galleanisti* welcomed the proposal but could not come up with the money. On September 28, Sacco was returned to his cell in Dedham. Waiting for him was a basket of peaches and apples sent by Cerise Jack. After more than a year's delay, the hearing on Moore's motions was just a few days away. Added to the four was a new one thought to be the most convincing yet.

While Sacco was at Bridgewater, Moore had hired a new ballistics expert. One of America's foremost criminologists, Albert Hamilton had analyzed hundreds of bullets and gun barrels with his Bausch and Lomb compound microscope, far more powerful than any used during the Dedham trial. His expertise had swayed many murder cases, most often in favor of the prosecution. In August, Hamilton had come to Boston to examine Bullet III and Vanzetti's revolver. Quickly convinced that Sacco and Vanzetti had been framed, he prepared an affidavit exonerating them. But a more startling piece of Moore's fifth motion came from a cop's confession.

Captain William Proctor, a thirty-six-year veteran of the Massachusetts State Police, had helped test-fire Sacco's gun during the trial. Asked in court about Bullet III, Proctor had testified, "My opinion is that it is consistent with being fired by that pistol." Both Katzmann and Judge Thayer had taken the captain's testimony as an unequivocal "yes." In his charge to the jury, Thayer said *two* prosecution witnesses linked gun and bullet. Ever since, however, the words "consistent with" had haunted the white-haired police veteran. "I'm getting to be too old to want to see a couple of fellows go to the chair for something I don't think they did," he told Albert

Hamilton. Some have charged that Proctor resented Katzmann for firing him as his chief investigator and for not paying him $500 for his ballistics work, but whatever his motive, the captain was soon adding his own affidavit to the pile.

Proctor now swore that his test firing had turned up no evidence linking the fatal bullet to Sacco's gun. Throughout the trial, Proctor added, Katzmann had asked him "repeatedly" about such a link; the captain had repeatedly said he had found none. If asked point-blank in court, Proctor told Katzmann, he would deny any connection. As a result, Proctor swore, Harold Williams had "framed his question accordingly," asking only "have you an opinion" about the bullet. In answering that it was "consistent with," Proctor meant only that Bullet III had passed through *some* Colt automatic, not necessarily Sacco's. "Had I been asked the direct question," Proctor now swore, "whether I had found any affirmative evidence whatever that this so-called mortal bullet had passed through this particular Sacco's pistol, I should have answered then, as I do now without hesitation, in the negative."

Moore's fifth motion seemed solid, yet the day before going to court, he bolstered the Ripley motion with one final revelation. No one knows how Moore met William Daly, but his story was all a lawyer could ask for. A few days before the trial, Daly had spoken with Walter Ripley. The ex–police chief who would soon be jury foreman had told Daly he would "be leaving you for a couple of weeks" to serve on a jury. Daly asked whether the trial was the famous one of those two "guineas" charged with murder. When Ripley said it was, Daly told his old friend he did not think the men guilty. Why would a man, in broad daylight, rob a factory where he had worked and would be recognized? And Ripley had answered, "Damn them, they ought to hang them anyway!" With charges that the jury foreman was biased and the prosecution had suborned perjury, the hearing was called to order.

The first Monday in October was a crisp autumn day, much like the day of Moore's initial appeal for a new trial. But nearly two years had passed, two deadening years marked by madness, starvation, protests across two continents, and another seven hundred days behind bars. Now, as if stuck in some endless film loop, Sacco and Vanzetti were again marched into court. There was Judge Thayer sitting like an alabaster statue on the bench. There was Moore, arguing with the judge. There was Katzmann in all his pomp and pride. There were the McAnarneys, whose precise mannerisms always made Sacco and Vanzetti chuckle. But here was Ines in a pink dress being placed in Sacco's arms while Vanzetti beamed. And here on their behalf was the new lawyer, a Harvard man himself, recommended by "Auntie Bee" and hired by Moore to argue the latest motions.

In a broad Brahmin accent marking him as anything but an "outsider," William Thompson began. "It is supposed that these defendants hold radical opinions. Mr. Hill and I do not hold such opinions and we are not here in support of such opinions. . . . We are here because we think that the proper administration of the law is the only safeguard of human society. We think that nothing could be worse than that persons who talk about government by law are not willing to stand by the law—excepting when the law is in their favor." Listening to the tall, fair-haired lawyer in the impeccable gray suit, both defendants realized their case had finally moved beyond the bitterness of *Thayer v. Moore*. Thompson continued, arguing the Ripley motion. He quoted the late foreman: "Damn them, they ought to hang them anyway!" "That's why Mr. Hill and I are here," Thompson said. "It's because some of our friends have talked in the way Daly says Ripley talked." For two days, Thompson parried Katzmann's assertions, cited the Constitution, and argued that Ripley's comment alone merited a new trial. And when, after a three-week postponement allowing Katzmann and Williams to file affidavits swearing they had never coerced Captain Proctor, there was Thompson again on the attack. Turning to stare down Katzmann and Williams, Thompson shouted, "They knew—and don't deny it!—that Captain Proctor didn't believe that bullet went through that gun! And when they put him on the stand they gave him no opportunity to tell the truth and all the truth!"

Dragging on into November, the hearing turned to ballistics.

Huge photos of bullets and cartridges stood beside the witness stand. Microscopes sat on the bench. Moore's new ballistics expert, Albert Hamilton, told the court that Vanzetti's revolver did *not* have a new hammer because it had been Vanzetti's all along. Hamilton had Judge Thayer examine the screw holding the hammer in place, noting it was shiny and unmarked by repair. And Bullet III had *not* come from Sacco's gun, Hamilton insisted. Superimposing cross sections of the fatal bullet and a bullet he had test-fired himself, Hamilton rotated them like wheels, showing the court how the lands and grooves, the firing pin indentations, the flowback from the bullet's discharge simply did not match. Backing Hamilton's claim, a professor from the Massachusetts Institute of Technology added his own measurements proving "that the so-called mortal bullet never passed through the Sacco gun."

Fighting back, the prosecution called Captain Charles Van Amburgh and an engineer from the Winchester Repeating Arms Company. Each offered his own measurements, his own expertise proving the mortal bullet *had* been fired from the Sacco pistol. And the arguments, awash in technical terms and splitting hairs to ten-thousandths of an inch, raged for two days. Peering through Hamilton's microscope, Judge Thayer examined bullets, cartridges, the hammer of Vanzetti's pistol, and the firing pin of Sacco's gun. The judge's stone face revealed not the slightest favor to either side, yet when the hearings finally closed on November 8, Sacco and Vanzetti could almost imagine freedom.

"Mr. Thompson is a quick and penetrating intelligence, a tongue wonderful," Vanzetti wrote the Brinis. "With a few words he was able to destroy the elaborated sophistry, the mixing and twisting to make a truth seem a lie or a lie a truth. . . . At least I have had the moral satisfaction to see my framers unmasked, called liars— as they are." Sacco was equally inspired. "Just a few lines to say that behind these dark shadows the beautiful light it is begin to come upon me and will be light, more light, and always more bright," he wrote to Cerise Jack. "Believe me Mrs. Jack that these today Mr. Thompson was in court he did relief the soul of the sad reclus." Sacco's goal—to end his ordeal—had been thwarted. He found himself "alive in this terrible hole! Here, where there is no live and no vegitation: but I live!" Having been through the deeper hell of hunger and insanity, he allowed himself the luxury of a faint hope. "I will live for humanity and for the solidarity and for the fraternity and for gratitude to all the friends and comrades who have worked for Sacco and Vanzetti!" he wrote. In the light of the moment, neither Sacco nor Vanzetti suspected that their case was about to backslide into its own lunacy.

CHAPTER ELEVEN

"These So-Called Alleged Facts"

The inevitable conclusion to be drawn from an analysis of all the expert testimony [in the Sacco-Vanzetti case] is that what might have been almost indubitable evidence was in fact rendered more than useless by the bungling of the experts.

—1935 textbook *The Identification of Firearms from Ammunition Fired Therein*

On December 4, 1923, Albert Hamilton went to the courthouse in Dedham to take another look at Sacco's gun. While boxy black cars grumbled past the common, the short, bespectacled man strode beneath a plume of his own breath up the courthouse steps. Once inside, his unannounced arrival startled a clerk.

Ballistics had been the bedrock of the verdict. Witnesses had seen everything and nothing, yet as one juror recalled: "the bullets—there was no getting around that evidence." The bedrock, however, was shakier than jurors suspected. In the early 1920s, ballistics was far from an exact science. Within a few years, comparison microscopes would align grooves in bullets and gun barrels, "fingerprinting" a fatal slug. But the jury in Dedham had examined this crucial evidence with a low-power microscope and a magnifying glass. Once jurors had eyeballed Bullet III and Sacco's Colt, rival experts had recited long lists of measurements, "precise" statistics that varied up to twelve percent. Such ambiguities had allowed each expert to peer into his microscope and see precisely what he wanted to see. The trial's ballistics battle had since spilled into the appeals. Throughout 1923, prosecution and defense inundated Judge Thayer with data. Firing pin indentations, flowback, shell casings, ejector cuts—all were pinpointed in pages of bone-dry affidavits:

Land Mark No.	Inches	Groove Mark No.	Inches
1	.050	2	.1050
3	.045	4	.1050
5	.050	6	.1025
7	.0475	8	.1025

Filed with the affidavits, black-and-white enlargements of shells and bullets only deepened the dispute. Prosecution and defense experts disagreed on everything, right down to the width of Sacco's gun barrel.

By the winter of 1923, the defense seemed to be winning the battle. When Captain William Proctor swore he had never believed Bullet III had come from Sacco's gun, the prosecution's other expert, Captain Van Amburgh, was left hanging out in the breeze. The defense, meanwhile, still had its two trial experts plus an MIT professor and Albert Hamilton, whom *Scientific American* called "the foremost micro-chemical examiner and criminologist in the country." Having made one test firing, Hamilton hoped to do another, but when he came to Dedham that icy December morning, the battle bogged down in a quagmire of scandal.

When Hamilton asked for the "Sacco pistol," the surprised court clerk disappeared into an adjoining room. Moments later, he returned with the gun—in pieces. Hamilton was not surprised to see this critical evidence broken down into hunks of cold metal. He knew a .32 Colt was easily disassembled without tools. During the last hearing on November 8, he had taken apart Sacco's Colt and his own revolvers, then reassembled all three guns to the satisfaction of everyone watching. Judge Thayer had then ordered the guns impounded. But when Hamilton now inserted a plug gauge into Sacco's barrel, he noticed something strange. The plug gauge slipped right in. The barrel was *wider* than the last time he measured it, and its gunmetal gray, once clogged with rust and grime, was spotless and shiny. Hamilton did not immediately suspect foul play. He knew a barrel could be slightly enlarged if cleaned with hydrochloric acid and might be polished by repeated insertion of a plug gauge. After making more measurements, he returned the gun and stepped out into the cold. Two days later, he filed another affidavit replete with additional measurements and an observation: "Since November 8 the interior of the Sacco pistol has been quite thoroughly cleaned." The barrel's diameter, he added, had increased from .2920 to .3045 inch. Despite the changes, Hamilton asked permission to test-fire a hundred shots. Then winter tightened its lock on the Commonwealth and no one touched Sacco's gun—at least no one leaving fingerprints.

Early in February 1924, Captain Van Amburgh entered a Boston courtroom to find an ongoing discussion about Sacco's Colt. When Judge Thayer handed Van Amburgh the gun, the captain immediately noticed "something queer" about the barrel. The following day, he made his own measurements. Fred Moore was soon informed of what he would term "these so-called alleged facts," and on February 15, Judge Thayer called a hearing to learn who had switched the barrel on Sacco's gun.

The barrel switch suggested how the stakes had risen. The case was no longer about two murders; it was about prevailing. Someone was willing to jeopardize the case in order to win it. Someone had risked imprisonment to free Sacco and Vanzetti or else send them to the electric chair. But who? Opening the hearing, Judge Thayer lectured lawyers and ballistics experts, asking "whether there has been any tampering here, any evil intent by way of substitution. If anybody will give me any evidence tending to prove it, I want it!" Three weeks of private hearings began with a washing of hands. DA Harold Williams swore he had not seen Sacco's gun since November. William Thompson, assuming a larger role in the defense, said no one on his side could have switched the barrels "unless they wanted to run their necks into a noose." Hamilton swore he had only taken the gun apart under the watchful eyes of the judge. And the judge, studying the guns on his bench, insisted, "I never had those in my possession."

This much was certain: Sacco's pistol had been taken apart as often as a toy gun. Three times during 1923, the prosecution had taken the Colt to Bridgeport, Connecticut—where Captain Van Amburgh worked for the Remington Arms Company. Each time, measured and photographed, the gun had been broken down into some three dozen parts. It was also taken apart during the November 8 hearing. Four days later, Harold Williams had broken it down in the judge's chambers. When not under examination, Sacco's gun had been locked in a courthouse cupboard. Hamilton's own revolvers, from which Sacco's shiny new barrel seemed to have come, had been kept nearby in two red shoeboxes tied with string. All the rest was as chaotic as the arguments before the fuming judge.

How could the barrels have been switched? What could anyone hope to gain from a cheap trick sure to be detected, as Thayer said, "in a minute"? Switching barrels in front of the judge would have been "a bit risky," Thayer and Thompson agreed. Had someone broken into the courthouse in the dead of night? Had a duplicate key been made? Or had it been the innocent mistake of a befuddled clerk? Arguing, posturing, shuffling papers and theories, the lawyers could not even agree which barrel was which. Was the shiny barrel in Sacco's gun really new or had the original barrel been cleaned? Had the rusty barrel on one of Hamilton's pistols come from Sacco's Colt or from some other gun? With guns and barrels littering his bench, the judge struggled for order.

"That one there belongs in here, doesn't it?" Thayer asked of two barrels. "You look at it and tell me if I have got them right."

"It is the one that is in here," Hamilton said. "It isn't the one that belongs with that."

"No, no."

"That is the one that is in there," Hamilton continued.

After lunch, however, Thayer still labored to keep the evidence straight. "Where is the blame thing now?" he asked of the barrel.

"You have it in your right hand," Harold Williams said.

"That is the plug gauge."

Amidst spreading confusion, motives emerged. If detected, a switch would have given the defense grounds for a new trial. And if undetected, Hamilton could have fired his hundred shots and come back with bullets bearing no resemblance to Bullet III. William Thompson protested the implications, asking why "people whose lives may depend on whether or not a certain pistol will strike the firing pin in the middle or won't . . . [would] deliberately set to work to ruin their own chances?" The prosecution, too, had dual motives. Switching barrels, then "discovering" the tampering, would derail further tests on Sacco's gun. Even if the correct barrel were replaced, Captain Van Amburgh assured Judge Thayer, another firing would prove nothing. And if the switch could be blamed on the highly touted Albert Hamilton, all his meticulous measurements proving Sacco's innocence would be worthless.

As the hearings entered their second week, the press got word of this "bombshell." Reporters in thick coats and fedoras gathered outside the judge's chambers, but the judge, refusing to "try the case in the newspapers," kept the hearings private. While a snowstorm blanketed Boston, reporters begged for leaks but had to settle for accusations. Moore charged the defense with trying to scuttle his test firing. Williams suggested Hamilton had made the switch at the November 8 hearing. After a few days of dead ends, reporters and their editors turned to a meatier scandal unfolding in Washington, D.C. The secretary of the interior had been caught selling access to federal oil reserves in Teapot Dome, Wyoming. Raging on into summer, the Teapot Dome scandal denied readers any further mention of Sacco, Vanzetti, and this high-stakes twist to their case. The hearings went on in secret, with the judge, lawyers, and experts peering through microscopes and studying gun barrels in the light from the window. Each day the doubts grew.

Barred from the hearings, Sacco and Vanzetti remained in their cells. As their fifth year in prison approached, the men's contrasting characters, like the gun barrels, switched. Once the even-tempered monk, Vanzetti now began to rage at his fate. The tedium of prison life finally stamped upon him a funereal truth—that no stack of books, no eloquent letters, no amount of courage would ever free him. The previous summer, Vanzetti had witnessed a preview of his own execution. On July 14, 1923, a convict named Paul Pappas was to be electrocuted at midnight. The electric chair sat in a prison annex called the Death House, but the hulking generator pumping out its lethal current was just twenty feet from Vanzetti's cell. From 9:00 p.m. on, the generator hummed and crackled, sending live current through Vanzetti's nerves. He had vowed never to tremble, but now he was gripped with terror, wide-eyed, and tempted to smash his cell door. His dreams of revolt were never more fevered, yet he could do nothing. Finally, midnight arrived. "I saw the darkness enlight by a spark," Vanzetti wrote to Mrs. Evans, "a lightning followed by a dumb thunder. Few seconds after another lightning and another thunder, but not so strong as the first. And Pappas was dead. And he die bravely. Now everybody are satisfy; the Commonwealth is save." Though shaken and haunted, Vanzetti preferred electrocution to life in prison. "Two lightnings are much better than life in chains," he wrote. "We here know it. Many will kill others and theyselves before to come back here for a long sentence."

Despite mounting despair, Vanzetti thrived as much as anyone can in prison. Death, looming like footsteps on the floor above him, heightened his desire to read everything, to know everything, to write all he could in the time remaining. One day Moore visited the prison, finding Vanzetti emerging from the tailor shop "simply reeking with sweat." It was not a warm day, but Vanzetti had been driving himself to press his daily quota of pants so he could have more time for his studies and a novel he was writing about his long labors. Where once he had seen two "I's" in himself, now he became a prism of personalities, his letters presenting a different "Bartolo" to each correspondent. To his sister he called for courage and predicted vindication. Writing Sacco, he was defiant. They would win their freedom "in spite of our cold blooded murderers enemies, and of every crook, prostitute and perjurer of the world." But to his surrogate mothers, Vanzetti was not so sanguine. Their optimism worried him. Lest they be crushed by the inevitable, he assured them he expected nothing from Judge Thayer "other than some ten thousand volts divided in few times; some meters of cheap board and a 4x7x8 feet hole in the ground."

Word of the gun barrel switch further embittered Vanzetti. He called Judge Thayer's investigation "a joke." "Since the last hearing, the defense has not seen the revolver and the prosecution had asked for it many times," he wrote Luigia. "So who could have changed the barrel if not the prosecution?" Convinced the Commonwealth would stop at nothing in order to kill him, he dreamt only of revolution and revenge. Revolution would come "by thousands of strikes, gradually, one more powerful than the other, and through the centuries." Revenge he saw as more immediate. "I will ask for revenge. . . . I mean 'eye for an eye, ear for an ear,' and even more since to win it is necessary that 100 enemies fall to each of us."

The lone light in Vanzetti's life was his English teacher. The previous fall, he had written Virginia MacMechan, hinting at his growing affection. Now, after a dozen more visits and scores of endless nights in his cell, the "wild bear" found himself thinking of this married, middle-aged woman as the lover he never had. When MacMechan left for Europe, Vanzetti was heartbroken. The day after her departure, he barely concealed his feelings:

> There were so many things that I would have said and told to you—and I was unable; unable. What would I say if I thank you with all my heart for your goodness to me? Nothing. I have never saw you so beautiful as the last time: pale, tired, throbbing and yet so brave. I have been so near to you. . . . O, the great communion of our soul, Virginia, beloved one—I have touch your wrap in an unconsciouse impulse to grasp your hands.

Sacco, by contrast, became a boyish innocent and budding scholar. Having stared into the face of madness, he emerged docile: "The cookies Mrs. Jack they are so wonderful that I eta the two especial ones that had a little butter between, and really they were so nice and warm that they were almost delicious." He was reading biographies of Debs and Gandhi, Tennyson's poetry, and Bertrand Russell's *Why Men Fight*. Reveling in the attention of his surrogate mothers, he promised to improve his English until he "could be really a Shakespeare, ha ha." His cell was filled with gifts—flowers, cookies, an overcoat from Mrs. Evans, honey from his "honey," Mrs. Jack. By day, Sacco seemed resigned to his fate, but each evening when the lights went out, memories engulfed him like the darkness. Then he began pacing—one, two, three, four steps, until "these sad bars" turned him back. Often he harkened back to Italy, remembering his father's vineyards, his mother, and the songs he had sung while bringing her baskets of fruit. One night he dreamt he was in a Pennsylvania miners' strike where militiamen were driving mothers and children from their homes. Amidst the chaos, he saw himself pleading with the militia: "Brothers . . . remember that everyone of us we have mother and child, and you know that we fight for freedom which is your freedom." But as he finished speaking, a soldier shot him through the heart. Waking with a hand clasped over his chest, Sacco turned and looked out his barred window, seeing "the stars it bright my face and the shadow soon disapear."

During a second week of gun barrel hearings, everyone with access to Sacco's gun was summoned to Judge Thayer's chambers. Night watchmen and a courthouse janitor had seen no suspicious activity. Sheriff's deputies swore no one had touched the gun. Two women Thayer called "matrons of the courthouse" said the same. Such testimony steered suspicion toward the men who had the most to gain—the experts whose success in this front-page case might make or break their careers. For three days Captain Van Amburgh and Albert Hamilton were examined and cross-examined. Each studied gun barrels through a microscope, showing Judge Thayer revealing marks, but the judge seemed more interested in the men's backgrounds.

Albert Hamilton had a distinguished career in ballistics, at least according to Albert Hamilton. A pompous man in his early sixties, prone to referring to himself in the third person, Hamilton had graduated from the New York College of Pharmacy, which had since affiliated with Columbia University. During thirty-seven years as a criminologist, he had testified in 164 trials from Maine to Arizona. Enhanced by write-ups in *Scientific American* and in newspapers—Hearst's *Boston American* called him "America's Sherlock Holmes"—Hamilton's was an impressive résumé. At the hearings, Judge Thayer acknowledged such expertise, bidding Hamilton to "make any kind of an examination you see fit—forward, backward, or any way." The prosecution, however, was suspicious.

Upon learning Moore had hired "America's Sherlock Holmes," Harold Williams sent an investigator to Auburn, New York, Hamilton's hometown. The investigator found Hamilton more self-promoter than criminologist. Hamilton's courtroom experience resulted in part from a self-published pamphlet entitled *That Man from Auburn*. The pamphlet touted Hamilton as an expert in nearly two dozen forensic fields, including fingerprints, toxicology, nitroglycerin, blood and other stains, and "embalming and fluids." Before becoming an expert for hire, Hamilton had run a drugstore peddling "Hamilton's Kidney Cure" and "Hamilton's Cream Hair Balsam." But more damaging to the expert's reputation were several acquaintances—a former DA, a chemistry professor, a physician, another criminologist—who accused him of inept testimony in various murder trials. In 1915, Hamilton's linking of fatal bullets to a defendant's gun resulted in a death sentence. The condemned man was later proven innocent and Hamilton's testimony judged "worthless." Among lawyers in his county, one attorney swore, Hamilton was regarded as "a professional expert . . . [whose] testimony should not be accepted in any court of record." Hearing that his old enemies had filed affidavits, Hamilton filed explanations of how each accuser, outsmarted in a court case, had become "very bitter ever since against Hamilton." It all added up to more charges and countercharges piled on Judge Thayer's desk.

Early in the hearings, Hamilton called the gun barrel switch "an innocent mistake," blaming the court clerk who had hastily brought him Sacco's Colt. He soon changed his mind. Citing his enemies' affidavits, he saw the switch as another "attempt to thoroughly discredit Hamilton." Judge Thayer reserved his opinion, but clouds over Hamilton's reputation suggested him as capable of making the switch.

Charles Van Amburgh, whom colleagues called "Van," presented a simpler picture. The captain, a gaunt, bespectacled man with thin lips and prominent nose, had learned ballistics on the job. A graduate of Springfield (Massachusetts) Technical High School, he spent nine years testing weapons at the Springfield Armory. During the war, he was commissioned an army captain to teach marksmanship. At forty-one, the captain was a latecomer to the courtroom. Apparently he had not enjoyed testifying in Dedham. Asked during the gun barrel hearings how often he had appeared in a capital case, Van Amburgh replied, "The Sacco case was my first, praise the Lord." Now here he was again on a witness stand with his credibility and perhaps his career on the line. The defense offered no affidavits questioning Van Amburgh's expertise. Moore would take care of that, with help from Hamilton.

The previous fall, Hamilton and Van Amburgh had fired at each other in affidavits. Now the two experts faced off before the judge, disparaging each other's techniques, measurements, and conclusions. The duel also went on behind the scenes. Watching Van Amburgh in the witness stand, Hamilton began handing notes to Moore: "He wants court to understand sulphur makes oxides," Hamilton scribbled. "*Sulphur makes sulfides.*" Van Amburgh had never studied microscopy, Hamilton noted. The man did not even have the proper device—a stage micrometer—to make measurements in court. Hamilton suggested that Moore have Van Amburgh set up his microscope and measure a bullet. Look closely, he told Moore. Van Amburgh would read his measurements from the Colt manual right there in his lap. "You'll find he will do the same as yesterday,"

Hamilton scribbled. "He will look in his book before he is through."
Moore decided to put Van Amburgh to this test.

"I make it five plus," Van Amburgh answered, looking up from
his microscope. "In other words fifty-odd thousands, approximat-
ing sixty."

"Fifty plus or sixty?" Moore asked.

"Well, I should call it sixty, taking the maximum measure-
ment."

"You made it as fine and as accurate as it is possible for you to
make with all of the equipment that you named as using at the
time of the trial?" Moore asked. When Van Amburgh said "yes,"
Moore closed in. "Now Captain," he said. "Isn't it a fact that the
measurements that you pretended to give upon the trial of this case
were simply the standardized measurements, factory standards
that you took from the Colt automatic pistol people out of the
book you have been using right here during these proceedings?
Haven't you the book right in your possession out of which you
took those measurements?"

"No, I haven't any such measurements," Van Amburgh answered.

"With the Remington U.M.C. label on the cover of the book?"

"I haven't any such measurements in there."

Moore pressed on, asking what the captain had meant earlier in
saying "you caught me off my guard" and whether he could accu-
rately measure anything without a stage micrometer. Under attack,
the captain called a stage micrometer "a minor detail," then fell
back on statistics, citing streams of measurements until court adjourned for lunch. But when Van Amburgh returned to the stand,
Moore returned to the offensive, this time with a possible motive.
Hadn't the captain applied for a job as a state ballistics expert?
Yes, he had. Wouldn't his testimony in the Sacco-Vanzetti case—
his first trial—bear heavily on whether he got the job? And had he
gotten the job? Judge Thayer excluded this final question, but moments later Van Amburgh left the stand, his reputation seeming as
tarnished as Hamilton's.

A final few days only deepened the mystery. Hamilton announced

that the new barrel on Sacco's Colt had been treated with a chemi-
cal to make it look older, then said he had found a human hair on
the barrel. The hearings finally ended, but not before a court clerk
affirmed that the three pistols had only been together at the November 8 hearing where Hamilton—in plain view of Thayer,
Thompson, and the clerk himself—had correctly reassembled them.
Moore demanded time to call another witness, but the judge, finding it all "very, very disturbing," brought down his gavel.

Two weeks later, Judge Thayer released his findings. He ordered
the barrels restored to their original guns. Casting no aspersions
on Captain Van Amburgh, the judge wondered why Hamilton had
asked for new tests even after noting changes in Sacco's barrel. If
Hamilton knew the barrel had been switched "and did not com-
municate the fact to the Court or to counsel, that would be important evidence upon guilty consciousness," Thayer wrote. Yet his
finding was offered "without prejudice to either side." Moore appealed, arguing for the right to test-fire Sacco's Colt.

"We have got to fire it," he had told Thayer, "and your honor
has got to ultimately make an order for it."

"Don't tell me what I must do," Thayer had snapped. The hearings were closed; the judge had ruled. And Albert Hamilton would
conduct no more tests on Sacco's gun.

Hamilton soon disappeared from the case, leaving a bill for
$2,813.85. He continued to testify in murder trials, with occasional
blunders. Captain Van Amburgh, however, took a different road.
Shortly after the hearings, he got the job Moore had mentioned,
heading the Commonwealth's new ballistics lab. That summer, he
too made a courtroom error, linking a fatal bullet to his own test
bullet in a Connecticut trial. Van Amburgh was proven wrong and
a man convicted of murder was released. Van Amburgh continued
to work for the Commonwealth. The mystery remained. Who had
switched the barrels? More clues did not emerge until years later.

In 1935, when the case was just a bitter memory, the pulp mag-
azine *True Detective Mysteries* published "The Hidden Drama of
Sacco and Vanzetti." Alongside such lurid articles as "Behind the
Scenes of Michigan's Baffling Love Murder," the six-part serial

unfolded in purple prose. ("This is a tremendous thing!" Harold Williams tells Van Amburgh when the barrel switch is detected. "We must not be hasty. Captain, we must be *sure*.") The "hidden drama" emphasized the craftiness of Chief Stewart and the ballistics work of Van Amburgh. One installment closed by asking, "What staggering discovery was to be made by Captain Van Amburgh at the crux of this mystery of mysteries?" According to the author, the "staggering discovery" had come in 1932 when Van Amburgh asked Judge Thayer, "Just what did take place that day the pistol barrels were switched?" Looking back, the judge recalled the November 8 hearing. He remembered Hamilton reassembling three guns, then slipping them in his pocket and heading out of the courtroom. "Just a minute, gentlemen!" Thayer recalled shouting. "Come here, Mr. Hamilton. Hand me your pistols!" Thayer then impounded the guns. Several historians have recounted this discovery, ignoring the most staggering thing about it—that it never happened. Judge Thayer had impounded the guns, but neither three weeks of hearings nor his own findings mentioned any attempt by Hamilton to walk off with them. Back in 1924, Thayer agreed the barrel switch had not been made on November 8. The name of the pulp author spinning this scenario added a curious footnote to the mystery—it was Charles Van Amburgh.

The captain retired in 1943, yet he did not leave the crucial evidence from his career-making case to the whims of future experts. Claiming Judge Thayer had entrusted him with all Sacco-Vanzetti ballistics evidence, he took the guns, bullets, and shells to his home. Consciousness of guilt? Or a call to duty? After Van Amburgh died, his son kept the evidence in a sealed package "so that no future tampering with the exhibit may be possible." Only in 1960, following a *Boston Globe* exposé, were the exhibits returned to the custody of the Commonwealth.

Throughout the spring and summer of 1924, the confusion surrounding the gun barrels was mirrored in efforts to save Sacco and Vanzetti. In early May, Felicani walked in on a meeting a few blocks from his North End office. There he saw Moore, a grim-faced Mrs. Evans, and other longtime supporters seated around a table. "What is this?" Felicani asked. "Explain this to me. The Sacco-Vanzetti Defense Committee is still alive, still fighting, still interested in the case. What is this?" "This," Felicani learned, was the Sacco-Vanzetti New Trial League. Felicani assumed the schism was about money, but it ran deeper. Moore had given up working with the defense committee. The anarchists refused to listen to him, and Felicani "has tried my patience to the utmost in a thousand petty details." By then, the committee was taking in only $100 a week. "They are not merely financially bankrupt but likewise intellectually and spiritually," Moore observed. With bills piling up and no new leads, Moore hoped this new committee might shock his case back to life.

The Sacco-Vanzetti New Trial League would not outlast Moore's few remaining months in Boston. His withdrawal began that summer. On July 7, when Felicani refused to pay new bills, Moore tendered his resignation, offering to stay on until another lawyer could be hired. All summer, delay after delay spread the confusion. Since the first of the year, Judge Thayer's decision on the five motions had been expected any moment, but in June, Thayer had an appendectomy. Suddenly no one knew when his ruling might come. July passed, sluggish and sweltering. Vanzetti lamented receiving few letters from his beloved Virginia in Europe. When August's humidity baked the prisoners in their cells, Sacco's docility melted. Finally, he lashed out at Moore. "I am telling you that you are goin to stop this dirty game!" Sacco wrote. "You hear me? I mean every them words I said here, because I do not want have anything to do any more with 'New Trail League Committee,' because it does repugnant my coscience." Calling Moore "the obstacle of the case," Sacco accused him of playing his dirty game solely for "such sweet pay that has come to you right long." He wanted his case finished. What was Moore waiting for now? "Do you wait till I hang myself? That's what you wish? Let me tell you right now don't be illuse yourself because I would not be surprise if somebody will find you some morning hang on lamp-post." The letter was signed, "Your implacable enemy, now and forever, Nick Sacco."

By fall, no one seemed to know who was in charge. "I think that Moore has left the Defense," Vanzetti wrote, "but I am not sure of it." Overtures were made to Clarence Darrow, but since the Red Scare, America's most famous lawyer had stopped defending radicals, finding it "hopeless to get acquittals. I'm just taking cases of murderers and other respectable criminals," Darrow said. "I can sometimes get them off." With certainty dissolving into enigma, with another year evaporated, it fell to Judge Thayer to act decisively.

On October 1, 1924, the judge ruled on all five motions.

Motion one—Ripley: Thayer saw the issue as involving more than the cartridges carried by the jury foreman during the trial. The motion threatened "to invade the private sanctity of the jury room." Citing precedents, Thayer ruled that Ripley's "hearsay" comment did not override the affidavits of eleven jurors, each swearing the cartridges had hardly been seen and never discussed. "I am not willing to blacken the memory of Mr. Ripley and to pronounce those eleven surviving jurors as falsifiers under oath by claim of counsel that are so weak, so fragile, and so unsatisfactory," Thayer ruled. As to Ripley's comment—"Damn them, they ought to hang them anyway!"—Thayer said . . . nothing. The motion was denied.

Motion two—Gould/Pelser: To Judge Thayer, razor paste salesman Roy Gould was only "one more eye witness to the passing of the bandit automobile." Noting how testimony had been at odds, the judge claimed the verdict had not rested on eyewitnesses but on "consciousness of guilt." Thayer went on to argue the Commonwealth's entire case. He recounted the finding of the abandoned car, the shotgun shells, Sacco's cap, and Vanzetti's gun. The defendants' lies were crucial, for lies were "searchlights in a great many cases that assist in identifying the perpetrator of crime." Stronger still were their attempts to draw guns on the arresting officers.

Thayer dismissed the defendants' denials of the threats by noting, "the jury had a right to believe the officers." Then as if speaking to the nameless throngs who had created an international cause célèbre, Thayer asked, "Is it not somewhat remarkable that there are those who are so gifted as mind readers and heart interpreters that they can tell exactly what the verdict of a jury should be, when they never even saw the defendants themselves, nor heard a word of the evidence, nor saw a single witness upon the stand?" Driven by his arguments on the Commonwealth's behalf and finding Louis Pelser's confession of perjury "not at all satisfactory," Thayer handed down his second ruling. The motion was denied.

Motion three—Goodridge: As Thayer saw it, Carlos Goodridge had been "successfully impeached" during the trial. Tawdry attempts to reveal his shady reputation therefore meant less than Moore's conduct, "a cruel and unjustifiable attempt to scare Goodridge into swearing to something that was false against the District Attorney's office." Moore had hoped he would be tried in order to free "the boys." Thayer obliged. "I have tried to look at this conduct of Mr. Moore with a view of finding some justification or excuse of it," the judge wrote. "I can find none. I attribute it, however, to an over-enthusiastic interest in his client's cause, based upon the fact that belief in the innocence of one's client justifies any means to any desired end." Motion denied.

Motion four—Andrews: "It is a very unpleasant duty for me to pass judgment upon this motion," Thayer began. "This is so because charges of unprofessional conduct are made against counsel on both sides. A correct decision, however, of this motion is exceedingly easy." Thayer believed precisely what Lola Andrews had told Katzmann. He found nothing credible in her earlier claim that she had been coerced into identifying Sacco. "The master mind that procured this affidavit was Mr. Moore," Thayer wrote. "My relationship with him has been very pleasant, although at times it would seem, as was very natural, that he was quite unfamiliar with our trial evidence and practice in this state." His judicial restraint exhausted, Thayer accused Moore of "coercion, intimidation, fraud, and duress." The use of Andrews's son he found appalling.

"Could anything worse be done than the filling up of a nineteen-year-old boy by counsel for defendant with attacks upon the history of his mother's past life?" Conjuring the image of a lone, weeping woman surrounded by Moore's men in the Hotel Essex— "an unusual place for signing legal papers"—Thayer denounced such a "deep-laid scheme." Motion denied.

Motion five—Hamilton/Proctor: Caught in the crossfire of ballistics experts, Thayer relied more on character than measurements. He acknowledged Albert Hamilton's "skill and qualifications" but questioned his "over enthusiastic willingness to adapt himself to almost any condition that may arise within his line of professional inquiry." As an example, Thayer challenged Hamilton's claim that someone had marked the Ripley cartridges in the jury room. How could anyone tell when ink marks had been made? But did Vanzetti's gun have a new hammer? Was its screw head, as Hamilton said, free from marks showing repair? Thayer countered that a new screw might have been installed or the old screw tightened with care. Thayer cited other minutiae but relied more heavily on his respect for duty. To the patriotic judge, Hamilton's nationwide reputation paled in comparison to the military service of Captain Van Amburgh. If Hamilton was right, then Van Amburgh and the prosecution's other expert—also a veteran—were perjurers. "In cases of such tremendous importance can we attribute perjury or malice to these two men both of whom were selected by the United States Ordnance Department at Washington during the late war?" Judge Thayer asked. "I cannot force myself to come to that conclusion."

On William Proctor's retraction, the judge cited the captain's ample opportunity to offer his opinion in court. Why had he said Bullet III was "consistent with" being fired by "*that* pistol" if he only meant it was "consistent with" being fired from some random .32 Colt? Had Proctor been under some mental strain? And why hadn't the defense pressed him on this point? The judge regretted that the police veteran had accused Katzmann and Williams of "framing" questions. Only on evidence "clear, satisfactory, and convincing" should a public servant's reputation be tarnished.

And having watched Katzmann and Williams at work, Thayer had seen only "the highest standard of professional conduct." The motion was denied.

Five denials had ended a yearlong muddle. When word reached Charlestown, Vanzetti reflected his fleeting hopes through his many facets. To his sister, he saw "no reason to be discouraged." He predicted taking his case all the way to the U.S. Supreme Court. But writing to his American mothers, Vanzetti simmered, boiled, burned. During his laboring life, he had cut down trees. Now he relished the thought of using an axe "on the necks of those who seem to have the evil in their head." To the "hanger judge," Vanzetti had only one message: "Long live anarchy!" Sacco's response was more childlike. "We are always keep in our soul the hope and faithful in our innocent," he wrote Vanzetti, "and I am sure that we will keep this hope and faithful till the bright day of our triumph."

As Thayer's denials burrowed into the convicted, the judge blurted out words that would forever haunt all claims of his fairness. Shortly after his decision, "Web" Thayer ran into a professor, a former Massachusetts lawyer, at a Dartmouth football game. Instantly bringing up Sacco and Vanzetti, Thayer snapped, "Did you see what I did with those anarchistic bastards the other day? I guess that will hold them for a while! Let them go to the Supreme Court now and see what they can get out of them!" The outburst remained a secret until 1927 when the phrase "anarchistic bastards" would echo around the world.

Thayer's denials marked the end of Moore's efforts. As a farewell act, Moore sent his bill of exceptions—2,200 pages—to the Massachusetts Supreme Judicial Court. With the arduous task finished, with Sacco calling him a *carogna* (swine), and the case more hopeless than ever, Moore submitted his resignation to the court on November 8. He would hang around Boston for another two months, firing off angry letters dunning the defense committee for back pay. He would get only $500 before driving a beat-up car home to California. "At least I kept them alive," he said. After destroying his declining career, losing during the struggle another wife, his father, his dream of ending the "frame-up system," and the last shreds of his reputation, Moore never tried another major case. "He was not a bad man," Vanzetti concluded, "but he lacked character and moral courage." Back in Los Angeles, Moore lived with his widowed mother and worked as an ad salesman, but he had not given his final word on Sacco and Vanzetti.

Desperate to find someone to carry on, Felicani and Elizabeth Gurley Flynn begged William Thompson to take over. Thompson hesitated. A defense of Italian anarchists was not a task readily shouldered by a man whose New England ancestry dated to the 1600s.

William Goodrich Thompson was the opposite of Fred Moore in every respect. Where Moore was radical, Thompson was a buttoned-down conservative. Where Moore saw law as a street fight, Thompson considered it one of mankind's highest endeavors. Moore had politicized the trial. Thompson would moderate it, opposing public protests, reaching out not to unions and radicals but to lawyers, bankers, and businessmen. And while the abrasive Moore had aroused animosity on both sides, the gentlemanly Thompson would earn nothing but respect. A Phi Beta Kappa graduate of Harvard Law School who still lectured there, Thompson was one of Boston's most esteemed attorneys. He had never taken a criminal case. At sixty, he was tall and broad-shouldered, with thinning gray hair, arched eyebrows, and large glasses that made him look owlish. Thompson commanded courtrooms with his wit, self-assurance, and the eloquence Vanzetti called "a tongue wonderful." Such a man might easily have ignored pleas to entangle the firm of Matthews, Thompson, and Spring—its senior partner a former Boston mayor—with the fate of two Italian anarchists. Thompson knew taking their case would drive away other clients. He did not share Moore's suspicion of a frame-up. "I do not think that the jury's mistake was an unnatural one," he had written Moore, "or that the government was actuated by any ulterior purpose in bringing the charge against them. They ought to realize that the circumstantial evidence against them was certainly enough to excite grave suspicion."

Thompson scoffed at the men's politics. Sacco and Vanzetti, he wrote one banker, were "half educated dreamers and fanatics," easily swayed by "Tolstoi, Prince Krapotkin [sic], Bakunin, Proudhon and others. They seem not to have felt the influence of American ideas in the slightest degree." Yet Thompson did not care for Judge Thayer either. As a Worcester native, he had known Thayer all his life. Thompson considered the judge "full of prejudice [and] carried away with this fear of Reds. . . . His categories of thought are few and simple—Reds and conservatives, and 'soldier boys.' No margin between them." Convinced Sacco and Vanzetti were innocent, Thompson felt his own call to duty. "I have been fortunate in accumulating some of this world's goods," he later observed. "But what I have accumulated will be not good to myself or to anybody else if the precedent is established in this state that the humblest and least popular of the persons within its borders can be deprived of life by the methods followed in this case."

When the ultra-radical Flynn and the anarchist Felicani entered his office in Boston's elegant Tremont Building, Thompson asked for $25,000 up front. He expected the fee would end all discussion. "Well, here we were with not one penny," Felicani recalled. "So we left the office and said, 'What now? Where are we going to get the money? We need him.'" An emergency meeting in the North End scrounged up $5,000. Meanwhile, Flynn contacted the American Fund for Public Service in Manhattan. The fund, bankrolled by the heir of a Wall Street tycoon, specialized in social causes. Within days, Flynn brokered a no-interest $20,000 loan, and by Thanksgiving Thompson was preparing his appeal to the Supreme Judicial Court. At last, Sacco and Vanzetti had a lawyer they could trust.

As 1925 promised either execution or another gray year inside the same gray walls, Vanzetti turned to a scheme he had contemplated for months. Always a hellhole, Charlestown State Prison was getting worse. With the Commonwealth cracking down on crime, the inmate population had risen fifty-five percent since Vanzetti's arrival. Packed into the "barbaric and antiquated" old prison, inmates were lashing out like caged animals. To the hum of the generator and flickering of lights, Vanzetti had witnessed another execution. He had to get out—somehow. Having learned from Sacco's stint at Bridgewater that insanity could give a condemned man a bigger cage, Vanzetti decided to fake his own paranoia. He had warned his sister, "I can assure you that I am completely well. If you hear that I am ill do not believe it: understand? Only be sure that I want to win." Shortly after Thayer's ruling, Vanzetti began ranting that Mussolini had come to America to kill him. Just before Christmas, he smashed a chair in his cell and propped his table against the bars. Again, psychiatrists diagnosed "prison psychosis," but this time there would be no hearings, no periods of observation. On January 2, 1925, Vanzetti was sent to Bridgewater.

Sacco had recovered at the "State Farm," but Vanzetti had no delirium to cure. The country air was better for his scarred lungs and he reveled in the songs of birds. During a total solar eclipse that January, he stood at his window reading Marcus Aurelius, noting how "the sun's spectrum colored its page." But he spent five weeks in solitary confinement before being moved to an open room where inmates were forbidden to speak. He had to eat with his hands—knives and forks were potential weapons—and was rarely allowed in the spacious yard. Guards taunted him, calling his supporters "fools and cheaters" and asking whether he believed in God. Only Vanzetti's will kept his spirit afloat until a doctor concluded he had never been insane. In late April, he was returned to his cell in Charlestown.

Throughout 1925, confusion gave way to inertia and business as usual. President Calvin Coolidge proclaimed, "The business of America is business," and the stock market soared. Sacco and Vanzetti were still in jail. A book by a Madison Avenue mogul praised Jesus as "the founder of modern business." The book topped best-seller lists. *The Great Gatsby* got mixed reviews and sold poorly. Sacco and Vanzetti were still in jail. William Thompson spent much of his time winning a million-dollar patent suit. On May Day, Eugene Debs came to Boston to fire up a rally for Sacco and Vanzetti. The heroes of the Lawrence strike, Ettor and Giovannitti, reunited for similar rallies. Throughout the happy-go-lucky nation, craze followed craze—crossword puzzles, flagpole sitting, dance marathons. Ads for Old Gold cigarettes boasted, "Not a cough in a carload." On Broadway, the Marx Brothers starred in *The Cocoanuts* while Al Jolson crooned "If You Knew Susie Like I Knew Susie." Sacco and Vanzetti were still in jail.

Back in his cell, Vanzetti became "a living hurricane of thoughts, feelings and sentiments." Reading Emerson and Thoreau, translating an anarchist tract by Proudhon, he saw the world "going to hell by radio." Fascist Italy was "weeping tears of blood" while his own case had become "a tragic laughing stock." Transferred from the tailor shop to the paint shop, where fumes tortured his lungs, he found himself "lusting for death." He imagined dying "beautifully in an open and heroic rebellion that would signify something inspire and create. The enemy would ponder a little before to frame others."

Sacco remained the radical naïf. "I wish I could be out Mrs. Jack," he wrote one spring day, "for bring you near your bed a big bunch of odorous narcissus and violet—and try to relieve your noble soul with my warm words." Yet on that same day, he sent a letter to an anarchist newspaper praising Luigi Galleani and thanking his followers for their "audacious revolt." Martyrdom was still his dream, yet unlike Vanzetti, Sacco had another legacy—he had children. When they came to visit, he found Dante as tall as Rosina. Four-year-old Ines, with pudgy cheeks and bobbed brown hair, was getting to know her father. During one visit, guards allowed the family into the cellblock. Before Sacco could step from his cell, his little girl ran past the bars to hug his legs. "Why don't you come home, Papa," Ines said, "and play with me out in the yard?"

1925 continued to crawl by. John Scopes was found guilty of teaching evolution in Tennessee and fined $100. Charlie Chaplin's *The Gold Rush* flickered on movie screens. Still in jail, Sacco and

Vanzetti had vanished from public view, but behind the scenes, another bombshell was in the making. In July, both Thompson and the prosecution learned of Judge Thayer's rants at the University Club toward the end of the trial. Attorney George Crocker quoted Thayer: "These two men are anarchists; they are guilty. . . . They are not getting a fair trial but I am working it so that their counsel will think they are." If Thompson went public with the revelation, Norfolk County's assistant DA warned his boss, it would cause "the biggest scandal that has occurred in our judiciary for many years." Thompson kept the charge hidden, like an ace up his sleeve. That August, white-hooded Ku Klux Klansmen capped their surge to nationwide power with a march of forty thousand strong past the Capitol in Washington, D.C. On the edge of Boston, white sailboats skimmed along the Charles River. Come autumn, the boats turned to sculls rowed by the Harvard crew. And Sacco and Vanzetti were still in jail.

Watching the seasons pass, Vanzetti wrote, "Since an execution has become a little too shameful and dangerous, my enemies have just resolved to keep us in prison, all our lives. Exactly that." Then suddenly the inertia ended. A week before Thanksgiving, a prisoner sent Sacco a note slipped inside a magazine. Reading it, Sacco leaned against one wall, trembling, his eyes filling with tears. The note began, "I hear by confess . . ."

CHAPTER TWELVE

"A Vulgar Contest"

The earth is given into the hand of the wicked;
He covereth the face of the judges thereof:—
If it be not he, who then is it?

—Job 9:24

Beneath the towering rotunda of the Norfolk County Jail, three men huddled around a table fleshing out a confession. In his striped prison uniform, Sacco sat beside the nattily dressed William Thompson. Slouching in the opposite seat was another prisoner, lanky and curly-haired, his face dulled by the banality of the seasoned killer. It was November 20, two days after a slip of paper had left Sacco in tears, and through the jail's double-arched windows he could see bare branches and a bleak sky. Sacco occasionally urged this third man to tell the truth "for Jesus' sake!" but mostly he just listened to words he had surrendered hope of hearing.

The prisoner was saying he had been there. In South Braintree. On April 15, 1920. He had ridden in the back of the Buick. He had been eighteen years old, drunk, and "scared half to death when I heard the shooting begin." As the man continued, Thompson scribbled notes:

—4 Italians picked him up Apl. 15, 1920 on N. Main St., Prov. . . .

—Left Hudson car in woods and took it again after job, leaving Buick in woods in charge of one man who drove it off. . . .

—They talked like professionals.

—Sd. had done lots of jobs—freight cars.

—2 young, 20 to 25, one abt. 40, other 35. . . .

—I sat on back seat of auto.

—Had Colt auto. 38, but did not use it—to hold crowd back.

—Curtains flapping—don't remem. shot-gun. . . .

—Money in black bag—think.

Toward the end of the confession came the words Sacco needed to hear: "Sacco and Vanzetti had nothing to do with this job."

The confession lit candles among friends, family, and the defense committee. Finally. Finally, after five and a half years, there would be vindication, a new trial, perhaps even clemency. Supporters wanted to shout the news from the rooftops, as Fred Moore would have, but Moore was only a bad memory now. His successor was more cautious. When word leaked to the *Boston Post* and *Boston Globe,* Thompson convinced reporters not to publish anything until he had filed a motion based on the confession. First he had to check out some troublesome details.

The trouble began with timing. The prisoner claimed his gang had driven that morning to Boston, then back to Providence, then back toward Boston again, arriving in Braintree at about noon. Then what two "funny looking strangers" had been seen near the Buick at midmorning? And what about the "black bag"? Could two strongboxes be mistaken for one bag? The man knew few details of Pearl Street. He remembered the Buick's flapping curtains but said nothing about a water tower, railroad tracks, or men digging a foundation. He claimed his accomplices were Italians but refused to name names other than "Mike and Bill." "The names of these men don't amount to anything," he told Thompson. "They change them whenever they want to." Finally, there was the man himself.

Celestino Medeiros was a "good killer," all right. Driven out of school by epilepsy and bad eyesight, he had taken to crime at fourteen. Psychiatrists found him a "psychopathic personality" fascinated by firearms. Medeiros once shot flies off a friend's ceiling and gunned down his landlady's kittens. The only job he ever held had been a sham—wearing a fake army uniform while soliciting funds for a bogus American Rescue League, funds he spent on liquor and women. By 1924, Medeiros had a dozen convictions ranging from larceny to breaking and entering. When he blew away a bank cashier with a .45, he added murder to his record and was sentenced to the electric chair. Such was the man on whom hope now hinged.

Shortly before sending his note to Sacco, Medeiros had been granted a new trial because the judge had neglected to tell his jury he was innocent until proven guilty. A second trial granted on such a technicality enraged Vanzetti, but it also meant that publicity of the confession might prejudice Medeiros's second jury. So the press remained silent; the defense committee wrote no bulletins. Vanzetti could not even share the confession with his sister, hinting only of "secrets that are important proofs." Thompson alerted the prosecution to the confession, then continued preparing his argument before the Supreme Judicial Court. As Christmas gave way to New Year's, optimism strained at its leash. The day before Thompson's appeal, a friend visited Vanzetti. "He was convinced of victory," Vanzetti wrote, "so convinced that he cried with joy. Well, we'll see."

On January 11, 1926, *Commonwealth v. Sacco and Vanzetti* ascended to a higher court. The Massachusetts Supreme Judicial Court, established in 1692, was the oldest appellate tribunal in the Western Hemisphere. Its former chief justices included John Adams and Oliver Wendell Holmes; its landmark decisions ranged from abolishing slavery in the Commonwealth to acquitting British soldiers of the Boston Massacre. Now with a huge map of Pearl Street near the bench, with Rosina, her children, and Mrs. Evans in the standing-room-only gallery, the court took up the thorniest case in its history. Stepping before five aged judges, Thompson faced a daunting task. In contrast to several other states, Massachusetts's highest court could not rule on evidence or the overall fairness of a case. Thompson had to base his appeal on judicial errors. He cited thirty-four, presenting what the *Boston Globe* called "one of the most powerful arguments made before the Supreme Court for years."

Thompson began by attacking the late-night roundup of potential jurors, claiming deputies had chosen men prone to convict. Ignoring the Andrews and Goodridge motions with their stench of blackmail, he revived the "Gould motion," accusing Katzmann of concealing this key witness. He reviewed the Red Scare and Palmer Raids, explaining how lingering fears of radicalism, Katzmann's cross-examination, and a courtroom guarded like a fortress had biased the jury. As the Dedham trial dragged on, he argued, "It wasn't so much a question whether Sacco and Vanzetti had committed this murder as whether they were not, as radicals, men too dangerous to be allowed at large in the community."

Thompson noted his clients' good reputations and lack of previous arrests. Calling Judge Thayer "confused," he accused him of repeating one "sneering question"—had the roundup of radical literature been "in the interest of the United States"? Turning to Captain Proctor's retraction, Thompson charged Katzmann with fooling the jury. "I don't believe the District Attorney is elected for the purpose of playing a game with human life as a stake, that he is there to see how many convictions he can obtain," Thompson told the judges. Then there was the stolen money—never recovered—the numerous questions about identity excluded by "the learned judge," and the widely conflicting stories of the gun repairmen and other witnesses. His clients' political views were "ignorant and misguided," Thompson argued, yet "the way to recommend our institutions is not to trip these men up on exceptions, not to hurry them off to the chair, but to show them that we have sufficient confidence in our institutions to give them every opportunity." After comparing the case to France's Dreyfus affair, Thompson wrapped up eight hours of argument by echoing the jury foreman—"Damn them, they ought to hang them anyway!" "That," he concluded, "was the whole spirit of the trial."

Rising on the Commonwealth's behalf was the new assistant DA. A Harvard grad and World War I veteran with wavy black hair and a movie-star smile, Dudley Ranney was the son of a prominent Boston lawyer. Ranney would later admit he considered the Commonwealth's case "not proven," yet doubt would not interfere with what he called "my duty." After highlighting the prosecution's evidence—Bullet III and Shell W, the eyewitnesses, Sacco's cap, Vanzetti's gun, the lies upon arrest—he denounced Thompson's "bitter attack" on Katzmann and the persistent claim that Sacco and Vanzetti had been convicted as radicals. Radicalism had only entered the trial with the eighty-fifth witness, Ranney said. A defense witness. Finally, he suggested that Katzmann's cross-examination had helped the defendants, letting them explain their "consciousness of guilt." After three days, days that saw Boston papers leak the news of Medeiros's confession, the appeal ended and the wait began.

The high court's decision was expected in February. The high court's decision was expected in March. After its chief justice had an appendectomy, the decision was expected in April. In anticipation of the first ruling by a court other than Thayer's, optimism mounted, even behind bars. Vanzetti, now whiling away the hours carving penholders he sent as gifts, at last began to believe. Thompson's erudition, friends' hopes, and Medeiros's second trial granted on "an insignificant trifle" persuaded Vanzetti that "this time we will finally get justice." And then there was the simmering protest overseas. Denying a new trial "could change the proletarian Jobs into a Sampson, the proletarian rabbit into a lion," Vanzetti wrote. "There would be flames. Fatally. Nor I believe the five men capable of such a monstrosity."

The high court's decision was expected in early May. When it did not come, Vanzetti talked of a hunger strike, but Thompson talked him out of it. The self-taught anarchist and the Harvard-educated lawyer were becoming good friends, sharing long intellectual chats during prison visits. "To have known you 6 years ago!" Vanzetti replied after Thompson thanked him for a penholder. "I would never have been a convict." In Dedham, Sacco waited in stoic silence. The men who had expected imminent execution in 1921 had just begun their seventh year in prison when the high court handed down its decision.

On a sparkling spring afternoon, Rosina was sitting outside her small home in Millis, ten miles west of Sacco's cell. Ines was playing in the backyard. Dante was in his seventh-grade classroom. Across the street at the general store, the phone rang. A clerk beckoned "Mrs. Sacco." The call was from her husband's defense committee. With her red hair glinting in the sun, Rosina crossed the muddy street in what must have been the longest walk of her life. In a matter of seconds, she could expect to be shouting the incredible news, or else crushed, a living widow awaiting only the end. Inside the store, she stood, receiver in hand, listening to a tinny voice read a telegram. Moments later, her face drawn and somber, she made the long journey home, stopping to tell a neighbor. She had heard the words but could barely grasp the message. "I wonder if Nick knows about it yet," she said. "He'll be disturbed when he hears the news. He's been so optimistic lately."

While the news flashed through Boston, police guarded the homes of Chief Justice Arthur Rugg and Judge Thayer. The defense committee scheduled an evening meeting with Thompson, who, stunned and confused, was off to see his clients. Each of the thirty-four points unanimously overruled by the court deepened Thompson's bewilderment. A biased jury foreman. A politically charged courtroom. A vindictive trial judge. How could the high court ignore such palpable injustice? Did judges fear, as Vanzetti often said, that a second trial would undermine the courts by revealing the evils of the first? Was he right when he said, "They must kill us to save the dignity and honor of their Commonwealth"? Nothing Thompson had learned at Harvard, nothing in his lifetime at the bar helped him understand. Talking to his grim-faced clients, he did his best to explain. That the Commonwealth's highest court considered the late-night jury roundup justified in avoiding delay. That the five judges bowed to Thayer's discretion on Captain Proctor's testimony. That despite the jury foreman's "Damn them!" comment, his answers during jury selection "showed him to be unprejudiced." That Katzmann's grilling of Sacco did not "excite and intensify prejudice against him." In short, all aspects of the trial and appeals were held as within Judge Thayer's discretion. The words "discretion" and "sound discretion," laced throughout the ruling, buttressed the decision that no legal errors had been committed, no rights denied, and there would be no new trial.

For Vanzetti, this was the beginning of the end; for Sacco, it was the end. Let them do to him what they had always planned, he told Thompson. He would have nothing to do with any further appeal. Vanzetti's moods were more nuanced. "Yesterday, we got the last stroke," he wrote Alice Stone Blackwell. "It ends all. We are doomed beyond any kind of doubts." At his writing table, he again heard the crackling hum of the prison generator "preparing for an execution, maybe for my execution—and that noise cuts my being all over." The following day, however, he vowed to go on. "Be of brave heart," he wrote to Mrs. Evans. "Our comrades, the good people are still with us and they will never quit us. And history is galloping! Who can know the incognitas of the future near and remote?" Vanzetti's lone unwavering mood, shared by Sacco, was a mounting hunger for revenge. Their joint letter to a new defense committee bulletin concluded with a veiled reference to Luigi Galleani's bomb manual: "Remember, *La Salute è in Voi.*" But Vanzetti also targeted his fury. "I will try to see Thayer death, before his pronunciation of our sentence," he seethed. "I will put fire into the human breaths."

Handed down on May 12, the denial shoved the case onto a fast track. The day after the ruling, Norfolk County DA Winfield Wilbar, a stout, balding man with wire-rimmed glasses, set the sentencing for May 15 at 11:00 a.m. Thompson filed a hasty appeal breaking the momentum, but he could not douse the rising determination across the Commonwealth to close this malingering case, to be rid of Sacco and Vanzetti. The following week, as a bomb blamed on Sacco-Vanzetti supporters damaged the American embassy in Buenos Aires, Celestino Medeiros was retried. In five days, with Medeiros slouching in the cage glaring at judge and jury, he was again found guilty. After a six-month wait, Thompson could finally detail the confession. With it, the defense committee awoke from quiet despair.

Volunteers had come and gone, but six years after emerging from Gruppo Autonomo, the committee remained dominated by anarchists. With time running out, these diehards finally realized they needed help. Aldino Felicani was still the committee's soul, his tall, gentlemanly figure always in the office, his deep baritone swaying most decisions. Mrs. Evans, when not helping Rosina, was still the group's heart. But now the committee tapped minds who knew America and knew how to make Americans listen. Leading the newcomers was Mary Donovan.

Raised an Irish Catholic, the forty-year-old Donovan had been an Irish rebel since college when she was excommunicated for becoming a Socialist. Pompously independent, unafraid of authority, she had worked as a factory inspector, labor leader, and organizer for Sinn Fein in Boston. Joining the defense committee, she was instantly seen everywhere—in courtrooms, at the State House, planted at her office table firing off letters to editors, contributors, to Sacco and Vanzetti. She was "plain as an old shoe, with no figure worth a damn, straight, stringy hair in a bob, a creased kind of face," wrote another newcomer, Gardner Jackson. Yet Donovan's dynamism and intellect charmed the committee. "Every guy that came near that place just went beside himself, Felicani among them," Jackson recalled. Before the fight was over, Donovan would be arrested and harassed, would meet her future husband among the protesters, and would be fired from her job with the Commonwealth. But she would not surrender her dream of justice until it was reduced to ashes.

While Donovan supplied the energy, Jackson supplied the words that now poured from the committee's office. Known to all as "Pat," Gardner Jackson was raised far from Boston, farther still from social causes. The son of a Colorado banker, he had grown up in privilege, attending prep schools and Amherst College. After serving in World War I, Jackson sold bonds and worked for his father's firm. In the summer of 1921, he was writing for the *Boston Globe* when his wife urged him to look into the Dedham trial. "Pat, I don't think that they're getting a fair break," she said. "Will you try to find out?" Jackson approached *Globe* reporter Frank Sibley, who congratulated Mrs. Jackson on her assessment. "It's an outrage that's being perpetrated here," Sibley said. For the next few years, Jackson wrote part-time for the committee. Then in 1926, Felicani convinced him to take over all publicity. "We were now able to reach people we never could have dreamed [of] reaching before," Felicani recalled. "Jackson brought in a respectable, social, liberal element." Jackson's arrival angered Mary Donovan. Once, after he had held forth during a meeting, she burst into tears. "I hate you!" she cried. "You've taken my Italians away from me!" But the two reconciled their contrasting styles, turning the committee into an efficient machine, part publishing house and part clearinghouse for all the money and passion about to be spent to free Sacco and Vanzetti.

With all of Boston buzzing about the case, Felicani and friends began working day and night. Amidst the chaos of rumors, ringing phones, and time ticking away, new volunteers sat on bundles of pamphlets opening letters from Cuba and Belgium, Yugoslavia and Paris. While Donovan made call after call, Jackson banged out the new *Official Bulletin* and the committee's first solicitation in more than a year. "We still have a fighting chance," he wrote. "When it seemed that all hope had gone valuable new evidence came forward—adding fresh proof of the innocence of Sacco and Vanzetti. Chief Defense counsel William G. Thompson and his associates are now making investigations. . . ."

Ten days after the denial, a third newcomer was driving toward Rhode Island to investigate the confession. Hired by Thompson, who had taught him at Harvard, thirty-four-year-old Herbert Ehrmann carried little but the names "Mike and Bill," the name of an inn where Celestino Medeiros had been a bouncer, and his own doubts. Ehrmann did not know whether Sacco and Vanzetti were innocent, but recalling the Red Scare, he sensed they had not received a fair trial. Still, he considered Medeiros's story a "death house confession." Planning to be back at his law firm within days, unaware he had entered a case that would obsess him for the rest of his life, Ehrmann stopped to ask directions to the Bluebird Inn.

During Prohibition, many an "inn" was more than an inn. The Bluebird Inn, a faded old farmhouse on a back road just east of the Rhode Island line, doubled as a speakeasy, a dance hall, and no one dared say what else. Strangers told Ehrmann that police had closed the joint, but he finally found it, parked his car, sidestepped some chickens, and knocked on a rickety front door. He was soon inside, talking to a statuesque blonde who reminded him of a heroine from a Wagner opera. The woman did not flinch at the names Sacco and Vanzetti, but at the mention of Medeiros she came alive. How was "Fred" doing? Was there any chance of his avoiding execution? Did Mr. Ehrmann consider it fair to execute a man who wasn't quite sane? Told of Medeiros's confession, May Monterio shook her head. "Fred couldn't have been in it," she said. "I believe he was in Mexico at the time." She remembered him heading south with "a circus girl" who had sent back letters telling of gifts Medeiros lavished on her. Mrs. Monterio still had the letters. Checking their postmarks, Ehrmann saw that Medeiros's trip had begun months after the Braintree murders. Its length—two years— led him to ask how much money the Bluebird Inn's ex-bouncer had taken along.

"He said he took twenty-eight hundred dollars with him." Ehrmann divided $15,000 by six—five men in a Buick plus one waiting in the woods beside the Hudson. He headed on, less skeptical. Next stop was Providence, where police had initially investigated the Braintree murders before Chief Stewart steered them to his hometown. At police headquarters, two cops listened to Ehrmann's story. They seemed dubious until one dropped a name that would parallel the case forever. In fact, the cop said, there had been a local gang of Italians robbing freight cars. "The Morell gang."

The name had been Anglicized, but Fred Moore would have recognized it. Back in 1923, a convict in Atlanta had written the Boston Bar Association about his cellmate, Joe Morelli. Late one sleepless night, Morelli had described in brutal detail how his gang had pulled off the Braintree murders. Morelli had forced his cellmate to swear, if ever asked, that on April 15, 1920, they had been together playing poker in Manhattan. Learning of the letter, Moore had written Congressman La Guardia suggesting "somebody put their shoulder to the wheel with a little aggressiveness to put this man Morelli on the street." La Guardia had not replied, leaving Moore to wander his wilderness of other leads. Joe Morelli was transferred to the federal penitentiary in Leavenworth, Kansas, and his name was not mentioned again until Ehrmann learned about the "Morell gang." There were five Morell brothers, Providence cops now told him—all yeggs. A police blotter listed three brothers arrested in October 1919, but three had been out on bail the following April. "From now on it was possible to believe Medeiros," Ehrmann recalled. Returning home, he phoned Dudley Ranney. The new prosecutor was an old Harvard classmate, and Ehrmann felt he could level with him. Sharing his discoveries, Ehrmann suggested the prosecution might have to drop its case. "Over my dead body!" Ranney replied.

Three days later, Ehrmann returned to Providence with his wife, Sara. While she checked federal court records, Ehrmann dropped in on the lawyer who had defended the brothers he now knew as the Morellis. Learning of their specialty—stealing shoes—Ehrmann wondered how the Morellis knew which shoe factories were shipping on a given day. Their lawyer told him the Morellis used "spotters" to stake out factories and railroad stations. Did the lawyer know any particular factories the Morellis had "spotted"?

"Well, I remember one place," Daniel Geary said. "The Rice and Hutchins shoe factory." When Ehrmann told him of the Braintree connection, Geary whistled. "That brings it home, doesn't it?" he said. Feeling on the verge of breaking the case wide open, Ehrmann returned to his hotel to find his wife in the lobby, eager to shove a paper into his hands. Her notes listed nine indictments— *"United States v. Joseph Morelli et al."* The first four counts listed thefts from "Rice and Hutchins, at South Braintree." The eighth count was from Slater and Morrill. And the trial, Ehrmann noted, had been in May 1920, suggesting a desperate need for ready cash to pay a lawyer.

Ehrmann's investigation kept steering him straight toward the Morellis. In New Bedford, Massachusetts, a cop dug out his notebook from April 1920. Ellsworth "Jake" Jacobs had spotted "Mike Morrell" driving a new Buick touring car a few days before the Braintree murders and again on April 15 at about 5:30 p.m. The cop never saw the car again. Jacobs told Ehrmann he had initially suspected the brothers of the murders. Then he offered another clue. Nine days after the crime, Jacobs had noticed the Buick's plates on another car outside a restaurant. Entering, he approached four Italians at a table. One reached for his hip pocket. Then Frank "Butsy" Morelli spoke.

"What's the matter, Jake?" he asked. "What do you want with me? Why are you pickin' on me all the time?"

When Jacobs mentioned the car with the Buick plates, Butsy shrugged it off. It was a dealer's plate. He was in the automobile business. "We just transfer plates from one car to another."

As clues spiraled into more clues, Ehrmann assembled a possible cast of characters in the Buick, thugs known to drift in and out of the gang. Albert "Bibba" Barone. Joseph "Gyp the Blood" Imondi. Anthony "Tony" Mancini. Ehrmann relayed each discovery to Thompson, who was beginning his "first adventure into the mysteries of the so-called underworld." In Charlestown Prison, Thompson deposed Medeiros's accomplice in his fatal bank robbery. "Medeiros often told me about the South Braintree job," James Weeks said. "He said that it was arranged by the Joe Morell gang." Corroborating Medeiros on several details, Weeks assured Thompson that Sacco and Vanzetti were innocent: "It is well known and has long been well known among a certain crowd who did that job."

The day after interviewing Weeks, Thompson moved for a new trial, then wrote the state attorney general and DA Wilbar suggesting a joint inquiry. With the prosecution already sniffing around, Thompson worried that parallel investigations would become "a vulgar contest of affidavits." The attorney general approved of Thompson's suggestion; the DA refused. The vulgar contest was under way. State detectives were soon following the trail blazed by Ehrmann and Thompson. At Charlestown, detectives deposed James Weeks, offering him Camel cigarettes and hinting his sentence might be commuted if he refused to sign an affidavit for Thompson. Weeks signed anyway. In Providence, detectives met with lawyer Daniel Geary and various cops, then spoke with three Morelli brothers, who denied everything. In New Bedford, they met Medeiros's sister, who remembered her brother saying, "You think I am tough because I am in this case? Well, there is a fellow in here over five years who killed two men in a job."

With a race under way to get the truth—or a usable version of it—Ehrmann and a U.S. marshal boarded a train for Kansas. As the Santa Fe chugged across the Midwest, the marshal told Ehrmann about the gangster they were about to meet. Joe Morelli considered himself "a high class man," too sophisticated to steal shoes. Joe often claimed he was in "the piano business," but along with robbery, his gang dabbled in drugs, counterfeiting, and prostitution. Shortly before his arrest, this "high class man" had swindled his invalid mother out of her home, leaving her to live in a state almshouse. Explosively violent—he had shot a deputy sheriff and threatened the marshal's life—Joe was also wily enough to turn evidence and enemies in his favor. Ehrmann and the marshal agreed that Joe Morelli seemed a more likely murderer than either Sacco or Vanzetti.

At Leavenworth, Ehrmann told the warden why he had come all the way from Massachusetts. Worried an accusation of murder might get Morelli, a prison trusty, "all worked up," the warden sat in on the interview. For the next hour, scowling and grunting, Joe Morelli was a portrait of denial. He did not know the hotel where Medeiros claimed he had met "Mike and Bill" on the morning of the murders. He did not know any Portuguese men. He did not know any Tony Mancini. He had never heard of South Braintree, Rice & Hutchins, Slater & Morrill. Reminded of his convictions for robbing those factories, Morelli scoffed. That was six years ago. A guy couldn't remember all his indictments. This was just another frame-up. When the marshal mentioned Joe's other activities in Providence, Morelli said, "You are trying to spoil my record with my warden, my good warden." The good warden agreed. "How would you like to have such things said to you?" he asked.

Before leaving, Ehrmann mentioned Sacco and Vanzetti. Morelli seemed to recognize the names. "Sacco? Sacco?" he said. "See Mancini about that!" Still puzzling over the comment, Ehrmann and the marshal headed back to Boston with little more than denials, yet they had noticed something startling. Though his face was slightly thicker, the expression more severe, Joe Morelli looked remarkably like Sacco.

While Ehrmann was in Kansas, the story that had begun with dynamite seven years earlier exploded again. Shortly after midnight on June 1, a blast heard ten miles away demolished a farmhouse in Bridgewater. When dawn came, a farmer in overalls stood beside his bedraggled wife and children, puffing his pipe and surveying the wreckage of his home. "I didn't know I had an enemy in the world," Samuel Johnson said. Police, however, understood. Samuel's brother was Simon Johnson, the mechanic who had repaired Mario Buda's car. At the trial, Simon's wife, Ruth, had placed Sacco and Vanzetti at her home an hour before their arrest. Police and press speculated that the bombing—mistakenly aimed at the wrong Johnson—was payback. Thompson objected. Such speculation raised "serious prejudice" against his clients, he told the press, but the accusation lingered. Three days later, another bomb splintered the American embassy in Uruguay. In Paris, the same American ambassador targeted by a mail bomb in 1921 received more death threats.

The new wave of threats and explosions dredged up new fears. On the evening after the Bridgewater bombing, key prosecution witness Mary Splaine was startled to find a stranger at her door.

The stranger was Ehrmann's assistant, holding a stack of photos. Shown a mug shot of Joe Morelli, Splaine said, "This is a picture of the man who did the shooting! It's a picture of Sacco, isn't it?" When told the photo was of another man, Splaine said she never saw such lookalikes. After the stranger left, she called the police, who came to guard her home. Splaine was the last prosecution witness to be so welcoming. Lewis Wade singled out Morelli's mug, calling him "strikingly like the man whom I saw shooting Berardelli," yet when Ehrmann went to get a sworn statement, Mrs. Wade opened the door just a crack. Her husband refused to say any more. Hadn't he been fired for his trial testimony? Wasn't that enough? Ehrmann then called on a Mrs. Hewins, at whose house he believed the fleeing gang had stopped for directions. Through a locked screen door, Mr. Hewins said neither he nor his wife wanted to get involved. Jimmy Bostock also singled out Morelli, but when told who he was, the mechanic who had refused to identify either gunman in court began ranting. Sacco and Vanzetti were guilty, Bostock shouted. He had seen Sacco gun down Berardelli, then take his gun. He had seen Vanzetti driving the Buick. And Vanzetti was guilty of the Bridgewater crime too! With prosecution witnesses clamming up, Ehrmann searched out defense witnesses. Glassblower Frank Burke identified Morelli as "the man I saw sitting next to the driver." Several Italians who had been digging the foundation on Pearl Street flipped through photos until one shouted, "Sacco! Sacco!" Others took up the cry. The photo was of Joe Morelli.

On June 5, Thompson heard that police and witnesses were being paid to protect the verdict. That afternoon, Dudley Ranney phoned Thompson to discuss the rumors. Ranney "understood a sum of about $15,000 was to be paid," Thompson wrote in his diary. "Denied that state police would share in this. Could not say who was to share." Thompson passed the rumors on to the state attorney general but heard no more about them.

By mid-June, the contest of affidavits had become a game of blindman's bluff. For the prosecution: Joe Morelli's girlfriend swore he had been home every morning till 10:00 a.m. throughout

April 1920; Mary Splaine denied she had mistaken Morelli for Sacco; and a psychiatrist swore Medeiros told him the Braintree robbery took place in 1918 and that he had gotten no money from it. For the defense: Two women told of watching the Buick's driver through their factory window, but after telling Katzmann neither Sacco nor Vanzetti was the man, they never heard from the DA again; May Monterio's husband, Barney, swore Medeiros had often boasted of the Braintree robbery; and another convict remembered Medeiros telling him in 1920, "I am working with a good mob in Providence." On top of his heap, Thompson added an affidavit from a glove maker. Mary Splaine had insisted the gunman had "a good sized hand," but the glove man had measured Sacco's hands, finding them "what men in the glove trade would call small hands."

As the filing deadline for affidavits approached, Medeiros changed his story. He had been in the Buick's *front* seat for part of the trip, he said. All the men had carried .38s. And he had confessed because "I seen Sacco's wife come up here with the kids and I felt sorry for the kids." More affidavits were needed. By the time the contest ended, Thompson had filed sixty-four, the Commonwealth twenty-six. Judge Thayer, reeling from a bout with pneumonia, set the hearing for September, giving Thompson time to chase a new lead all the way to the nation's capital.

During the first week of July, former agents of the Bureau of Investigation approached Thompson. Fred Moore had always suspected the federal bureau of meddling in his case. Knowing agents had planted "a stool pigeon on Sacco," Moore had fired off indignant letters but never proved anything else. Now the ex-agents confirmed Moore's suspicions. Even before April 15, 1920, Fred Weyand and Lawrence Letherman told Thompson, federal files listed Sacco and Vanzetti as "radicals to be watched." A dozen G-men had been in on the pretrial investigation, infiltrating the defense committee and giving Katzmann background information even though the "general opinion" in the bureau was that Sacco and

Vanzetti "were not highway robbers, and had nothing to do with the South Braintree crime." A murder conviction, the bureau had concluded, "would be one way of disposing of the two men." The Boston bureau's files, Weyand and Letherman said, contained further details. Thompson immediately wrote the U.S. attorney general asking to see the files.

Within days, J. Edgar Hoover was on the phone to Harold Williams, now a federal attorney. Williams advised against letting Thompson see any files. Boston's bureau chief agreed, assuring Hoover the files contained nothing on Sacco and Vanzetti prior to their trial. Yes, the bureau had planted an informer near Sacco's cell following the Wall Street bombing. And the bureau had investigated anarchists on the defense committee. But until their mug shots hit the front pages, the bureau had known nothing of Sacco and Vanzetti. The ex-agents spreading this "figment of imagination" were just angry at being fired in 1924. Letherman, a bureau report noted, suffered from "senile dementia," while his drinking buddy Weyand had "falsified reports." Sacco and Vanzetti might be found *somewhere* in the file on Boston anarchists, Hoover was told, but until their arrest, the men were "not sufficiently active to come to the attention of the office." When the bureau chief told Thompson the same, the mild-mannered lawyer began shouting into the phone. Did federal agents think they could railroad men to the electric chair just because they were anarchists? Asked to specify what information he was seeking, Thompson yelled, "Specify nothing! I want every damn thing in your files and you better telephone Washington without delay!"

Throughout July, letters and phone calls flew between Washington, D.C., and Boston, but the Weyand and Letherman affidavits—corroborated by a third ex-agent—were the only evidence of conspiracy Thompson would ever get. That fall, Hoover received Boston's Sacco-Vanzetti files. He was alarmed. "I am considerably concerned to note that certain papers and documents have been taken from this file," he wrote his bureau chief. Yet Hoover refused to release any Sacco-Vanzetti papers. Thompson, furious, disillusioned, and convinced his own government was harboring secrets, could only add the affidavits to his stack. Then, working from his summer home in Maine, he continued preparing his next appeal.

As surely as if granted by a judge, the case had changed venues. It had been a small-town crime staged on gravel roads, tried in a county courthouse beside a quaint common. But by the summer of 1926, the focus had shifted to Boston, stirring its urban cauldron. As the summer dragged on, three centuries of pride and outrage, pomposity and indignation inflamed the city's factions. Boston newspapers returned Sacco and Vanzetti to the front pages, and as word spread that the same Italian anarchists whose case had ignited Europe and Latin America back in 1921 were *still* in jail, *still* shouting about their innocence, prosecution and defense dug in for a dirty, drawn-out battle.

On July 27, District Attorney Wilbar wrote to "Friend Dud" Ranney: "You can stake your last dollar on the proposition that I will *never* consent to a motion for a new trial." Wilbar found public sentiment "about 10 to 1, to place it very conservatively, for having Sacco and Vanzetti sentenced and executed." Had justice been swifter, the DA added, the condemned men "would have long since been shoveling smoke in Hades." And as that "10 to 1" sentiment against Sacco and Vanzetti mounted, newspapers began tallying the years, the taxpayer dollars, the effort this single case had cost the Commonwealth. In August, the *Boston Telegram* denounced the "notorious anarchists"

> found guilty before the ablest judge who ever sat on a Massachusetts bench, Webster Thayer. But they are not dying! Reprieve has followed reprieve; delay has crowded delay . . . [and] today, five years after conviction, the Reds in every Communist nest in the world are contributing money to keep up the fight. They bomb embassies and threaten ambassadors; they hold mass meetings and train orators while the army of lawyers continue the battle.

The average citizen, chimed in the *Gloucester Times,* "beholds with amazement the vast concerted attempt to free these two murderers."

With Bostonians calling for their execution, Sacco and Vanzetti also entrenched. While Sacco stonewalled all legal efforts, Vanzetti funneled white-hot rage through his pen. He called his enemies "hangers," "murderers," and "ugly company." The press, having "presented the case and ourselves to the public in the worst of every possible way," was guilty of a "journalistic lynching." And Judge Thayer? "He would refuse us a new trial even if Christ came down from the cross for us. If he were dead or if he dies, we would be free. If not, no. . . . Thayer is capable of any bestial ferocity." Fury turned Vanzetti into human radar. Somehow he got his hands on dozens of newspapers and magazines, culling a wide range of opinions, speeches, and rumors that left him with one conclusion: "How thirsty for our blood all of them are!" He began planning a book on the "capitalist reactionary hyenas" who had ruined his life. "Of course I will make a list honor of the perjurers who murdered us and I will illustrate the 'Defalco' case, etc. All this if I will not get disgusted to death."

From the North End, the defense committee spread its own gospel truths—that Sacco and Vanzetti had been convicted solely as radicals, that the federal government was covering up conspiracy, that the men were "philosophical anarchists" incapable of sanctioning violence. With the case's notoriety spreading, these charges soon ignited intellectuals and iconoclasts across the Charles River and across America.

As a former federal attorney who had investigated both the Mooney trial and the Palmer Raids, Harvard law professor Felix Frankfurter was easily aroused by injustice. Yet Frankfurter had not immediately sensed parallels between the Mooney and Sacco-Vanzetti cases. Only when Captain Proctor recanted did the professor take notice. "If what [Proctor] said was true," Frankfurter wrote, "it was reprehensible beyond words, and it undermined any confidence in the conduct of the case." He began telling his law students about Sacco and Vanzetti, harping on it until they mocked him. In 1924, one Harvard society's Christmas dinner roast gibed:

> *And Felix doesn't think it right*
> *That you should throw confetti*
> *When gloating o'er the sorry plight*
> *Of Sacco and Vanzetti.*

Frankfurter donated $1,000 to the defense committee, lent another $1,500, and went to New York to broker a second loan from the American Fund for Public Service. He also lobbied his Harvard colleagues, convincing the historian Arthur Schlesinger, law school dean Roscoe Pound, and others. In the coming year, Frankfurter would risk his reputation, but only after more strident voices spoke up.

Come August, John Dos Passos, fresh from the triumph of his experimental novel *Manhattan Transfer,* came from New York to cover the case for the *New Masses.* Interviewing witnesses in Plymouth, he found the eels alibi more believable than testimony from the Bridgewater trial. He found Sacco and Vanzetti still more convincing. Seeing in Sacco "the good citizen which his character witnesses described," Dos Passos considered it "barely possible" he might have considered homicidal robbery "a justifiable act in the class war." In Charlestown, the novelist was struck by Vanzetti's "aloofness from egotistical preoccupations." The fish peddler seemed too gentle to take part in a deadly holdup, Dos Passos remembered, and "nobody in his right mind who was planning such a crime would take a man like that along." While Dos Passos stayed in Boston to write a pamphlet on the case, others turned up the volume.

All that summer, meetings were held in labor halls across America. Union locals—carpenters, bakers, bricklayers, plasterers— demanded justice for Sacco and Vanzetti. Communists demanded much more. At gatherings of the party faithful, Sacco and Vanzetti became symbols of capitalist cruelty. Enraged speakers thumped podiums. Fellow workers dug into their pockets. Stark backdrops featured two figures beside an electric chair, the slogan SACCO AND VANZETTI MUST NOT DIE! and the words "International Labor Defense." The ILD, based in Chicago with ties to Moscow and Berlin, distributed a quarter million Sacco-Vanzetti pamphlets and raked in contributions, sending some $6,000 to the defense committee and small sums—five or fifty dollars—to the prisoners. Yet Sacco and Vanzetti were far more useful to Communists than Communists would be to them.

Though Red-baiters linked the two anarchists with the Communists who rallied for their release, they were poles apart. In principle, Vanzetti had considered Communism "the most humane form of social contract," but distrusting Lenin as much as he distrusted all politicians, he was not surprised when the Bolshevik Revolution descended into tyranny. "The communists want power," he wrote, "and this explains all: the ruin of the revolution." Yet American Communists, far fewer in number than their foreign counterparts, needed martyrs. THREE THOUSAND YOUNG WORKERS PROTEST THE UNFAIR TRIAL GIVEN SACCO AND VANZETTI, the Young Communist League of America telegrammed Massachusetts governor Alvan T. Fuller that summer: WE DEMAND IMMEDIATE GRANTING OF NEW TRIAL YOUR DELAY IS SIGN OF YOUR SERVILITY TO LABOR HATING RICH.

The proletariat's rage was genuine, but Communist leaders quickly fell under suspicion. Peppered by rumors of siphoned funds, Felicani demanded a full account of contributions to the ILD. The Communist front stopped sending money and, in the gathering frenzy, the backbiting intensified. Claiming Communists were the rightful representatives of two class-warfare victims, the ILD offered to merge with Felicani's committee, moving it to Chicago and hiring Clarence Darrow. Darrow still wasn't interested, nor was Vanzetti, who felt Darrow's presence would inflame "the black-gowned hangers." Rejected, the ILD accused Felicani's committee of selling out "the class birthright of the Sacco-Vanzetti case for a mess of liberal milk and pap." Felicani soon told supporters to stop donating to Communists. Years later, one repentant Communist confirmed that funds had been siphoned. "Some of the money went to the *Daily Worker* . . . and the rest was spent on campaigning to enhance the prestige of the Party," Benjamin Gitlow recalled.

By the end of the summer, the case was sweeping over Boston like a nor'easter—dominating talk on Beacon Hill, sparking arguments in men's clubs, spawning impassioned letters to editors. Sacco and Vanzetti even surfaced in classified ads. On September 12, Boston papers advertised the "Sacco-Vanzetti car," a 1920 Buick complete with "bullet holes in side." The price: $100. The following day, all of Boston again turned its attention to the Dedham courthouse.

Hearings on the eighth motion for a new trial had all the suspense of a black-tie dinner. Held in the same courtroom before the same judge, the hearing's outcome was foretold even before the same gavel came down on the same bench. There were new onlookers— Mary Donovan, Gardner Jackson, Felix Frankfurter, and reporters from New York, Pittsburgh, and Chicago. Rosina was there, but Sacco and Vanzetti were not. They knew the ending of any act starring Judge Thayer.

Outlined in sixty-four affidavits, the appeal came down to two points. First, Thompson detailed the Morelli scenario: Medeiros picked up by the gang; Medeiros in the Buick "scared half to death"; Joe Morelli firing a .32 Colt like the one police had found in his apartment; Tony Mancini firing the fatal shots from a foreign pistol; the Buick fleeing; Morelli shouting, "What the hell are you holding us up for?" As mortar cementing these pieces, Thompson cited corroborations by Medeiros's friends and accomplices. The prosecution had countered parts of the confession, Thompson granted, but remember—Medeiros had been a drunken kid. "Called upon to relate the details of this crime six years afterwards . . . his mind is in a strained condition . . . and to say that because he cannot be sure whether they stopped at South Braintree in the morning or only stopped in the afternoon his whole story must be discredited is simply not dealing with the evidence fairly."

Then, arguing as if defending democracy itself, Thompson blasted the federal government for concealing its conspiracy to help Katzmann. "A government which has come to value its own secrets more than it does the lives of its citizens has become a tyranny, whether you call it a republic, a monarchy, or anything else!" Still fuming, he muttered, "Secrets! Secrets!" Rising to refute the charges, the debonair Dudley Ranney said, "We have heard much here . . . of the rottenness of Massachusetts—a statement to which we will never agree." Ranney then called Medeiros a "surly, morbid brute," and denounced the ex-agents' affidavits as "insulting and traitorous." Judge Thayer surely knew the importance of secrecy in police work. "Secrecy is a watchword, a byword," Ranney said. " 'Do not betray the secrets of your departments.' And if the secrets were broadcast, what would be the result? There would be no crime detected and punished."

With Boston hanging on his decision, Judge Thayer did not delay. On October 23, he let loose with all the righteousness that had brought a sixty-nine-year-old man through his own ordeal. Thayer's opinion of Medeiros—"without doubt, a crook, a thief, a robber, a liar, a rum-runner, a 'bouncer' in a house of ill-fame, a smuggler, and a man who has been convicted and sentenced to death"—telegraphed his decision, but determined to make his word stick, he attacked the confession point by point. Why did this "crook" not recall anything of South Braintree? How could this "thief" claim the money had been taken in a black bag? How could anyone trust a "liar" who said the black bag had not been opened in the Buick when sixty-two cents had been found in the front seat? Or a robber who claimed the gunmen had used .38s when everyone knew Berardelli had been killed by a .32 Colt? "Is it not asking altogether too much of human credulity to believe this story?" Thayer wondered.

Disbelieving Medeiros, Thayer found no reason to value the considerable case against the Morellis. Thompson had claimed "ten times the evidence" necessary to hold the Morellis for a grand jury, but judging by Medeiros's character alone, Thayer found the gang innocent. To overturn the verdict, he ruled, "would be a mockery upon truth and justice." But the judge did not stop with denial. His patience exhausted by incessant appeals, Thayer lamented "a new type of disease," one he called " 'lego-psychic neurosis' . . . a belief in the existence of something which in fact and truth has no such existence." As symptom, he cited Thompson's federal conspiracy. Where was the proof? The two ex-agents who thought Sacco and Vanzetti innocent had never attended the trial, never even reviewed the evidence, hence their opinions "were valueless and incompetent as evidence before any court in the world." Prejudiced affidavits, which "seem to be quite easily obtained nowadays," Thayer sneered, were not enough to overturn a verdict upheld by the Supreme Judicial Court. As to the suggestion that Katzmann and federal agents had "stooped so low [as] to convict two innocent men of murder by the concealment of evidence," Thayer only posed the question, holding its absurdity self-evident. After another recitation of the prosecution's evidence, the motion for a new trial was denied.

Three days later, Boston's simmering civil war over Sacco and Vanzetti erupted. Its Fort Sumter came in the conservative *Boston Herald*. On October 26, the *Herald* editorial page praised the pro-Republican comments of Henry Cabot Lodge Jr. and urged America to hold firm in the Philippines. Then came the editorial that would win the Pulitzer Prize. Headlined "We Submit," it began:

> In our opinion Nicola Sacco and Bartolomeo Vanzetti ought not to be executed on the warrant of the verdict returned by a jury on July 14, 1921. We do not know whether these men are guilty or not. We have no sympathy with the half-baked views which they profess. But as months have merged into years and the great debate over this case has continued our doubts have solidified slowly into convictions, and reluctantly we have found ourselves compelled to reverse our original judgment.

Claiming Judge Thayer's recent denial "carries the tone of the advocate rather than the arbitrator," the *Herald* reviewed the litany of doubt and called for a new trial.

For the next month, the *Herald*'s "Mail Bag" overflowed. Many lauded the paper's courage—"the best lesson on Americanism that any foreigner could receive"—but others urged the Commonwealth to uphold the rule of law. A prominent lawyer warned, "If what was done in this case is disregarded in order that Sacco may be restored to liberty . . . the lives and property of Massachusetts citizens are no longer safe." As letters poured in, rumors suggested other Boston papers would follow the *Herald*'s lead. None did. The letters had just begun to dwindle when the Worcester Bar Association gave Judge Thayer flowers and a plaque thanking him for his steadfast conduct. Heading into 1927, with Sacco-Vanzetti crowds marching in Paris and Berlin, with the Communist International in Moscow warning against execution, and American newspapers starting to question the case, Bostonians watched in dismay as "outsiders" circled the "Athens of America."

One more appeal was filed, but no one, not even Thompson, expected much to come of it. Only public outcry or a governor's mercy seemed likely to save Sacco and Vanzetti. "Auntie Bee" put her faith in the former. "The time of your crucifixion is drawing to a close," Mrs. Evans wrote Sacco. Showing the *Herald* to Dante, she assured him the day would soon come "when he would understand that his father was a great man who has suffered and suffered for his ideals." A tear rolled down the boy's cheek. Vanzetti found solace in endurance. "We are still alive," he wrote Luigia. "Life is a victory, thus we are victorious." But those hoping for clemency saw only ill omens. In December, Governor Fuller published an article entitled "Why I Believe in Capital Punishment." Then early in the new year, Boston watched another notorious murder case end with the throwing of a switch. Three young men had gunned down a night watchman in a car barn. All three were veterans, all repentant Irish Catholics. After six months of controversy, three mothers, backed by a petition of 120,000 names, appealed to the governor on bended knee. On January 6, 1927, the

Carbarn Bandits were electrocuted at Charlestown. The following morning, the prison generator was quiet, but at the mere mention of Sacco and Vanzetti, all of Boston crackled with electricity. And three men—Sacco in Dedham, Medeiros and Vanzetti in Charlestown—sat in their cells awaiting the lightning.

CHAPTER THIRTEEN

"Flowers to the Fallen Rebels"

I beseech you, in the bowels of Christ, think it possible you may be mistaken.

—Oliver Cromwell

Midway through an average life's journey but sensing the end of his own, Sacco awoke on a crystalline winter morning and took out his pen.

February 4, 1927   Dedham Jail

Dear Bartolo:

Here I am always in this narrow sad cell walking up and down, up and down while I were trying to give an idea to each one of the dear images that very often they cross my mind. . . . After all these long persecution years instead to open our prison door, the storm continues to pass upon our shoulder one more cruel than another. But there between these turbulent clouds, a luminous path run always toward the truth, and here under the blue radiant skies a little beloved sweet home in my eyes appear, while two lovely children seeking and calling their dear father. . . . This morning, just soon I were sitting I took my pen and I begin to write you these lines, with certain that you would be pleased to get it and to know that through all these long way cross road, I am still alive.

Though their names were now inseparable, Sacco and Vanzetti had not seen each other since 1923. Yet together they sensed the new year as a watermark. On January 1, Vanzetti had written to supporters, "We are convinced that our would-be murderers are determined to burn us within this year 1927, and that it is most probably that they will succeed." The momentum was plain, the appeals all but exhausted. Approaching its seventh year, the case had worn down lawyers, judges, the public, and the prisoners themselves. Still, as in some bloodied warrior clinging to life, there remained enough fury for a death struggle.

A week before Sacco wrote Vanzetti, William Thompson stood again before the Supreme Judicial Court. Appealing Judge Thayer's latest denial, Thompson detailed Mcdeiros's confession, denounced the federal conspiracy, and submitted photos of Sacco and Joe Morelli. "We do not claim these men are twins," Thompson told the five judges, "but we do claim they are strikingly similar." Fleshing out this scenario, he offered a brief comparing suspects of the Braintree murders.

	Medeiros-Morelli	Sacco and Vanzetti
Character of Accused	Typical gangsters and gunmen of the worst type	One of them an industrial workman with a family and a savings bank deposit, and no previous criminal record. The other a fish peddler never before his arrest accused of a crime. Both unpopular as pacifists and radicals.

	Medeiros-Morelli	Sacco and Vanzetti
Motive	Desperate need of funds for lawyer and bail before trial for serious Federal offense . . .	Robbery for private gain alleged. No claim or evidence that either defendant ever received or had any part of the stolen money.
Stolen Money	Medeiros' possession of $2,800 immediately thereafter (about his "split" of the total sum stolen)	None . . .

The chart also contrasted consciousness of guilt, ballistics, and six other categories. Moving on, Thompson accused Katzmann of "delivering the goods" to federal agents and Judge Thayer of prejudice and personal hostility. The judge, Thompson reminded the court, had accused him of "fraud in obtaining the affidavits" and of insanity "because I believed in the innocence of my clients." Then, steeling himself for one last appeal to reason, Thompson urged the high court to "wipe out the stain of the most outrageous transaction that has ever disgraced the courts of Massachusetts." After Dudley Ranney reviewed the prosecution's case—bullet, shell, cap, gun, lies—and the inconsistencies in Medeiros's confession, another agonizing wait began.

Back in his office, Thompson seemed upbeat. Puffing on his pipe, he told Herbert Ehrmann that a new trial should be awarded on any number of points. Ehrmann left the office in a buoyant mood, but when he slipped back in to get a bag, Thompson thought a partner from his firm had entered. Without looking up, he muttered, "There is no hope, Mr. Mears. There is no hope."

Shielded from Thompson's pessimism, inspired by the doggedness of the men and women working tirelessly to save them, Sacco and Vanzetti clung to a half-waking dream. "I don't expect much good, but it could be I'm wrong," Vanzetti wrote his sister. "It's certain that the cause seems to be going better now." Another winter in jail dragged by, each day a tedium of pacing, writing, reading, each week leading deeper into this decisive year. Then in March, the case blossomed when Felix Frankfurter leveled a *"J'accuse"* at the Commonwealth.

Frankfurter's *Atlantic Monthly* article, "The Case of Sacco and Vanzetti," was concise, detailed, and as sharp as a scalpel. Suddenly, Americans who had considered the affair too complex to merit their attention had a primer on Sacco and Vanzetti. Women basking on Miami beaches read from Katzmann's cross-examination of Sacco. Chicago businessmen weighed evidence against the Morelli gang. Denver bankers discussed Bullet III and pondered the words "consistent with." Manhattan lawyers read the Harvard professor's opinion of Thayer's recent denial—"a farrago of misquotations, misrepresentations, suppressions, and mutilations"—and his charge to the jury that "directs the emotions only too clearly." And readers everywhere learned that Red Scare zealotry had resulted in forty-four convictions since overturned for misconduct of judge or public prosecutor. Why not this one, Frankfurter implied.

The *Atlantic* article resonated from coast to coast. J. Edgar Hoover got a copy from his Boston bureau chief, who, noting its attacks on the Department of Justice, sent it on as "of considerable interest to you." U.S. Supreme Court chief justice William Howard Taft privately called the article "vicious propaganda" and blasted Frankfurter as "an expert in attempting to save murderous anarchists from the gallows or the electric chair." Frankfurter received congratulations from the old muckraker Ida Tarbell and future Supreme Court justice Benjamin Cardozo. When outraged alumni stiffed Harvard's annual fund, college president A. Lawrence Lowell claimed Frankfurter "stopped dead the Law School drive." Frankfurter responded, "This school does not exist for the collection of money. This school exists for the perpetuation of certain professional and ethical ideals." Reading the *Atlantic,* Sacco and Vanzetti celebrated. Sacco "enjoyed to see an competent lecture man to demolish all the frame-up," while Vanzetti told his sister

Frankfurter had "broken down much indifference and hostility."
Indifference had long since vanished; hostility was only in hiding.

The backlash was swift and personal. In Boston's fine restaurants, even Frankfurter's old friends turned away. Rumors soon
spread that the article had earned Frankfurter $50,000 and that
the professor worked for the defense committee (Frankfurter advised the committee but was never on its payroll). Judge Thayer
called Frankfurter "Professor Frankenstein." "Criticism of me in
the conservative circles in Boston," Frankfurter observed, "is com-
pounded of the fact that I am supposed to be a 'radical' . . . and
that it so happens I am not only an outsider in this community, but
also a Jew." When Frankfurter expanded the article into a slim
book, Boston bookstores faced a dilemma. *The Case of Sacco and
Vanzetti* was not banned in Boston—as were sixty-eight books
that year—but bookstores in the Hub kept the incendiary tome
behind the counter, available only by request. "How tenuous and
doubtful an instrument human reason is," Frankfurter often pos-
tured. In the coming months, he would learn how tenuous, how
doubtful.

In 1926, the state's high court had dawdled four months over its
denial, but 1927 demanded a speedier response. By the end of
March, Vanzetti was mocking the justices as "just-ices," saying
their cold refusal to render their decision "means that it is negative
and that they are just afraid and ashame to announce it." Sacco
was long past caring. Instead, like a condemned man a few steps
from the gallows, he found himself gazing intently at the miracle
of life all around him. Letter after letter mentioned "blue radiant
skies," "the spring come always more vivid," and "the tepid ray of
sunlight warming my heart." And it was on a vivid spring day,
with blue sky and tepid sunshine, that armed guards surrounded
courthouses and judges' homes, triggering news that spread, according to the *Boston Globe,* "like wildfire."

Again the door slammed shut. Again the justices were unanimous. Again, lacing their decision with the word "discretion,"

they found not a single legal error. Medeiros's confession, they ruled, "would not be admissible upon a trial of the defendants." All affidavits citing Medeiros's boasts of the Braintree crime were dismissed as "pure hearsay." Evidence against the Morellis "fell short of furnishing adequate proof of their guilt." The justices did not rule on other evidence, because "it is not for us to determine what is to be believed." The only question was, "Could the judge conscientiously, intelligently and honestly have reached the result he has reached?" The answer was implicit. As an exclamation point, the oldest appellate court in the Western Hemisphere added a statement that read like the trial scene in *Alice in Wonderland*: "It is not imperative that a new trial be granted even though the evidence is newly discovered, and, if presented to a jury, would justify a different verdict." As precedent for this startling opinion, the court cited a civil case, applying it freely to the capital murder trial.

In March, Dudley Ranney had promised Thompson he would wait a week between a denial and sentencing. Now Ranney broke his promise. The denial came on April 5. Four days later, Vanzetti was awakened before dawn. He enjoyed his favorite breakfast—hot dogs and potatoes—then donned a black overcoat and gray cap and walked with a guard to the prison rotunda, where he waited, smoking his pipe while sunrise gilded the brick smokestacks of Charlestown. An hour later, he arrived at the jail in Dedham. He and Sacco kissed each other on both cheeks. Police were surprised to see them calm, smiling, utterly at peace.

While the men waited, an unusual number of cars passed through downtown Dedham. Slowing alongside the courthouse, drivers gazed at the throng gathering on the steps. Once spectators were admitted—by ticket only—several hundred mingled outside. This time there would be no march of handcuffed prisoners through tranquil streets. At 9:50 a.m., a black, snub-nosed bus pulled up at the courthouse. Three policemen with rifles and several grim men in overcoats spilled out of it. Then, stepping onto the overflowing sidewalk came the two world-famous convicts, handcuffed to a deputy. In their natty coats and ties, Sacco and

Vanzetti seemed headed for a wedding, not a death sentence. Hustled toward the courtroom, they might have passed the crowd in a blur, but someone asked them to halt. Sacco inched closer to Vanzetti and muttered something. Then, while shutters clicked and newsreel cameras cranked, both obligingly took off their caps. They looked so much older, their balding foreheads prominent, their weariness as palpable as their wonder at all the attention. Vanzetti beamed while Sacco looked gently bemused in the midst of the crowd, in the center of the whirlwind. Finally, led by police, who were all over the courthouse inside and out, the men climbed the steps. When they passed between the pillars, girls stood on each other's shoulders to peer in windows while boys in floppy caps called out, "Hey, Sacco!" and "You shall be hanged by the neck!"

Entering the courtroom, Sacco and Vanzetti nodded to friends. Rosina, overcome with grief, remained at home, but Mrs. Evans dropped her frown and threw out her arms to greet her surrogate sons. Moments later as a clock struck ten, Judge Thayer, in dark coat and derby, hurried up the courthouse steps. The cry of "Hear ye, hear ye" rang out. The judge took his place.

The prosecution had waited nearly six years. As if it could not wait another minute, District Attorney Wilbar recommended execution "sometime during the week beginning Sunday, July 10 next." A clerk then asked, "Nicola Sacco, have you anything to say why sentence of death should not be passed upon you?" Sacco rose.

As he began to speak, the slow, steady tapping of his foot could be heard throughout the courtroom. Sacco apologized for his English, saying, "my comrade Vanzetti will speak more long." Then he aimed his words at the judge and fired: "I never know, never heard, even read in history anything so cruel as this court. After seven years prosecuting they still consider us guilty. And these gentle people here are arrayed with us in this court today. I know the sentence will be between two class, the oppressed class and the rich class, and there will be always collision between one and the other. We fraternize the people with the books, with the literature. You persecute the people, tyrannize over them and kill them. . . . That is why I am here today on this bench, for having been the oppressed class. Well, you are the oppressor. You know it, Judge Thayer—you know all my life, you know why I have been here, and after seven years that you have been persecuting me and my poor wife, and you still today sentence us to death!" Calming himself, his foot still tapping, Sacco sighed. "I would like to tell all my life," he said, "but what is the use?" He spoke for another minute, praising Vanzetti—"the kind man to all the children"—and thanking his supporters. "Judge Thayer know all my life," he concluded, "and he know that I am never been guilty, never—not yesterday nor today nor forever."

"Bartolomeo Vanzetti. Have you anything to say . . ."

Vanzetti got to his feet. How many long nights had he tossed and turned, imagining this scene? Arrested after writing a speech that might have drawn fifty people, he now stood before a gallery of hundreds with reporters ready to send his words around the world. Yet he had not written a speech, merely some notes scribbled in pencil on the back of an old letter.

1. *Innocente delle due accuse*
2. *Mai rubato o sparso sangue*
3. *Astenuto del furto e l'omicidio legalizzati e santificati. . . .*

Gripping his notes, Vanzetti began. "I am not only innocent of these two crimes, but in all my life I have never stole and I have never killed and I have never spilled blood. . . . Everybody that knows these two arms knows very well that I did not need to go in between the street and kill a man to take the money. I can live with my two arms and live well." While onlookers fought back tears, Vanzetti reined in his rage and stared straight at Judge Thayer. He noted how the case had aroused "the flower of mankind of Europe . . . the greatest scientists, the greatest statesmen of Europe have pleaded in our favor." Was it possible, he asked, that the jury could be "right against what the world, the whole world has say it is wrong? . . . You see it is seven years that we are in jail. What we have suffered during these seven years no human tongue can say, and yet you see me before you, not trembling. You see me looking you in your eyes straight, not blushing, not changing color, not ashamed or in fear."

Vanzetti recounted the Bridgewater trial, how his lawyer "sold me for thirty golden money like Judas sold Jesus Christ." He recalled the Red Scare, the hatred of "people of our principles," then accused Katzmann and Thayer of doing everything in their power "to agitate still more the passion of the juror, the prejudice of the juror against us." Turning to the trial, he picked apart Katzmann's role—his telling the jury that Coacci had taken the stolen money to Italy and brokering the agreement to strike all record of Vanzetti's good reputation in Plymouth. Barely controlling his fury, Vanzetti called such tactics "plain murder" and "a frame-up with which he has split my life and doomed me."

Glancing at his notes, sometimes slapping them against the railing, Vanzetti spoke for forty-two minutes. He lamented hiring a lawyer "from California . . . ostracized by you and by every authority." He blasted Judge Thayer—"we have proved that there could not have been another judge on the face of the earth more prejudiced and more cruel." As the stocky, mustachioed man spoke from the cage, the judge stared into space or studied his bench, but the gallery remained riveted. "This is what I say," Vanzetti concluded. "I would not wish to a dog or to a snake . . . what I have had to suffer for things that I am not guilty of. But my conviction is that I have suffered for things that I am guilty of. I am suffering because I am a radical, and indeed I am a radical; I have suffered because I was an Italian, and indeed I am an Italian. I have suffered more for my family and my beloved than for myself, but I am so convinced to be right that if you could execute me two times, and if I could be reborn two other times, I would live again to do what I have done already. I have finished. Thank you."

In the silence, Vanzetti turned to see women with brimming eyes and men fighting back every feeling. The hushed anticipation lasted only seconds before Judge Thayer spoke. As if to the ticking of the clock above him, he read the sentence: ". . . verdicts of the jury should stand . . . not a matter of discretion . . . a matter of statutory requirement . . . first the court pronounces sentence upon Nicola Sacco . . . ordered by the court that you, Nicola Sacco, suffer the punishment of death by the passage of a current of electricity through your body . . ." When the judge turned to Vanzetti, the condemned man stood and asked to speak with his lawyer.

"I do not know what he wants to say," Thompson announced.

"I think I should pronounce the sentence," Thayer continued. "Bartolomeo Vanzetti, suffer the punishment of death—"

Sacco could stand no more. Pointing at the judge, he shouted, "You know that I am innocent! That is the same words I pronounced seven years ago! You condemn two innocent men!"

"—by the passage of a current of electricity through your body within the week beginning on Sunday, the tenth day of July . . ."

By 11:00 a.m., it was all over. With the final gavel, friends gathered around the men. Lawyers congratulated Vanzetti on the speech he felt was a failure because he had forgotten his eulogy to Sacco. Mrs. Evans called out, "There's lots to hope for yet!" As he was led away, Vanzetti spotted Mary Donovan, her face streaked with tears. "Do not cry, Mary," he said. "Keep a brave front." Then the men were rushed down the steps to the waiting bus, driven along the common, past the graveyard, back to the jail. Judge Thayer sat in his chambers asking reporters to be fair to him, saying he had "done my duty as God gave me the power to see it." Outside, the streets were quiet. Cars passed without slowing, and the tepid spring sun did its best to warm the peaceful little town of Dedham.

The death sentence reverberated around the world "like the shot fired at Concord Bridge" (the *Nation*). All that spring, the world's scorn mounted. From Germany: "Sheer madness . . . an act of sadism." From Sweden: "A deep offense of the general sense of justice. . . ." From the Netherlands: "In the gracious name of Jesus Christ we beseech you. . . ." From twenty members of the British

Parliament: "We view with horror the violation of justice. . . ." Judge Thayer and Massachusetts were also vilified in France, Italy, Argentina, Uruguay, Paraguay, Ireland, Canada, Switzerland, and New Zealand. Albert Einstein signed a protest sent to President Coolidge. George Bernard Shaw said the case certainly looked like "a frame-up." H. G. Wells called Katzmann "tricky and evil," and Judge Thayer "extremely obtuse mentally and morally." A variety of protests broke out. In Los Angeles, the police department's "Red squad" broke up an "auto parade" of motorists holding Sacco-Vanzetti banners. Marchers were routed in London, Brussels, and Stockholm. From Australia came threats of a boycott of American goods. Communists in Moscow denounced "the new crime of the American bourgeoisie."

Eminent Americans quickly added their voices. Jane Addams called the sentence "inevitable when an individual is judged not by his own acts but upon his group and racial affiliations." Upton Sinclair wrote Governor Fuller, "When you execute these two Italian workingmen you will execute also the legal system of your State." Sacco-Vanzetti committees sprang up across America. In the North End, Felicani's committee resolved to raise the loudest outcry the world had ever heard. They *had* to be saved. If there was any justice left on earth . . . If enough people could be alerted . . . If every outrage was exposed . . . The committee was soon swamped with contributions. A Brooklyn man sent ten dollars, wishing he could send a million. Even if Sacco and Vanzetti were "murdered on July 10th," the man wrote, "their names are now immortal, foremost heroes in the great fight constantly waged with the forces of evil." Such letters were passed around the office where Mary Donovan and new volunteers frantically sent telegrams, fielded phone calls, and mailed ten thousand copies of John Dos Passos's pamphlet *Facing the Chair*. Calls arose for a national Sacco-Vanzetti conference, but the committee opted for a petition drive to gather a million signatures. "You cannot imagine the strength of the movement gathering in your behalf," Mrs. Evans wrote Vanzetti. "From every side it comes."

By mid-April, newspapers across America were weighing in:

> If they had been Smith and Brown, Democrats and Republicans and supporters of the war, the jury would have taken two minutes to acquit them.
>
> —*Duluth* (Minnesota) *Herald*

> This rotten business in Massachusetts about Sacco and Vanzetti is now too old by far for temporizing. . . . Why should any of us consent now to be polite about Judge Webster Thayer and the dirty work in Dedham.
>
> —*Macon* (Georgia) *Telegraph*

Further reproof came from the *New York World*, the *Brooklyn Eagle*, the *St. Louis Post-Dispatch*, and the *Baltimore Sun*. Only the most conservative papers sided with the Commonwealth. In Massachusetts, however, newspapers bristled with umbrage.

> Sacco and Vanzetti have been denied nothing that anyone could have in such a cause . . . and the case against them has withstood every attack of any kind.
>
> —*Springfield Union*

> The degree of deliberation in the treatment of this case has been almost unexampled. The defendants have had every possible chance. . . . The end of the road has been reached.
>
> —*Boston Transcript*

A week after the sentencing, eight thousand people packed Manhattan's Union Square. Above a swarm of hats and heads, speakers stood at podiums draped with Stars and Stripes. Cheering Sacco and Vanzetti, booing Calvin Coolidge, workers roared in agreement to walk off their jobs on June 5. Overseas, the tide of

outrage surged again. General strikes shut down Buenos Aires and
Asunción. In Berlin, in Rome, in Paris, American tourists overheard "Sacco and Vanzetti" among foreign chatter. Across open
plazas, along columns of marchers, the familiar names bobbed on
placards in a Babel of languages: *Sacco y Vanzetti*, САККО
ИВАНЦЕТТИ, *Heraus mit Sacco und Vanzetti, Sauver deux In-
nocentes Sacco & Vanzetti.*

When the initial shock subsided, all attention turned to Governor Fuller. Debate swirled about what he might do, but Alvan T.
Fuller was a hard man to read. The quintessential self-made man,
Fuller had dropped out of school at sixteen, worked in a shoe factory, raced and sold bicycles, then started one of the first car dealer-
ships in Massachusetts. After amassing a fortune selling Packards,
Fuller followed his idol, Teddy Roosevelt, into politics. Congressman Fuller was a moderate Republican except during the Red
Scare, when he advocated "the execution of the whole red scum
brood of anarchists, Bolsheviks, IWWs, and revolutionaries." Re-
lentlessly upbeat and impishly independent, he enjoyed standing up
to party bosses. He served as lieutenant governor, then was elected
governor in 1924. Said to be worth $40 million, Fuller lived in a
Beacon Hill mansion packed with fine art, including many Gains-
boroughs. The ex–car dealer with the broad forehead and quick
smile saw himself as a businessman in the State House. From his
first day in Congress to his last as governor, he returned every pay-
check he earned as a politician. Such autonomy brought the forty-
nine-year-old Fuller a bipartisan popularity and made many wonder
whether he might just free Sacco and Vanzetti.

Mrs. Evans and the other surrogate mothers assured the convicted men that Fuller would give their case impartial consideration. Vanzetti thought otherwise. The governor, he wrote his
sister, "is an ass overloaded with gold and vanity." When Vanzetti
heard that Fuller hoped to follow Coolidge to the White House, he
added, "To be choised to such candidature, one must prove himself a hanger to the appointing and overulling American Plutocracy." Hadn't Fuller electrocuted the Carbarn Bandits just so he
could do the same to him and Sacco? "To expect that Fuller will

stand against the judiciary, the middle class, the big money of Massachusetts in behalf of two damned dagos and anarchists seems absurd to me," he warned Mrs. Evans.

Beyond prison walls, few were so cynical. The day after the sentencing, letters began pouring into the State House. Six secretaries were hired to handle the influx. Letters from Bishop William Lawrence and other respected Bostonians suggested an independent commission study the case. Echoing this call came letters from clergy, social workers, and faculties at Harvard, Yale, Johns Hopkins, Wellesley, Princeton, Columbia, and the University of California. Pleas for clemency came from the American Negro Labor Congress, the Ladies' Auxiliary of the Workmen's Circle in St. Louis, the Christian Social Justice Fund in Baltimore, and dozens more organizations. But with each call for mercy, the governor received another letter urging him to "stand firm." "Calvin Coolidge stands for law and order and will be remembered by that expression," one man wrote. "Let your name ring through the land as the savior of justice for all." A woman added, "We taxpayers wonder for what purpose are laws if not to be upheld amid pressure and foolish sentiment or gush."

Furious and indignant, earnest and prayerful, the seventeen thousand letters sent to the governor suggested that the men who straddled two nations had each acquired dual profiles. Beyond lambs and wolves, Sacco and Vanzetti were becoming the symbols Americans needed to make sense of a dizzying decade.

The 1920s were the boldest of times, if not the best. Since 1919, the chaotic country frightened of its own shadows had blossomed into a brash, confident nation. The self-assurance peaked in 1927 when suddenly it seemed Americans could do anything. During this annus mirabilis, a handsome Minnesotan would throw five sandwiches and a jug of water into his tiny plane and fly from Long Island to Paris. A New Yorker in blackface would croon "Mammy" in the first talking motion picture. A big, beefy man from Baltimore would hit sixty home runs, more than any other team in the American League. And ordinary Americans would drink and carouse, invest and spend as if the good times would never end. "We were the most powerful nation," F. Scott Fitzgerald recalled. "Who could tell us any longer what was fashionable and what was fun?" But what about justice? Would people who spoke of "liberty and justice for all" ignore every doubt, squelch every suspicion of a frame-up in Massachusetts? Would America really kill Sacco and Vanzetti? To millions around the world, such "sheer madness" did not seem possible.

From beyond its borders, America looked like a single country, but in 1927, as John Dos Passos would write, it was "two nations." "Coolidge Prosperity" had filled homes with radios and refrigerators, a toilet *inside* the house and a car out front. Prosperity, however, had bypassed "Main Street" and much of Massachusetts. Since 1919, textile and shoe firms had been fleeing the Commonwealth in search of nonunion labor down South. The result, in a boom decade, was a loss of 154,000 jobs and a deepening distrust of modern times. In Massachusetts, as in rural America where farmers struggled, the "Jazz Age" seemed a curse. With its "short-haired women and long haired men," its crime waves and corruption, modernity seemed to be running amok. For the first time, more Americans lived in big cities than in small towns, creating a cultural standoff between the urban and the rural. In cities, smug socialites discussed Freud and talked frankly about sex. In small towns, people discussed the newest A&P and never mentioned "you know what." Urbanites bought stock in RCA and reached out to the future. "Ma and Pa" kept their money in savings and loans and remained rooted in the past. As the most confidently American year in the whole American century unfolded, Sacco and Vanzetti came to symbolize this schism. Opinions on their guilt or innocence soon separated sophisticate from "rube," liberal from conservative, and those who feared authority from those who implicitly trusted cops, judges, and juries.

To their own detriment, they had ceased to be mere men. Supporters, marveling at their quiet dignity, sanctified them. *New York World* columnist Heywood Broun called Vanzetti a "Jeffer-

sonian Democrat, even if he dies in the shadow of Bunker Hill."
Sacco and Vanzetti, noted a flyer passed out in Union Square,
"represent the highest aspirations of mankind." Felix Frankfurter's
wife, Marion, saw in them "a sense of beauty of spirit that abides
above the bitterness and ignorance and confusion that gives us so
much pain." To the dreamer, the skeptic, the die-hard Progressive,
the pending execution of these saintly innocents was proof that
something had gone terribly wrong with the American dream. But
to the businessman, the banker, the small-town "Babbitt," Sacco
and Vanzetti personified all things anti-American, and as their
notoriety spread, total strangers came to loathe them.

To some, the men stood for immigrant rabble. After decades of
rising xenophobia, Congress had slashed immigration quotas in
1924, drying up the foreign tide as if turning off a faucet, but here
were these two "Wops" still harping on their innocence. To finish
off "the immigrant problem," the American Legion and Ku Klux
Klan urged Governor Fuller to send the men straight to "the chair."
To those frightened by the Red Scare, Sacco and Vanzetti suggested a resurgence of the radicals long since silenced, jailed, or
deported. All efforts on their behalf, the Sons of the American
Revolution warned Fuller, were "part of a definite, well-organized
program by Communists and Anarchists to weaken the fundamental institutions of our form of government and pave the way
for world revolution." Finally, to those frightened by the relentless
crime wave that in 1927 gave Al Capone America's biggest income,
the swift execution of Sacco and Vanzetti symbolized a crackdown
long overdue. "Both are cold-blooded murderers and should have
been hung years ago," an Ohio doctor wrote.

To "Cold Roast Boston," Sacco and Vanzetti were more than
symbols; they were the line between the venerated Victorian age
and the chaotic twentieth century. If a Massachusetts judge and
jury could be overruled by a worldwide radical uprising for "these
two murderers," then the old Commonwealth and all its institutions would be fair game for modern mayhem. "No two lives," one
lawyer told a civic club, "are of greater import than the stability of
our courts." In the prideful state there were few dissenters, very

few. Writing to Governor Fuller, twenty-six distinguished New Englanders, including a Cabot, the head of the Boston Women's City Club, and several Harvard professors, asked probing questions. Had any judge other than Thayer weighed the fairness of the case? How could just one bullet be traced to Sacco's gun? Where was the stolen money? Why hadn't the men fled the area? But the vast majority in Massachusetts—from old Yankee farmers to First Families—just wanted an end to this endless case. Touring New England, the populist editor William Allen White sensed only "bitterness and hate" toward the demonized men. Before visiting Massachusetts, White wrote Fuller, "I had no idea that one could let their passions so completely sweep their judgment into fears and hatreds, so deeply confuse their sanity. I now know why the witches were persecuted and hanged by upright and godly people."

Within a week of the sentencing, bizarre scenes on opposite ends of the Commonwealth revealed an urgent desire to silence all doubts. On April 15, the seventh anniversary of the murders, Henry James's nephew headed to South Braintree. The eccentric Edward Holton James, mocked in the Boston press as "the millionaire pacifist," arrived on Pearl Street in midafternoon. Hundreds gazed out factory windows watching police follow him and a friend as they took measurements from witnesses' windows to the precise spots on the gravel where Parmenter and Berardelli had fallen. After being denied access to Mary Splaine's window, James left. Returning a few days later, he was given fifteen minutes to leave town. When he refused, he was arrested.

On April 19, professors in Northampton planned an evening meeting on the case. Because President Coolidge had once been its mayor, the charming college town eighty miles west of Boston was itself a symbol. Its prominent citizens were not about to see a call for clemency come from their midst. At 7:00 p.m., Smith College students filled the high school auditorium, while hundreds of townspeople lined the back wall or waited outside. Following a review replete with scathing denunciations of Judge Thayer, professors read a resolution urging clemency. Just before the vote, a former DA spoke up from the back. Any show of hands would be unfair, he shouted, because locals had been kept outside while outsiders filled the seats. The hall erupted, with college "girls" booing and hissing while townspeople shouted back. The near riot ended when the 10:00 p.m. curfew called students to their dorms. Locals rushed into the vacated seats and voted down the resolution.

Accustomed to seeing its name venerated and its judgment revered, the old Commonwealth bristled at the rising chorus of critics. Massachusetts had taught the world lessons about freedom; how dare anyone question its fairness. Every attack on the Commonwealth led Proper Boston to a deeper entrenchment and determination to uphold the law. In the state legislature, a bill asking Governor Fuller to appoint a review commission was defeated 146 to 6. Private clubs in Boston banned all discussion of Sacco and Vanzetti. A Brockton high school teacher refused to let her students debate the case. And in a statement that echoed from Cape Cod to the Berkshires, a banquet speaker in Boston told the disparaging world, "We would respectfully ask you to mind your own business!" The audience leapt to its feet, cheering.

By late April, Boston's most conservative newspaper led the resistance. Too respectful of Puritan blue laws to publish on Sundays, too proper to print any word referring to the human body, the *Boston Transcript* had been a Back Bay institution since the heyday of John Quincy Adams. Even as other papers added photos, crosswords, and other features, the *Transcript* remained a gray ledger sheet filled with legalistic articles, puritanical editorials, and obituaries that were must reading among Boston Brahmins long said to have "grandfather on the brain." Back in the nineteenth century, the *Transcript* had branded Boston native Edgar Allan Poe "snobbish and dirty," while dismissing Emerson in a huff: "Original thinkers are not always practical men." Now the paper brought its rectitude to bear upon this new threat.

Not content with editorials, on April 25 the *Transcript* ran a front-page attack on Felix Frankfurter. Far from the pressure cooker of Boston, Dean John Wigmore of Northwestern University had read the *Atlantic* article. Wigmore, a widely known legal expert, told dinner companions, "Sacco and Vanzetti are dangerous to society. I am sure the facts are not as Frankfurter says they are. I will write Judge Thayer and find out what the facts really are."

As Wigmore defined them in the *Transcript,* the facts were: (1) a certain "plausible pundit," whom Wigmore coyly avoided naming, had committed "a gross libel" on the honor of Massachusetts; (2) contrary to the pundit's assertion, the jury had not been "specially selected" but was properly screened and empaneled without protest; (3) the "plausible pundit" had not mentioned Sacco's cap that "appeared to fit him"; (4) at the close of the "unfair trial," J. J. McAnarney had stated that Sacco and Vanzetti "have had every opportunity here; they have had every patience and every consideration;" and (5) all the "palaver" about radicalism was "a cruel and libelous falsity," while the idea of a government conspiracy was "ridiculous." Wigmore then detailed the bombings and strikes overseas, calling the two anarchists "valued members of a powerful international fraternity" that had perpetrated "the most extensive system of international terrorism that the world has known for a century past." Was it not "an intolerable state of things that American justice should be subject to the dictates of international terrorists?" The "plausible pundit," Wigmore concluded, could be disbarred for filing a brief as inaccurate as his article, while "the heroic judge" deserved praise.

Boston newspaper circulation was hitting record highs. While congratulations rained down on the *Transcript,* Frankfurter's terse rebuttal in the next day's *Herald* was read throughout the city. The respected dean, replied the "plausible pundit," had studied neither the trial record nor the *Atlantic* article. In fact, the defense *had* objected to the jury selection. In fact, Frankfurter's book *had* discussed the ill-fitting cap in detail. And when J. J. McAnarney called the trial fair—a customary legal nicety—he had not known of concealed witnesses, Captain Proctor's opinion hidden by a "calculated ambiguity," and other irregularities. In arguments breaking out all over Boston, Frankfurter's points were championed by one side, Wigmore's by the other, ratcheting the bitterness to yet a higher level.

Early in May, Governor Fuller began his own investigation. The Commonwealth followed his every move. Would Fuller side with the "sob sisters, pacifists and Reds"? Would he appoint a commission? Or would he stand for law and order? On May 12, the humorist Will Rogers visited the governor, finding him in his high-ceilinged office beneath portraits of Samuel Adams and John Hancock, studying the trial transcript. "I don't know what he is going to decide, of course," Rogers told a crowd at the Boston Opera House that night, "but I do know that he isn't going to be 'skeered' into decidin' it." Yet in his syndicated column, Rogers wrote, "It should not take a nation or a State seven years to decide whether anyone committed a crime." The humorist was glad Sacco and Vanzetti had been young when arrested, "otherwise they wouldn't live long enough for justice to make up its mind."

With his clients under relentless attack, Thompson finally went public with revelations about Judge Thayer. Now Boston learned of Robert Benchley's allegation—that Thayer had called Sacco and Vanzetti "Bolsheviki" and said he "would get them good and proper!" Benchley's claim was refuted by the judge's old friend, shocked to see private comments at the Worcester Golf Club made public. Yet no one questioned attorney George Crocker's account of Thayer's tirade at the University Club, nor two reporters' charges that Thayer, during the trial, had assured them the men's guilt would become obvious. Such transparent bias, coupled with Thayer's now public "anarchistic bastards" comment, had Sacco-Vanzetti supporters gloating. Imagine the wrinkled old judge presenting a pretty young reporter with his autographed picture! Could anyone still claim the trial had been fair? Glee was cut short by newspaper headlines:

EXTRA! EXTRA! BOMB ATTEMPT ON FULLER'S LIFE FAILS!

On May 10, a package containing a pound of dynamite was plucked from bags of mail addressed to the State House. An attached note read:

> Mr. Governor of Massachusetts:
>   I have succeeded in getting one fourth of a ton of this. If Sacco and Vanzetti are going to be murder, I am going to get more and use it.
>   —A Citizen of the World.

With another Frankfurter-Wigmore exchange and scorching letters to editors dissecting every last detail, many were relieved to have Charles Lindbergh's stunning transatlantic flight knock Sacco and Vanzetti off the front pages. Lindbergh even promised to come to Boston in late July. By then, most people figured, Sacco and Vanzetti would be dead. By then, "normalcy" would be restored.

The only people in Massachusetts not consumed by the case were the men themselves. Journalists visiting Sacco and Vanzetti found them trading quips and comments. Two months from the electric chair, they seemed content to imagine themselves the latest martyrs in the anarchist pantheon. Vanzetti summed up their spirit in an interview with the *New York World*. The reporter later admitted he had taken hasty notes and possibly enhanced them. Vanzetti would not have called Sacco "the good shoemaker." But with slight embellishment, the "poor fish peddler's" impromptu soliloquy became immortal:

> If it had not been for these thing, I might have live out of my life, talking at street corners to scorning men. I might have die, unmarked, unknown, a failure. Now we are not a failure. This is our career and our triumph. Never in our full life can we hope to do such work for tolerance, for justice, for man's understanding of man as we now do by dying. Our words, our lives, our pains— nothing! The taking of our lives—lives of a good shoe-

maker and a poor fish peddler—all! That last moment belongs to us—that agony is our triumph!

Adding to their ennobled purpose, the men were enjoying each other's company. Following the sentencing, Vanzetti had remained in a cell beside Sacco's. Each afternoon they spent an hour in the yard. One day, a guard overheard them arguing about who had the better voice until Vanzetti threw his head back and crooned, "Let me call you sweetheart, I'm in love with youuuu!" Friends sent them a bocce set, and each day the men lofted the shiny spheres until sweat darkened their striped uniforms. They feasted on home-made tagliatelle brought by local Italian women. Their cells bloomed with flowers—tulips, pink carnations on a bare table, yellow blossoms brushing against gray granite walls. "My window . . . is a riot of blissing colors and beauties forms," Vanzetti wrote his unrequited lover Virginia MacMechan, inviting her to send him "the whitest flowers of your soul and the reddest flowers of your heart within the folds of letters." One afternoon when another bouquet arrived, Vanzetti overheard Sacco say, "Date fiori ai rebeldi caduti." Both men knew the phrase from an old anarchist hymn.

> *Date fiori ai ribeldi caduti*
> *collo sguardo rivolto all'aurora*

> Give flowers to the fallen rebels
> with a glance turned toward the dawn.

But no matter how much they romanticized martyrdom, beneath their calm lurked a mounting terror and the burning lust for revenge. "Death for death," Vanzetti wrote. "I think that the times require to bring with us some enemies, some blackguards—I should say the more that is possible." Vanzetti was also furious with Sacco, who still refused to do anything in his own behalf. After Vanzetti labored over a fourteen-page letter to Governor Fuller, painstakingly reviewing each doubt, explaining anarchism, citing Jefferson, Lincoln, Kropotkin, and finally asking for clemency, Sacco would not sign it. Nor would Sacco heed his surrogate mothers. "Mrs. Ehrmann, dear, I am innocent," he told his lawyer's wife. "I cannot, even for the sake of my family, say that I am guilty. I cannot beg for mercy."

On a Saturday evening during Memorial Day weekend, Vanzetti was eating an apple when Thompson strode up to his cell. "Vanzetti," the lawyer announced, "I've come to tell you that the governor has finally decided to appoint an investigative commission. Professor Lowell, head of Harvard University, is one of the members. And there will be a public hearing. Then the governor and the commission will come here to speak with you!" Vanzetti handed Thompson a cigar, then fished out an anarchist pamphlet to give Fuller in case "some enemy has given the governor a false definition of anarchism." The next morning, he passed on the good news: "Courage, dear Luigina. If they can't kill us, neither will they be able to keep us locked away forever, you'll see."

Formally announced on June 2, news of the governor's commission promised to prolong the tension. Because two of three appointees had to close out the academic year, no investigation could begin until late June. A July 10 execution would have to be postponed. Or would it? With less than a month left, Sacco and Vanzetti rode a roller coaster of expectation and despair. "Is this double investigation going to be another mockery?" Vanzetti asked Mrs. Evans. "Spitting on our faces? Sponge of vinager and bitterness on the top of a lance?" Yet on better days, when the sun tanned him during a bocce game, when still more flowers arrived, "the poor fish peddler" could almost see himself outside the walls. During frequent conferences with the men, Gardner Jackson noted their contrasts. Sacco, Jackson remembered, "never thought anything would work. He was always convinced that he was a goner." Vanzetti never stopped studying the possibilities. "It was as if he was outside of himself, looking at himself and the circumstances, conferring with us about himself and those circumstances while he wasn't in himself. It was very impressive."

As summer approached, the death throes of the case kept Boston on an uneasy watch. Governor Fuller, laboring fourteen-hour days, was interviewing the trial's principles—J. J. McAnarney,

Michael Levangie, five jurors one day, two more the next. Leaving the governor's office, each met a pack of reporters. Each refused comment, spawning gossip about what secrets might have been revealed. The defense committee sent telegrams to Los Angeles calling Fred Moore back to Boston, but Moore had disappeared again. Thompson and Ehrmann wrote long letters to Fuller explaining every point of contention. Fuller interviewed Thompson, Judge Thayer, and Lola Andrews's son. Overwhelmed by details, the governor surprised the *Herald*'s editor during the Boston University commencement, saying he found his position "abhorrent" and that, to his surprise, "the prosecution testimony was breaking down." Learning of the conversation, former Boston mayor John "Honey Fitz" Fitzgerald, grandfather of John F. Kennedy, phoned the *Herald* to get inside word. When Fitzgerald said he expected the sentence to be commuted, the editor did not disagree. Elsewhere, others were choosing sides.

The Harvard Law School faculty and student body were solidly behind a new trial, as were a former state attorney general and the prominent retailer Edward Filene. But far more agreed with the Kiwanis Club of Lawrence. Members in the textile city cheered a state official's speech, "Sacco-Vanzetti and the Red Peril," which linked the men to the nationwide conspiracy by "Reds, Socialists, Pacifists, and their college professor allies . . . having for their purpose the destruction of our government by force, the tearing down of religion, the weakening of our Army, Navy and other defenses, the destruction of the home, the Boy Scouts, and all the institutions that Americans hold dear."

On June 22, Mary Donovan and Gardner Jackson trudged up the State House steps hefting two thick paper rolls. On them were 474,842 signatures calling for a pardon. The signatures had come not just from big cities but from Evansville, Indiana; Piney Fork, Ohio; and Yerrington, Nevada. Some supporters apologized for not being able to do their part. A Sheldon, Iowa, man wrote, "I'm doing the best I can to overcome the prejudices of a community to whom 'them Eye-talians are a lot of bomb-throwers and cut-throats in general.' But it is hard, slow work." An elderly Fort Lauderdale woman had walked on crutches to the nearest gas station. Meeting men hanging around the pumps, she read portions of *Facing the Chair* and asked for contributions. But the men compared Sacco and Vanzetti to Italian mobsters in Chicago and said their huge defense fund proved them guilty. She sent back no signatures. "Pardon me, I feel as if I have not been able to do my duty to two human beings," she wrote the defense committee. "I include a dollar. I cannot do more."

By the final week of June, a stay of execution seemed inevitable. A reprieve promised more than additional time; it would let Sacco and Vanzetti remain in Dedham instead of enduring the dog days of July in Charlestown Prison, where even guards were known to faint from the heat. Rosina worried that a transfer would cause her husband to relapse into insanity. The remaining days dwindled— to thirteen, twelve, eleven. Finally, on June 29, Governor Fuller postponed the execution until August 10. To Sacco, the reprieve meant only "thirty-one more day living death." Vanzetti, however, welcomed the chance to remain where "we have at least some air, light, a slice of land and of sky to contemplate." His relief was not allowed to linger.

On June 30, Vanzetti stayed up after lights-out reading an American history text by moonlight. Two hours after he retired, he and Sacco were jolted awake, shackled together, and driven through the night to Charlestown. Bleary-eyed, terrified, livid, they were led through the gates of the prison Sacco knew solely from Vanzetti's horror stories. While being admitted, Sacco explained his reason for coming to America. "Some friends were here and on account of the free and comfortable life here as told by them." Then he and Vanzetti were led to the prison's Cherry Hill wing, segregated from the regular block. Each was given a windowless cell, still warm and threatening to become an oven. Vanzetti found the midnight transfer "the most dreadful of all the dreadful experiences of my dreadful ordeal."

The following day, members of the governor's commission were spotted leaving the State House carrying copies of the trial transcript. On July 2, the three men were driven to South Braintree.

There they spoke with factory workers, stood by the water tower where Parmenter and Berardelli fell, and looked down Pearl Street to imagine the Buick's getaway. They made no comments to reporters; they did not have to. Everyone watching now—and that was everyone—knew there would be no more homemade meals, no more singing contests, no more bocce in the sun. Everyone knew that these eminent men and a matter of weeks were all that stood between the fallen rebels and the flowers at their funerals.

CHAPTER FOURTEEN

"The Judgment of Mankind"

All right you have won you will kill the brave men our friends tonight . . . all right we are two nations.

—John Dos Passos

The summer of 1927 was a season of peace. Aside from small uprisings by Chinese Communists and Nicaraguan guerrillas, for the first time in modern memory not a single war was under way anywhere on earth. With battlefields silent, humanity poured its passions into a bitter fight for the lives of two men. The struggle rocked every settled continent, every industrialized country, every major capital. Fought in teeming open squares, fought in newspapers, in parliaments, in the petitions and telegrams by the thousand, the battle for Sacco and Vanzetti gripped humanity like no cause célèbre before or since. As headlines would note, "Reds" spearheaded most marches, but protestors also included statesmen, authors, scientists, clergymen, and untold numbers of rank-and-file workers. Before the crusade ended, bombs and bomb threats would make the world as jittery as in 1919. Hopes would plummet, rebound, hover. In the judgment of the watching world, one American city would stand for America itself, one court case for the universal dream of fairness, two men for all men staring into the naked face of power. And as the battle raged, the days ticked away toward a deathwatch that had millions clinging to their faith in justice as midnight approached.

On August 2, a Boston tabloid, claiming Vanzetti was raving in a padded cell, ran a "composite photo" of him in a straitjacket. Yet it was not Vanzetti but Boston that flirted with insanity. Viewing outsiders as a siege army, digging in, determined to uphold the rule of law, the city was consumed by a gut-wrenching tension that drove some to the breaking point. Before the siege ended, arguments over Sacco and Vanzetti would break into knife fights. There would be threats to dynamite a tunnel leading into Boston. A man overhearing a young woman discussing the case would threaten to kill her if Sacco and Vanzetti were executed. All this, despite the judgment of three eminent men who began their work just as a murderous heat wave settled over that last, lunatic summer.

For his advisory commission, Governor Fuller had picked prominent men whose verdict would convince the doubting world. Probate judge Robert Grant was also a novelist whose works championed "the New England conscience against the forces of easy-going but efficient modernity." Scion of a deeply rooted Boston family, old enough to recall boyhood chats with Longfellow, Grant was a dour man, his mournful eyes topping a white mustache as ragged as Vanzetti's. The defense committee raged against Grant, citing anti-Italian passages from his memoir. Now he sat in the State House listening to attacks on the integrity of his beloved Commonwealth. Beside him sat Samuel Stratton, physicist and engineer. A native of Illinois, Stratton was a precise thinker best known for creating and heading the National Bureau of Standards. The stout, silver-haired gentleman had been the president of MIT since 1923. Beyond this, little was known about him, and he said almost nothing during the hearings.

But everyone knew who was in charge of the commission. He was the man who asked almost every question, the man to whom the other members deferred, the man who, though seventy, jogged up the State House steps each morning to be seated before his colleagues arrived. His name was a composite of Boston's bedrock families—Abbott Lawrence Lowell. His were the Lowells who, in "the land of the bean and the cod . . . spoke only to Cabots who spoke only to God." Generation after generation, the Lowells had towered over Boston's aristocracy, producing judges, lawyers, professors, poets, and now a president of the university where all had graduated—Harvard. In eighteen years heading the university, Lowell had quintupled the endowment and modernized the curriculum to stress "an ability to use information rather than a memory stocked with facts." Lowell had also fought for a Jewish quota at Harvard and served as vice president of the Immigration Restriction League, yet his reputation trumped these hints of bias. "Now we can sleep nights in the thought that the president of Harvard is on the committee," a friend told Herbert Ehrmann. Even Vanzetti was impressed. After the commission visited him on July 8, he praised Lowell and Stratton as "men impartial and well-intentioned who will not decide against us for no other motive than their honest conviction of our guilt." Vanzetti could not say the same of Judge Grant, whom he considered "another Thayer." On Monday, July 11, the commission called its first witness.

To William Thompson, the committee headed by the president of his alma mater offered a shoal of reason in a sea of hatred. Throughout June, Thompson had deluged Lowell with evidence—protracted letters detailing each doubt, newly revealed Pinkerton reports, newspaper clippings, and a law journal article on Captain Van Amburgh's inaccurate testimony in a 1924 case. Now, in a sweltering room across the hall from where Governor Fuller continued his interviews, the Harvard lawyer stood face-to-face with the Harvard president. Confident that Lowell would surely see the light to which Judge Thayer had closed his eyes, Thompson began.

During the next two weeks, Lowell, Grant, and Stratton met every skeptic Thompson could call before them. The defense summoned thirty-six witnesses to Dudley Ranney's thirteen. Yet the prosecution had one distinct advantage—privacy. Ranney's first witness, Judge Thayer, spoke with the commission for two hours—

alone. "I wish I could have cross-examined him," Thompson lamented, "because I do not think he could have stood up for five minutes." When ten jurors met the commission, Thompson was again excluded. Only Frederick Katzmann, after private questioning, volunteered to face Thompson. Amidst caustic exchanges, Katzmann denied concealing witnesses, denied any federal conspiracy, denied being told "anarchists do not commit crimes for money," and blamed Captain Proctor's retraction on "a rift in the relations between us."

Thompson dominated the rest of the hearings. Watching the seasoned lawyer lay out each reasonable doubt, Stratton sat in silence. Judge Grant challenged each "very grave charge" against Thayer and Katzmann. Lowell, despite sagging jowls and spaniel eyes that made him look sleepy, was alert, inquisitive, skeptical. Why were *four* men needed to round up radical literature? he asked. Hadn't Captain Proctor said Bullet III was "consistent with going through *that* particular gun?" Witness after witness described a blatantly biased judge, an overzealous DA, and a jury foreman who wanted all "Dagos" kept out of America. *Boston Globe* reporter Frank Sibley recalled the mood of the trial: "There was always 'danger' in the air, the very atmosphere of the courtroom. The danger these prisoners might do." When Judge Grant asked whether Thayer had displayed any bias before the jury, Sibley replied, "Only his whole manner." Others told of Thayer's tirades. To the Dartmouth professor recounting the judge's "anarchistic bastards" diatribe, Thompson asked, "What did you do, Professor Richardson, when he made this remarkable demonstration of impartiality?" Albert Hamilton accused the prosecution of tampering with Vanzetti's gun, and everyone who had the chance denigrated Fred Moore—"a slum worker," "so out of his element," "irritating beyond words."

At the close of the first week, the defense reeled when Lowell played his own game of "Gotcha." In broken English, Professor Felice Guadagni told of lunching with Sacco in the North End on the day of the murders. Like other alibi witnesses, the bespectacled, goateed professor remembered April 15, 1920, because he had been invited to a banquet that day. Lowell then produced a newspaper clipping about the banquet—dated May 14. Flustered, groping for words, Guadagni admitted he had only heard about the event. "I was so sure of that day," he said. Thompson was even more shaken. "There must have been two banquets," he insisted. If he believed anyone had crafted Sacco's alibi, "I do not think you would see me around here very much longer." Judge Grant wondered whether the defense committee had concocted the alibi. But moments later, Albert Bosco told the commission that his newspaper had covered the banquet on April 15. Lowell protested, "It is perfectly obvious that it is not so!" Bosco promised to bring in a clipping, and Lowell, charging that a serious alibi had been destroyed, called the next witness.

Reporters waiting in the hall could hear Carlotta Tattilo through the door. "I deny that statement!" her shrill voice snapped. A Boston lawyer had recommended Tattilo to the prosecution, but she had not testified in Dedham, and the commission quickly saw why. She began by saying she had known Sacco at Rice & Hutchins not in 1917 when he briefly worked there, but in 1908, the year he arrived in America. "I must have a pretty good brain to remember away back to 1908," she boasted. Her good brain also recalled seeing Sacco on Pearl Street the day of the murder. "Oh goodness," she remembered telling herself. "I think that's the fellow that worked here in 1908."

For the next two hours, the commission heard the volatile woman's take on the truth. Prompted by Lowell, Tattilo accused Moore of offering her $500 to leave the state. When Thompson read from Moore's notes suggesting it had been the other way around—that she had been seeking hush money—the woman went off like a firecracker. "I will make you prove your statement!" she shouted. "It is a dirty, nasty lie!" Complaining that her character was being "overhauled," Tattilo ranted until Judge Grant shouted, "Keep quiet!" She would not. Thompson struggled to calm the witness while revealing her as mendacious, perhaps insane. She insisted Sacco had once thrown a shoe last at her, but when asked what else she remembered about him, she began rambling. "My head is too full of music and things like that to remember. . . . I can't remember everything, and you don't. If you do you are a pretty smart man, both of you over there." She told of hearing a gunman on Pearl Street shout, "Hurry up, there, I have got to get through at half past three. I have some clams to dig." Raving, yapping, denying her own words that Thompson read from the inquest, she finally blurted out, "This is the most sickening case I ever heard of!" When she left, reporters trailed her down the hall. "I have nothing to say!" she shouted. "I have nothing to say!" The commission adjourned for a long, hot weekend.

Thompson was beginning to believe. The sudden doubt circling Sacco's alibi was disturbing, but how could six witnesses detailing Judge Thayer's bias not sway the president of Harvard? Sacco and Vanzetti, however, had inside information. On July 11, after speaking with the commission, Rosina had met with Governor Fuller. The following day she visited her husband. The governor, she told him, seemed to believe Lola Andrews and could not stop asking why Vanzetti had failed to testify at his first trial. Beltrando Brini then told Vanzetti what the governor thought of the eels alibi. Why couldn't Vanzetti have committed the Bridgewater holdup, then raced to Plymouth to sell eels, the governor had asked. Vanzetti was stunned. "If the Governor does not believe Beltrando," he lamented, "he neither believes all the other of my witnesses." On July 17, as the death toll from Boston's heat wave reached nineteen, Sacco and Vanzetti began hunger strikes. Calculating that twenty-four days of starvation in sweltering cells might cheat the executioner, they pushed away meals and sat welcoming death on their own terms. Sacco's spirits lifted when his daughter wrote him for the first time, but hunger reminded him that he could expect no more mercy from the governor than from the sun. Vanzetti, certain now that he would be dead within weeks, asked Felicani to send for his sister.

During the Lowell Commission's closing week of hearings, Governor Fuller visited the condemned. Sacco refused to see him—"He didn't want any grace, any part of it," Felicani recalled—but Vanzetti spoke with Fuller for ninety minutes, explaining particulars of the case, defending his alibi, waxing eloquent on his innocence. "What an attractive man," Fuller told the warden as he hurried off to ride in Lindbergh's motorcade through Boston. Vanzetti was equally enthusiastic, especially when the amiable governor returned four days later to resume their discussion, then shook his hand upon parting. Vanzetti feared the ex–car salesman could not master the case's complexities, but he wrote to Mary Donovan, "I don't think he is going to burn us."

As the hunger strikes ground on, the defense committee pleaded for public hearings. "Sacco and Vanzetti are starving themselves to death," Gardner Jackson wrote Fuller. "They see you interviewing a long list of witnesses, hostile and friendly, in private. . . . The reputations of these men are being killed by rumor." But the governor and his commission continued their work behind closed doors. On Monday, July 18, when Harvard's president again jogged up the State House steps, his game of "Gotcha" blew up in his face.

As promised, Albert Bosco handed Lowell a clipping about the disputed banquet. Had it taken place in April or May? The clipping from *La Notizia* detailed the banquet "In Onore Del Direttore Dei 'Boston Transcript.'" It was dated *Venerdi 16 Aprile 1920*. After reading the article in Italian, Lowell called the *Transcript*. The editor had previously assured Lowell he had attended one banquet—in May—but now he suddenly remembered the April affair. Lowell apologized to Bosco and Guadagni. Thompson said the incident proved how easily New Englanders doubted foreigners. Even he had been inclined to believe Lowell and not the Italians, Thompson admitted. Didn't that strengthen Sacco's alibi?

"You are just back where you were before," Judge Grant said.

That same Monday, the commission learned more about the cap a witness had "found beside the body" of Berardelli. Braintree's ex–police chief told of being handed the cap a full day after the murders. After keeping it in his car, Chief Gallivan had decided to look for the owner's name. "I took and ripped that lining right down myself," he confessed. Hence the hole the prosecution claimed was made by Sacco hanging his cap at the factory. Gallivan doubted that the cap, when found, had been in the street "for thirty hours with the State Police, the local police, and two or three thousand people there." Before leaving, Gallivan also called Carlotta Tattilo "a nut" whose promiscuity, when she had been "a mighty pretty girl," sent many Braintree men to the doctor. The Dedham trial, the ex-chief added, had impressed him as a contest "to see who could tell the biggest lies."

Final days brought still more skeptics. A criminologist said the marks on the base of Bullet III differed dramatically from those on other bullets, "as though they were made with a different tool." A shoe worker, hired by Moore to investigate, claimed that a dozen witnesses had clammed up under orders from factory bosses. The repairman of Berardelli's gun told the commission he had seen only "a very slim possibility" it had become Vanzetti's, but Harold Williams "did not seem to want to have that at all. . . . There are thousands of times more chances that it was not than that it was." Finally, another *Transcript* editor, assigned to the case presuming the men guilty, found himself tormented by doubt. The Buick had skirted a passing train in Braintree shortly after 3:00 p.m., James King noted, then stopped more than an hour later at the crossing twenty-two miles south. During long, sleepless nights, King had studied train schedules, getaway routes, and testimony. The timing of the getaway convinced him that the bandits had either changed cars in the woods or they had driven 14.65 miles per hour. Given widespread testimony that the car had been flying along, King assured the commission that Medeiros had told the truth.

On July 25, Thompson summed up. He blasted Thayer as "narrow minded . . . half educated . . . violent, vain, and egotistical." He called Lola Andrews "a hysteric" and Carlos Goodridge "a professional criminal," and accused Katzmann of violating fairness standards common in several states, "even in Texas." He revealed his latest discovery—clerk Shelley Neal's inquest testimony that he had seen *two cars* that morning on Pearl Street. "There is your Hudson, and there is your Buick, and there is Medeiros' story," Thompson said. Turning to his clients, Thompson praised Vanzetti as a "gifted man" who could have been a college professor. Sacco, he added, could not be both cold-blooded murderer and dutiful worker with $1,500 in savings, nor could he have leapt around South Braintree to be in all the places wearing all the different clothes witnesses described. Then there was the cap, now discredited, the alibi banquet, now affirmed, and the trial atmosphere. "Everybody in South Braintree wanted to see somebody punished for the most shocking and cold-blooded murder ever heard of," Thompson said. Resting, mopping his brow, he allowed Herbert Ehrmann to make the boldest accusation.

How strange, the young lawyer posited, that witnesses had seen a gunman pump bullets into Berardelli, that *four* bullets had been extracted but only *one* was linked to Sacco's gun. How "very peculiar" that Katzmann, having promised he would not use ballistics evidence, had changed his mind in midtrial. Sensing the implication, Judge Grant became as stiff as his collar.

"Are you suggesting that the Colt bullet was invented for the occasion?"

Ehrmann was careful not to accuse Katzmann or Williams, but he did not hesitate to blame police. Captain Proctor, he suggested, "apparently did something that he was mightily ashamed of," and doubting the case, was replaced by "the country policeman, Stewart." Dudley Ranney laughed at the term "country policeman," but Grant, Lowell, and Stratton sat like statues. Thompson then concluded, arguing for a pardon. "We have to stomach it, to stand it; there is no way out of it," he said. "Everybody is familiar with the case, all over the world. This evidence has been translated into every European language. They are as familiar with it in Germany and France as we are. We are up against the wall."

In a third the time taken by the defense, Ranney summed up a case he had barely argued. Judge Thayer's prejudice was just a "fanciful argument." No more than a dozen guards had been at the trial, their weapons concealed. Medeiros was "a twice-convicted murderer," Captain Proctor's affidavit "a play on words," and the last-minute suggestion of a substituted bullet was without the slightest evidence. Despite worldwide outcry, Ranney concluded, freeing Sacco and Vanzetti as "public policy" would "destroy our courts." The hearings were adjourned. Three days later, on July 28, Grant, Lowell, and Stratton were seen carrying brown binders into the State House. Their report. Lowell raced down the steps to dodge the press. The governor's decision was promised in early August.

On the evening of August 3, a crowd swarmed the sidewalk fronting the State House. A few blocks away, hundreds gathered before the outdoor bulletin board where the *Boston Globe* posted fresh headlines. Governor Fuller had said his decision would be announced at 8:30 p.m., yet he did not arrive at the State House until 8:26. An hour later—still no word. From the sidewalk below, crowds looked up at the light burning in the governor's office window. Nine forty-five. Ten. Ten-fifteen.

In the week since his commission had adjourned, Fuller visited South Braintree, staring up and down Pearl Street and then rattling along the dusty getaway route with Chief Stewart. He saw more witnesses—Judge Thayer again, Officer Connolly, and Vanzetti's first lawyer. "Big Chief" Mede, having told the governor he helped plan the Bridgewater burglary, returned to confess to a state deputy but was turned away. Sacco and Vanzetti broiled in their cells, refusing to eat no matter how friends and family begged them. Shortly after the heat wave broke into thunderstorms, a Sunday afternoon rally on the Boston Common drew a flotilla of straw boaters and impassioned calls for clemency. The defense committee had tried to bring Clarence Darrow but settled for reading his telegram aloud—"It would be a terrible mistake not to grant a pardon." Then, on the evening before Fuller's decision was due, the governor was handed a yellowed slip of paper.

"I'm a business man," Fuller had told Gardner Jackson. "I want to see documentary evidence on everything." Vanzetti claimed he had been selling eels during the Bridgewater burglary. Where was the proof? When Jackson mentioned sixteen witnesses swearing they had bought eels, Fuller answered, "Oh Mr. Jackson, those are Italians. You can't accept any of their words." To satisfy the governor, Ehrmann, with Felicani as interpreter, began visiting fish stalls. Roaming Boston's wharf, the men finally found one fisherman who knew Vanzetti as a customer, not just a cause. Most of his old receipts had been destroyed, the man said, but some were upstairs. In a filthy office strewn with boxes, Ehrmann and Felicani began tearing through papers. They found nothing. They tried other boxes. Still nothing. Then in a box deep in the attic . . . Signed "B. Vanzetti, Plymouth Mass.," the receipt listed "1 bbl" valued at forty dollars and dated "Dec. 20, 1919." Shipped that Saturday, the eels would have arrived in Plymouth on Monday or perhaps Tuesday, in time to be sold Wednesday, Christmas Eve. Ehrmann rushed the receipt to Thompson, who took it to the governor on the eve of his decision.

Later that night, Sacco, Vanzetti, and Medeiros were marched across the prison yard. Weakened by seventeen days without food, Sacco walked on his own, his numbed gaze leveled at the prison walls. Beside him, Vanzetti sighed and glanced up at the sky. "It was so long I did seen it before," he later wrote, "and thought it was my last glance to the stars." Reaching the far wall, the men stepped from the warm night into the most chilling place on earth—the prison Death House. They crossed a shiny white tile floor, then skirted a screen hiding three mortuary slabs. Across the room stood the electric chair shrouded in dark canvas. Passing through another door, they came to three narrow cells beneath a bare bulb. Medeiros entered the first, Sacco the second, Vanzetti the third. And that was the order in which, eight midnights later, each was to make the dead man's walk.

On the morning of August 3, Rosina entered the Death House and spoke to Sacco from behind a black line outside his cell. Distraught at seeing her husband just a short walk from the electric chair, Rosina told Warden William Hendry she could not stand to face the press. The warden, a rotund, kindly man who barely knew Sacco but had come to respect Vanzetti, helped Rosina evade reporters. She was then driven through a city bristling with anticipation. At the *Boston Herald*, a reporter was giving ten-to-one odds favoring a pardon. Rumors from the State House also suggested clemency. Lowell and Stratton, rumors said, favored leniency. Dudley Ranney had been seen leaving the governor's office "greatly agitated." The front page of that morning's *New York Times* proclaimed, "Nicola Sacco and Bartolomeo Vanzetti will not die in the electric chair on the date set. Neither will they be pardoned." The *Times* predicted the state legislature would grant a new trial. The Associated Press spread the same news along its wires.

All day, the minutes ticked away as if on a time bomb. Nearly four months had passed since the sentencing, four months of simmering doubt across America and boiling outrage around the world. Now all the doubt, all the delays came down to one man's decision. In the fading twilight, the governor arrived at the State House. "Quite a delegation," he said, smiling at the fifty reporters and photographers outside his office. As journalists took up watch, as crowds mingled outside, the tension hung like the fog bank off the coast. Newspapers had wired telegraph lines inside the State House. By 9:00 p.m., telegraphers sat on the third floor, nervously tapping their keys. Across town at the defense committee office, Felix Frankfurter crouched in his shirtsleeves, refusing comment, while Rosina sat in a corner, emotionally exhausted. The battery of typewriters was silent. The office was jammed with somber men and women, smoking, worrying, watching a tall, gentlemanly Italian pace the floor. "My heart is in my shoes," Felicani said. A clock on the wall inched past 10:30, then several hours later, 11:00. Mary Donovan fielded calls, saying "No news, no news." Italian callers heard "Ancora niente." On Beacon Hill, guards surrounded the governor's home and the hospital bed where his son was recuperating from an appendectomy. Finally, at

11:26, the governor's secretary emerged from his office with a stack of envelopes. Hands snatched at them and tore them open as reporters ran down the hall to the makeshift press gallery. The *Times* man won the race. Arriving at the bank of telegraphs, he shouted, "They die!"

Sacco and Vanzetti were among the last to learn. As the news stunned the waiting world, they slept soundly in the Death House. The following morning, leaning against the bars, they got the word from Felicani. "Vanzetti really took it very hard," Felicani remembered. "He looked at me for minutes with eyes that were just out of this world, like a person who was losing his mind. He wouldn't believe it." In Cell 2, Sacco just kept saying, "I told you so!"

After more than seven years, a mere six days remained. Vanzetti's response was his usual. The jagged script of his first letter suggested a trembling hand and a fevered mind.

> August 4, 1927
>
> Dear Friends of the Committee:
>   Please telegraph immediately to the people all over the world for immediate mobilization of a million of men. Keep me informed continually. Make a flag. Have all my witnesses act as quick as the light. Make your motto justice and freedom. Tell all I am ready to take the lead and die or change the human destiny in earth.

As execution crept closer, Vanzetti would again rant about "the million men," but by afternoon his mania had given way to a cry for justice. "I am innocent!" he wrote Luigia. "No death sentence, no Judge Thayer, no Governor Fuller, no reactionary state of Massachusetts can change the innocent into a murderer." Sacco preferred defiance to another "Sono innocente!" "We are proud for death and fall as all the anarchist can fall," he wrote. Only an uprising could save them now, "for we have always know that the gov. Fuller, Thayer and Katzmann are the murder."

William Thompson resigned that afternoon. After years of arguing for mercy, the governor's decision convinced him that his own state had none to offer. In his report, Fuller saw "no evidence of prejudice in his [Thayer's] conduct of the trial." As to the judge's outbursts, Fuller wrote, "that he had an opinion as to the guilt or innocence of the accused after hearing the evidence is natural and inevitable." Fuller believed the jurors—"thoroughly honest men"— and the "clear-eyed witnesses" for the prosecution. He did not believe Medeiros, nor any Italians. He outlined evidence against the men—their guns, their "tissue of lies," the eyewitnesses—but said nothing about Captain Proctor, the jury foreman, Sacco's cap, or any receipt for eels. Reading the ruling, Thompson lost his will to challenge the Commonwealth, its lockstep courts, its congenial governor. He stepped down in favor of new lawyers "less disturbed by a sense of injustice." The case, he told reporters, "is remitted to the judgment of mankind."

The judgment of mankind depended on the jury. Among those who had urged Alvan T. Fuller to "stand firm," the decision seemed heroic. Eighty percent of telegrams to Fuller congratulated him. With Calvin Coolidge having just announced, "I do not choose to run" for reelection, some backed the governor for president, comparing him to Lincoln. Others thanked him for "upholding law and civilization." Even former doubters agreed that, with the governor and his commission finding Sacco and Vanzetti guilty, they must be guilty. Ten months after calling for a new trial, the *Boston Herald* editorialized, "Upon the conclusion now reached we can afford to stand and tell the rest of the world that we are executing these two men because we believe them guilty of an atrocious murder and not because of their political or other views or of their attitude toward the war."

But farther from Boston, judgment was unforgiving. "What the world demanded was a new trial in open court before a jury of peers of the indicted men and an impartial judge," wrote the *New York Herald Tribune*. "What it finally got from Governor Fuller and his commission was a trial in star chamber and a public statement of a decision based on secret hearing of evidence." Fuller's mail echoed widespread denunciations in the press. "Conviction is a great national calamity," a Long Island woman wrote. "Shame on you!" A Denver man added, "Deservedly you will go down in history as another Pilate." Overseas, newspapers denounced the "barbarous decision" (Paris's *Le Soir*), the "tragic jest" (Rome's *La Tribuna*), and the "base, inhuman extermination" (*Pravda*). Marches and general strikes were planned all over the world. Closer to Boston, judgment burst forth in the familiar, audacious method.

Subway stations in midtown Manhattan were empty as midnight approached on August 5. Suddenly a deafening roar came from beneath Broadway. Smoke and flames belched from sidewalk grates. Inside the 28th Street station, the ticket booth was blown in front of an oncoming train. Ten minutes later, blocks away, another explosion lifted sidewalks "as if by a giant hand." Crowds poured onto the scene. Some told of hearing "Revenge for Sacco and Vanzetti!" Eighteen people were injured, but none were killed. That midnight, a bomb hollowed out a Philadelphia church. The next evening, "infernal devices" destroyed the home of Baltimore's mayor and a Washington, D.C., printing plant that had published a Klan newspaper. "Prevent the murder of these comrades," the note in D.C. warned, "or you will a find about what the mean of anarchy is." By August 7, J. Edgar Hoover was warning of "depredations made by alleged anarchists in behalf of Sacco and Vanzetti." Hoover soon learned of threats in Omaha—"We will blow this building if they die!"—and in Manhattan, where letters threatened to destroy skyscrapers. In Chicago, a bomb set for midnight was defused. Guards soon patrolled every subway station in New York and Boston. Police surrounded federal buildings nationwide. The guard around President Coolidge, on a working vacation in South Dakota, was tripled.

The defense committee denounced the bombings, but there was little time to debate responsibility. With just days remaining, the North End office became "the Hub" of the global uprising. Messages scribbled in pencil were rushed to Western Union, then telegraphed to any famous person who might speak out—to Lindbergh, Jane Addams, Congressman La Guardia, fourteen U.S. senators, H. L. Mencken, William Allen White, New York governor Al Smith. Appealing to "the conscience of America," the committee called all sympathizers to Boston.

> Comrades:
>
> There are just four days before Sacco and Vanzetti will be electrocuted. We call upon you to use every means at your disposal to prevent the legal murder of our two friends! We urge you to demonstrate your solidarity behind these two workers by organizing strikes immediately, by holding mass meetings of protest, and by coming to Boston—as many of you as can—for assignment to picket duty at the State House and elsewhere. The time is terribly short. . . . Make yourselves heard and felt! Save Sacco and Vanzetti! Save Sacco and Vanzetti for the honor of your class! Save them for the honor of justice and life!

Terribly short, time also rubbed fraying nerves. At a Brooklyn construction site, an argument over Sacco and Vanzetti led to a gunfight in which an Italian was killed. In Bucharest, a disabled veteran showed up at the American embassy offering to be executed in lieu of Sacco. At Boston Psychopathic Hospital, a discussion of the case sent a patient on a knife-wielding rampage, and in Denver, a man police said had "worked himself into a frenzy" over the case put a bullet through his head.

On Sunday, August 7, Boston papers released the Lowell Commission report. Reviewing the case, Lowell, Grant, and Stratton reasoned away each reasonable doubt. Katzmann's cross-examination of Sacco, while "unnecessarily harsh," had been justified to determine whether the men were frightened radicals. The jurors, "an unusually intelligent and independent body of men," had convinced the commission of Judge Thayer's fairness. Of Thayer's tirades, the commission lamented, "We are forced to conclude that the Judge was indiscreet in conversation . . . but we do not believe that he used some of the expressions attributed to him." The commission scoffed at a substituted bullet: "The case of the defendants must be rather desperate on its merits when counsel feel it necessary to resort to a charge of this kind." The ranting Carlotta Tattilo was "eccentric . . . but the Committee believe that in this case her testimony is well worth consideration." The man who heard the jury foreman say "they ought to hang them anyway" "must have misunderstood him." But jurors had not misunderstood Captain Proctor's "consistent with" because it was "plain English." Examining ballistics, the commission agreed with Captain Van Amburgh, distrusted Albert Hamilton, and noted that the same type of obsolete shells had been found on Pearl Street and in Sacco's pocket. The cap, "found on the ground near the body . . . fitted" Sacco. The tear admitted by Chief Gallivan was "trifling . . . by no means a ground for a new trial." James King's train timetable corroborating Medeiros's confession was based on "somewhat uncertain data." That left the lies, the witnesses, and men "armed for quick action when arrested. . . . Carrying fully loaded firearms, where they can be most quickly drawn can hardly be common among people whose views are pacifist." Sacco's alibi, the report noted (without mentioning Lowell's attempt to discredit it), was not credible. He was "guilty beyond reasonable doubt." Evidence against Vanzetti was weaker, but he was "in the same group as Sacco," had the guard's gun—the commission did not mention the repairman's doubts—and was identified by witnesses. "On the whole, we are of opinion that Vanzetti also was guilty beyond reasonable doubt."

As Fuller had hoped, the commission's ruling satisfied many doubters. Lowell received dozens of congratulatory letters. The *New York Times* thanked the commission for "assuring the American people and the world that no intentional or notorious injustice has been done," while the *Chicago Tribune* predicted the ruling "will be accepted by the American conscience." But the divided nation had more than one conscience. Lowell also received dozens of irate letters—"a shame and a blot on the old Bay State"—and telegrams—SINCERELY HOPE YOU LIVE TO LEARN SHAME FOR

YOUR PART IN LEGAL MURDER OF SACCO AND VANZETTI. Reading the report, wrote Harvard graduate John Dos Passos, "the suspicion grows paragraph by paragraph that its aim was not to review but to make respectable the proceedings of Judge Thayer and the District Attorney's office." Heywood Broun called his alma mater "Hangman's House" and snapped, "It is not every prisoner who has a President of Harvard University throw on the switch for him." Broun continued sanctifying Sacco and Vanzetti—"shining spirits . . . they are too bright, we shield our eyes and kill them"— until the *New York World* yanked his column, causing him to resign in protest. Others observed that Lowell was perhaps not the fairest judge of Italian anarchists. "They never had a prayer with that committee," one Bostonian told the critic Edmund Wilson. "Grant is *non compos mentis,* and of all the prejudiced people in Boston—and everybody in Boston is more or less prejudiced— Lowell is probably the most so. . . . It would be hard to find anyone less suitable for conducting an impartial investigation into something like this where the men accused are attackers of authority and property." Lowell dismissed the rising uproar as "mob psychology provoked by energetic propaganda."

That Sunday, Vanzetti's sister arrived in Paris. Summoned by her brother, Luigia had struggled to get a passport, finally appealing to Mussolini. She had not left Villafalletto until the day of Fuller's decision. Vanzetti had resigned himself to never seeing his "Carissima Luigina" again, but she pressed on. In Paris, the shy homebody led eight thousand protesters through the Bois de Vincennes. Another hundred thousand paraded elsewhere through the city, chanting, shouting, waving banners. Meanwhile, protesters in London staged a mock execution in Trafalgar Square. A few hours later on the Boston Common, long known as a haven of free speech, police began stifling all dissent. Mounted officers scattered crowds listening to speakers and arrested those handing out a flyer that read, "Massachusetts is disgraced in the eyes of the world!" Mary Donovan, carrying a sign reading, DID YOU SEE WHAT I DID TO THOSE ANARCHISTIC BASTARDS?, was also arrested, and was dragged from a platform by her ankles. Told that "bastard" was no word for a lady to use, Donovan replied that it was no word for a judge to use either. The following day, the source of the epithet was back in Dedham for his final ruling.

With Thompson's resignation, Arthur D. Hill had taken over for the defense. Hill, a Boston blueblood, friend of Frederick Katzmann, and former counsel for the city of Boston, cared more for the honor of Massachusetts than for "these draft-dodgers." Uncertain of their innocence yet certain they deserved a new trial, he had worked briefly for Moore in 1923, earning cold shoulders at his Beacon Hill gentlemen's club. With the marathon now ending in a sprint, he and three other lawyers began papering courtrooms with motions—for a stay of execution, a revocation of sentence, a writ of habeas corpus, a writ of error. Predicting appeals to the U.S. Supreme Court, Hill made plans well beyond August 10. His hopes were slim. Highest among them was his request that some judge other than Thayer be assigned the case. The Supreme Judicial Court quickly dismissed the writs; Hill just as quickly filed appeals. Then, to rule on Judge Thayer's alleged bias, the high court appointed . . . Judge Thayer.

On Monday, August 8, Thayer sat in the Dedham courtroom to judge whether he had shown any prejudice toward Sacco and Vanzetti. Hill argued for common sense. "No man is so wise, clear-headed and dispassionate that he can sit on the question whether he was actuated by prejudice," he said, but Thayer proceeded. "Prejudice?" he declared. "There isn't any now and there never was at any time." In denying a second trial, however, he cited a higher authority. Massachusetts law forbade a new trial once sentence had been passed. Hill appealed. The legal machinations ground on. Sacco and Vanzetti were two days from the electric chair.

On Tuesday, August 9, pickets began marching in front of the State House. The women wore bowl-shaped hats and skirts to midcalf; the men wore suits, ties, and boaters. Their picket signs were printed in block letters:

GOVERNOR FULLER! If Your Conscience is Clear
Why Did You Keep Investigation Secret?

GOVERNOR FULLER! Why Did You Call
All Our Witnesses Liars?

Had Fred Moore been present, he might have asked where these people had been for the last six years. Lost in the mad dance of the Twenties, many had been too busy or too disillusioned to pay attention. Still, these were the children of the Progressive Era, raised to believe in justice and the intervening power of government. Saving Sacco and Vanzetti meant more to them than "the honor of justice and life"; it meant saving their own idealism. If the men were executed, an entire generation's dream of social progress would die with them. Many who had believed devoutly in America, not just the America of Washington and Lincoln but the America of Eugene V. Debs, would never believe again.

The picketing began at 8:00 a.m. Beneath the towering gold dome, men and women strode the length of the sidewalk, turned, and walked back again. Clunky Model Ts slowed to watch. Boxy cameras on tripods took newsreel footage. All morning and into the afternoon, the picketing continued, like an endless drive chain of dissent. By 4:00 p.m., police had seen enough. Thirty-nine picketers were led to the police station on Joy Street to be booked for "sauntering and loitering." After filling the station with cheers and clapping, all were bailed out by Mary Donovan.

That Tuesday, the New York anarchist paper *L'Adunata dei Refrattari* again reminded its readers, "La Salute è in Voi!" But one did not have to understand veiled hints of bombings to sense the threat. Boston corporations had taken out $100 million in bomb insurance. Boston, however, was just the eye of the storm. In Manhattan's garment district, where the *Jewish Daily Forward* distributed half a million copies of a special Sacco-Vanzetti edition, "not a stitch was sewn." Strike leaders—Communist, Socialist, and mainstream—claimed three hundred thousand had walked out. Thousands overflowed Union Square, then marched south threatening to burn City Hall. En route, policemen battled marchers while bricks and flowerpots rained down from windows above. Walkouts bordering on riots rocked Philadelphia, Chicago, Rochester, and Baltimore. In Omaha, a truck carrying a hooded man in "an electric chair" was ordered off the street. The international outcry could be charted in datelines from the *New York Times*: MANILA. MOSCOW. WARSAW. COPENHAGEN. OSLO. ROME. AMSTERDAM. BRUSSELS. PARIS. LONDON. MONTEVIDEO. BUENOS AIRES. ASUNCION. MONTREAL. The Italian dateline could have read TORREMAGGIORE, where Sacco's father cabled Rome pleading with Mussolini to do *something*. "Il Duce" had already sent the Italian consul in Boston to meet with Fuller and urge a pardon, but the fascist dictator would make no public statement on behalf of anarchists. The Vatican was also silent, but for anyone on any street in the industrialized world, dodging the case proved more difficult.

In Paris, a vacationing Chicago judge strolled through the Latin Quarter, where cafés were filled with American writers and artists. At one of Hemingway's haunts, the Café Select, the judge was sipping a mineral water when a striking red-haired woman asked him, "Just what is your opinion of the Sacco-Vanzetti case?" The judge, shocked by radical protest attempting to sway an American court, said as much. The woman, the dancer Isadora Duncan, flew into a rage. She called the case "a blot on American justice" that would "bring a lasting curse on the United States." During the ensuing argument, other Americans gathered around, challenging the judge. After several edgy minutes, the judge stood to leave. A bearded man told him to expect visitors at his hotel. They would be eager to "inspect a representative of the American judicial system and show him what they think of it."

With just one full day remaining, the New York Sacco-Vanzetti Emergency Committee telegraphed a last-minute plea for marchers to gather outside the prison. The urgent call went out to everyone from Sinclair Lewis to Mother Jones, Carl Sandburg, and a former warden of Sing Sing. That afternoon, telegraph lines were installed near the Death House. Floodlights went up around the prison walls and police cordoned off adjacent streets, turning

Charlestown into a ghost town. As evening arrived, a final salvo in the ballistics battle hit the newsstands. *Boston Transcript* readers now learned of tests conducted at the Dedham courthouse on June 3. Using a new invention—the comparison microscope—Major Calvin Goddard had examined Bullet III and Shell W. Aligning microscopic grooves, Goddard concluded both shell and bullet had been fired by Sacco's Colt "and no other." Thompson, who had learned of the tests just before they began, had sent MIT professor Augustus Gill as a witness. Gill had previously filed affidavits for the defense, but now he agreed with Goddard and withdrew from the case. Other witnesses—Ehrmann and a *Herald* reporter—had not been convinced, nor was Thompson, who considered Sacco's gun barrel "so altered by rust and age as to render such experiments wholly valueless." After the tests, Thompson had invited Major Goddard to his office, where the expert admitted he had considered Sacco guilty even before coming to Dedham, and had entered the case chiefly to attract more ballistics work. Goddard offered no opinion on whether Bullet III had been substituted but agreed with Thompson that its markings were different from those on other bullets. Thompson would detail his doubts in the following evening's *Transcript,* but by then Sacco and Vanzetti would have just a few hours left.

August 10, the date that had driven Boston to the brink, began in quiet desperation. At 8:00 a.m., picketers assembled outside the State House. By noon, thirty-nine more, including John Dos Passos and Dorothy Parker, had been arrested. When she had decided to protest, Parker had endured taunts from fellow cynics at the Algonquin Round Table. Now, led away by police, she heard counterprotesters across the street shout, "Bolsheviki!" "Guinea lover!" and "New York Nut!" More picketers were on their way from Manhattan on a "death watch" bus. At lunchtime, Governor Fuller summoned his executive council, needed to approve any last-minute stay of execution. All afternoon the men waited while around the world workers shut down cities, closed factories, and encircled American embassies. In Rome, Giuseppe Andrower assured reporters he had seen Sacco in the Italian consulate on April 15. A bomb exploded at the Palace of Justice in Buenos Aires. Another bomb injured fifteen on a streetcar in Switzerland. Back in the Death House, Sacco and Vanzetti spent the day writing sad fare-wells to their surrogate mothers. Vanzetti signed a petition for a writ of habeas corpus; Sacco refused. "They have been driving nails into us for seven years," he said. "Let's have it over."

Toward 2:00 p.m., Arthur D. Hill and William Thompson rushed a writ of habeas corpus to America's most venerated judge. Supreme Court justice Oliver Wendell Holmes, vacation-ing on Boston's North Shore, had followed the case since reading Frankfurter's article. Sensitive to the possible injustice, the white-haired judge nonetheless considered Sacco-Vanzetti supporters too extreme, their grievances not so worthy as those of "the blacks." Hill and Thompson argued for two hours, but Holmes refused to intervene. "Prejudice on the part of the presiding judge, however strong," he said, did not give him authority "to interfere in this summary way with the proceedings of the State Court." As lawyers were leaving, Holmes told Thompson that Sacco and Vanzetti "did not get a square deal," but said he could not toss aside the separation of state and federal courts. Later, Holmes's secretary asked him whether justice had been done. "Don't be foolish, boy," Holmes answered. "We practice law, not 'justice.'"

With sunset circling the globe, throngs gathered in capital cities, feeling powerless, drained, on the verge of shattered illusions. Wait-ing to board the *Aquitania* in Cherbourg, France, Vanzetti's sister prayed. In Charlestown, police stood shoulder to shoulder at the prison gates. Silhouetted by floodlights, mounted police rode along empty streets, the hoofbeats of their horses echoing off brick walls. Searchlights swept the prison, spotlighting guards perched atop the embattlements against the black of night. Nearby rooftops, bridges, railroad yards, and the Charles River were heavily patrolled. At the Death House door, guards toted machine guns and tear gas bombs. Back at the State House, the governor finally convened his execu-tive council to hear Hill argue for a stay of execution pending his appeal to a writ of error. While the lawyer spoke, calls poured into newspaper offices. Were they still alive? Throughout that evening, not a single crime marred Boston police blotters.

At 9:00 p.m., Sacco and Vanzetti heard the executioner in the next room testing the electric chair. An hour later, they were led from their cells. Their heads were shaved, their pants slit to allow the clamp of electrodes. Then a sudden call alerted Warden Hendry. The execution had been postponed! Before the news leaked, however, the warden learned the call was a hoax. No stay had been granted. Sacco and Vanzetti had ninety minutes left.

Toward 11:00 p.m., Dorothy Parker somehow slipped inside the prison. There she heard prisoners screaming, "Let them out! Let them out!" She quickly found a phone and called the defense committee but was overheard and escorted outside. Moments later, with witnesses waiting in the Death House, with reporters needing only the condemned's last words to lead their stories, the warden received a second call. Thirteen minutes later, an order signed by the governor arrived by taxi. Smiling as he strode into the pack of reporters, Warden Hendry announced, "It's all off, boys!" and passed out cigars. The news spread. In London and Paris, crowds still assembled at dawn sent up cheers. Vanzetti announced he was "damn glad" for the chance to see his sister, who would surely arrive before August 22. Sacco said nothing. No one knows how the men slept that night, and their thoughts upon waking can only be imagined.

The following morning, Sacco, Vanzetti, and Medeiros walked back across the prison yard. Returned to his steamy cell, Vanzetti added postscripts to good-byes not yet mailed, confessing his amazement to be alive. He had begun sampling broth and toast, but Sacco, though dazed by heat and hunger, still refused to eat. "Why should I fatten myself for the execution?" he asked. Told there might not be an execution, Sacco answered, "We will see." On August 12, he wrote a final letter to "Auntie Bee"—"this good old dear mother, that I like always and in the death house more than ever." Having written to Ines, he pondered his farewell letter to his son.

Luigia Vanzetti's steamship embarked on August 13. Certain she would reach her brother in time, she began mustering her words, her prayers. When she had left Villafalletto, her father had said, "Bring Barto back with you," but although a devout Catholic, Luigia did not expect a miracle. She hoped only to convince her brother to accept a personal savior and last rites from a priest.

For the next few days, the watching world seemed to relax. In America, police stood down from federal buildings and subway stations. Across Europe and South America, strikers returned to their jobs. In London, once and future prime minister Ramsay MacDonald declared, "All friends of America pray there will be no execution." Consensus in France held clemency to be Fuller's next move. "One can scarcely believe that his intervention should have no other effect than a prolongation of the torture," wrote the conservative *Journal des Débats*. Across Italy, millions trusted that America would soon free the men, but elsewhere the suspicion lingered that the reprieve was merely "another turn of the rack." Radicals, convinced their protests had forced the latest reprieve, called for bigger rallies. In New York, Carlo Tresca's *Il Martello* claimed the stay of execution would be "a crude prolonging of agony" unless a general strike paralyzed America, "tearing Sacco and Vanzetti from the hands of the executioner and giving them to their families, to us, to the world." Days passed with little news other than what the men had or had not eaten. Then the countdown began again, set off by yet another fuse.

Shortly after the trial, juror Lewis McHardy had received a threatening letter. The middle-aged mill worker put the threat out of his mind, but at 3:33 a.m. on August 16, he awoke to a shattering explosion, the pungent smell of sulfur, and his son shouting, "That Sacco!" McHardy staggered through rubble and stood beneath trees stripped of their leaves, surveying the remains of the house he had built. An American flag was soon draped from the shell of the juror's home. Captain Van Amburgh investigated but found no clues. Neighbors saw only sinister intent and a "living God" sparing a family and leaving a crucifix hanging on a wall above the debris. McHardy's hometown started a relief fund that would eventually build him a new house, and guards took their posts outside other jurors' homes, at public buildings, and in the minds of those who saw such violence as the best reason to get rid of "those Reds."

Communists took the lead in denouncing any connection between the case and the bombing. But they were also finding new ways to exploit Sacco and Vanzetti. The *Daily Worker* was printing "Sacco and Vanzetti Shall Not Die!" on every page of every issue. The Communist party paper also peddled a "Sacco-Vanzetti Anthology of Verses" and hyped its subscription drive as "a necessary and vital part of the campaign for the freedom of Sacco and Vanzetti." Such tactics gave Red-baiters added evidence that the condemned were dangerous subversives, yet supporters remained suspicious of the Communists in their midst. Ever since Communists and labor organizers had come to blows at a Sacco-Vanzetti rally in Manhattan, the rift had widened. As party members grew increasingly shrill, their callousness appalled sincere supporters. Communists flocking to Boston, Gardner Jackson remembered, unquestionably "preferred Sacco and Vanzetti dead [rather] than alive." Arriving to picket the State House, the writer Katherine Anne Porter told one Communist she hoped Sacco and Vanzetti could be saved.

"Saved?" the woman asked. "Who wants them saved? What earthly good would they do us alive?"

On the day of the McHardy bombing, Arthur D. Hill made his final appeal before the Supreme Judicial Court. With six days remaining, the court's decision promised to be painfully quick. The battle for Sacco and Vanzetti was nearly spent.

Approaching midnight on August 18, Charlestown Prison suddenly went dark. Inmates shouted in the pitch-black. Guards, fearing an attack from outside, scrambled for flashlights. Only Vanzetti suspected what had happened. To buy a few more days, he had taken advantage of widespread sympathy for him throughout the prison by bribing an electrician. The man was to cut all power as Vanzetti's execution approached. In preparation, the electrician was toying with circuit breakers when he crossed wires. Power was quickly restored, and Vanzetti gave up on the scheme.

As the final weekend began, Sacco and Vanzetti dominated the front page of newspapers around the globe, and full-page ads in major American papers. On August 19, the *New York World* gave its entire editorial page to Walter Lippmann's plea—"Doubts That Will Not Down." "Everywhere there is doubt so deep, so pervasive, so unsettling that it cannot be denied and it cannot be ignored," Lippmann wrote. "No man, we submit, should be put to death where so much doubt exists." While newspapers and pundits obsessed about his fate, Sacco surrendered to Rosina's pleas and agreed to eat. The day before, Rosina had brought Dante for a last visit. The little boy who had played catch over the jail wall had grown taller than his father. Sacco called Dante "my giant." "I want you to work for humanity," he told his son. For an hour, he held his emotions in check, but when his children walked out of his life, Sacco lay on his cot and sobbed. Now he began a farewell letter to "My Dear Son and Companion." "Seven dolorous years" had not weakened "the heart-beat of affection," he assured Dante before making his own plea for courage. "Don't cry, Dante, because many tears have been wasted, as your mother's have been wasted for seven years, and never did any good. So, Son, instead of crying, be strong so as to be able to comfort your mother."

Sacco was interrupted by attorney Michael Musmanno. A lean, bushy-haired lawyer from Pittsburgh, Musmanno had arrived in May bearing an appeal from the Sons of Italy. He had stayed on all summer, infused with a furious energy. Approaching Sacco and Vanzetti that morning, Musmanno was crestfallen. He had just come from the Supreme Judicial Court, where judges had upheld Thayer's last ruling. Musmanno spoke of appeals to the U.S. Supreme Court, but Vanzetti was already pacing, talking about "the million men." Sacco set aside his letter to Dante. "I can't go on," he said. "I'm too tired." Guards soon arrived to take the men back to the Death House. Crossing the open yard, Sacco could only mutter, "They crucify me." Back in Cell 3, Vanzetti wrote to

Thompson. Dated "New Era Year I," his letter suggested delirium. "Big corps of men are in march. . . . Take all the protective measure to the crossing of Rio Grande and Panama Canal. . . . Renew my notes to the King of Italy and the Pope." He soon recovered his control. Long after midnight, he and Sacco stayed up talking loudly. That same evening in Binghamton, New York, the Ku Klux Klan, beside blazing crosses, protested any further delay in the executions.

The weekend was filled with tears, anguish, and frantic dashes to find a sympathetic judge. On Friday afternoon, Luigia Vanzetti arrived in New York. Met at the gangplank by a contingent of two hundred, the tall, gaunt woman dressed like an old "schoolmarm" was sped toward Boston. Crossing her path on his way south was attorney Musmanno, taking a train to Washington, D.C., to file an appeal with the Supreme Court. On Saturday morning, Luigia arrived at the Death House. Against regulations, Warden Hendry allowed her brother to step from his cell. His eyes melting, his heart aflame, Vanzetti approached the younger sister whom he had consoled with calls for *coraggio*. When they embraced, Luigia swooned. Helped to a chair, she spoke with her brother for an hour, time to talk about the family garden, the grown siblings Vanzetti barely knew, his father weeping at home, and the savior the anarchist steadfastly refused to summon. While they talked, "Nick and Rosie" spoke nearby. When Luigia left, she glanced back, then walked off leaning on the shorter and stronger Rosina.

That morning in Washington, Michael Musmanno discovered he did not have the necessary papers for an appeal. Promising to send them by Monday, he hurried to the Department of Justice to demand the opening of federal files on the case. A nationwide clamor for their release had arisen among professors and civil libertarians. The acting attorney general, a Massachusetts lawyer, assured Musmanno the files contained nothing absolving Sacco and Vanzetti. The files remained sealed, and Musmanno left that evening. While the train bore him back toward Boston, appeals for a second stay of execution poured into the State House, signed by social workers, professors, district court judges, scientists, doctors, writers, and hundreds whose jobs were as simple as their pleas for mercy.

On Sunday, Sacco finished his letter to his son: "Dante, I say once more to love and be nearest to your mother and the beloved ones in these sad days, and I am sure that with your brave heart and kind goodness they will feel less discomfort. And you will also not forget to love me a little for I do—O, Sonny! thinking so much and so often of you." His postscript offered greetings from Vanzetti, who was already writing his own farewell to the boy. Late that afternoon, the men sent a joint good-bye to supporters:

> Friends and Comrades, now that the tragedy of this trial is at an end, be all as of one heart. Only two of us will die. Our ideal, you our comrades, will live by millions. We have won. We are not vanquished. Just treasure our suffering, our sorrow, our mistakes, our defeats, our passion for future battles and for the great emancipation. Be all as of one heart in this blackest hour of our tragedy. . . .
>
> We embrace you all and bid you our extreme goodbye with our hearts filled with love and affection. Now and ever, long life to you all, long life to liberty.
>
> Yours for life and death
>
> > Nicola Sacco
> > Bartolomeo Vanzetti

Vanzetti saw his sister again that day, softly kissing her cheeks through the bars.

With execution set for the following midnight, the defense committee renewed its call for picketers. From throughout the Northeast, writers, artists, social workers, and social gadflies flocked to Boston. One woman had already begun walking from the tip of Cape Cod carrying a banner reading, SAVE SACCO AND VANZETTI! IS JUSTICE DEAD? Cursed, threatened, and occasionally complimented along her hundred-mile march, Paula Holladay arrived on the common that Sunday. Parading with her sign, she was quickly arrested. Up the hill at the State House, other new arrivals joined the chain of protest. Policemen herded 108 picketers to jail. As the sidewalk protest continued, the American Legion, having backed Governor Fuller, could be heard nearby singing "The Star-Spangled Banner."

Many last-minute arrivals gathered at the Hotel Bellevue, where a new Citizens' National Committee for Sacco and Vanzetti had set up headquarters. Members, including college presidents, former muckrakers, and prominent liberal lawyers, peppered the Department of Justice with demands for the release of federal files. Among the committee's stenographers was a state police informer. The prim, inconspicuous woman began filing daily reports. She overheard rumors that Governor Fuller's wife, who did not believe in capital punishment, was about to leave him. She found it "perfectly appalling the way the Reds are using this to play upon the ignorant workers," but discovered few secrets. A wiretap on Felix Frankfurter's phone was another dead end. Phone calls revealed no subversive activity, just a Harvard professor desperate to save the men. In these final days, Frankfurter phoned journalists asking them to highlight certain points of evidence, lamented that "extreme left-wingers came from New York and are raising hell," and regretted that Thompson was "pretty heartbroken. . . . He is a fine human being."

All that Sunday, Boston police surrounded some twenty thousand protesters on the common. Sailors and soldiers circled, their fists poised to give any Sacco-Vanzetti supporter a "sock on the nose." Police arrested anyone handing out leaflets, carrying a sign, or saying anything derogatory about the Commonwealth. As the weekend waned, the search for an intervening judge quickened.

Justice Holmes had again refused but told lawyers a colleague might see the case differently. On this hope, attorney Hill leapt into his car and sped toward the elbow of Cape Cod, where Supreme Court justice Louis Brandeis was vacationing. Brandeis turned Hill away without even inviting him inside. Because Rosina had been a guest at his home, Brandeis could not consider the case.

Hill turned around and drove past Boston, heading up the coast. By sunset, he had crossed into Maine, bound for the vacation home of Justice Harlan Stone on the tiny island of Isle au Haut, another hundred miles and two ferry rides away. While Hill drove on toward midnight, Musmanno sent a courier to Washington, D.C., with papers for the Supreme Court, then wired President Coolidge in Rapid City, South Dakota. Receiving no reply, Musmanno phoned the president and spoke with his secretary. A plane was waiting to take him to South Dakota for a personal plea, Musmanno said. The secretary coldly replied that the president would not interfere in the affairs of his home state. Musmanno then telegraphed Chief Justice Taft, who was vacationing near Quebec. On into the night, the lawyer awaited a reply. Toward midnight, Sacco and Vanzetti lay down for their last night of sleep. They slept well, guards reported.

For the second time in as many weeks, dawn brought a day that seemed set to explode at midnight. Yet August 22 was eerily different. Twelve days earlier, there had been a sense of possibility. Appeals had been pending. The governor's hand seemed unsteady, ready to rely on his executive commission. But now, another bombing and several frustrated appeals later, the Commonwealth had exhausted its senses—its sense of possibility, of patience, of mercy. Only a sense of the inevitable remained.

The inevitable could be heard in Governor Fuller's greeting that morning. "It's a beautiful morning," he told reporters as he strode into the State House. The inevitable was seen in Judge Thayer's stare as he sat in a Worcester court handing down harsh sentences—fifteen to twenty years for breaking and entering—as if to prove duty had prevailed. The inevitable could be felt in Boston's meager protests, the usual pickets joined by just a few hundred workers while thousands more ignored calls for a general strike. The inevitable was spoken by Boston's police chief asking some of the 162 picketers arrested that day, "What good do you expect to do?"

President Lowell embodied the inevitable when, being told federal files were open to Massachusetts authorities on request, refused to make such a request. And beyond Boston, the inevitable saw America enjoying another Monday in August, as if no approach of death could scar a summer day.

President Coolidge took in the scenery at Yellowstone National Park that day. Charlie Chaplin's wife was granted a divorce, and betting was heavy on the upcoming rematch between heavyweights Jack Dempsey and Gene Tunney. Babe Ruth hit home run number forty. Lindbergh, continuing his nationwide tour, flew the *Spirit of St. Louis* to Madison, Wisconsin. Compared with the global reaction, American protests were small. Crowds from a few thousand to twenty-five thousand—in Manhattan, Chicago, Detroit, San Francisco—were dispersed in chaos. Along the Allegheny River near Pittsburgh, striking miners planned a picnic and Sacco-Vanzetti rally. As soon as a speaker mentioned the names, state troopers began circulating, saying, "No meeting today." A scuffle over a flag led to fights, clubs, tear gas. Women and children screamed, troopers swarmed, some shouting "dirty wop sons of bitches!" One miner, clubbed on the knees, pulled his gun. Elsewhere across America, guards searched packages outside federal buildings. On Wall Street, where stocks soared to record highs, a car backfired and pedestrians took cover. Marshals with riot guns protected the Capitol Building in Washington, D.C., but the Pennsylvania trooper shot by a miner was the day's lone fatality.

No one knows how Sacco and Vanzetti spent their last day. Rosina and Luigia visited that morning. Unwilling to say good-bye, they promised to return and departed arm in arm with Mrs. Evans. After seven years, four months, and seventeen days—Vanzetti had tallied the time in his letter to Dante—did the men talk of Italy? Anarchism? Martyrdom? Did Vanzetti speak of "the million men," Sacco of being "proud for death"? Other than Luigia and Rosina, the prison chaplain was the only one to see the men before sundown. Father Murphy entered the Death House several times to

Sacco and Vanzetti

offer salvation, but was politely refused. Undaunted, he waited in his office, certain the condemned would summon him.

The legal machine that had kept Sacco and Vanzetti alive broke down that day. Reaching Rockport, Maine, after midnight, Arthur D. Hill waited for a ferry. By nine, he was on the windswept coast of Isle au Haut. Justice Stone spoke with Hill for more than an hour before sending him back to the ferry, rejected again. By then, Musmanno had his answer from Chief Justice Taft. With his appeal filed in the Supreme Court, Musmanno could not imagine an execution before the case could be considered on the first Monday in October. But to intervene, Taft wired, he would have to make a long journey to the American border. If he did, "I would feel constrained to conform to Justice Holmes' decision." There were more appeals that Monday—a third denied by Holmes, and one before U.S. District Court judge James Lowell, cousin of the Harvard president. "Did you ever see a Norfolk County farmer?" Judge Lowell asked the petitioning lawyer. "Well, if you did, you would have more appreciation of that jury." With night descending, a plane waited to take lawyers to a federal judge vacationing in the Berkshires. The plane was not allowed to take off after dark. As the lawyers headed for their car, a stranger strode up to them. From out of the night came the words "It would give me pleasure to shoot you."

"What is that?" one lawyer asked. The stranger repeated his remark and disappeared.

Governor Fuller, having kept the day open to all appeals, smugly offered to explain to a string of doubters why he knew the men were guilty. But by afternoon he had grown testy. "Have you interviewed the witnesses?" he asked Arthur Garfield Hays, who had worked on the Scopes trial. "I have. Presumably I know more about the case than you do." Arriving by chartered plane, Fiorello La Guardia also spoke with Fuller. As he emerged from the governor's office, La Guardia shook his head. "There is one chance in a thousand of reprieve," he said.

Toward 6:00 p.m., Thompson left his summer home. Summoned by Vanzetti, the elite Boston lawyer went to the Death

House to say good-bye to his good friend, the Italian anarchist. Stepping into Cell 3, Thompson shook Vanzetti's hand and sat. Hunched over in the cramped cell, seated knee to knee, neither man said much for a moment. Then Thompson stated he still believed his clients innocent, but there was a chance he might be mistaken. Could Vanzetti, in this late hour when nothing could save him, offer reassurance? Vanzetti, "with a sincerity which I could not doubt," declared his innocence, and Sacco's, one more time. The men discussed Vanzetti's readiness to die for "the upward progress of humanity and the elimination of force from the world." Then Vanzetti, his dark eyes brimming, said, "clear my name." No one knows what Thompson replied, but he advised the anarchist to make a public statement against violent retaliation. Vanzetti hesitated. History had shown him that "every great cause for the benefit of humanity had had to fight for its existence." Should seven years of unrelenting cruelty go unpunished? Talk then turned to Christ's crucifixion. (Thompson would later say Vanzetti was the most Christlike figure he had ever met.) When Vanzetti asked if he, like Christ, should forgive his enemies, Thompson replied, "In the long run the force to which the world would respond [is] the force of love and not of hate." Vanzetti said he would consider Thompson's advice. Concluding an hour punctuated by grave silences, the men shook hands and parted. Thompson said a few words to Sacco, who thanked him for his efforts. Neither man, Thompson marveled, seemed at all afraid of death.

Crushed and despondent, Thompson stepped from the Death House into the living world beyond. On his way out, he passed Luigia and Rosina. Moments later, grasping hands through the bars, their tears glistening in the glare of the bare bulb, Luigia said good-bye to her brother, "Rosie" to her Nick, her husband, her "man."

"I love you and always will," Sacco said.

"Nick," Rosina replied. "I am dying with you." Somehow the women found the strength to leave. Hurrying into the night, they headed for the State House.

At 7:55 p.m., the "dead line" went up around the prison. Anyone crossing it would be shot. Floodlights made the surrounding area as bright as day. Mounted police and the battalion of guards resumed their patrol. At 8:40, Warden Hendry entered the Death House. Sacco was writing to his father when interrupted. "I am sorry," the warden said through the bars. "It is my painful duty to tell you that you have to die tonight. Your lawyers have exhausted their efforts." Sacco stared at the letter, then asked the warden to be certain it was mailed. Hendry moved to Vanzetti's cell. "I am sorry but it is my painful duty . . ." Vanzetti stood staring at the floor. Finally he flung his arms out. "We must bow to the inevitable," he said. He sat, hearing the tramp of guards outside, then the pulsing hum of high voltage. Father Murphy entered again but both men refused him. He would try one more time, then go home toward midnight, saying, "I guess they don't want me now."

Again Boston was quiet that evening. From the Hotel Bellevue, the state police informer had reported a plan to storm the prison: "They will make an attempt on Warden Hendry. They really mean this, it is no fantastic idea." But a ragtag march of a few hundred, easily halted by police, was the only disturbance near the dead line. Downtown, crowds mingled outside the *Globe* and the State House. Boston's five radio stations broadcast O'Leary's Irish Minstrels, a debate on the blue laws, and a lecture entitled "Massachusetts Cares for Its Citizens." Stations promised to stay on the air until the "news flash." At the defense committee office, worn-out volunteers paced and watched the clock, afraid to answer the phone, afraid to believe any longer. "You never can tell," one woman said. "Look what happened last time." "You're crazy," another answered. "It's all over this time." Yet Boston was not so much a city as a mood that night, and as the fugitive minutes fled, its mood of inevitability rippled around the world, casting gloom across crowds already in mourning.

In the final three hours, efforts focused on the governor. All day, telegrams had arrived—nine hundred from America, a thousand from overseas—two-thirds pleading for clemency. The governor stood firm. Evening brought a letter from Edna St. Vincent Millay. Arrested while picketing, released on bail, the Pulitzer Prize–winning poet had pleaded with the governor in person that afternoon. Now her letter asked him, "Which way would He have turned, this Jesus of your faith? I cry to you with a million voices: answer our doubt. Exert the clemency which your high office affords. There is need in Massachusetts of a great man tonight. It is not yet too late for you to be that man."

Shortly after 9:00 p.m., Michael Musmanno raced past onlookers and up the steps of the State House. Massachusetts's attorney general had just agreed to consider a reprieve and Musmanno had come seeking Fuller's assent, but first he had to interpret for Rosina and Luigia. On bended knee, with Luigia fingering rosary beads, the sobbing women pleaded for mercy. The governor, repeating phrases verbatim from his decision, apologized for being unable to ease their sorrow and turned them away. Musmanno then camped outside the governor's office. He waited an hour. A few minutes before eleven, he was called in. The attorney general, Fuller said, had changed his mind. No stay of execution was recommended.

"And what do you say, Governor Fuller?"

"That is my decision."

"And on that decision will you stand for all time?"

"For all time."

Outside the prison, a small crowd peered up at a light in a watchtower. Rumor had it that the light would dim with each jolt from the electric chair. In the surreal glow of floodlights, the crowd watched and waited as all the effort, all the passionate pleas, all the world's cries for justice ended in the winking of the light.

At precisely midnight on August 23, Celestino Medeiros was led from Cell 1. Six times since his confession, Medeiros's execution had been postponed so that he might testify if a second trial was granted. Slouching, often sleeping whole days in his cell, he had lingered on, insisting on the innocence of the men in whose shadow his life played out. Entering the execution chamber, Medeiros looked at no one, said nothing, sat down. Across the room, the executioner, a tall, skinny electrician from the Bronx, stood beside a white panel with two dials above two switches. At 12:03, he threw both switches.

Minutes later, guards came for Sacco. While Vanzetti watched in dazed disbelief, his friend marched through the Death House door. Sacco walked on his own to the chair and sat amidst its serpentine clamps. As guards strapped him in, he suddenly noticed witnesses and a reporter. His eyes grew wild and he shouted, "Viva l'anarchia!" Calming himself, he said, "Farewell, my wife and child and all my friends!" With adjustments still being made, he eyed the witnesses and said, "Good evening, gentlemen." Guards hastily fitted the skullcap, slipped a mask over his head, and fell back. Seconds before the end, Sacco uttered, "Farewell, *mia madre*!" His body jolted. The killing charge was close to two thousand volts, higher than usual due to Sacco's loss of fluids from fasting. When the smoldering body slumped in the chair, a medical examiner felt the flaccid wrist. At 12:19 a.m., Ferdinando Nicola Sacco was pronounced dead. Guards headed for Cell 3.

Vanzetti entered the Death House appearing strangely calm. But his eyes bore the burden of years, those just endured and those not to be lived. Hunched over like a man twice his age, he approached two guards, shook their hands, and thanked them for their kind treatment. He shook the hand of Warden Hendry, whose eyes were filled with tears. Finally led to the chair, Vanzetti sat. As straps were tightened and electrodes clamped on, he said, "I wish to tell you that I am innocent. I never committed any crime but sometimes some sin. I thank you for everything you have done for me. I am innocent of all crime, not only of this one, but all. I am an innocent man." Pausing as guards finished their work, he slowly announced, "I wish to forgive some people for what they are now doing to me." The mask was slipped over his head. Minutes later, he was carried from the room.

As if from an earthquake, a shock wave rippled from the epicenter of Boston. Outside the prison, sobbing or silent witnesses slowly dispersed. "Life felt very grubby and mean," Katherine Anne Porter remembered, "as if we were all of us soiled and disgraced." When she said as much to a stranger, he shot back, "What do you mean? There's no such thing as disgrace anymore." At the defense committee office, the telephone had rung twice—the signal. A reporter said simply, "They're gone." Holding the phone, Gardner Jackson nodded to the crowd. Mary Donovan shouted, "I can't believe it!" Others wept, clung to each other, dropped to the floor. After a few minutes, wrenched, shaken, and instantly so much older, people filed down the stairs and onto the street to begin the rest of their lives. Many would walk the empty streets until dawn.

Shortly after midnight in Manhattan's Union Square, a sign was posted in the window of the *Daily Worker*—SACCO MURDERED. The overflow crowd was stunned into silence. But when another sign proclaimed VANZETTI MURDERED, people gasped, moaned. Some tore their dresses or hats. Others sobbed. Across Europe, where the midnight execution had been a dawn execution, a great wave of grief gave way to cathartic violence. All that day in Paris, tanks surrounded the American embassy while mobs raided cafés, turning tables and chairs into barricades, tearing up lampposts and hurling them through plate-glass windows. The façade of the Moulin Rouge was smashed. Riots in Germany claimed three lives. In London, bobbies on horseback routed protesters in Hyde Park. Mobs in Geneva ransacked American targets—Model Ts, shops selling Lucky Strikes, and theaters showing Mary Pickford and Douglas Fairbanks films. Across South America, widespread walkouts idled factories and left cities without taxis and buses. American businesses in Buenos Aires were stoned. Around the world, protesters swarmed through capitals from Amsterdam to Tokyo. In South Africa, the American flag was set ablaze outside Johannesburg's city hall. The riots continued for two days before the truth set in and protest seemed pointless. Sacco and Vanzetti were dead. In Torremaggiore and

Villafalletto, families wept. "They have killed my innocent son," Michele Sacco cried when Sabino ran to him with the news. While neighbors gathered around, the old man fell to cursing and sobbing.

For the next few days, visitors on the Boston Common noticed men working on adjacent streets, blocking some with trucks, digging up others. Boston was preparing for a funeral. While the city braced itself, the bodies of Sacco and Vanzetti lay in a North End mortuary. For two full days, a stream of mourners filed through a dimly lit room past the men they had seen only in photos. There was the walrus mustache, the broad forehead, the fiery, flashing eyes closed, the hungry mind stilled, the famous "fish peddler" now at rest. Beside him, also in a dark suit and tie, was the "shoemaker," his features calm, his hands folded. Death masks were made, but even white plaster was not as serene as the faces themselves. Before the funeral home was finally closed to the public, a hundred thousand people had paid their respects, their feet wearing a notch in a marble step outside. Mary Donovan was arrested for carrying her "anarchistic bastards" sign through the line. (Convicted of inciting a riot, she would be given a year in prison.) But otherwise all was peaceful, somber, final. A few days later, the mad, fearful, scorching summer ended beneath a gray drizzle.

On Sunday morning, August 28, Boston police arrested six newsboys selling magazines critical of Massachusetts. A few hours later, twin mahogany caskets were loaded into hearses in the North End. Dozens of huge horseshoes billowing with red carnations were placed beside adjacent cars. Crowds jammed the narrow sidewalks. Upper windows filled with heads gazing down at the flowers, the cars, the throngs. For the next two hours, the funeral of Sacco and Vanzetti, a mournful remembrance in anarchist red and black, took over Boston. Surrounded by marchers, the hearses inched over glistening brick cobblestones. Behind them, Rosina and Luigia rode in one car, defense committee heads in another. Then came the flowers—flowers and more flowers for the fallen rebels. A few floral pieces bore ribbons. One read, "The Committee," another "Martyrs of Massachusetts," a third simply "Rosa." The procession was absolutely silent, tens of thousands marching with arms locked, each coat sporting a red carnation, each arm bearing a red band reading, REMEMBER—JUSTICE CRUCIFIED AUGUST 22, 1927.

Flanked by police on horseback, the parade wound out of the North End, through the openness of Scollay Square, into the labyrinth of downtown and toward the common. Lining the route, two hundred thousand people lowered their heads, doffed their hats, or wept. Plans had been made to pass the State House, but all streets leading toward its gold dome were blocked. As the procession advanced, streets were littered with petals, laying a red carpet in its wake. On they marched in what the *Boston Globe* called "one of the most tremendous funerals of modern times."

No one knew who started the trouble. Police later claimed they were just controlling the crowd. Marchers insisted police opened up on them. Farther back in the procession, people heard cries up ahead. Coming up Washington Street, they entered the melee. Women screaming. Men running. Police grabbing armbands with one hand, flailing clubs with the other. Some marchers buried bruised faces in their hands. Others were on the ground, recoiling from nightsticks, defenseless against boots. The funereal red was now a bloody scarlet—streaming from split chins, smearing the hands of men running. The trouble lasted fifteen minutes. When it was over, just a few hundred remained to accompany the hearses through the gates of Forest Hills Cemetery. There, in a deepening drizzle, Mary Donovan, her careworn face longer than ever, stood before a small gathering pierced by open umbrellas, with Rosina and Luigia off to the side, and read the eulogy.

"Nicola Sacco and Bartolomeo Vanzetti, you came to America seeking freedom. In the strong idealism of youth you came as workers searching for that liberty and equality of opportunity heralded as the particular gift of this country to all newcomers. You centered your labors in Massachusetts, the very birthplace of American ideals. And now Massachusetts and America have killed you—murdered you because you were Italian anarchists." Comparing the executions to the Salem Witch Trials, Donovan called Sacco and Vanzetti "victims of the crassest plutocracy the world has known since ancient Rome" and their execution "one of the blackest crimes in the history of mankind." She quoted Vanzetti's eulogy of their agony and triumph. Rising to find some meaning in the bleakness of the moment, Donovan concluded, "In your martyrdom we will fight on and conquer."

While the crowd drifted away in a driving rain, the bodies were taken to the crematorium. Within the hour, ash and a thin plume of smoke were all that remained. All week, there had been talk—and a few arguments—about what to do with the ashes. Plans were made to send them on tour, to London, Paris, and on across Europe. The day after the funeral, hundreds in Manhattan waited in vain for the ashes to arrive. They had to settle for seeing the death masks and for a quick appearance by Rosina, cheered by ten thousand in Union Square. Sacco's widow had considered circulating her copper urn but chose instead to divide its contents, giving some to the Brinis, keeping some, and sending the rest back to Italy with Luigia, who wanted no part of any tour. Two urns, each containing a mixture of the men's ashes, crossed the Atlantic with Vanzetti's sister. When she arrived in Villafalletto, nearly the entire town met her train and followed her to the cemetery amidst the flat fields with the Alps in the distance. There, one urn was entombed beside the remains of Vanzetti's mother. Another was sent south to Torremaggiore, where the Sacco family buried it in the cemetery overlooking soft green olive groves like those young "Nando" had once tended. In ashes and sorrow, forever intermingled, Sacco and Vanzetti had come home.

Epilogue

We have seen the best of our time. Machinations, hollowness, treachery, and all ruinous disorders follow us disquietly to our graves.

—Shakespeare, *King Lear,* act 1, scene 2

On the morning after the executions, Katherine Anne Porter stepped into the elevator of her hotel. After watching the winking of the tower light, she had stayed up until dawn, "brought to a blank pause, keeping a vigil with the dead in the first lonely long night of death." Numbed and defeated, she rode the elevator to the lobby. Three elderly gentlemen in suits rode with her. No one uttered a word. Then, as the elevator neared the ground floor, one man said, "It is very pleasant to know we may expect things to settle down properly again." The other gentlemen nodded. The elevator door opened.

Neither in Boston nor in world opinion would things ever "settle down properly." The massive struggle to save Sacco and Vanzetti had failed, but it spawned a massive effort for vindication and a counterattack among those still judging the men guilty. More than eighty years after their executions, Sacco and Vanzetti haunt American history. Lauded as poster boys of injustice, they have also been denounced as "liberal martyr-saints" whose "mythical" innocence became "the private drama of the intellectuals." Denied a second trial, they have been tried and tried again in absentia while decade by decade new interpretations and new evidence have deepened their saga. "Clear my name," Vanzetti begged William Thompson, but the names remain entangled in forensic minutiae and sentenced in rushes to judgment based on personal politics.

The tug-of-war between redemption and repression began shortly after the funeral. Many who had given up jobs to work for Sacco and Vanzetti drifted back to their lives, but others dedicated themselves to creating a legacy. The defense committee continued its monthly bulletin while a new Sacco-Vanzetti National League arranged publication of the prisoners' letters and the trial transcript. The two-volume transcript plus four thick books of affidavits, appeals, judicial opinions, and other documents came out in 1928, its publication funded by John D. Rockefeller Jr. and other prominent men. Yet it was the letters that made men out of symbols. Reading *The Letters of Sacco and Vanzetti,* anyone could know the prisoners as their supporters had—as dual personalities, sentimental militants, hopeful, bitter, resigned.

Not everyone cared to consider, in the flesh of their words, the lives the electric chair had snuffed out. At the 1929 inauguration of his successor, Governor Alvan T. Fuller was descending the steps of Boston's State House when Gardner Jackson thrust a copy of the letters into his hands. Fuller read the title and threw the book to the sidewalk. Others simply refused to believe two Italian convicts could have written such stirring missives. The *Boston Transcript* described the letters as "said to have been written" by Sacco and Vanzetti. The Paris edition of the *New York Herald Tribune* wondered "how far these documents have been dressed up or perhaps even forged." Despite the publisher's lawsuit, which elicited a retraction, critics have continued to charge that the letters were edited to show the men in a favorable light. The most noted elision, they aver, was the removal of the phrase "Revenge our blood!" from a joint letter of August 1927. Vanzetti's statement—"I will try to see Thayer death before his pronunciation of our sentence"—was cut from another letter. However, having read the originals of every letter in the collection, this author has not found other significant omissions. As written and as published, the letters contain virulent anarchist diatribes as well as gentle paeans to nature. In one's awkward English, in the other's lyrical prose, the letters remain the strongest statement of innocence. "If Sacco and Vanzetti were professional bandits," wrote Walter Lippmann, "then historians and biographers who attempt to deduce character from personal documents might as well shut up shop. By every test that I know of for judging character, these are the letters of innocent men."

Reaction to the letters was mild, however, compared to the calculated amnesia of the Commonwealth. "Boston has a bad conscience," the *New Republic* noted, and whether motivated by conscience or concern for law and order, Boston spent decades trying to forget Sacco and Vanzetti. Worldwide opinion continued to condemn the Commonwealth and its capital. A Swedish newspaper branded Massachusetts "the shame of the world," while the French writer Romain Rolland said the Commonwealth had a heart of stone. City leaders remained unrepentant. As the first anniversary of the executions approached, supporters hoped to purchase a building in the shadow of the State House to be dedicated to Sacco and Vanzetti. Inside would hang a bronze bas-relief by Gutzon Borglum. Having just begun sculpting Mount Rushmore, Borglum took time out to craft a plaster model of the plaque featuring the men's profiles and a statement by Vanzetti. But there would be no such memorial building, nor an official anniversary. On August 22, 1928, denied the use of any meeting hall, five hundred people milled on a downtown street corner, blocking traffic while listening to speakers incant the names. The following evening, two thousand gathered in Scenic Hall. Mrs. Evans, Gardner Jackson, and other supporters were on hand. So were Boston police. Hearing a former Harvard lecturer proclaim, "If Sacco and Vanzetti were anarchists, Jesus Christ was an anarchist," police charged the man with blasphemy. William Thompson agreed to defend the case, but it was dismissed without trial.

Ten weeks later, a picketer carrying a sign reading FULLER—
MURDERER OF SACCO AND VANZETTI was charged with criminal
libel. At his trial, lawyers insisted their client had only meant the
governor was "morally responsible" for the executions, but all testimony about Sacco and Vanzetti was excluded and the man received a year in jail. The following August, on the execution's
second anniversary, protesters were denied use of Faneuil Hall, the
Old South Meeting House, and several other venues. The memorial meeting was finally moved to New York. Gutzon Borglum
again offered his bas-relief to the city of Boston; he received no
reply.

While Boston closed down, the rest of America opened its eyes
to new evidence. In the fall of 1928, Frank Silva, a.k.a. Paul Martini, whom Moore had interviewed in Atlanta six years earlier,
confessed to the Bridgewater holdup. Silva's mea culpa in the *Outlook and Independent* detailed how, in 1919, he and three accomplices had set out Christmas Eve morning in a Buick touring car to
do "the job." Silva knew every detail of the bungled burglary, right
down to a basement where the men had shot pool after casing the
town. Moore's other lead on Bridgewater, Jimmy "Big Chief"
Mede—in on the planning but not the burglary—backed the confession. So did the editors of the *Outlook and Independent,* who
toured Bridgewater with Silva before publishing his story. The only
doubt came from an accused accomplice. Joseph Sammarco had
known Vanzetti in prison—"he wasn't any stickup guy. . . . I always knew he wasn't guilty"—but denied he had helped Silva, even
passing a lie detector test. Still, the confession convinced the press,
which hailed it as proof that Vanzetti had been framed.

As the 1920s careened to a close, sentiment for Sacco and Van-
zetti was mounting. Annual memorials were held in many cities.
Socialists, union leaders, writers, artists, and intellectuals lauded
them as modern martyrs. One man pasted their pictures in his Bi-
ble "so that others looking at it may count them among the saints."
Many put the men in a pantheon of martyrs ranging from John
Brown to Joan of Arc. Then the stock market crashed, the Jazz
Age soured, and fresher causes arose. "I am afraid that people are

rather tired of hearing about the Sacco-Vanzetti case," William Thompson wrote to Mrs. Evans. Only in the Soviet Union, where Stalin considered their executions the most important event since the Bolshevik Revolution, were they a vital part of public history. The Soviet navy christened one ship the *Sacco,* another the *Vanzetti.* Streets were named for the men, and even as Stalin's purge trials made the Dedham proceeding look like a paragon of justice, a Soviet factory made Sacco-Vanzetti pencils. Translated into Russian, *The Letters of Sacco and Vanzetti* sold 130,000 copies. (The book was also among those burned by the Nazis in 1933.) But in the America of soup lines and hobo jungles, Sacco and Vanzetti were just two Wops who got in a jam during a distant era called the Twenties. *Liberty* magazine turned them into a contest, offering a $1,000 prize for the best solution of ten famous murder mysteries, among them the "Mystery of Sacco-Vanzetti." Then, just when it seemed the long saga might end, it burst again onto the front pages.

In 1928, a bomb destroyed the home of the electrician who had served as executioner. Undeterred, Judge Thayer continued to revel in his own fearlessness. Without being asked, the proud old judge often shared his disdain for Sacco, Vanzetti, and their supporters. At public gatherings throughout Massachusetts, Thayer was hailed as "the peacetime soldier fighting for his country." Standing ovations led him to bow or tip his hat. "I have had hundreds of letters from all over this country and from foreign countries," the judge told one crowd, "and have noticed a great many newspaper articles referring to the great courage required to go through what I went through for seven long years under the most vicious attacks."

During the fall of 1932, Thayer's Victorian home in Worcester was being remodeled. The contractor was due to finish the job one September day, but a stranger finished it for him. Mrs. Thayer was asleep upstairs. The judge was sleeping in a separate room. The bomb was on the porch beneath him. At 4:08 a.m., the blast caved in the rear of the house. Among the debris the judge hurled off his bed was the Worcester Bar Association plaque congratulating him on his firm stand. Given that his wife's face was cut and his maid was in shock, Thayer considered it "marvelous" that he emerged unscathed. The rising sun caught him in overcoat and slippers, hat in hand, sadly surveying the rubble. "I hate to think that because a man does his duty before mankind and God that the penalty is this," he told reporters. Noting the nearly finished remodeling, the judge managed a chuckle, but the shock stayed with him. Seven months later, he suffered a fatal stroke.

In the wake of the Worcester bomb, guards surrounded President Lowell's home in Cambridge. No suspicious activity was reported, but guards could not shield Lowell from his share of controversy. At Harvard's 1936 tercentenary, angry alumni published *Walled in This Tomb: Questions Left Unanswered by the Lowell Committee in the Sacco-Vanzetti Case*. The pamphlet reprinted Lowell's committee report, citing its omissions and "discrepancies" as evidence "of the incredible and destructive twists of men's minds—even the mind of a president of Harvard University." Unlike Thayer, Lowell rarely commented on the case. "In my opinion, the men were undoubtedly guilty," he had written in 1928, "and the evidence would have been deemed by everyone conclusive had it not been for the sympathy excited by the claim that they were 'Reds.'" He did not respond to the pamphlet. The year after it was issued—the tenth anniversary of the executions—Gutzon Borglum again offered his bas-relief to Boston. He had designed it with a special alloy, bulletproof and resistant to axes. Again there was no reply.

Dragged off podiums, denied meeting halls, fading from the press, crusaders for redemption turned to arts and letters. In the two decades following their electrocution, Sacco and Vanzetti were eulogized in 144 poems, six plays, eight novels, the now classic portraits by Ben Shahn, and an album by Woody Guthrie. The quality of these varied widely. Guthrie visited Boston and Plymouth to feel closer to the men, but his dozen repetitive ballads were far from his best work. Many poems about Sacco and Vanzetti were ruined by rage or sentimentalism. Dozens of poets saw the executions in biblical terms—the crucifixion of two "dago Christs" and a thief, Massachusetts as Golgotha, Governor Fuller as Pilate washing his hands. In purpled verse, Sacco and Vanzetti rose to be exonerated by God while Thayer and Katzmann were banished to hell or the harsh judgment of history. A few poems, however, remain powerful statements of mourning and loss. In "Justice Denied in Massachusetts," published in the *New York Times* on the day of the executions, Edna St. Vincent Millay wrote:

> What from the splendid dead
> We have inherited—
> Furrows sweet to the grain, and the weed subdued—
> See now the slug and the mildew plunder.
> Evil does overwhelm
> The larkspur and the corn;
> We have seen them go under

Novelists used the story as a backdrop for suffering and redemption. Upton Sinclair's seven-hundred-page novel *Boston*, published a year after the executions, was long-winded but historically accurate. The book savaged Proper Bostonians, resulting in its being banned in Boston. The best fictional account, however, came in *U.S.A.,* by John Dos Passos, who conceived his classic trilogy on the eve of the executions. In the third volume, Dos Passos's stream-of-consciousness interlude defined the divide the executions had widened.

> America our nation has been beaten by strangers who have turned our language inside out who have taken the clean words our fathers spoke and made them slimy and foul
> their hired men sit on the judge's bench they sit back with their feet on the tables under the dome of the State House they are ignorant of our beliefs they have the dollars the guns the armed forces the powerplants
> they have built the electricchair and hired the executioner to throw the switch
> all right we are two nations

Poets, playwrights, and novelists made Sacco and Vanzetti tragic heroes. None hinted that the men were militant revolutionaries, that the slightest evidence had been presented against them, or that they had been fully armed when arrested. By dodging these inconvenient facts, the posthumous sanctification left the case wide open for later critics.

With their martyrdom established, Sacco and Vanzetti might have rested quietly in their graves, yet theirs had become what Herbert Ehrmann called "the case that will not die." On the twentieth anniversary of the executions, dozens picketed the State House and a new memorial committee issued a manifesto. Among 150 signatories were Eleanor Roosevelt, the theologian Reinhold Niebuhr, United Auto Workers president Walter Reuther, Oregon senator Wayne Morse, and Harvard historian Arthur Schlesinger. At a public reading of the manifesto, the Sacco-Vanzetti Memorial Committee displayed the plaque by Gutzon Borglum. Mount Rushmore had since become world famous and many cities would have welcomed one of the late sculptor's works, but when again offered his bas-relief, Boston gave no reply. That same year, Albert Einstein wrote, "Everything should be done to keep alive the tragic affair of Sacco and Vanzetti in the conscience of mankind. They remind us of the fact that even the most perfectly planned democratic institutions are no better than the people whose instruments they are."

In 1950, a journalist tracked down seven former jurors. Despite all subsequent doubts—the retracted testimony, Judge Thayer's caustic comments, the Morelli scenario, and so on—the reporter found all living jurors still "of the same mind, the same opinion." "The more I've seen and heard, even after the trial, the more I am convinced they were guilty," one said. Another wished there had been a second trial because "there was no doubt in my mind a second jury would have found them guilty." Jurors had been long dismayed by charges that Sacco and Vanzetti were convicted for their radical politics. "As far as I know, the prosecution never offered any evidence they were Communists or slackers," one juror said. Another wondered, "Who are these people who keep bringing up the case and complaining about the verdict? If they say the country was witch-hunting those days, it must have escaped me. I don't remember all the radical talk."

Two years later, the same reporter found a white-haired Chief Michael Stewart eager to reminisce. Nothing he had seen since the 1920s had changed the chief's mind, but time had embellished his story. When he had first questioned Vanzetti, Stewart now remembered, the anarchist had asserted his belief in overthrowing the government, standing and proclaiming, "By force!" The chief also claimed that after Sacco injected radicalism into the trial, Vanzetti never spoke to him again. And recalling how Vanzetti sang en route to his first trial, Stewart said—apparently with a straight face—that when the Buick fled down Pearl Street, "the curtains were swinging in the wind and a strong voice was singing." The reporter also contacted Frederick Katzmann, but having never commented publicly on the case, the former DA had "no intention of doing so now." Katzmann continued in private practice until in 1953 when, while trying a civil case in the Dedham courthouse, he suffered a heart attack. He died the same evening.

Meanwhile in Braintree, where common sentiment still held Sacco and Vanzetti guilty, rumors sprouted to vindicate the verdict. On April 15, 1920, Rosina Sacco had been seen at a gas station in South Braintree; Sacco and Vanzetti had been spotted around town for days prior to the crime; Sacco had confessed to one of his lawyers; and J. J. McAnarney, on his deathbed, had told a friend both men were guilty. So the rumors said.

While Boston suffered amnesia and Braintree wallowed in rumors, supporters, like Vanzetti in his final year, became human radar. Whenever the case was mentioned in print, Felicani, Jackson, Donovan, and surviving surrogate mothers responded with furious letters to editors. By contrast, the families of both men tried to put the tragedy behind them. Luigia never recovered from her grief. "My sister became prematurely old," Vincenzina Vanzetti recalled. "She suffered and cried so much that something went out in her brain. She kept getting more and more depressed. She could not move her legs, her back. She had a total nervous breakdown, but she was conscious to the end." Luigia died in 1950, nineteen years after Vanzetti's father. Vincenzina blamed Gian Batista Vanzetti's death on "heartbreak from the tragedy."

Little is known about the fate of Sacco's children. Dante led as anonymous a life as his surname allowed. Working as a truck driver and airplane mechanic, he raised three sons in the Boston area. He tried to forget his father's fate but often overheard comments: "That's Sacco's son." Dante died in 1971, on August 22, the anniversary of the deathwatch. Ines Sacco is still alive and lives in the Greater Boston area. She has never commented publicly on the case or the father she saw only behind bars. But the family's stoic survivor was Rosina. So close to returning to Italy when the long death spiral began, she remained in America, her scars never healing. "Mrs. Sacco cut herself off from the world," Sara Ehrmann remembered. "She couldn't bear it anymore, and that frightful thing just ruined their lives. She forbade her children from talking about it at all." Two years after the executions, Rosina moved in with another anarchist who had fallen in love with her while working to save her husband. The two married in 1943 and started a small poultry farm. Rosina remained a devout anarchist, once telling Dante's wife, "Don't pray. I tried it once and it didn't work." When her second husband died in 1985, Rosina moved to a nursing home, where she passed away early in the 1990s. She never spoke about the case. Dante's son Spencer did not know of his family's history until his Cub Scout master said, "Did you know that your grandfather was electrocuted?" When a neighbor told Spencer's brother, "Your grandfather was a murderer!" Dante sat his family down and shared the sad story.

Throughout the 1950s, America said little about Sacco and Vanzetti. In 1956, television networks refused to air *The Male Animal,* James Thurber's play about a small college polarized by a classroom reading of Vanzetti's famous eulogy. Sponsors considered the topic too controversial. Three years later, Massachusetts politicians learned just how hot the case remained. Because the state legislature had recently pardoned the Salem witches, one member proposed pardoning Sacco and Vanzetti. A stormy committee hearing resulted. Michael Musmanno, having since served at the Nuremberg trials and on the Pennsylvania Supreme Court, denounced Judge Thayer and called the prosecution "unscrupulous, unethical, and diabolically skillful." When one legislator asked Musmanno whether he had brought his supporters in "by bus or by train," boos and hisses came from the crowd. Only one witness—an attorney for a deceased juror—spoke against the bill, but proponents repeated the mistakes of the 1920s, infuriating the committee by attacking the Commonwealth. After a thirteen-hour hearing, the bill was defeated on the house floor without debate.

By 1960, when NBC aired a mournful Reginald Rose teleplay about the case, the widespread certainty that justice had been crucified in Massachusetts was ripe for attack. With the cold war at its height, cold warriors began to chisel away at "the myth" of Sacco and Vanzetti. Liberals had long believed "they *had* to be innocent." Now conservatives claimed they *had* to be guilty. The opening salvo of revision was *Sacco and Vanzetti: The Murder and the Myth* by Boston corporate lawyer Robert H. Montgomery. As if he were the reincarnation of Frederick Katzmann, Montgomery highlighted incriminating evidence and downplayed each doubt, convicting Sacco and Vanzetti of the Braintree crime and Vanzetti of the Bridgewater burglary. Both trials had been fair, both verdicts just, Montgomery wrote. Reds and radicals had exploited the case "for revolutionary purposes and propaganda, mass agitation, and the breaking down of the American judicial system and American institutions generally."

With the backlash begun, liberals and conservatives began blasting each other in reviews of each new book "proving" innocence or guilt. Innocence was touted in the *New Republic, Saturday Review,* and the *Nation.* Guilt was propounded by *American Heritage, Commonweal,* and the *National Review,* whose editor, William F. Buckley, called the case "a human vehicle through which to indict the existing order, condemn our institutions, dramatize the cause of proletarian socialism, scrape away at the Puritan ethic, tear and wrench the nation and cause it to bleed across the pages of history." Creating myths of their own—that Communists alone had rallied for Sacco and Vanzetti, that there had been no bias against them as anarchists—Buckley and his followers equated Sacco's and Vanzetti's so-called innocence to that of Alger Hiss and the Rosenbergs. A compromise of sorts emerged when Francis Russell's *Tragedy in Dedham* concluded that Sacco was guilty, Vanzetti innocent. This "split guilt" theory was backed by the first of many ghosts to step from the shadows of history. The former radical Max Eastman revealed that in 1942, Carlo Tresca had told him, "Sacco was guilty, Vanzetti was not." Defenders instantly impugned Tresca, claiming he had been angered by his lifelong feud with *Galleanisti*. Tresca's daughter insisted he had never hinted of Sacco's guilt.

Like the tirades of the 1920s, the cold war debate became an exercise in mutual contempt. Those calling the men innocent were "left-wing intelligentsia" duped by Communists. A book insisting on guilt was dismissed as "one long sneer." The two sides were as bitter as Moore and Katzmann in Dedham. "Consciousness of guilt" was the key! No, it was worthless! The men had been heavily armed! But they were scared! They were persecuted as radicals! But jurors denied radicalism played any part in the verdict! Again the fine points of ballistics were debated in exhausting detail. During the gun barrel hearings, Charles Van Amburgh had discounted any further tests of Sacco's gun as meaningless, but Francis Russell arranged new tests in 1961. Again Bullet III and Shell W were linked to *that* .32 Colt. Critics doubted anything could be proven by a rusty old gun and bullets that had been in the care of Van Amburgh and his son. Besides, before even testing Sacco's Colt, these latest experts had written, "There can be no doubt Sacco's pistol fired one cartridge case and one of the fatal bullets." So much for their impartiality, critics said, but the charge weakened claims of Sacco's innocence.

In 1969, Supreme Court justice William O. Douglas proffered a higher court's opinion. Innocent or guilty, Douglas wrote, Sacco and Vanzetti deserved a second trial. Those reading the courtroom transcript, Douglas noted, "will have difficulty believing that the trial with which it deals took place in the United States. All the 'i's'

were dotted and all the 't's' crossed. The game was played according to the rules. But the rules were used to perpetuate an awful injustice." Although the Supreme Court had refused to intervene in
1927, had Sacco and Vanzetti been tried in the 1960s, Douglas concluded, the court would have taken the case on several grounds—
the judge's patriotic exhortations, the manner of jury selection, the
identification of suspects without a police lineup, Captain Proctor's
retraction, and "the saturation of the trial with the radicalism of
the defendants."

In the last three decades, shouts over Sacco and Vanzetti have
diminished to occasional stirrings, yet historians continue to seek
the final word, the last clue, proof positive. The search has been
complicated by more ghosts.

A year after the executions, while researching *Boston*, Upton
Sinclair met Fred Moore in a Denver hotel. Asking for the truth
about Sacco and Vanzetti, Sinclair got the surprise of his life when
Moore said he had come to the conclusion the men were guilty. Confused and shaken, Sinclair consulted Moore's ex-wife, who assured
him, "Fred is embittered because he was dropped from the case and
it has poisoned his mind." When Sinclair shared Moore's opinion
with friends, they begged him to keep it a secret. *Boston* contains no
hint of Moore's change of heart. In 1953, Sinclair revealed it in a
social studies journal, but more details emerged in a letter only discovered in 2005. "He then told me that the men were guilty, and he
told me in every detail how he had framed a set of alibis for them,"
Sinclair wrote. Sacco and Vanzetti had never uttered the slightest
hint of their guilt, Moore said, but they had told him they were hiding dynamite on the night of their arrest. And he had come to believe they had taken to robbery to raise funds for their "idea."
Sinclair remained unconvinced. Noting Moore's drug use and dismissal from the defense, he wondered whether the lawyer's opinion
could be attributed to "his brooding on his wrongs." In 1963, Sinclair wrote, "Those who believe or declare Sacco was guilty get no
support from me." But Moore clung to his opinion until he died of
cancer in 1932. In contrast, William Thompson, who died three
years after Moore, remained convinced of the men's innocence.

As if to counter Moore, additional ghosts emerged, including two named Morelli. In 1931, Joe Morelli had confessed to a New York lawyer. Grilled on the details of April 15, 1920, Morelli passed easily. The lawyer "left completely satisfied that the gang chieftain was in the murder car and knew all the details of the planning of the robbery, the details of the shooting, and the technique of escape." Four years later and behind bars again, Morelli resumed his denials. After reading *The Untried Case*, Herbert Ehrmann's book on his investigation of the Morellis, Joe responded with a rambling ninety-six-page rebuttal that only became public in 1998. Ehrmann's book, Morelli wrote, was "childish foolishness" and "a jumble on nothingness." He belittled "smart Mr. Ehrmann" and his "trash, manufactured against me without one substantial fact to bolster them up." No, he had not been in South Braintree that day but "most likely in some cabaret, with some girl friend." And Sacco and Vanzetti? "I was personally acquainted with them, and I knew of their racket," Morelli wrote. Vanzetti had stuck up the Pawtucket Mill in 1918 and "got away clean." He "always played the greenhorn but he was one of the shrewdness 'Dago' that was known to many gangsters. Sacco was something alike, but not quite as shrewd." More than twenty "reliable gangsters" had assured Morelli that Sacco and Vanzetti "were vicious, cold-blooded killers." And the book by "smart Mr. Ehrmann" was "just something for dumb nuts like himself to read. Its stupid editorials stink. Ehrmann ought to burn the whole damn mess and then it would still stink."

If Joe Morelli wanted to absolve his gang, he should have told his brother Frank, a.k.a. Butsy. In a 1973 memoir, an ex-mobster recalled Frank Morelli's confession: "'We whacked them out, we killed those guys in the robbery,' Butsy said. 'These two greaseballs [Sacco and Vanzetti] took it on the chin.'" When his fellow mobster asked whether the Morellis were really guilty of the Braintree murders, Joe's brother "looked at me, right into my eyes, and said: 'Absolutely, Vinnie. These two suckers took it on the chin for us. That shows you how much justice there really is.'"

Yet in a case that will not die, ghosts can argue as fiercely as lawyers. Nine years after Butsy Morelli's confession was revealed, Francis Russell received a letter from the son of a North End anarchist. Ideale Gambera shared with Russell what his father had told him: "Everyone [in the Boston anarchist circle] knew that Sacco was guilty and that Vanzetti was innocent as far as the actual participation in the killing. But no one would ever break the code of silence even if it cost Vanzetti's life." How the elder Gambera knew this and why he revealed it only after decades of secrecy remains in doubt. One final ghost rose from the dead when the historian Paul Avrich interviewed a friend of Mario Buda. In 1955, Buda had talked of the Braintree robbery, saying, "Sacco c'era" (Sacco was there). Buda said nothing about Vanzetti. Was the slippery Buda finally coming clean? Had time muddled his mind or made him eager to further muddle the case? Whether true or false, Buda's surprising accusation brought to eight—himself, Carlo Tresca, Louis Pelser, Lola Andrews, two Morelli brothers, Frank Silva, and Fred Moore—the number of people who had changed their stories. Who to believe? Who to believe?

When the fiftieth anniversary of the executions approached, many in Massachusetts believed it was time to wipe away the stain. Across the Commonwealth, August 23, 1977, was declared "Nicola Sacco and Bartolomeo Vanzetti Memorial Day." Governor Michael Dukakis, who as a young law student had attended the raucous 1959 pardon hearing, signed a proclamation declaring "any stigma and disgrace should be forever removed from the names of Nicola Sacco and Bartolomeo Vanzetti." While admitting the Dedham trial had been "permeated by prejudice," Dukakis stopped short of a pardon. "We are not here to decide whether these men were guilty or innocent," the governor told the press. "We are here to say that the high standards of justice, which we in Massachusetts take such pride in, failed Sacco and Vanzetti." Standing beside the governor, Spencer Sacco brushed away tears, but the partisan politics continued. Massachusetts Republicans denounced Dukakis—"You would have thought these men were victims of a lynch mob"—and urged the anniversary be set aside to remember the Parmenter and Berardelli families, who had said nothing throughout the seven-year ordeal and still remained silent. Alvan T. Fuller Jr. said Dukakis had "disgraced himself, his office, and his state by attempting to honor the memory of two convicted murderers." New York mayor Abe Beame planned a similar memorial day but backed down when it proved too contentious.

The fiftieth anniversary revived hopes of finding some dark secret buried in the papers of participants. Under the Freedom of Information Act, FBI files on the case had been released in 1975, but those looking for a huge federal conspiracy were disappointed. Files from the National Archives revealed a federal investigation of Sacco, Vanzetti, and the *Galleanisti* late in 1920, following the Wall Street bombing. New York agents had requested information on Sacco and Vanzetti, while Katzmann asked the bureau to investigate whether any stolen money ended up in the bank account of Carlo Tresca. (None did.) But federal files contained no evidence that the bureau shared with Katzmann what it knew about Sacco and Vanzetti, nor vice versa. The files revealed: (1) prior to the Dedham trial, the bureau knew Sacco and Vanzetti only as subscribers to *Cronaca Sovversiva*; (2) an undercover agent had attended the trial, submitting reports to Washington, D.C.; and (3) federal agents also attended the appeals hearings. The FBI's Sacco-Vanzetti papers—2,189 pages now available on the Internet—begin three months after the guilty verdict and show no conspiracy to convict. Still, some papers were deemed too sensitive for public viewing. FBI files for the summer of 1926, when William Thompson was demanding access to them, note twenty-eight pages withheld. Many files from the Boston bureau read "Contents removed." Scores of pages are illegible, and hundreds have portions blacked out. As the fiftieth anniversary arrived, historians awaited new papers.

The anniversary opened both the Abbott Lawrence Lowell papers and the Massachusetts State Police Files, but certainty again proved elusive. The Lowell papers revealed little more than the

Harvard president's many letters of praise and condemnation and his own certainty that his commission had performed "an important public service." The Massachusetts State Police Files likewise contained no smoking guns, but they did offer hints that Vanzetti's gun had been his all along.

Among state police papers was a memo written by Chief Stewart. On February 16, 1921, while preparing for the trial, Stewart had visited a Brockton hardware store. Rifling through sales records, the chief had discovered Parmenter's purchase of a .32 Harrington & Richardson revolver. Parmenter had bought the revolver the previous October just after Berardelli had been hired. Sarah Berardelli had often said Parmenter bought her husband's gun for him. Had this .32, whose serial number differed from that on Vanzetti's .38, really been Berardelli's gun? Although proof of ownership was lacking, the memo led the historians William Young and David Kaiser to conclude that Berardelli's gun was a .32 and had never fallen into Vanzetti's hands. Both Stewart and Katzmann, the historians wrote, knew this before the trial. Spurred by this suggestion of misconduct, Young and Kaiser found further papers in the state police files suggesting a bullet substitution. At the grand jury hearing, examining doctor Charles McGrath had testified that all four bullets removed from Berardelli's body "looked exactly alike." Since the contrasting leftward grooves on Bullet III were plainly visible to the naked eye, Young and Kaiser concluded the fatal bullet was substituted. Both Bullet III and Shell W, they wrote, must have been planted several months before the trial, probably by Chief Stewart and his assistant.

And so the convoluted case that started with dynamite, expanded into reams of testimony, descended into denial and innuendo, then burst into protests around the world now rests in the microscopic realm. Grooves and calibers, professions of innocence, proclamations of guilt—all have been cited as definitive. Yet eight decades after the executions, there is little concrete proof in the case of Sacco and Vanzetti. There are only shifting stories and gut feelings. No one should be sent to the electric chair on gut feelings, which are the essence of reasonable doubt. And reasonable doubt cries out that Sacco and Vanzetti clearly deserved what is now granted for even a fraction of the anomalies surrounding their case—a second trial. In a different time, a different state, they might have earned another day in court, yet a deadly combination, including the pride of an old commonwealth, the zealotry of a judge and DA, the indifference of too many Americans, and the flexible morals of too many witnesses, led to a denial of justice. Still, no matter how much one wants to shout their innocence, questions remain.

If they were innocent, why did Bullet III and Shell W implicate Sacco? If these were substituted, could such a crime be kept a secret for so long? What were the men really doing, armed to the teeth, on the night of May 5? If they were rounding up radical literature, why didn't they hide the radical literature in their own homes? Why did their roundup wait until five days after Vanzetti returned from New York with warnings of imminent raids? Why did their anarchist friends halt Fred Moore's search for the real murderers? Were the ghosts who claimed Sacco guilty simply telling tales? Then again . . .

If one or both men were guilty of savage murders, how did they get so many people—casual witnesses, an Italian consulate clerk, total strangers—to lie for them? What happened to the money? Why did those who heard the bandits speak insist they had no accents? If "Sacco c'era," why did he blithely allow his gun to be test-fired? If witnesses saw *one* gunman pump bullets into Berardelli, how could Sacco have fired *one* of four bullets found in the guard? Would Vanzetti, guilty of a high-profile murder, have planned a public speech before "fellow workers"? Would Sacco have taken the day off for a payroll robbery, then returned to work the next day? But the most crucial questions probe the depths of human nature. If either man was guilty, wouldn't seven years of relentless, impassioned pleas—from Sacco's "Sono innocente!" to Vanzetti's "In all my life I have never stole and I have never killed"—qualify them as the most incredible liars and con men in world history?

Returning to the scenes of crime and punishment, one finds only collective amnesia. Boston is noted for preserving its heritage, yet its public treasures ignore Sacco and Vanzetti. There are no monuments, no memorials, no markers. In 1997, Boston mayor Thomas Menino formally accepted a plaster model of the Gutzon Borglum plaque and promised it would be cast in bronze and put on public display. But so far, one still has to wind deep into the Boston Public Library to find the model hanging outside the third-floor Special Collections Room. Beyond Boston, most of the settings from the case have been erased. Charlestown State Prison was torn down in the 1970s to make way for a community college. The Pearl Street shoe factories are gone, replaced by strip malls. In Dedham, the Norfolk County Jail has been converted to upscale condominiums where a photo of Sacco and Vanzetti hangs in the lobby across the street from the graveyard. Two blocks away, the courthouse is still in use, but when it was designated a National Historic Monument, selectmen voted not to put up a plaque. For the final word on the two gentlemen from Italy, one must return to the source—their source.

Even in these days of the Internet, rental cars, and Italy's amazing Autostrada, Torremaggiore is still "a hell of a way out towards the Adriatic." Much has changed in Sacco's hometown. Muddy streets were long ago paved, and tractors, not donkeys, head each morning toward the surrounding fields. The abandoned castle near Sacco's birthplace has been magnificently restored, becoming the centerpiece of a town whose pride rivals that of the old Commonwealth. The main street climbing gently toward the castle is called Via Sacco-Vanzetti, one of dozens of streets so named in Italy. But Torremaggiore is also a timeless town. Just as when Sacco was a boy, grapevines and olive trees still carpet the surrounding hills, church bells still ring out each morning, and residents still stroll arm in arm during the traditional *passegiata* each Sunday evening. A few hours before one *passegiata*, strolling up to greet me comes Fernanda Sacco. Pleasingly plump with huge glasses and hair as red as Rosina's, Signora Sacco is a lifetime resident of Torremaggiore and the town's lone living descendant of its lamented native son.

Born in 1932, Fernanda Sacco never met the uncle for whom she is named. But her father, Sacco's older brother Luigi, told her the entire story, and since childhood she has shared the family's grief and outrage. Now she is not five minutes inside her apartment, just off Via Sacco-Vanzetti, when she begins to swell with emotion. Along with coffee and cookies, she serves memories and family stories. From her stream of sonorous Italian, familiar names echo through her apartment—*Il giudice* Thayer, *Il procuratore* Katzmann, *Il avvocato* Moore. As if the ordeal happened yesterday, she knows the intimate details, the sad ending, the shock that sealed the Sacco family in silence. Punctuating her speech with hands that plead for answers, the retired elementary school teacher asks the lingering questions.

"They changed the bullets, they changed the gun barrel," she says. "And they say it was a fair trial. Why did they do this? Why did they kill two innocent people? *Perché? Perché?*" Words like *fiasco* and *scandolo* flow freely. Later, having invited interested friends—two teachers, a journalist, and the town's mayor—to share in the discussion, Signora Sacco brings out memorabilia. She passes around Italian newspaper clippings and photos of her trip to Boston in the summer of 2004. She tells of visiting the Dedham courthouse, where she was allowed to sit at Judge Thayer's bench. "I felt I was not myself," she remembers. "I was crying, overcome, tingling all over." Photos show her on Pearl Street and in the North End. Reliving the trip is hard for the septuagenarian, and her friends try to change the subject, but she has more to share. She reads an article from a conservative Italian paper calling her uncle a criminal. Her voice rising, she reads the letter she fired back, asking how Sacco, raised in a good family, could have been a murderer. "How can they say my uncle was a criminal?" she asks. "I know my own blood! I know who we are!"

On into the night, the talk turns to justice, redemption, and how sad it is that young people in Torremaggiore know so little about Sacco and Vanzetti. The following morning, Signora Sacco serves coffee and apologizes for having been so emotional. Then she leads the way to the cemetery. Overlooking an olive grove, the cemetery is crammed with monuments, but none commands the attention more than a tall slab near the entrance. Etched into its black marble are the words of Michael Dukakis: *Io dichiaro che ogni stigma ed ogni onta vengano per sempre cancellati dai nomi di Nicola Sacco e Bartolomeo Vanzetti.*

When the monument was installed in 1998, hundreds gathered at the site. While press from throughout Italy scrambled for photos, Signora Sacco carried the urn of ashes from the original tomb to the striking new monument. She watched as the ashes were transferred to a new urn that was interred at its base below a small photo of Sacco and a bas-relief of Torremaggiore's castle. During Mussolini's reign, she says upon departing, it was illegal to even photograph her uncle's tomb. Now his photo and his monument greet each visitor to the cemetery.

A three-course lunch and a few farewells later, "lo scrittore Americano" is on the last leg of the long trip. In both distance and ambience, Villafalletto is as far from Torremaggiore as Sacco's temperament was from Vanzetti's. Flat instead of hilly, in the snowy north instead of the sunlit south, Villafalletto is a blink of a town offering few visible reminders of its most famous native. The main street, Via Sacco-Vanzetti, leads to the large house where, as a plaque notes, Vanzetti was born. From the house one can see the squat nineteenth-century bell tower dominating a low skyline. Sepia walls, green shutters, and tile roofs line winding streets that occasionally straighten to reveal nearby fields as manicured as those in sketches by Van Gogh. There are no Vanzettis left in Villafalletto, just rumors of a niece in Turin who does not care to be contacted. But each year, Villafalletto does more to remember the boy who won prizes in its schools only to return in ashes.

In 1977, Italian anarchists converged on the little town, hoping to rename it. Town officials refused, but for months road signs leading to Villafalletto featured bright red graffiti proclaiming "Villa Vanzetti." Anarchists also left a plaque in the town's only piazza announcing that Sacco and Vanzetti were "Killed by the state because they were anarchists. Their sacrifice reinforces our will and our struggle." Yet only recently has Villafalletto begun celebrating Vanzetti as a person, not just a political symbol. Since the seventy-fifth anniversary of the execution in 2002, conferences, plays, and readings from new Italian books on the case have been held here. There is talk of more memorials, including perhaps a statue in Turin. For now, however, one must wind through the fields to the cemetery to pay final remembrance.

Intermingled with Sacco's, Vanzetti's ashes remain where his sister laid them in sorrow upon her return from America. Luigia, too, lies in the tomb beside the rest of the family. Aside from Vanzetti's mother and devoted sister, other Vanzettis lived to ripe old ages. Brother Ettore, just three when Bartolomeo left, lived into his seventies, his father into his eighties, and sister Vincenzina into her nineties. Yet the eye is drawn to an innocent photo of a mustachioed young man, the name Bartolomeo, and the stark span of his shortened life—1888–1927. And with those numbers, here on this flat plain with the bell tower in the distance and the Alps beyond, the deepening saga ends. Aside from ashes, a haunted tragedy—shaded by doubts, shrouded by scandal and the equivocal judgment of mankind—is what remains of two anarchists, two gentlemen who lived the dream and the nightmare of Italy's most famous exile.

> You shall be forced to leave behind those things
> You love most dearly, and this is the first
> Arrow the bow of your exile will shoot.
> And you will know how salty is the taste
> Of others' bread, how hard the road that takes
> You down and up the stairs of others' homes.
> But what will weight you down the most will be
> The despicable, senseless company
> Whom you shall have to bear in that sad vale;
> And all ungrateful, all completely mad
> And vicious, they shall turn on you, but soon
> Their cheeks, not yours, will have to blush from shame.
> —Dante, *Paradiso*

Acknowledgments

The chronicling of such a massively documented case cannot be taken on by a lone writer with a laptop. I am therefore grateful to numerous enthusiasts who came from out of the woodwork or the stacks to assist me. The list begins with Tyler Hauck, a recent college grad with a love of history, who volunteered to dive into the microfilm at the Boston Public Library. When I was utterly overwhelmed by the mountain of materials ahead, Tyler got me started by digging up new details revealing how Sacco and Vanzetti were being perceived even before their trial. I am grateful for his interest, patience, and attention to the context of the case.

Keepers of library special collections in this forward-facing country are keepers of the culture, and for their help in cataloging and opening the vast archives on Sacco and Vanzetti, I am indebted to Roberta Zonghi and Eric Frazier at the Boston Public Library, and David Warrington and Sally Vermaaten at the Harvard Law School Library. Robert D'Attilio, the widely acknowledged master of this case, helped steer me from certain dead ends and toward more open highways. Thanks to lawyer Jenny Daniell for insights into legal matters. Again, I offer *mille grazie* to my friend, the artist and proud anarchist Pietro Spica, for insights into immigration, "the idea," and all things Italian. And in the same flavor, *devo ringraziare la Signora Fernanda Sacco, nipote di Nicola, che mi ha fato sentire benvenuto nel mio soggiorno a Torremaggiore, e Ivano Bellario che mi ha fato lo stesso favore a Villafalletto.*

I owe thanks to my agent, Jeff Kleinman, my former editor at Viking, Ray Roberts, and his successor, Cliff Corcoran, for realizing that an oft-covered subject could still yield new nuggets and again be brought alive. Finally, I thank my family for allowing me to talk altogether too much about Sacco and Vanzetti and their plight and for accepting my Italian detour from the glory that was Rome to the more modest confines of Torremaggiore, where there were few three-star Michelin sites. To my wife, Julie, I owe the greatest thanks for permitting me to indulge my interests and for again being my first line of defense against suffocating detail. Details of her patience, love, and support would themselves fill a vast archive, one where I intend to continue my research.

Notes

PROLOGUE

5   Enveloped in brown paper: *New York Times,* May 1, 1919, 3.
6   "infernal machine"; "Negro servant": *Atlanta Constitution,* April 30, 1919, 1.
6   Sealed with a red sticker: Ibid., 3.
6   "I do not recollect": Ibid.
7   "disgruntled anarchists": *Atlanta Constitution,* May 1, 1919, 6.
7   "vigorous prosecution": Stanley Coben, *A. Mitchell Palmer: Politician* (New York: Columbia University Press, 1963), 205.
7   "I trust Washington will buck up": *New York Times,* May 2, 1919, 3.
7   Tragic stories: "The Influenza Pandemic of 1918," http://www.stanford.edu/group/virus/uda/.
7   The dead, their bodies turned a ghastly blue: John M. Barry, *The Great Influenza: The Epic Story of the Deadliest Plague in History* (New York: Viking, 2004), 4–5.
9   "The world is coming to an end!": Coben, 205.
9   "The powers that be": Paul Avrich, *Sacco and Vanzetti: The Anarchist Background* (Princeton, NJ: Princeton University Press, 1995), 81.
10   "a few free treatments": Robert K. Murray, *Red Scare: A Study in National Hysteria, 1919–1920* (Minneapolis: University of Minnesota Press, 1955), 80.
10   "If I had my way": Ibid., 83.
10   Headlines stoked the fear: Ibid., 116.
10   CITIES PREPARE FOR REDS: *Los Angeles Times,* July 3, 1919, 1.
10   "There is hardly a respectable citizen": Coben, 196.
11   "the sharp tongues of the Revolution's head: Francis Russell, *Sacco and Vanzetti: The Case Resolved* (New York: Harper and Row, 1986), 82.

CHAPTER ONE: "LAMBS AND WOLVES"

13 "We always had the idea": *The Sacco-Vanzetti Case* (Mamaroneck, NY: Paul P. Appel, 1969), 2067. Hereafter referred to as Trial Transcript.

13 Prostrated with grief: Marion Denman Frankfurter and Gardner Jackson, *The Letters of Sacco and Vanzetti* (New York: Penguin, 1997), 10.

13 "that one will end on the gallows!": Francis Russell, *Tragedy in Dedham* (New York: McGraw-Hill, 1962), 80.

13 "I remember when wi youst": Frankfurter and Jackson, 12.

14 "I was a 'Dago,'": Avrich, *Sacco and Vanzetti: The Anarchist Background*, 35.

14 "The thought of getting married": Bartolomeo Vanzetti, *Il Caso Sacco e Vanzetti: Lettere ai familiari* (Rome: Editori Riuniti, 1971), 53. This is a collection of Vanzetti's letters in Italian.

14 "A little roof, a field": Frankfurter and Jackson, 82.

15 "my spiritual son": Ibid., 178.

15 "For some boys it was Ty Cobb": Paul Avrich, *Anarchist Voices: An Oral History of Anarchism in America* (Princeton, NJ: Princeton University Press, 1995), 104.

15 "a great anarchist": Avrich, *Sacco and Vanzetti: The Anarchist Background*, 160.

15 "plant[ed] the poof": Ibid., 103, 158.

16 "our master.": Russell, *Tragedy in Dedham*, 84.

16 "Dynamite is a paste": Avrich, *Sacco and Vanzetti: The Anarchist Background*, 98, 75.

16 "a rag of a paper": Robert D'Attilio, "La Salute è in Voi: The Anarchist Dimension," in *Sacco-Vanzetti: Developments and Reconsiderations—1979, Conference Proceedings* (Boston: Boston Public Library, 1982), 81.

16 "the most rabid, seditious, and anarchistic sheet": Avrich, *Sacco and Vanzetti: The Anarchist Background*, 95.

16 "To hell with the Constitution!": *Cronaca Sovversiva*, June 6, 1914, 6.

16 "We will dynamite you!": Paul Avrich, "Sacco and Vanzetti's Revenge," in Philip Cannistraro and Gerald Meyer, eds., *The Lost World of Italian-American Radicalism* (Westport, CT: Praeger, 2003), 164.

16 "under grave charges": Vanzetti Correspondence, Sacco-Vanzetti Case Papers, Boston Public Library (hereafter BPL).

17 "about as far away from murderers": Robert H. Montgomery, *The Murder and the Myth* (New York: Devin-Adair, 1960), 434.

17 "A man who is in his garden": Roberta Strauss Feuerlicht, *Justice Crucified: The Story of Sacco and Vanzetti* (New York: McGraw-Hill, 1977), 13.

17 "loved flowers, he loved birds": "The Reminiscences of Gardner Jackson [oral history]," 1955, on p. 209 in the Columbia University Oral History Research Office Collection (hereafter referred to as CUOHROC).

17 "believed in and taught violence": Avrich, *Sacco and Vanzetti: The Anarchist Background*, 161.

18 "They *had* to be innocent": Russell, *Tragedy in Dedham*, xii.

18   "My life cannot rise": Vanzetti, *Il Caso Sacco e Vanzetti*, 21.

18   "We knocked down mountains": Ibid., 62.

19   "it takes a poet of first magnitude": Frankfurter and Jackson, 207.

19   "unspeakably beautiful": Ibid., 223.

19   "In the evening, when I quit work": Vanzetti, *Il Caso Sacco e Vanzetti*, 39.

19   "the good, the worshipped mother": Ibid., 22.

19   "the fever of knowledge": Frankfurter and Jackson, 110.

19   "I came to understand": Vanzetti, *Il Caso Sacco e Vanzetti*, 31.

20   "There was nothing for me to do": Avrich, *Sacco and Vanzetti: The Anarchist Background*, 19.

20   "rotten food hardly fit for dogs": Vanzetti, *Il Caso Sacco e Vanzetti*, 25.

21   "in general, rather ignorant": Ibid., 50.

21   "the paternal home": Franco Ramella, *I documenti personali e la storia dell'emigrazione: Le lettere americane di Giovanni Batista Vanzetti, contadino cuneese* (Cuneo, Italy: Rivista dell'Istituto Storico della Ressitenza in Cuneo e Provincia, n.d.), 151.

21   "the immense hell pit": Vanzetti, *Il Caso Sacco e Vanzetti*, 62.

21   "I came to believe": Ibid., 32.

21   "perambulating philosopher": Frankfurter and Jackson, 242.

22   "I have had to suffer": Vanzetti, *Il Caso Sacco e Vanzetti*, 49.

22   "a dumbling": Frankfurter and Jackson, 32.

23   "La Mcrica": Barry Moreno, *Italian Americans* (New York: Ivy Press Limited, 2003), 501.

23   "I was crazy to come to this country": Trial Transcript, 1818.

23   "like a puppy": Feuerlicht, *Justice Crucified*, 11.

23   "Sacco was a genius at his work": Avrich, *Anarchist Voices*, 23.

24   "I don't know anybody in Milford": Ibid., 95.

25   "The nightmares of the lower classes": Frankfurter and Jackson, 68.

25   "watched over, inspected": George Woodcock, *The Anarchist Reader* (Glasgow: Fontana/Collins, 1977), 13.

26   And yet our idea: Pietro Gori, "Addio a Lugano," http://www.nelvento.net/addio-lugano.html.

26   "mankind's tormentors": Barbara Tuchman, *The Proud Tower: A Portrait of the World Before the War, 1890–1914* (New York: Macmillan, 1966), 69.

26   "mutual aid": Woodcock, 22.

26   "If men were angels": Alexander Hamilton, James Madison, and John Jay, *The Federalist Papers* (New York: New American Library, 1961), 322.

27   "a crime against the whole human race": Tuchman, 106–108.

27   "red-handed, unwashed foreigner": John Dos Passos, *Facing the Chair: Story of the Americanization of Two Foreign Born Workmen* (Boston Sacco-Vanzetti Defense Committee, 1927), 56.

27   "That government is best": Henry David Thoreau, "Civil Disobedience," in *The Selected Works of Thoreau* (Boston: Cambridge Editions, Houghton Mifflin, 1975), 789.

27   "the propaganda of the deed": Tuchman, 71.

27   "Oh friend": Frankfurter and Jackson, 99.
27   "no government, no police": Avrich, *Sacco and Vanzetti: The Anarchist Background*, 28.
27–28 "In whatever concerns *Cronaca Sovversiva*": *Sacco-Vanzetti: Developments and Reconsiderations*, 84.
28   "If you don't know any better": *Cronaca Sovversiva*, August 19, 1916, 4.
28   "as if she did not care": Ibid., January 6, 1917, 3.
28   "soldier who prostitutes himself": Ibid., May 26, 1917, 1.
29   "I cannot describe": Vanzetti, *Il Caso Sacco e Vanzetti*, 57.
29   Twelve-year-old Lefevre Brini: Avrich, *Anarchist Voices*, 106.
30   mysterious bombings: Avrich, *Sacco and Vanzetti: The Anarchist Background*, 104–107.
30   "I leave my wife here": Trial Transcript, 1820.
30   "a volcano": Vanzetti, *Il Caso Sacco e Vanzetti*, 58.
30   Sniffed out by a dog: Avrich, *Anarchist Voices*, 199.
30   Agents also seized: Avrich, *Sacco and Vanzetti: The Anarchist Background*, 197.
31   "I have seen human greed": Vanzetti, *Il Caso Sacco e Vanzetti*, 62–63.
31   "Stop talking, Nick": Trial Transcript, 2006; and Avrich, *Sacco and Vanzetti: The Anarchist Background*, 69.

CHAPTER TWO: "A GUNMAN JOB"

34   Suddenly its driver called out: Trial Transcript, Vol. VI, 429.
34   "Some funny looking people": Russell, *Tragedy in Dedham*, 31.
34   "Buick Baby Six": *Boston Herald*, April 16, 1920, 2.
35   "They had that character": Trial Transcript, 455.
35   "I don't think I owe you fellows": Ibid., 452.
35   "Go ahead, never mind the car": William Young and David E. Kaiser, *Postmortem: New Evidence in the Case of Sacco and Vanzetti* (Amherst: University of Massachusetts Press, 1985), 86.
35   "the roll": Trial Transcript, 432.
35   "Bostock, when you go up by": Trial Transcript, 187.
37   "Put them up!": Ibid., 5005.
37   "Get out of the way": Russell, *Tragedy in Dedham*, 40.
37   "I seen a glance": Trial Transcript, 5567.
38   The chief found witnesses of little use: Russell, *Tragedy in Dedham*, 41–42.
38   "laughing and talking some foreign gibberish": George Chisholm, statement to Michael E. Stewart and Albert Brouillard, June 1, 1921, Massachusetts State Police Files.
39   "What the hell": Trial Transcript, 603.
39   "a dark complected man": Ibid., 597.
40–41 "the most homogeneous": Cleveland Amory, *The Proper Bostonians* (New York: E. P. Dutton, 1947), 324.
41   "Nothing is clearer": Albert Bushnell Hart, ed., *Commonwealth History*

of Massachusetts, Colony, Province, and State, Vol. 5 (New York: States History Company, 1927), 675.

41 **"We are vanishing"**: Richard D. Brown and Jack Tager, *Massachusetts: A Concise History* (Amherst: University of Massachusetts Press, 2000), 204, 240–244.

42 **"The Italian experiences no difficulty"**: Wayne Moquin and Charles Van Doren, eds., *A Documentary History of the Italian Americans* (New York: Praeger, 1974), 52.

42 **"This aggregation of assassins"**: Ibid., 181.

42 **"The underlying cause"**: Ibid., 169.

43 **"inferior stocks"**: Brown and Tager, 231.

43 **"stand firm and stamp out lawlessness"**: *Braintree Observer,* April 24, 1920, 4.

43 **"Dear Son, I know very well"**: Sacco Correspondence, Sacco-Vanzetti Case Papers, Harvard Law School (hereafter referred to as HLS), Box 41, Folder 62.

44 **The gang's leader**: *New York Times,* April 16, 1920, 18.

44 **"a broken heart"**: *Boston Post,* April 19, 1920, 6.

45 **"About a week before the shooting"**: Sarah Berardelli, statement to Michael E. Stewart, January 31, 1921, Massachusetts State Police Files.

45 **all that remained of the crime were rumors**: *Boston Evening Globe,* April 16, 1920, 1; *Boston Herald,* April 16, 1920, 2; and *Boston Globe,* April 16, 1920, 19.

45 **"one of the most irresponsible persons"**: Pinkerton Report on the South Braintree Holdup, BPL, 7, 25.

45 **"cold blooded shootings"**: *Boston Post,* April 16, 1920, 1.

45 **"Berardelli fell at the first shot"**: *Boston Globe,* April 16, 1920, 19.

45 **"closed in on Parmenter"**: *Boston Herald,* April 16, 1920, 2.

45 **"fusillade of bullets"**: *Boston American,* April 16, 1920, 2.

45 **"Tony the Wop"**: Pinkerton Report on the South Braintree Holdup, BPL; Trial Transcript, 4539.

46 PALMISANO NOW IN AUBURN PRISON: Massachusetts State Police Files.

46 **descriptions at the inquest**: Trial Transcript, Vol. VI, 433–460.

46 **Taking back routes**: *Boston Globe,* April 18, 1920, 2.

47 **"a drug fiend"**: Prosecution Papers, Massachusetts State Police Files.

47 **"The men who did this job"**: Feuerlicht, *Justice Crucified,* 8.

48 **"5'8", 150 pounds"**: Trial Transcript, Vol. VI, 363–389.

48 **"Reds and Bolsheviks"**: Russell, *Tragedy in Dedham,* 49–51.

49 **"There is nothing the matter with her"**: Michael E. Stewart, "Commonwealth vs. Nicola Sacco and Bartolomeo Vanzetti—Two Murders, a Robbery, and the Eternal Myth," private paper, 1964, Michael E. Stewart Papers, BPL, 4.

49 **"The dates involved"**: *New Bedford Standard-Times,* August 24, 1952, 15.

49 **"It would not be surprising"**: *Boston Globe,* April 19, 1920, 1.

49 **"bad people"**: Stewart, 5.

50 **"carefully raked over"**: Ibid.

51 **"He had red spots"**: Trial Transcript, 4985.

51   He dreaded the journey: Elizabeth Gurley Flynn, *The Rebel Girl: An Autobiography—My First Life (1906–1926)* (New York: International Publishers, 1973), 298.
51   "the mopping up": Trial Transcript, xxx.
52   "The best way to take": Ibid., 1850.
52   "Is it not early?": Ibid., 4987.
52   Only when the dead man's lawyer blabbed: *Boston Herald,* May 4, 1920, 2.
52   "I was afraid": Trial Transcript, 1808.
53   money for "propaganda": Ibid., 1715.
53   "that it was terrible to be deported": Ibid., 4952.
53   "I've come for the milk!": *Boston Herald,* May 8, 1920, 2.
54   Testifying at an inquest: Young and Kaiser, *Postmortem,* 69.
55   "Proletarians, you have fought all the wars": Trial Transcript, 2120.
55   "If I was arrested": Mary Heaton Vorse, *A Footnote to Folly* (New York: Farrar and Rinehart, 1935), 333.

CHAPTER THREE: "YEGGS"

56   mug shots made the front page: *Boston Evening Globe,* May 7, 1920, 1; and *Boston Herald,* May 7, 1920, 1.
57   "yeggs": *Boston Herald,* May 9, 1920, 1; and *Braintree Observer,* May 8, 1920, 1.
57   FEELS HE HAS BRAINTREE BAND: *Boston Evening Globe,* May 7, 1920, 1.
57   "Am fish peddler": Trial Transcript, 842–846.
58   "we go into the woods": Ibid., 842–850.
58   "To give a name": Bartolomeo Vanzetti, *Background of the Plymouth Trial* (Chelsea, MA: Road to Freedom Group, 1926), 11.
58   "Are you a Communist?": Trial Transcript, 2112.
59   "I don't know myself": Ibid., 1844–1845.
59   "got Sacco and Vanzetti": Russell, *Tragedy in Dedham,* 5.
60   "shrewdness and cleverness": *Brockton Evening Enterprise,* October 16, 1953, 22.
60   He *knew* Sacco was guilty: Russell, *Tragedy in Dedham,* 67–68.
60   "Do you know Berardelli?": Trial Transcript, 1945.
61   "I read in the *Boston Post*": Nicola Sacco, statement to Frederick Katzmann, Massachusetts State Police Files.
61   "I am ashamed": Bartolomeo Vanzetti, statement to Frederick Katzmann, Massachusetts State Police Files.
61   "the man who was driving": Identification of Defendant Bert Vanzelli [*sic*], Sacco-Vanzetti Case Papers, HLS, Box 3, Folder 19.
62   "I never saw that man before": Ibid.
62   "That looks like the man": Identification of Defendant Nicolas Sacco, Sacco-Vanzetti Case Papers, HLS, Box 3, Folder 19.
62   "not like Sacco or Vanzetti": David Felix, *Protest: Sacco and Vanzetti and the Intellectuals* (Bloomington: Indiana University Press, 1965), 46.

62   "That man Sacco might know me": Ricardo Orciani, statement to Frederick Katzmann, Massachusetts State Police Files.

62   "obsessed with the desire to get somebody": Young and Kaiser, *Postmortem*, 159.

62–63 "the unemotional exterior of an American Indian": *Boston American*, May 9, 1920, 3.

63   Now state police knew: Young and Kaiser, 125.

63   "shot up the peaceful town": *Boston American*, May 9, 1920, 3.

63   "admits to being a radical": *Boston American*, May 7, 1920, 2; and *Boston Post*, May 7, 1920, 13.

63   "comparatively easy": *Boston American*, May 9, 1920, 3.

64   "We couldn't believe": Avrich, *Anarchist Voices*, 106.

64   Among his many cellmates: "The Reminiscences of Aldino Felicani [oral history]," 1954, on p. 19 in CUOHROC.

65   "Sacco was a man of action": Ibid., 64.

65   "Due to the relationship": Avrich, *Anarchist Voices*, 48.

65   Strewn with typewriters: Harold Blumenfeld, *Sacco and Vanzetti: Murderers or Murdered* (New York: Scholastic Book Services, 1972), 32–33.

65   "THIS IS A BATTLE": Sacco-Vanzetti Defense Committee Correspondence, BPL.

65   Initial contributions: *Financial Report of the Sacco-Vanzetti Defense Committee*, Boston, 1925, 12.

66   "The defendant has nothing to offer": Trial Transcript, Vol. VI, 34.

66   "the following information": Vanzetti Correspondence, BPL.

67   one shocking report after another: *Boston Herald*, March 8, 1920, 1; March 10, 1920, 4; March 13, 1920, 1; March 25, 1920, 1; and April 7, 1920, 1.

67   "There is hardly a burial": *Boston Globe*, August 1, 1920, 6.

68   "a training-school for anti-Americanism": "Crime and the Movies," *Literary Digest*, May 7, 1921, 19.

68   "giving them no quarter": *Dedham Transcript*, June 18, 1921, 4.

68   "He had quite a voice": Russell, *Tragedy in Dedham*, 19.

68   "I feel sure": Louis Joughin and Edmund M. Morgan, *The Legacy of Sacco and Vanzetti* (Chicago: Quadrangle Books, 1948), 36.

68   "I have seen him since in Brockton": Trial Transcript, Vol. VI, 49.

68   "I did not get much of a look": Ibid., 94.

68   "a short, well trimmed mustache": Ibid., 76.

69   "The ends had been cut off": Ibid., 90.

69   "He struck me immediately": Ibid., 76.

69   "He was some kind of foreigner": Ibid., 116.

69   "I could tell he was a foreigner": Ibid., 133.

69   "whether finding a shell": Ibid., 353.

70   "The thing I remember most": Russell, *Tragedy in Dedham*, 19.

70   he wrote again to Felicani: Vanzetti Correspondence, BPL.

70   the Pinkerton report: Trial Transcript, Vol. VI, 363–365.

70   Vanzetti would later wonder: Vanzetti, *Background of the Plymouth Trial*, 20.

71   "That is just the same story, isn't it?": Trial Transcript, Vol. VI, 268–269.
72   "One fifteen, was it?": Ibid., 273.
73   "It had nothing to do": Ibid., 263–276.
73   "Of course you know": Ibid., 297.
73   "The Dagos stand together": Vanzetti, *Background of the Plymouth Trial*, 21.
74   "I told him": Ibid., 28.
74   "I was willing to take the stand,": Ibid., 34.
74   According to James Graham: James M. Graham letter to Robert H. Montgomery, March 13, 1958, Michael E. Stewart Papers, BPL.
75   "You may go to your homes": Trial Transcript, Vol. VI, 336.
75   "Coraggio!": Russell, *Tragedy in Dedham*, 105.
75   "He did not want it known": Trial Transcript, Vol. VI, 356.
75   "If I had known": Felix, *Protest*, 51.
75   Back in Italy: Luigi Botta, *Sacco e Vanzetti: Giustiziata la verità* (Cavallermaggiore, Italy: Edizione Gribaudo, 1978), 255.
75   When Vanzetti finally wrote about his first trial: Vanzetti, *Background of the Plymouth Trial*, 6, 17, 27–28.
76   "barbaric and antiquated": *Boston Globe*, March 11, 1923, 1.
76   Noting him as "a man of much greater intelligence": Charlestown State Prison Records, Massachusetts State Archives.
76–77 "I heard the iron door": Vanzetti, *Background of the Plymouth Trial*, 37.
77   five hundred pounds of iron sash weights: Ron Chernow, *The House of Morgan: An American Banking Dynasty and the Rise of Modern Finance* (New York: Atlantic Monthly Press, 1990), 212.
78   Windows rained shards of glass: Ibid., 212.
78   "I think we had better stop trading": *New York Times*, September 17, 1921.
78   Thirty-eight people were dead or dying: Chernow, 212.
78   Once accident had been ruled out: *New York Times*, September 17, 1920, 8.
79   "The plot was conceived": Avrich, *Sacco and Vanzetti: The Anarchist Background*, 206.
79   "They have accused me": Federal Bureau of Investigation, Sacco-Vanzetti Case, File Number 61–126 (hereafter called FBI Files), 12a–14.
79   Within weeks, Mario Buda: Avrich, *Sacco and Vanzetti: The Anarchist Background*, 207.

CHAPTER FOUR: "SHOUT FROM THE ROOFTOPS"

81   "this long and dolorous Calvary . . . this terrible and iniquitous Bastile": Frankfurter and Jackson, *The Letters of Sacco and Vanzetti*, 8, 28.
82   "Now they are accusing me of murder": Vanzetti, *Il Caso Sacco e Vanzetti*, 64.

82 **Sacco was not in jail long:** Ralph Colp Jr., "Sacco's Struggle for Sanity," *Nation*, August 16, 1958, 65.

83 **"Elizabetta, I know you":** Flynn, *The Rebel Girl*, 303.

83 **"To steal money":** Ibid., 304.

84 **"a friendly way":** Vorse, *A Footnote to Folly*, 333.

84 **"What have I worked for in my life?":** Ibid.

84 **"Wouldn't that go against Nick?":** Flynn, 305.

84 **"the masterpieces of art and science":** Vanzetti, *Il Caso Sacco e Vanzetti*, 65.

84 **his stinking chamber pot:** Victor Nelson, *Prison Days and Nights* (Garden City, NY: Garden City Publishing Co., 1933), 11.

84 **"wretches":** Vanzetti, *Il Caso Sacco e Vanzetti*, 65.

85 **"prison stupor":** Nelson, 161, 223.

85 **"Do not keep my arrest hidden":** Vanzetti, *Il Caso Sacco e Vanzetti*, 65.

85 **"He lived cases":** Dorothy Gallagher, *All the Right Enemies: The Life and Murder of Carlo Tresca* (New Brunswick, NJ: Rutgers University Press, 1988), 84.

86 **Moore did not like to admit:** Geoffrey Cowan, *The People v. Clarence Darrow* (New York: Times Books, Random House, 1993), 158.

86 **simultaneous midwestern cases:** Joseph R. Conlin, *At the Point of Production: The Local History of the IWW* (Westport, CT: Greenwood, 1981), 158–160; and William Haywood, *Bill Haywood's Book: The Autobiography of Big Bill Haywood* (New York: International Publishers, 1929), 342–343.

87 **"keep your eye on the ball"; "Talk to me on white man's basis!":** Moore Correspondence, BPL; and Trial Transcript, 3881.

87 **"the frame-up system":** Moore Correspondence, BPL.

88 **seeking respite from the pressure:** John L. Spivak, *A Man in His Time* (New York: Horizon, 1967), 115.

88 **"We didn't know what to do":** Felicani oral history, CUOHROC, 60.

88 **"busy as the devil":** Moore Correspondence, BPL.

88 **"at least someone":** Ibid.

88 **"to keep out of this thing":** Trial Transcript, 5215.

89 **"we have decided":** Moore Correspondence, BPL.

89 **"a mixture of bad Italian":** Ibid.

89 **"My itinerary has been as follows":** Motion for Continuance, Fred Moore, Sacco-Vanzetti Case Papers, HLS Box 4, Folder 33.

89 **"a man of faith and ability":** Vanzetti, *Il Caso Sacco e Vanzetti*, 68.

89 **"an Italian in Massachusetts":** Moore Correspondence, BPL.

90 **"Money talks more effectively":** Moore to W. J. Ryan, Sacco-Vanzetti Case Papers, HLS.

90 **$2,350 in September:** *Financial Report of the Sacco-Vanzetti Defense Committee*, 12–14.

90 **"Moore was . . . an honest person":** Felicani oral history, 87.

90 **"ability and fairness":** Montgomery, *The Murder and the Myth*, 69.

91 **"There is grave danger":** *Shall There Be a Mooney Frame-up in New*

England? Sacco-Vanzetti Defense Committee, 1921, Massachusetts State Police Files.

91   **On July 22, 1916:** Richard H. Frost, *The Mooney Case* (Stanford, CA: Stanford University Press, 1968), 87, 25–35, 298, 293, 304, 311–318. Mooney was finally pardoned in 1939.

92   **"an atmosphere of viciousness":** John Nicholas Beffel, "Eels and the Electric Chair," *New Republic,* December 29, 1920, 129.

92   **"Italian labor organizer":** Art Shields, *Are They Doomed?* (New York: Workers Defense League, 1921), 11.

92   **December—$6,634.85:** *Financial Report of the Sacco-Vanzetti Defense Committee,* 16–22.

92   **"The people proclaim my innocence":** Vanzetti, *Il Caso Sacco e Vanzetti,* 64.

93   **"Sacco does not smoke":** Prosecution Papers, Sacco-Vanzetti Case Papers, HLS, Reel 20.

93   **"like a Turk":** Frankfurter and Jackson, *The Letters of Sacco and Vanzetti,* 250.

93   **"the sight of blood":** Young and Kaiser, *Postmortem,* 74.

93   **Sacco "could speak good English":** Massachusetts State Police Files.

93   **"notorious Galleani group":** Trial Transcript, 4570.

94   **"Burn this as soon as you read it":** Interview with John Ruzzamenti, Sacco-Vanzetti Case Papers, HLS, Box 5, Folder 69.

94   **"My Dear John":** Trial Transcript, 4502, 4489–4490.

94   **"right hard up against it":** Ibid., 4493.

94   **"I haven't got a case":** Interview with John Ruzzamenti, Sacco-Vanzetti Case Papers, HLS, Box 5, Folder 69.

95   **"a figment of imagination":** FBI Files, part 8, 63–72.

95   **"this evil inquisition":** Sacco Correspondence, BPL.

95   **"The poor Nick":** Vanzetti Correspondence, BPL.

95–96 **"There will be a mock trial":** Herbert B. Ehrmann, *The Case That Will Not Die: Commonwealth vs. Sacco and Vanzetti* (Boston: Little, Brown, 1969), 163.

96   **"Of course," DeFalco answered:** Herbert B. Ehrmann Papers, HLS, Box 5, Folder 16.

96   **Late that evening:** Russell, *Tragedy in Dedham,* 120.

96   **"we have a little society of our own":** *Boston Post,* January 28, 1921, 1.

96   **"fix those anarchists":** *Boston American,* February 3, 1921, 8.

96   **"If those two victims":** *Boston Post,* February 2, 1921, 2.

97   **"I have heard all the testimony":** *Boston American,* February 3, 1921, 8.

97   **"reprehensible to the last degree":** *Boston Post,* February 4, 1921, 8.

97   **In 1931, she was convicted:** Russell, *Tragedy in Dedham,* 121.

97   **"Neither in this case":** *Boston Globe,* February 2, 1921, 2.

97   **"It was front page stuff":** Ehrmann, *The Case That Will Not Die,* 165.

97   **"What a pigsty!":** Vanzetti, *Il Caso Sacco e Vanzetti,* 68.

97   **"Getting started is damned hard":** Motion for continuance, February 23, 1921, Sacco-Vanzetti Case Papers, HLS, Box 4, Folder 33.

98   "a nice fellow": Moore Correspondence, BPL.
98   "Sure enough the 15th": Ibid.
99   "The boy is as innocent": Ibid.
99   "The fellow is mighty agreeable": Ibid.
99   "We will take care": Ibid.
100 "The chief charge": Ibid.
100 "I have done my duty": Ibid.
100 "Stop bothering with the Saccos": Eugene Lyons, *Assignment in Utopia* (New York: Harcourt, Brace, 1937), 26–27.

CHAPTER FIVE: "I SEEN THIS FELLOW SHOOT THIS FELLOW"

104 "painful, confining, and distressing": Trial Transcript, 3.
104 "more closely watched": *Boston Globe,* May 29, 1921, 12.
105 "Not lack of courage, is it?": *Boston Globe,* June 1, 1921, 20.
105 Gelotte, Otto: Defense Papers, Sacco-Vanzetti Case, HLS, Box 4, Folder 1.
106 no "capitalists": Trial Transcript, 5052.
106 Carter, Roscoe A: Defense Papers, Sacco-Vanzetti Case, HLS, Box 4, Folder 1.
106 "When we adjourned": Trial Transcript, 33.
107 "The jury is in bed": *Boston Globe,* June 4, 1921, 1.
107 dog-eared *National Geographic*s: Russell, *Tragedy in Dedham,* 137.
108 "pretty well burned": Trial Transcript, 139, 160.
109 "I thought they was Italian fruit peddlers": Ibid., 195.
109 "As I looked down there": Ibid., 188–189.
109 "the man who killed Berardelli": Identification of Defendant Nicholas Sacco, Sacco-Vanzetti Case Papers, HLS, Box 3, Folder 19.
109 "probably twenty-six or twenty-seven": Trial Transcript, 204–216.
109 was soon fired: Ehrmann, *The Case That Will Not Die,* 192.
109 "one of the most irresponsible persons": Pinkerton Report on the South Braintree Holdup, BPL, 7, 25.
110 made one juror wonder: John Dever Papers, BPL.
110 "He was a man": Trial Transcript, 223–224.
111 "His left hand": Ibid., 232–233, 240.
111 "Yes sir, I think I did": Ibid., 240.
111 Sacco leaned forward: Russell, *Tragedy in Dedham,* 144.
112 "Not since I saw him in Quincy": Trial Transcript, 255.
112 "The best I can remember": Ibid., 287.
112 "I can't say that they are": Ibid., 276.
112 "I seen this fellow shoot this fellow": Ibid., 292–294.
113 "Now, those windows": Ibid., 297.
113 "I seen everything happen": Ibid., 298–299.
113 "In other words," Moore said: Ibid., 300.
114 "falsehood!": Ibid., 306–310.
114 "And what peculiar quality": Ibid., 315.
114 "Things seem to be going well": Vanzetti, *Il Caso Sacco e Vanzetti,* 71.

114   Both blamed his stomach trouble on stress: Moore Correspondence, BPL.
115   "It was quite similar": Trial Transcript, 5047.
115   "in the West or in California": Ibid., 5049.
115   "Katzmann would say something": Ibid., 5380, 4982.
115   "I hope to heaven": Ibid., 4999.
115   "For God's sake": Ibid., 5062.
115   "I'll show them": Ibid., 4924.
116   "Did you ever see a case": Ibid., 4930.
116   "Mark you," and "What say?": Ibid., 4, 13.
116   "arnuchists": Russell, *Tragedy in Dedham,* 157.
116   "Bernadelli": *Boston Evening Globe,* June 9, 1921, 1.
116   "a self-conceited narrow-minded little tyrant," "part tiger and part ass": Frankfurter and Jackson, 117; and Vanzetti, *Il Caso Sacco e Vanzetti,* 107.
116–17 "the self-righteous unrighteousness": H. G. Wells, "Outrages in Defense of Order: The Proposed Murder of Two American Radicals," in *Sacco & Vanzetti,* ed. John Davis (Melbourne, Australia: Ocean Press, 2004), 100.
117   "a Thayer but not one of the 'right' Thayers": Upton Sinclair, *Boston* (New York: Albert and Charles Boni, 1928), 249.
117   "a sincere, honest, absolutely fair": John Dever Papers, BPL; and "Jurors Unshaken in Verdict: Sacco and Vanzetti Guilty," *New Bedford Standard-Times,* November 12, 1950, 12.
117   "a new propaganda": Young and Kaiser, *Postmortem,* 22.
117   If the "Reds" lurked outside: Russell, *Tragedy in Dedham,* 128.
118   "Gentlemen," he asked: *Brockton Times,* April 24, 1920, 15.
118   Reporters also considered a conviction unlikely: FBI Files, 11a-12, 12a-20.
118   "like a clap of thunder": *Boston Post,* June 12, 1921, 13.
119   "Do you see him": Trial Transcript, 337.
119   "Miss Andrews," the man reported: Memo from JNB, June 12, 1921, Sacco-Vanzetti Case Papers, HLS, Box 13, Folder 7.
120   "hopeless confusion": Trial Transcript, 371.
120   "The time for criticism": Ibid.
120   "It was obvious that Mr. Moore": John Dever Papers, BPL.
121   Katzmann caught her in his arms: *Boston Globe,* June 14, 1921, 1.
121   "dark complected man": Trial Transcript, 417.
121   "a foreigner with a black mustache": Ibid., 426.
121   "all coons look alike": Ibid., 432.
121   "That carload was a tough looking bunch": Ibid., 488–495.
122   Three more witnesses pinpointed Sacco and Vanzetti: Ibid., 490, 510, 519.
122   "the gentleman on the right": Ibid., 545.
122   Had Alta Baker: Ibid., 566, 583, 616.
123   young Filene's clerk John Dever: John Dever Papers, BPL.
124   'Keep your hands out on your lap': Trial Transcript, 752–753.
124   "You try to cooperate, Mr. Moore": Ibid., 660.
124   "Did you read *Commonwealth v. Snell*": Ibid., 663.
124   "in our State": Ibid., 85.

124   "You get the hell out of here!": Ibid., 5392.
125   "in light of the results": Ibid., 5319; and Ehrmann, *The Case That Will Not Die,* 256–258.
125   "Now, when you arrived": Trial Transcript, 798.
126   "property of Alex Berardelli": Ibid., 814.
126   "does not show": Ibid., 813–822.
126   "because the gun": Ibid., 824.
126   State Police captain William Proctor: Ibid., 884–895.
127   "consistent with": Ibid., 896.
128   "a wilderness of lands and grooves": Russell, *Tragedy in Dedham,* 158.

CHAPTER SIX: "I DO NOT THINK I EVER SAW THEM MEN IN THE WORLD"

129   "Bastille without bars": John Dever Papers, BPL.
130   "I am not positive": Trial Transcript, 1044, 1070.
131   "Did you think I asked you about that": Ibid., 988.
131   "All right," Katzmann said: Ibid., 1131.
132   "he had no mustache": Ibid., 1008.
133   "I did not see any of the men": Ibid., 1168–1172.
133   "I can't keep track": Ibid., 1181.
133   "always remember his face": Ibid., 1191–1196.
134   "You don't say a man": Ibid., 1279.
135   "I told the same story": Ibid., 1329.
135   "I do not think I ever saw them men": Ibid., 1331.
135   "We haven't got the right men": Ibid., 1348.
135   "I saw a man in the car": Ibid., 1353.
136   "it would be hard to identify": Ibid., 1372.
136   "had not seen the faces": Ibid., 1375–1377.
136   "reputation for truth and veracity": Ibid., 1404.
136   spewed statistics: Ibid., 1408.
136   "Was Bullet III fired": Ibid., 1414–1416.
137   "It isn't an honest question": Ibid., 1437.
137   bullets entered the trial: *Boston American,* June 29, 1921, 1; and *Brockton Enterprise,* June 29, 1921, 1.
137   "You fooled me yesterday": Trial Transcript, 1448.
139   "Haven't you tested him": Ibid., 1515.
139   "Was he away from there": Ibid., 1524.
139   Lefevre Brini had a fever: Avrich, *Anarchist Voices,* 106.
139   "seeking to be gentle": Trial Transcript, 1539–1540.
140   "Does that date mean anything to you": Ibid., 1546.
140   John Dever, and perhaps other jurors: Russell, *Tragedy in Dedham,* 171.
140   "I take it, Mr. Guidobone": Trial Transcript, 1589.
141   "I never saw a man": Ibid., 1606–1609.
141   "bore the reputation": Ibid., 1629.
141   Some historians speculate: Young and Kaiser, 132.
141   "Why didn't you answer": Trial Transcript, 1641.
142   "no doubt or uncertainty": Ibid., 2266f.

143   "April nineteenth, eighteenth, seventeenth": Ibid., 1683.
143   soup and pasta: Avrich, *Anarchist Voices*, 131.
144   One evening, they snuck: *New Bedford Standard-Times*, November 12, 1950, 13.

CHAPTER SEVEN: "I WAS CRAZY TO COME TO THIS COUNTRY"

145   "Oh dear": Trial Transcript, 1687.
145   "Will the defendant Vanzetti": Ibid., 1689.
146   "I realized it was liable": Ibid., 4996.
147   "for a quarry—stone": Ibid., 1694.
147   "In Plymouth I worked": Ibid., 1695.
147   "I met this man": Ibid., 1701–1702.
147   "How is that involved": Ibid., 1710.
147   "It was a very bad time": Ibid., 1715.
147   Vanzetti plunged in: Ibid., 1721–1722.
148   "Judge Thayer looked over": Ibid., 4997.
148   First Vanzetti spoke: Ibid., 1726–1727.
149   "So you left Plymouth, Mr. Vanzetti": Ibid., 1737–1738.
149   "I am not asking you that, sir!": Ibid., 1764–1766.
150   "Yes, I say in the Italian Boston hall": Ibid., 1747.
150   "Even if you ask me": Ibid., 1758.
150   "I don't tell he want": Ibid., 1760–1762.
151   "You have a good strong voice": Ibid., 1767.
151   "Will you answer my question?": Ibid., 1768–1769.
152   "Oh, did Sacco go with you too?": Ibid., 1777–1778.
152   The two squared off: Ibid., 1779–1800.
152   "He was killed before my arrest": Ibid., 1809.
153   people dragged chairs into shady streets: *Boston Globe*, June 25, 1921, 2.
153–54   "I was crazy to come to this country": Trial Transcript, 1818.
154   "buy elixir for physic": Ibid., 1826.
154   "We are going a good ways": Ibid., 1849.
154   "to find where you could put": Ibid., 1850.
154   Sacco tried on the cap: *Boston Post*, July 7, 1921, 6.
154   "Put that on again, please": Trial Transcript, 1851.
154   sketches in the *Boston Post* and *Boston Herald*: *Boston Post*, July 7, 1921, 1; and *Boston Herald*, July 7, 1921, 1.
155   "They watch pretty carefully": Trial Transcript, 1862.
155   "Did you say yesterday": Ibid., 1867.
155   Katzmann rained questions down on Sacco: Ibid., 1868–1869.
155   "Well, first thing": Ibid., 1869–1870.
156   It was time for the sermon: Ibid., 1875–1877.
157   At first, Sacco stood his ground: Ibid., 1887–1891.
158   "I don't want to destroy": Ibid., 1890.
158   "Probably I mistake": Ibid., 1892.
158   Katzmann stared at Sacco: *Boston Globe*, July 8, 1921, 8.

159   "You told me what was untrue": Trial Transcript, 1902.
159   "Oh, but it is too tight": Ibid., 1929.
159   "Will you let me see your left hand"; "Did you shave this morning?":
      Ibid., 1944, 1961.
160   the judge launched into a tirade: Ibid., 4928.
160   "N. Sacco, Stoughton": Ibid., 2039.
160   "I have my opinion about the cap": Ibid., 2010. Note: In the Massachu-
      setts State Police Files' transcript of the interview, Kelley is quoted as say-
      ing, "You know what my opinion is about that cap but I want to stand in
      right with these fellows and don't want a bomb planted *at my place*." (Ital-
      ics mine.—Au.)
160   "plenty of hope and courage": *Brockton Enterprise,* June 23, 1921, 1.
161   Called to the witness stand: Trial Transcript, 2065.
161   "the day my man went to the consul": Ibid., 2069.
161   "Well, gentlemen": Ibid., 2121.
162   "Save Nick": Lyons, *The Life and Death of Sacco and Vanzetti,* 77.
162   Moore laid out his case: Trial Transcript, 2122–2148.
163   stream of consciousness: Ibid., 2148–2179.
164   Stepping before the jury, the DA: Ibid., 2179–2237.
166   he badgered a stranger: Ibid., 5412.
167   he began as he had begun the trial: Ibid., 2239–2264.
167   glass door was labeled JURY: Russell, *Tragedy in Dedham,* 211.
167   betting on the verdict: John Nicholas Beffel, "The Sacco-Vanzetti Ver-
      dict," *New Republic,* August 10, 1921, 299.
168   jurors began with a straw poll: *New Bedford Standard-Times,* Novem-
      ber 12, 1950, p. 12.
168   "You can't depend on the witnesses": Ibid., 13.
168   "of the same mind": Ibid.
169   Moore tapping a pencil: Russell, *Tragedy in Dedham,* 213.
169   "Gentlemen of the jury": Trial Transcript, 2266.
169   "Sono innocente!": *Boston Globe,* July 15, 1921, 3.
170   "For God's sake": *Brockton Enterprise,* July 15, 1921, 11.
170   "Tough luck, Mr. Moore": Russell, *Sacco and Vanzetti: The Case
      Resolved,* 107.

CHAPTER EIGHT: "CORAGGIO"

174   "With the face in my hands": Frankfurter and Jackson, *The Letters of
      Sacco and Vanzetti,* 82.
174   The verdict pleased the Commonwealth: Attorney General's Office Files,
      Massachusetts State Archives; and Russell, *Tragedy in Dedham,* 216.
174   "as a crushing and wholly unexpected blow": Moore Correspondence,
      BPL.
175   "The worst part": Ibid.
175   "good and law-abiding citizens"; "a fair, just one": *Dedham Transcript,*
      July 23, 1921, 4; and July 30, 1921, 4.
175   "most unconvincing": FBI Files, 3b-45.

175   One reporter took the unusual step: Frank Sibley to J. Weston Allen, Attorney General's Office Files, Massachusetts State Archives.

175   The verdict incensed Italian papers: Eugene Lyons, "Italians in American Courts," *Survey*, November 1921, 238.

175   called the verdict "macabre": *Gazzetta della Massachusetts*, July 23, 1921, 4.

175   "And all of us are proud of you": Michael M. Topp, *The Sacco and Vanzetti Case: A Brief History with Documents* (New York: Palgrave Macmillan, 2005), 141–142.

175   "working like the Devil": Moore Correspondence, BPL.

176   "that we may be able": Russell, *Tragedy in Dedham*, 222.

176   She sent expansive lists: Moore Correspondence, BPL.

176   "They are keeping this thing on": Insanity Matters, Sacco-Vanzetti Case Papers, HLS, Box 6, Folder 7.

176   "They can put something under the skin": Ibid.

176   "officers," "authorities," "the State": Moore Correspondence, BPL.

176   "They have a couple of spies": Insanity Matters, Sacco-Vanzetti Case Papers, HLS, Box 6, Folder 20.

176   "We will never be abandoned": Vanzetti, *Il Caso Sacco e Vanzetti*, 76.

177   "Well, dear Tresca": Topp, 141.

177   *Fangs at Labor's Throat*: New York World, November 26, 1921, 6.

177   Felicani sought another lawyer: Aldino Felicani Correspondence, BPL.

177   "I love the anarchists": Moore Correspondence, BPL.

177   The radical Italian press: Mary Anne Trasciatti, "The American Campaign to Save Sacco and Vanzetti," in Jerome H. Delamater and Mary Anne Trasciatti, *Representing Sacco and Vanzetti* (New York: Palgrave Macmillan, 2005), 40.

177   "Good God!": Sacco-Vanzetti Defense Committee Correspondence, Sacco-Vanzetti Case Papers, BPL.

178   *militants libertaires*: FBI Files, 1a-30; 1a-32; 1a-19.

178   "Sachi und Vanzetti": Ibid., 1a-31.

178   "The United States government": *New York World*, November 23, 1921, 10.

178   "tear them away from the executioner": FBI Files, 1a-15.

178   "the peasants listened": "Our Communist Martyrs Disturbing the World," *Literary Digest*, December 10, 1921, 36.

178   screening each article: Felicani oral history, CUOHROC, 101.

178   his "crank box": *Boston Globe*, October 20, 1921, 1–2.

178   "Redemption springs from audacious revolt!": Avrich, *Sacco and Vanzetti: The Anarchist Background*, 98.

179   "Our committee wish to warn you": FBI Files, 4b-29.

179   "This affair is a challenge": *Boston Globe*, October 21, 1921, 12.

180   "Unless the two Italians": FBI Files, 1b-34.

180   "one of the most violent anarchists in Europe": Ibid., 1b-20-31.

180   "reign of terror": *New York Times*, October 27, 1921, 4.

180   "disturbances by the followers": FBI Files, 1b-42-85, 2a-1-5.

181   the mainstream press: "Anarchists and the Ambassador," *Literary Digest,* November 5, 1921, 9.

181   the rumor mill: *Boston Globe,* October 29, 1921, 1; and *Boston American,* October 29, 1921, 2.

182   "O, funny, humble": Frankfurter and Jackson, 86.

182   "have advertised himself": *Boston Herald,* October 30, 1921, 9.

182   Rosina Sacco, learning of the arrest: *Boston Evening Globe,* October 29, 1921, 1.

182   "want to know in detail": Ibid., 4.

182   "Mr. Moore, I am afraid": Argument of Mr. Moore on Motion for New Trial, October 29, 1921, Sacco-Vanzetti Case Papers, HLS, Box 4, Folder 41.

183   "apply Yankee, ordinary horse sense": Ibid.

183   A statement published overseas: Ibid.

183   a poster fanned the embers of rage: FBI Files, 4b-80-81.

184   "Appeal to the American People": John Davis, ed., *Sacco & Vanzetti* (Melbourne, Australia: Ocean Press, 2004), 64.

184   In Italy, Mussolini proposed a resolution: Cannistraro and Meyer, 46.

184   "the administration of justice": *Boston Herald,* November 6, 1921, 9.

184   Sacco erupted first: *Boston Globe,* November 6, 1921, B1; and *Boston Herald,* November 6, 1921, 1.

185   Finally, Katzmann resumed: *Boston Post,* November 6, 1921, 14.

185   "intelligent and righteous": Ibid.

186   "the kind of man": *Boston Herald,* June 12, 1921, 9.

187   "There goes the paymaster now": Trial Transcript, 3503.

187   "cranks on the subject of anarchy": FBI Files, 7b-12.

187   Katzmann urged federal agents: Ibid., 4b-38.

187   "the Sacco-Vanzetti crowd": Ibid., 2b-79.

187   "Thair is about five hundred": Ibid., 4b-51.

188   "sent to prison to rot": Ibid., 5-21; 4b-58-63.

188   "This was not a proper sort of meeting": *Boston Globe,* November 28, 1921, 4.

188   "Sacco and Vangetta": FBI Files, 6a-12.

188   "I cannot—as I must": Trial Transcript, 5563.

189   "The echo of shouts": Sacco Correspondence, BPL.

189   "If Christmas means peace": Vanzetti Correspondence, BPL.

CHAPTER NINE: "NICE PEOPLE AND GOOD KILLERS"

191   "You look like a white man": Trial Transcript, 5597.

191   "I said, 'No'": Trial Transcript, 5565–5575.

193   "One word led to another": Ibid., 5585–5586.

193   Harold Williams began: Ibid., 5587–5589.

193   From Boston's theater district: Moore Correspondence, BPL.

194   Upon his release: Nick Salvatore, *Eugene V. Debs: Citizen and Socialist* (Urbana: University of Illinois Press, 1982), 328.

194   "Rarely have death-dealing lies": Sacco-Vanzetti Defense Committee
       Correspondence, BPL.

194   Flynn's February 4 meeting: FBI Files, 6b-57, 6b-69.

195   "I hope the *New York Times*": Joughin and Morgan, *The Legacy of
       Sacco and Vanzetti*, 239.

195   "not a great deal of interest": FBI Files, 5–114.

195   "When they arrested us": Vanzetti, *Il Caso Sacco e Vanzetti*, 79.

196   "The world broke in two": Willa Cather, *Not Under Forty* (New York:
       Alfred A. Knopf, 1936), v.

197   "A light rattan": *Boston Herald*, June 4, 1921, 1.

198   "one of the most amazing scandals": Mayo DuBasky, *The Gist of
       Mencken: Quotations from America's Critic* (Metuchen, NJ, and Lon-
       don: Scarecrow Press, 1990), 430.

198   "If I am convinced of anything": Arthur M. Schlesinger Jr., *The Age of
       Roosevelt: The Crisis of the Old Order, 1919–1933* (Boston: Houghton
       Mifflin, 1957), 145.

198   "Presently we began to have our slices": F. Scott Fitzgerald, "Echoes of
       the Jazz Age," in *The Crack Up* (New York: New Directions, 1945), 14.

198   *Caro Barto*, "I am old": Alberto Gedda, *Gridatelo dai tetti: Autobiografia
       e lettere di Bartolomeo Vanzetti* (Asti, Italy: Editoriale Fusta, 2005), 168.

198   "il mio disgraziato figlio": Gian Batista Vanzetti to "Egregia Signora," Feb-
       ruary 19, 1922, Herbert B. Ehrmann Papers, HLS, Box 16, Folder 15.

199   "sadness is weakness": Vanzetti, *Il Caso Sacco e Vanzetti*, 78.

199   "My Ten Biggest Manhunts": *Boston Herald*, March 5, 1922, part 2, 10.

199   *AL SERVICIO DEL BOIA:* Vanzetti Correspondence, BPL.

200   Dante Sacco picked up the ball: Avrich, *Anarchist Voices*, 93.

201   "this beloved brittle soul": Frankfurter and Jackson, 45.

201   "You can imagine how happy I felt": Ibid., 6.

201   "Look," he wrote a friend: Sacco Correspondence, BPL.

201   "They're all nice people": Thomas Doyle to Fred Moore, August 27,
       1922, Sacco-Vanzetti Case Papers, HLS, Box 5, Folder 12.

202   "especially noted as a perjurer": FBI Files, 11a-21.

202   "The conviction of Vanzetti": Moore Correspondence, BPL.

202   "extremely interested": FBI Files, 7b-48.

202   "To us, playing the part of police": Vanzetti, *Il Caso Sacco e Vanzetti*, 83.

202   threatened to kill Moore: FBI Files, 6b-105-106.

203   "in response to some sort of force": Trial Transcript, 5564.

203   "The Committee is literally penniless": Fred Moore to Frank Bellanca,
       May 5, 1922, Sacco-Vanzetti Case Papers, HLS, Box 41, Folder 1.

203   "I am as innocent": Nunzio Pernicone, "Carlo Tresca and the Sacco-Vanzetti
       Case," *Journal of American History* 66, no. 3 (December 1979): 543.

204   "dark colored revolver": Trial Transcript, 544.

204   "a nice bird": Fred Moore to Steven Hornik, June 14, 1922, Sacco-
       Vanzetti Case Papers, HLS, Box 41, Folder 17.

204   "happy in Jesus": Trial Transcript, 3753.

204   "plays the religious game": Ibid., 3745, 3763, 3807.

205   "You have never served": Ibid., 3873–3886.

206   "Unless I hear from them tonight": Ibid., 3855.
206   her teenage son, John: Deposition, John Andrew Hassam, July 16, 1922, Sacco-Vanzetti Case Papers, HLS, Box 13, Folder 22.
207   "The consensus of opinion": Moore Correspondence, BPL.
207   "I have seen her 'die' ": Deposition, Martha Wellman, July 1922, Sacco-Vanzetti Case Papers, HLS, Box 13, Folder 27.
207   "Her word is not worth *that*!": Deposition, Mayhew Assam [*sic*], July 1922, Sacco-Vanzetti Case Papers, HLS, Box 13, Folder 21.
208   "the said Rachel A. Hassam": Affidavit, Stephen S. Lancaster, July 22, 1922, Sacco-Vanzetti Case Papers, HLS, Box 13, Folder 23.
208   "They ought to hang": Affidavit, Alderic Richard, August 21, 1922, Herbert B. Ehrmann Papers, HLS, Box 13, Folder 13.
208   the seedy Hotel Essex: Russell, *Tragedy in Dedham,* 232.
208   volunteered new information: Trial Transcript, 3898.
209   "We have melted her": Fred Moore to Upton Sinclair, September 3, 1922, Sacco-Vanzetti Case Papers, HLS, Box 41, Folder 38.
209   "You told a lie": "An Encounter with Lola Andrews, Dictated by John Hassam," September 24, 1922, Sacco-Vanzetti Case Papers, HLS, Box 13, Folder 15.
209   "an utterly and hopelessly unreliable": Trial Transcript, 3894.
209   he then wrote to Katzmann: Moore Correspondence, BPL.
210   *Dazzling of light:* Vanzetti Correspondence, BPL.
210   "the sad reclus": Frankfurter and Jackson, 8
210   "because I am joy": Ibid., 7.
210   "When I was home": Insanity Matters, Sacco-Vanzetti Case Papers, HLS, Box 6, Folder 20.
211   "tired of this life": Sacco Correspondence, BPL.
211   "Mr. Barrett," he asked: Insanity Matters, Sacco-Vanzetti Case Papers, HLS, Box 6, Folder 20.
211   "No Christ can convince me": Sacco Correspondence, BPL.

CHAPTER TEN: "FREE OR DIE"

212   "I feel so keenly": Moore Correspondence, BPL.
213   "The world will be cleansed": Howard Zinn, *La Guardia in Congress* (Ithaca, NY: Cornell University Press, 1958), 101.
213   "I am absolutely convinced": *Boston Advertiser,* June 21, 1923.
213   "demented": Arthur Mann, *La Guardia: A Fighter Against His Times, 1882–1933* (Philadelphia and New York: J. B. Lippincott, 1959), 260.
213   "Thirty-four months": Sacco Correspondence, BPL.
214   "I don't care if I die": *Boston Evening Globe,* March 2, 1923, 1.
214   "On the forty-fourth day": *Boston Globe,* March 7, 1923, 3.
214   "free or die": "Insanity Matters," Sacco-Vanzetti Case Papers, HLS, Box 6, Folder 20.
215   "flopped": Moore Correspondence, BPL.
216   "Some of my best friends": Trial Transcript, 3850–3855.

216   *Examination of Mrs. Lola R. Andrews:* Ibid., 3910–3938.
217   "We have them telling four stories each": Moore Correspondence, BPL.
218   front-page news: *Boston Globe,* March 13, 1923, 5; *Boston Globe,* March 14, 1923, 1; and *Boston Daily Advertiser,* March 15, 1923, 1.
219   "Today I saw Nick": *Boston Daily Advertiser,* March 5, 1923, 3.
219   "Did anyone ever hear": *Boston Globe,* March 12, 1923, 4.
219   "revolutionary spirit and courage"; "Nicola Sacco is dying!": Sacco-Vanzetti Defense Committee Correspondence and Moore Correspondence, BPL.
219   "Nicola's tragic determination": Vanzetti, *Il Caso Sacco e Vanzetti,* 92.
219   "This man's life is at stake": Insanity Matters, Sacco-Vanzetti Case Papers, HLS, Box 6, Folder 17.
220   "flatly refused": Ibid.
220   "I have been through": Ibid.
220   "this poor, half-starved man": Ibid.
220   "It has already come!": *Boston Evening Globe,* March 17, 1923, 1.
221   "I know that if they wish": *Boston Globe,* March 17, 1923, 1, 5.
221   "almost as good as Italian spaghetti": *Boston Globe,* March 21, 1923, 5.
221   "Tell my comrades": *Boston Evening Globe,* March 19, 1923, 1.
221   "I am innocent!": Russell, *Tragedy in Dedham,* 239.
221   "I did not smash my head hard enough": Insanity Matters, Sacco-Vanzetti Case Papers, HLS, Box 6, Folder 19.
221   "no evidence of insanity": Ibid.
222   "would furnish Sacco the weapon": Moore Correspondence, BPL.
222   "My Nick is not insane": *Boston Daily Advertiser,* April 14, 1923, 5.
222   "Haven't you known in this Commonwealth": Insanity Matters, Sacco-Vanzetti Case Papers, HLS, Box 6, Folder 7.
223   The prisoner, the judge stated: Ibid., Box 6, Folder 20.
224   squeaky, high-buttoned shoes: Russell, *Tragedy in Dedham,* p. 238.
224   "You are always surprise me": Nicola Sacco to Mrs. Cerise Jack, June 18, 1925, Sacco-Vanzetti Case Papers, HLS, Box 38, Folder 70.
225   "A player of golf and of tennis": Frankfurter and Jackson, 100.
225   "almost forgot to be in prison": Vanzetti Correspondence, BPL.
225   "Ah, my passion for the truth!": Frankfurter and Jackson, 181.
225   their own ways of helping: Laura Ann Haight, "Tenders of the Flickering Flame: Boston Brahmin Women in Defense of Sacco and Vanzetti, 1920–27," Honors Thesis, B.A. History and Literature, Harvard and Radcliffe Colleges, March 1, 1984, p. 40, Harvard University Archives, Harvard University.
225   "a nightingale of the English Language": Vanzetti to Virginia Mac-Mechan, May 10, 1923, Sacco-Vanzetti Case Papers, HLS, Box 40, Folder 57.
225   "Treat them as sisters": Vanzetti Correspondence, BPL.
225   "How many good souls": Frankfurter and Jackson, 134.
226   "poor relations": Elizabeth Glendower Evans Papers, Radcliffe Institute, Schlesinger Library.
226   "all the time there is": Ibid.

226 "as if a new 'world' were opened": Ibid.
226 "one of those old-fashioned Americans": Haight, 13.
227 "I could scarcely credit my senses": Ibid., 50.
227 "Her actions were childish": FBI Files, 6a-62.
227 "Since the day": Frankfurter and Jackson, 29.
227 "my dear mother": Elizabeth Glendower Evans, *Outstanding Features of the Sacco-Vanzetti Case* (Boston: New England Civil Liberties Committee, 1924), 40.
227 "Dear Mrs. Evans": Frankfurter and Jackson, 135–137.
229 "paupers," "drug addicts": *Annual Report of the Commissioner of Correction* (Boston: Commonwealth of Massachusetts, 1923), 65.
229 Of nearly nine hundred inmates: Ibid.
229 "My mind is clear": Russell, *Tragedy in Dedham,* 241.
229 causing Moore to suspect: Moore Correspondence, BPL.
229 "the name and address": Fred Moore to Chaim Shapiro, May 29, 1923, Sacco-Vanzetti Case Papers, HLS, Box 41, Folder 36.
229 *A Proletarian Life:* Vanzetti's autobiography was translated into English by Eugene Lyons. Lyons had balked at the job, claiming the short work was too repetitive. "To make it palatable to any but Latin taste would mean completely rewriting the thing," he told Moore. Given the job, he did plenty of rewriting, adding entire passages that are not in the original.
229 "one of the world's gentlest spirits": *San Francisco Examiner,* October 14, 1923, News-Features, 1.
230 Angelina DeFalco "could have saved them": Flynn, *The Rebel Girl,* 310.
230 The *Galleanisti* welcomed the proposal: Avrich, "Sacco and Vanzetti's Revenge," in Cannistraro and Meyer, eds., 165.
230 "I'm getting to be too old": Trial Transcript, 5413.
231 Some have charged that Proctor: Montgomery, *The Murder and the Myth,* 224.
231 "Had I been asked": Trial Transcript, 3642–3643.
231 "Damn them": Ibid., 3580.
232 "It is supposed": *Boston Globe,* October 2, 1923, 8.
232 He quoted the late foreman: Ibid.
232 "They knew—and don't deny it!" *Boston Globe,* November 3, 1923, 3.
233 "that the so-called mortal bullet": Trial Transcript, 3650.
233 "Mr. Thompson is a quick and penetrating intelligence": Frankfurter and Jackson, 112.
233 "Believe me Mrs. Jack": Ibid., p. 9.
234 "alive in this terrible hole!": Sacco Correspondence, BPL.

CHAPTER ELEVEN: "THESE SO-CALLED ALLEGED FACTS"

235 "the bullets": *New Bedford Standard-Times,* November 12, 1920, 13.
236 bone-dry affidavits: Trial Transcript, 3630.
236 "the foremost micro-chemical examiner": Norman G. Meade, "Practical Criminology at Work: Some of the Adventures of the Scientific Modern Detective," *Scientific American,* October 1923, 232.

236 a .32 Colt was easily disassembled: Marstar Canada Web site, http:// marstar.ca/c32s.htm.

236 When Hamilton asked for the "Sacco pistol": Transcript of Hearings Before Judge Webster Thayer, February 15, 1924, Sacco-Vanzetti Case Papers, Box 14, Folder 1.

237 "Since November 8": Trial Transcript, 3692.

237 "these so-called alleged facts": Transcript of Hearings Before Judge Webster Thayer, February 15, 1924, Sacco-Vanzetti Case Papers, HLS, Box 14, Folder 1.

237 "whether there has been any tampering here": Ibid.

238 "unless they wanted to run their necks into a noose": Ibid.

238 "I never had those in my possession": Ibid.

238 two red shoeboxes: Ibid.

238 "That one there belongs in here": Ibid.

239 "people whose lives may depend": Ibid.

239 another firing would prove nothing: Ibid.

239 "bombshell": Boston Post, February 18, 1924, 1.

240 "I saw the darkness": Vanzetti to Elizabeth G. Evans, July 17, 1923, Sacco-Vanzetti Case Papers, HLS, Box 40, Folder 9.

240 "simply reeking": Moore Correspondence, BPL.

241 "in spite of our cold blooded murderers": Vanzetti Correspondence, BPL.

241 "other than some ten thousand volts": Frankfurter and Jackson, 117.

241 "Since the last hearing": Vanzetti, Il Caso Sacco e Vanzetti, 108.

241 "by thousands of strikes": Vanzetti Correspondence, BPL.

241 "I will ask for revenge": Frankfurter and Jackson, 120.

241 "There were so many things": Vanzetti Correspondence, BPL.

242 "The cookies Mrs. Jack": Sacco Correspondence, BPL.

242 "could be really a Shakespeare": Sacco to Mrs. Cerise Jack, January 19, 1924, Sacco-Vanzetti Case Papers, HLS, Box 38, Folder 51.

242 One night he dreamt: Frankfurter and Jackson, 18–19.

243 "America's Sherlock Holmes": Boston American, February 24, 1924, 1.

243 "make any kind of an examination": Transcript of Hearings Before Judge Webster Thayer, February 15, 1924, Sacco-Vanzetti Case Papers, HLS, Box 14, Folder 2.

243 The investigator found: Affidavit of Joseph W. Keith, Sacco-Vanzetti Case Papers, HLS, Box 16, Folder 37.

243 Hamilton's testimony judged "worthless": Affidavit of Charles B. Bechtold, Sacco-Vanzetti Case Papers, HLS, Box 16, Folder 37.

243–44 "very bitter ever since against Hamilton": "History Upon Dr. Albert L. Hall," Sacco-Vanzetti Case Papers, HLS, Box 16, Folder 37.

244 "attempt to thoroughly discredit Hamilton": Transcript of Hearings Before Judge Webster Thayer, February 15, 1924, Sacco-Vanzetti Case Papers, HLS, Box 14, Folder 5.

244 "The Sacco case was my first": Ibid., Box 14, Folder 4.

244 Hamilton began handing notes: Albert Hamilton note to Fred Moore, n.d., Sacco-Vanzetti Case Papers, HLS, Box 15, Folder 5.

245 "I make it five plus": Transcript of Hearings Before Judge Webster Thayer, February 15, 1924, Sacco-Vanzetti Case Papers, HLS, Box 14, Folder 4.

246 a court clerk affirmed: Ibid., March 7, 1924, Box 14, Folder 12.

246 Judge Thayer released his findings: Trial Transcript, 3732jj.

246 "We have got to fire it": Transcript of Hearings Before Judge Webster Thayer, February 15, 1924, Sacco-Vanzetti Case Papers, Box 14, Folder 1.

246 Van Amburgh was proven wrong: Russell, *Tragedy in Dedham,* 250–251.

246 the pulp magazine *True Detective Mysteries:* "The Hidden Drama of Sacco and Vanzetti," *True Detective Mysteries,* September 1935, 120.

247 The name of the pulp author: Ibid.

247 "so that no future tampering": *Boston Globe,* July 24, 1960, 1.

248 "What is this?": Felicani oral history, CUOHROC, 107.

248 Felicani "has tried my patience": Moore Correspondence, BPL.

248 "I am telling you": Frankfurter and Jackson, 21–24.

249 "I think that Moore": Ibid., 127.

249 "hopeless to get acquittals": "Reminiscences of Roger Nash Baldwin [oral history]," 1954, CUOHROC, 237.

249 Motion one: Trial Transcript, 3594–3604.

249 Motion two: Ibid., 3513–3527.

250 Motion three: Ibid., 3887–3891.

250 Motion four: Ibid., 3950–3958.

251 Motion five: Ibid., 3698–3724.

252 "no reason to be discouraged": Vanzetti, *Il Caso Sacco e Vanzetti,* 117–118.

252 an axe "on the necks": Frankfurter and Jackson, 132.

252 "hanger judge": Vanzetti Correspondence, BPL.

252 "We are always keep": Frankfurter and Jackson, 24–25.

252 "Did you see what I did": Trial Transcript, 5418–5419. When Dartmouth alumni learned of the outburst, they offered to donate $10,000 to the college if the professor revealing it was fired. (See Ehrmann, *The Case That Will Not Die,* 476.)

252 He would hang around Boston: Moore Correspondence, BPL.

253 "At least I kept them alive": Russell, *Tragedy in Dedham,* 363.

253 "He was not a bad man": Vanzetti, *Il Caso Sacco e Vanzetti,* 163.

253 "I do not think that the jury's mistake": Moore Correspondence, BPL.

254 "half educated dreamers": William Thompson to Charles B. Rogers, November 19, 1926, Sacco-Vanzetti Case Papers, HLS, Box 41, Folder 64.

254 "full of prejudice": Trial Transcript, 5273.

254 "I have been fortunate": *New York World,* October 3, 1926, sec. II, 1.

254 "Well, here we were": Felicani oral history, CUOHROC, 111.

255 the inmate population: *Annual Report of the Commissioner of Correction,* 1925, 11.

255 "I can assure you": Vanzetti, *Il Caso Sacco-Vanzetti,* 128.

255 "prison psychosis": Dr. Charles B. Sullivan et al. to a Justice of the

Superior Court of Suffolk County, December 30, 1924, Sacco-Vanzetti
Case Papers, HLS, Box 6, Folder 13.

255   "the sun's spectrum": Vanzetti Correspondence, BPL.

255   "fools and cheaters": Frankfurter and Jackson, 148.

255   "the founder of modern business": William E. Leuchtenberg, *The Perils
of Prosperity: 1914–1932* (Chicago: University of Chicago Press, 1958),
189.

256   "a living hurricane": Vanzetti Correspondence, BPL.

256   "going to hell by radio"; weeping tears of blood"; "a tragic laughing
stock": Frankfurter and Jackson, 188, 128, 158–159.

256   "lusting for death": Vanzetti Correspondence, BPL.

256   "I wish I could be out Mrs. Jack": Sacco to Mrs. Cerise Jack, April 16,
1925, Sacco-Vanzetti Case Papers, HLS, Box 38, Folder 67.

256   "audacious revolt": *L'Adunata dei Refrattari*, May 23, 1925, 2.

256   "Why don't you come home, Papa": Sacco to Mrs. Cerise Jack, March
30, 1925, Sacco-Vanzetti Case Papers, HLS, Box 38, Folder 65.

257   "These two men are anarchists": Dudley P. Ranney to Winfield M.
Wilbar, July 22, 1925, Sacco-Vanzetti Case Papers, HLS, Box 23,
Folder 7.

257   "Since an execution": Vanzetti to Alice Stone Blackwell, September 15,
1925, Sacco-Vanzetti Case Papers, HLS, Box 39, Folder 65.

257   "I hear by confess": Russell, *Tragedy in Dedham*, 279.

CHAPTER TWELVE: "A VULGAR CONTEST"

258   "scared half to death": Trial Transcript, 4418.

258   "4 Italians picked him up": Ibid., 4543–4544.

259   "Sacco and Vanzetti had nothing to do with this job": Ibid., 4518.

259   Thompson convinced reporters: William G. Thompson, Massachusetts
Lawyer's Diary, 1925, BPL.

259   "The names of these men": Trial Transcript, 4418.

260   "secrets that are important proofs": Vanzetti, *Il Caso Sacco e Vanzetti*,
136.

260   "He was convinced": Ibid., 135.

261   "one of the most powerful arguments": *Boston Globe*, January 13,
1926, 1.

261   "It wasn't so much a question": *Boston Globe*, January 12, 1926, 12.

261   Calling Judge Thayer "confused": Ibid., 10.

261   "I don't believe the District Attorney": Ibid.

261   "ignorant and misguided": *Boston Herald*, January 12, 1926, 2.

262   "That," he concluded: Ibid.

262   "not proven"; and "my duty": Ehrmann, *The Case That Will Not Die*,
389, and *Harvard Class of 1912: Twenty-fifth Anniversary Report*
(Cambridge, MA: Common Press, 1937), 608–609.

262   "bitter attack": *Boston Globe*, January 14, 1926, 9.

262   "this time we will finally get justice": Vanzetti, *Il Caso Sacco e Vanzetti*,
140.

262 "There would be flames": Frankfurter and Jackson, *The Letters of Sacco and Vanzetti*, 186.

263 "To have known you 6 years ago!": Ibid., 187.

263 "I wonder if Nick knows": *Boston Globe*, May 13, 1926, 13.

263 "They must kill us": Frankfurter and Jackson, 234.

264 "excite and intensify prejudice against him": Trial Transcript, 4279–4280.

264 "Yesterday, we got the last stroke": Frankfurter and Jackson, 191–192.

264 "Be of brave heart": Vanzetti Correspondence, BPL.

264 "Remember, *La Salute è in Voi*": Robert D'Attilio, "La Salute è in Voi: The Anarchist Dimension," in *Sacco-Vanzetti: Developments and Reconsiderations*, BPL, 1979, 75–89.

264 "I will try to see Thayer death": Frankfurter and Jackson, 199; and Vanzetti Correspondence, BPL.

265 "plain as an old shoe": Jackson oral history, CUOHROC, 195.

266 "Pat, I don't think": Ibid., 114–115.

266 "We were now able to reach people": Felicani oral history, CUOHROC, 130.

266 "I hate you!": Jackson oral history, CUOHROC, 195.

266 "We still have a fighting chance": Sacco-Vanzetti Defense Committee Correspondence, BPL.

267 "death house confession": Herbert B. Ehrmann, "The Bouncer of the Bluebird Inn," *Survey Graphic,* August 1933, 398.

267 "Fred couldn't have been in it": Ehrmann, *The Untried Case,* 41–42.

268 "somebody put their shoulder": Moore Correspondence, BPL.

268 "From now on": Ehrmann, *The Untried Case,* 45.

268 "Over my dead body!": Ehrmann, *The Case That Will Not Die,* 413.

268 "Well, I remember one place": Ehrmann, *The Untried Case,* 50–51.

269 "What's the matter, Jake?": Ibid., 58–62.

269 "first adventure": *Boston Herald,* September 16, 1926, 8.

269 "Medeiros often told me": Trial Transcript, 4401–4403.

270 "a vulgar contest of affidavits": Ehrmann, *The Untried Case,* 127.

270 "You think I am tough": Trial Transcript, 4573.

270 "a high class man": Ibid., 4449–4551.

270 Joe was also wily enough: Russell, *Tragedy in Dedham,* 296.

271 "You are trying to spoil my record": Ehrmann, *The Untried Case,* 110.

271 "Sacco? Sacco?" he said": Ibid., 107–111.

271 "I didn't know I had an enemy in the world": *Boston Evening Globe,* June 1, 1926, 1.

271 "serious prejudice": *Boston Herald,* June 3, 1926, 16.

272 "This is a picture": Trial Transcript, 4471.

272 "strikingly like the man": Ibid., 4470.

272 Jimmy Bostock also singled out: Herbert B. Ehrmann to Governor Alvan T. Fuller, June 30, 1927, Felix Frankfurter Papers, HLS, Box 209, Folder 11.

272 "the man I saw": Trial Transcript, 4485.

272 Dudley Ranney phoned him: Thompson, Massachusetts Lawyer's Diary 1926, BPL.

273   "I am working with a good mob": Trial Transcript, 4555.

273   "what men in the glove trade": Ibid., 4526.

273   "I seen Sacco's wife": Ibid., 4663.

273   "a stool pigeon": Moore Correspondence, BPL.

273   Fred Weyand and Lawrence Letherman told Thompson: Trial Transcript, 4503–4506.

274   "senile dementia"; "falsified reports": Russell, *Sacco and Vanzetti: The Case Resolved*, 178–179.

274   "not sufficiently active": FBI Files, 8–51.

274   "Specify nothing!": Ibid., 8–58.

274   "I am considerably concerned": Ibid., 9–12.

275   "You can stake your last dollar": Winfield M. Wilbar to Dudley P. Ranney, July 27, 1926, Sacco-Vanzetti Case Papers, HLS, Box 23, Folder 13.

275   "would have long since been shoveling smoke in Hades": Winfield M. Wilbar to Dudley P. Ranney, July 23, 1926, Sacco-Vanzetti Case Papers, HLS, Box 23, Folder 13.

275   "found guilty before the ablest judge": *Boston Telegram*, August 6, 1926, 10.

276   "beholds with amazement": *Gloucester Times*, August 23, 1926, 8.

276   The press, having "presented the case": Bartolomeo Vanzetti, "Awaiting the Hangman: A Journalistic Lynching," *Official Bulletin of the Sacco-Vanzetti Defense Committee*, August 1926, 1.

276   "He would refuse us"; "Thayer is capable": Vanzetti, *Il Caso Sacco e Vanzetti*, 143, 149.

276   "How thirsty for our blood": Frankfurter and Jackson, 201.

276   "capitalist reactionary hyenas": Vanzetti Correspondence, BPL.

276   "If what [Proctor] said was true": H. N. Hirsch, *The Enigma of Felix Frankfurter* (New York: Basic Books, 1981), 91.

277   *And Felix doesn't think it right:* Francis T. P. Plimpton, *In personam: being a lyrical libel read at the Christmas dinner of the Lincoln's Inn Society, 1924* (Cambridge, MA: privately printed, 1925).

277   he found the eels alibi more believable: John Dos Passos, *The Best Times: An Informal Memoir* (New York: New American Library, 1966), 166.

277   Stark backdrops: *Brockton Times*, June 10, 1926, 3.

278   "the most humane form of social contract"; "The communists want power": Vanzetti, *Il Caso Sacco-Vanzetti*, 33; and Frankfurter and Jackson, 125.

278   THREE THOUSAND YOUNG WORKERS: Sacco-Vanzetti Defense Committee Correspondence, BPL.

278   "the black-gowned hangers": Vanzetti Correspondence, BPL.

278   "the class birthright": Max Schactman, *Sacco and Vanzetti: Labor's Martyrs* (New York: International Labor Defense, 1927), 49–50.

278–79 "Some of the money": Benjamin Gitlow, *I Confess: The Truth About American Communism* (New York: E. P. Dutton, 1940), 471–472.

279   "Sacco-Vanzetti car": *Boston Herald*, September 13, 1926, 8.

279   "Called upon to relate the details": Trial Transcript, 4373–4374.

280   "A government which has come to value its own secrets": Ibid., 4385.

280   "We have heard much here": *Boston Globe,* September 17, 1926, 28.
280   "Secrecy is a watchword": Felix Frankfurter, *The Case of Sacco and Vanzetti: A Critical Analysis for Lawyers and Laymen* (New York: Grosset and Dunlap, 1927), 71.
280   "ten times the evidence": *Boston Herald,* September 16, 1926, 8.
280   To overturn the verdict: Trial Transcript, 4748–4777.
281   "We Submit": *Boston Herald,* October 26, 1926, 20.
282   "the best lesson on Americanism": *Boston Herald,* October 29, 1926, 26.
282   "If what was done": *Boston Herald,* October 27, 1926, 26.
282   "The time of your crucifixion": Sacco Correspondence, BPL.
282   "We are still alive": Vanzetti, *Il Caso Sacco e Vanzetti,* 156.
282–83 the Carbarn Bandits were electrocuted: Russell, *Tragedy in Dedham,* 349–350.

CHAPTER THIRTEEN: "FLOWERS TO THE FALLEN REBELS"

284   "Dear Bartolo": Frankfurter and Jackson, 43–44.
285   "We are convinced": Vanzetti Correspondence, BPL.
285   "We do not claim": *Boston Herald,* January 28, 1927, 8.
285   a brief comparing suspects: Trial Transcript, 4791–4792.
286   "fraud in obtaining the affidavits": *Boston Herald,* January 28, 1927, 8.
286   "wipe out the stain": *Boston Herald,* January 29, 1927, 1.
286   "There is no hope": Ehrmann, *The Case That Will Not Die,* 449.
286   "I don't expect much good": Vanzetti, *Il Caso Sacco e Vanzetti,* 173.
287   Frankfurter's *Atlantic Monthly* article: Felix Frankfurter, "The Case of Sacco and Vanzetti," *Atlantic,* March 1927, 409–432.
287   J. Edgar Hoover got a copy: FBI Files, 9–79.
287   "vicious propaganda"; "an expert in attempting": Joughin and Morgan, *The Legacy of Sacco and Vanzetti,* 308, and Michael E. Parrish, "Sacco and Vanzetti Revisited: Russell and Young & Kaiser," *American Bar Foundation Research Journal* 12, no. 2/3 (Spring/Summer 1987): 579.
287   "stopped dead the Law School drive": Melvin I. Urofsky and David W. Levy, eds., *Letters of Louis D. Brandeis—Volume V (1920–1941): Elder Statesman* (Albany: State University of New York Press, 1978), 278.
287   "This school does not exist for the collection of money": Felix Frankfurter to Stoughton Bell, April 9, 1927, Felix Frankfurter Papers, HLS, Box 207, Folder 1.
287   Sacco and Vanzetti celebrated: Frankfurter and Jackson, 47; and Vanzetti, *Il Caso Sacco e Vanzetti,* 176.
288   "Professor Frankenstein": John F. Neville, *Twentieth-Century Cause Célèbre: Sacco, Vanzetti, and the Press, 1920–1927* (Westport, CT, and London: Praeger, 2004), 88.
288   "Criticism of me": Hirsch, 93–94.
288   "How tenuous and doubtful": Felix Frankfurter to Joseph Henry Beale, June 27, 1927, Felix Frankfurter Papers, HLS, Box 207, Folder 8.

288   "just-ices": Vanzetti to Alice Stone Blackwell, March 22, 1927, Sacco-
       Vanzetti Case Papers, HLS, Box 39, Folder 89.

288   Letter after letter: Frankfurter and Jackson, 48–50.

288   "like wildfire": *Boston Globe,* April 6, 1927, 12.

288   Again the justices were unanimous: Trial Transcript, 4892, 4890, 4893,
       4881.

290   "Hey, Sacco!": *Boston Transcript,* April 9, 1927, 15.

290   As he began to speak: Ehrmann, *The Case That Will Not Die,* 451.

291   some notes scribbled in pencil: Vanzetti Correspondence, BPL.

291   "I am not only innocent": Ehrmann, *The Case That Will Not Die,*
       450–458.

292   Judge Thayer spoke: Ibid., 458.

293   "There's lots to hope for yet!": Russell, *Tragedy in Dedham,* 362.

293   Judge Thayer sat in his chambers: Ehrmann, *The Case That Will Not
       Die,* 475.

293   "like the shot fired at Concord Bridge": George W. Kirchwey, "Sacco-
       Vanzetti," *Nation,* April 20, 1927, 415.

293   "Sheer madness": *Boston Evening Globe,* April 6, 1927, 15.

293   "A deep offense": *Boston Globe,* April 13, 1927, 13.

293   "In the gracious name": *Boston Globe,* June 3, 1927, 7.

294   "We view with horror": *Boston Globe,* April 9, 1927, 15.

294   George Bernard Shaw said: *Boston Herald,* June 3, 1927, 2.

294   H. G. Wells called: "The Cobbler and the Pedler [*sic*] Whose Fates Stir
       the World," *Literary Digest,* April 23, 1927, 5; and H. G. Wells, "Out-
       rage in Defense of Order: The Proposed Murder of Two American Radi-
       cals," in *Sacco & Vanzetti,* John Davis, ed. (Melbourne, Australia: Ocean
       Press, 2004), 101–107.

294   "the new crime": *New York Times,* April 9, 1927, 1.

294   "inevitable when an individual is judged": *Boston Globe,* April 13,
       1927, 13.

294   "When you execute these two": *Boston Evening Globe,* April 15,
       1927, 1.

294   "murdered on July 10th": Sacco-Vanzetti Defense Committee Corre-
       spondence, BPL.

294   "You cannot imagine the strength": Vanzetti Correspondence, BPL.

295   "If they had been Smith and Brown": Neville, *Twentieth-Century Cause
       Célèbre,* 89.

295   "This rotten business in Massachusetts": Ibid., 90.

295   Further reproof: "The Cobbler and the Pedler [*sic*] Whose Fates Stir the
       World," *Literary Digest,* April 23, 1927, 6.

295   "Sacco and Vanzetti have been denied": Ibid.

295   "The degree of deliberation": *Boston Transcript,* April 6, 1927, part
       2, 2.

296   "the execution of the whole red scum": Feuerlicht, *Justice Crucified,* 340.

296   "is an ass": Vanzetti, *Il Caso Sacco e Vanzetti,* 166.

296   "To be choised to such candidature": Vanzetti to Alice Stone Blackwell,
       January 10, 1927, Sacco-Vanzetti Case Papers, HLS, Box 39, Folder 87.

296–97 "To expect that Fuller will stand": Frankfurter and Jackson, 270.

297 "stand firm": *Boston Globe,* May 20, 1927, 3.

297 "Calvin Coolidge stands": *Boston Globe,* April 13, 1927, 13.

297 "We taxpayers wonder": *Boston Globe,* April 14, 1927, 10.

298 "We were the most powerful nation": Fitzgerald, *The Crack Up,* 14.

298 a loss of 154,000 jobs: Brown and Tager, *Massachusetts: A Concise History,* 40.

298 "short-haired women and long haired men": John Dos Passos, *The Big Money* (New York: New American Library, 1933), 499.

298–99 "Jeffersonian Democrat": *New York World,* May 10, 1927, 15.

299 "represent the highest aspirations of mankind": FBI Files, 10–39.

299 "a sense of beauty of spirit": Liva Baker, *Felix Frankfurter* (New York: Coward-McCann, 1969), 127.

299 "part of a definite, well-organized program": *Boston Globe,* May 7, 1927, 12.

299 "Both are cold-blooded murderers": *Boston Globe,* April 14, 1927, 10.

299 "No two lives": *Boston Globe,* April 13, 1927, 13.

300 twenty-six distinguished New Englanders: Joughin and Morgan, 267–268.

300 "bitterness and hate": *Boston Globe,* June 7, 1927, 3.

300 "the millionaire pacifist": Russell, *Tragedy in Dedham,* 370.

300 When he refused: Ibid.

301 "We would respectfully ask": John Davis, ed., *Sacco & Vanzetti,* 67–68.

301 the *Boston Transcript:* Amory, *The Proper Bostonians,* 335–336.

302 "Sacco and Vanzetti are dangerous": Baker, *Felix Frankfurter,* 125.

302 As Wigmore defined them: *Boston Transcript,* April 25, 1927, 1, 5.

302 Frankfurter's terse rebuttal: *Boston Herald,* April 26, 1927, 1, 11.

303 "sob sisters, Pacifists and Reds": *Boston Globe,* June 2, 1927, 8.

303 his high-ceilinged office: Russell, *Tragedy in Dedham,* 390.

303 "I don't know what he is going to decide": *Boston Globe,* May 13, 1927, 1.

303 EXTRA! EXTRA!: *Boston Traveler,* May 14, 1927, 1.

304 "Mr. Governor of Massachusetts": *Boston Evening Globe,* May 14, 1927, 1.

304 "If it had not been for these thing": *New York World,* May 13, 1927, 15.

305 "Let me call you sweetheart": Ehrmann, *The Untried Case,* 92.

305 "My window": Frankfurter and Jackson, 250; and Vanzetti to Virginia MacMechan, April 25, 1927, Sacco-Vanzetti Case Papers, HLS, Box 40, Folder 66.

305 "Date fiori": Vanzetti to Mrs. Cerise Jack, May 7, 1927, Sacco-Vanzetti Case Papers, HLS, Box 40, Folder 51.

305 "Death for death": Vanzetti, *Il Caso Sacco e Vanzetti,* 192; and Paul Avrich, "Sacco and Vanzetti's Revenge," in Cannistraro and Meyer, eds., 167.

306 "Mrs. Ehrmann, dear": Avrich, *Anarchist Voices,* 123.

306 "Vanzetti," the lawyer announced: Vanzetti, *Il Caso Sacco e Vanzetti,* 194–197.

306 "Is this double investigation": Frankfurter and Jackson, 286, 288.

306   "never thought anything would work": Jackson oral history, CUOHROC, 207.

307   the governor surprised the *Herald*'s editor: Robert Lincoln O'Brien, "My Personal Relations to the Sacco Vanzetti Case as a Chapter in Massachusetts History," Herbert B. Ehrmann Papers, HLS, Box 13, Folder 22.

307   "Reds, Socialists, Pacifists": Frank Goodwin, "Sacco-Vanzetti and the Red Peril," speech before the Lawrence Kiwanis Club, June 30, 1927 (Boston: Industrial Defense Association, Inc., 1927), 5–10. After reading this speech, Vanzetti began calling Goodwin "Orlando Furioso Goodwin."

307   "I'm doing the best I can": Sacco-Vanzetti Defense Committee Correspondence, BPL.

307   An elderly Fort Lauderdale woman: Ibid.

308   "thirty-one more day living death": Frankfurter and Jackson, 61.

308   "we have at least some air": Ibid., 290.

308   "Some friends were here": Charlestown State Prison Records, Massachusetts State Archives.

308   "the most dreadful": Vanzetti Correspondence, BPL.

CHAPTER FOURTEEN: "THE JUDGMENT OF MANKIND"

311   "the New England conscience": Robert Grant, *The Chippendales* (New York: Charles Scribner's Sons, 1909), 290.

312   "an ability to use information": Ferris Greenslet, *The Lowells and Their Seven Worlds* (Boston: Houghton Mifflin, 1946), 397.

312   "Now we can sleep nights": Ehrmann, *The Case That Will Not Die*, 484.

312   "men impartial and well-intentioned": Vanzetti Correspondence, BPL.

312   "another Thayer": Frankfurter and Jackson, 303.

312   Thompson had deluged Lowell: William Thompson to the Advisory Committee, July 7, 1927, Abbott Lawrence Lowell Papers, Harvard University Archive, Box 1, Folder 1.

313   "I wish I could have cross-examined": Trial Transcript, 5272.

313   Katzmann . . . volunteered to face Thompson: Ibid., 5074–5085.

313   "consistent with going through": Ibid., 4976.

313   "There was always 'danger' ": Ibid., 4958.

313   "What did you do, Professor Richardson": Ibid., 5066.

313   "a slum worker," "so out of his element," "irritating beyond words": Ibid., 5063, 5209, 5337.

314   Lowell then produced a newspaper clipping: Ibid., 5085–5106.

314   "I must have a pretty good brain": Ibid., 5110–5111.

314   For the next two hours: Ibid., 5111–5138.

315   "I have nothing to say!": *Boston Evening Globe*, July 15, 1927, 1.

315   "If the Governor does not believe": Frankfurter and Jackson, 301.

316   "He didn't want any grace": Felicani oral history, CUOHROC, 146.

316   "What an attractive man": Russell, *Tragedy in Dedham*, 394.

316   "I don't think he is going to burn us": Vanzetti Correspondence, BPL.

316   "Sacco and Vanzetti are starving themselves to death": Sacco-Vanzetti Defense Committee Correspondence, BPL.

316   "In Onore Del Direttore": Trial Transcript, 5256f.
316   "You are just back": Ibid., 5256d.
316   "found beside the body": Ibid., 798.
316–17 Braintree's ex–police chief told: Ibid., 5166–5184.
317   "as though they were made with a different tool": Ibid., 5225.
317   "a very slim possibility": Ibid., 5235.
317   Thompson summed up: Ibid., 5257–5314.
318   How "very peculiar": Ibid., 5319.
318   "Are you suggesting": Ibid., 5320.
318   "apparently did something": Ibid., 5320–5321.
318   "We have to stomach it": Ibid., 5333.
318–19 Ranney summed up a case: Ibid., 5334–5347.
319   "It would be a terrible mistake": Sacco-Vanzetti Defense Committee Correspondence, BPL.
320   "I'm a business man": Jackson oral history, CUOHROC, 221.
320   Signed "B. Vanzetti, Plymouth Mass.": Ehrmann, *The Case That Will Not Die*, photo insert.
320   Shipped that Saturday: If the eels had arrived in Plymouth on Monday, Vanzetti could have peddled them on December 23, as skeptics of his innocence have claimed. See Montgomery, *The Murder and the Myth*, 33.
320   "It was so long I did seen it before": Frankfurter and Jackson, 314.
321   "greatly agitated": *New York World*, August 3, 1927, 12.
321   "Nicola Sacco and Bartolomeo Vanzetti will not die": *New York Times*, August 3, 1927, 1.
321   "Quite a delegation": *New York Times*, August 4, 1927, 2.
321   "My heart is in my shoes": *Boston Globe*, August 4, 1927, 21.
322   "They die!": Russell, *Tragedy in Dedham*, 409.
322   "Vanzetti really took it very hard": Felicani oral history, CUOHROC, 148.
322   "I told you so!": *New York World*, August 5, 1927, 2.
322   "Please telegraph immediately": Vanzetti Correspondence, BPL.
322   "I am innocent!": Vanzetti, *Il Caso Sacco e Vanzetti*, 205.
322   "We are proud for death": Frankfurter and Jackson, 69.
323   In his report, Fuller: *Boston Globe*, August 4, 1927, 20.
323   "less disturbed by a sense of injustice": *New York World*, August 5, 1927, 2.
323   "I do not choose to run": Some have suggested that as presidential aspirant, Fuller, thought to be leaning toward a pardon, changed his mind based on Coolidge's withdrawal on August 2. See Feuerlicht, *Justice Crucified*, 383.
323   "upholding law and civilization": *Boston Transcript*, August 4, 1927, 5.
323   "Upon the conclusion now reached": *Boston Herald*, August 4, 1927, 12.
323   "What the world demanded": "The Sacco-Vanzetti Case," *Literary Digest*, August 13, 1927, 9.
324   "Shame on you!": *Boston Transcript*, August 4, 1927, 5.
324   Overseas, newspapers denounced: *Boston Transcript*, August 4, 1927, 11; *Boston Globe*, August 5, 1927, 6; and *Atlanta Constitution*, August 6, 1927, 9.

324　Suddenly a deafening roar: *New York Times,* August 6, 1927, 1; and *New York Herald Tribune,* August 6, 1927, 1.

324　"Prevent the murder of these comrades": *Atlanta Constitution,* August 8, 1927, 2.

324　"depredations made by alleged anarchists": FBI Files, 10c-16.

324　"We will blow this building"; destroy skyscrapers; a bomb set for midnight: Ibid., 10c-37; *Boston Globe,* August 9, 1927, 8; and FBI Files, 10c-54.

325　"Comrades: There are just four days": Sacco-Vanzetti Defense Committee Correspondence, BPL.

325　"worked himself into a frenzy": *Boston Globe,* August 8, 1927, 10.

325　the Lowell Commission report: Trial Transcript, 5378c–5378z.

326　The *New York Times* thanked; the *Chicago Tribune* predicted: *Literary Digest,* August 20, 1927, 6; and *Chicago Tribune,* August 5, 1927, 8.

326　dozens of irate letters: A Citizen of Massachusetts to A. Lawrence Lowell, n.d., Abbott Lawrence Lowell Papers, Harvard University Archives, Harvard University, Box 2, Folder 2.

327　"The suspicion grows": John Dos Passos, "An Open Letter to President Lowell, *Nation,* August 24, 1927, 176.

327　"Hangman's House": *New York World,* August 5, 1927, 11.

327　"They never had a prayer": Edmund Wilson, *The American Earthquake: A Documentary of the Twenties and Thirties* (New York: Octagon, 1971), 154.

327　"mob psychology": A. Lawrence Lowell to Frederick Lewis Allen, August 15, 1927, Abbott Lawrence Lowell Papers, Harvard University Archives, Harvard University, Box 2, Folder 2.

327　"Massachusetts is disgraced": *New York Times,* August 7, 1927, 22.

327　Told that "bastard": Russell, *Tragedy in Dedham,* 417.

328　"these draft-dodgers": Ibid., 235–236.

328　"No man is so wise": *Boston Globe,* August 9, 1927, 1, 7.

329　"sauntering and loitering": *Boston Globe,* August 10, 1927, 22; and *The Good Shoemaker and the Poor Fish Peddler,* newsreels, Robert D. Farber University Archives and Special Collections, Brandeis University.

329　"La Salute è in Voi!": *L'Adunata dei Refrattari,* August 9, 1927, 1.

329　"not a stitch was sewn": *New York World,* August 10, 1927, 2.

330　datelines from the *New York Times: New York Times,* August 9, 1927, 4, and August 10, 1927, 2.

330　Sacco's father cabled Rome: *New York Times,* August 10, 1927, 1.

330　"Il Duce" had privately sent: Cannistraro, "Mussolini, Sacco-Vanzetti, and the Anarchists," 57.

330　a vacationing Chicago judge: *Chicago Tribune,* August 10, 1927, 1.

331　"and no other": *Boston Transcript,* August 9, 1927, 10.

331　"so altered by rust and age": William Thompson to Felix Frankfurter, May 10, 1927, Felix Frankfurter Papers, HLS, Box 197, Folder 23.

331　Thompson had invited Major Goddard to his office: Russell, *Tragedy in Dedham,* 377. Russell also notes that Goddard made a major error in a later case, linking a fatal bullet to a gun subsequently proved to have been purchased after the murder in question.

331   "Bolsheviki!": Marion Meade, *Dorothy Parker: What Fresh Hell Is This?* (New York: Villard, 1988), 183.

331   In Rome, Giuseppe Andrower: *La Republica de Buenos Aires,* August 11, 1927, 1.

332   "They have been driving nails into us": Michael A. Musmanno, *After Twelve Years* (New York: Alfred A. Knopf, 1939), 298–299.

332   "the blacks": Baker, *Felix Frankfurter,* 608.

332   "Prejudice on the part of the presiding judge": *Boston Globe,* August 11, 1927, 11.

332   "did not get a square deal": Baker, 607.

332   "Don't be foolish, boy": Ibid.

333   "Let them out!" Meade, 183.

333   "It's all off, boys!": *New York Times,* August 11, 1927, 1.

333   "Why should I fatten myself": Musmanno, 304.

333   "this good old dear mother": Frankfurter and Jackson, 70.

334   "Bring Barto back with you": Musmanno, 337.

334   "All friends of America pray": *New York World,* August 12, 1927, 2.

334   "One can scarcely believe": Ibid.

334   "another turn of the rack": *New York World,* August 12, 1927, 2.

334   "a crude prolonging of agony": *Il Martello,* August 13, 1927, 1.

334   "That Sacco!": *Boston Globe,* August 17, 1927, 8.

335   "a necessary and vital part": *Daily Worker,* August 8, 1927, 5.

335   "preferred Sacco and Vanzetti dead": Jackson oral history, CUOHROC, 215.

335   "Saved?" the woman asked: Katherine Anne Porter, *The Never-Ending Wrong* (Boston: Atlantic Monthly Press, 1977), 19.

335   Charlestown Prison suddenly went dark: Jackson oral history, CUOHROC, 250.

336   "Doubts That Will Not Down": *New York World,* August 19, 1927, 12.

336   "my giant": *Boston Globe,* August 19, 1927, 7.

336   "My Dear Son and Companion": Frankfurter and Jackson, 71–72.

336   "I can't go on": *New York World,* August 20, 1927, 1.

337   "New Era Year I": Vanzetti to William G. Thompson, n.d., Sacco-Vanzetti Case Papers, HLS, Box 40, Folder 110.

338   "Dante, I say once more": Frankfurter and Jackson, 74.

338   "Friends and Comrades": Ibid., 320–321.

339   a state police informer: Massachusetts State Police Files.

339   A wiretap on Felix Frankfurter's phone: Ibid.

339   "sock on the nose": *New York World,* August 22, 1927, 2.

340   "It's a beautiful morning": *New York Times,* August 23, 1927, 1.

340   "What good do you expect to do?": Paula Holladay, "I Paraded," *New Republic,* October 19, 1927, 232.

341   "dirty wop sons of bitches!": Don Brown, "So This Is America!" *New Republic,* October 12, 1927, 202–203.

342   "I would feel constrained": Musmanno, 357.

342   "Did you ever see a Norfolk County farmer?": *Boston Globe*, August 23, 1927, 9.

342   "It would give me pleasure to shoot you": Louis Stark, "The Grounds for Doubt," *Survey*, October 1, 1927, 38; and Mrs. Walter Frank Papers, Brandeis University.

342   "Have you interviewed the witnesses?": Arthur Garfield Hays, "A Conference with Governor Fuller," *Nation*, September 21, 1927, 285.

342   "There is one chance in a thousand": *New York World*, August 23, 1927, 2.

343   Stepping into Cell 3: William G. Thompson, "Vanzetti's Last Statement," *Atlantic*, February 1928, 254–257.

343   "I love you and always will": Musmanno, 362.

344   "It is my painful duty": *Boston Globe*, August 23, 1927, 8.

344   "We must bow to the inevitable": Ibid.

344   "I guess they don't want me now": *Boston Globe*, August 23, 1927, 8.

344   "They will make an attempt on Warden Hendry": Massachusetts State Police Files.

344   Boston's five radio stations broadcast: *Boston Globe*, August 22, 1927, 18.

344   "You never can tell": *New York Times*, August 23, 1927, 4.

345   "Which way would He have turned": Allan Ross Macdougall, *Letters of Edna St. Vincent Millay* (New York: Harper and Brothers, 1952), 222.

345   "And what do you say": Musmanno, 389–390.

346   "Viva l'anarchia!": *New York Times*, August 23, 1927, 2; and *Boston Globe*, August 23, 1927, 8.

346   "I wish to tell you that I am innocent": Ibid.

347   "Life felt very grubby and mean": Porter, 44–45.

347   "They're gone": Felicani oral history, CUOHROC, 241.

348   "They have killed my innocent son": *New York World*, August 24, 1927, 2.

349   "one of the most tremendous funerals": *Boston Globe*, August 29, 1927, 1.

349   "Nicola Sacco and Bartolomeo Vanzetti, you came to America": Jeannette Marks, *Thirteen Days* (New York: Albert and Charles Boni, 1929), 61–64.

EPILOGUE

351   Katherine Anne Porter: Porter, *The Never-Ending Wrong*, 48–49.

351   "liberal martyr-saints"; "the private drama": *Los Angeles Times*, January 5, 2006; and Felix, *Protest*, 240.

352   "how far these documents": Gardner Jackson to Leonard Abbott, April 23, 1929, Sacco-Vanzetti Case Papers, HLS, Box 41, Folder 40.

352   The most noted elision: Frankfurter and Jackson, *The Letters of Sacco and Vanzetti*, xli.

353   "If Sacco and Vanzetti were professional bandits": "Those Two Men," *Lantern*, August 1929, 5.

353 "Boston has a bad conscience": "After Two Years," *New Republic*, August 21, 1929, 5.

353 "the shame of the world": "We Defend Boston!" *Lantern*, February 1928, 3.

353 "If Sacco and Vanzetti were anarchists": *New York Times*, August 24, 1928, 5; and *Chicago Tribune*, August 29, 1928, 17.

354 "morally responsible": *Boston Evening Globe*, May 23, 1929, 16.

354 Silva's mea culpa: "Frank Silva's Story," *Outlook and Independent*, October 31, 1928, 1056.

354 "he wasn't any stickup guy": Russell, *Tragedy in Dedham*, 323–325.

354 One man pasted their pictures: " 'Have Faith in Massachusetts'? Letters from our Readers," *Nation*, September 14, 1927, 254.

354 "I am afraid that people": Elizabeth Glendower Evans Papers, Radcliffe Institute, Schlesinger Library.

355 Only in the Soviet Union: Francis Russell, "The End of the Myth," *National Review*, August 19, 1977, 938.

355 "Mystery of Sacco-Vanzetti": Sidney Sutherland, "The Mystery of Sacco-Vanzetti," *Liberty*, March 15, 1930, 38–40, 45–48.

355 "the peacetime soldier": *Lantern*, December 1927 and January 1928.

355 "I have had hundreds of letters": *Boston Evening Globe*, September 27, 1932, 22.

356 "I hate to think": Ibid.

356 "of the incredible and destructive twists": *Walled in This Tomb: Questions Left Unanswered by the Lowell Committee in the Sacco-Vanzetti Case* (privately published, 1936), 4.

356 "In my opinion": "After Two Years," *New Republic*, August 21, 1929, 6.

356 Dozens of poets: Joughin and Morgan, *The Legacy of Sacco and Vanzetti*, 383; and Lucia Trent and Ralph Cheyney, eds., *America Arraigned* (New York: Dean and Co., 1928), 52, 62.

357 "Justice Denied in Massachusetts": *New York Times*, August 22, 1927, 2.

357 "America our nation": John Dos Passos, *The Big Money*, 468–469.

358 "Everything should be done": "The Case That Won't Die," *Nation*, August 16, 1958, 62.

358 seven former jurors: *New Bedford Standard-Times*, November 12, 1950, 13.

359 a white-haired Chief Michael Stewart: *New Bedford Standard-Times*, August 24, 1952, 15.

359 "no intention of doing so now": *New Bedford Standard-Times*, November 12, 1950, 13.

359 "My sister became prematurely old": Feuerlicht, *Justice Crucified*, 429.

360 "heartbreak from the tragedy": *Boston Herald*, April 1, 1959, 19.

360 "Mrs. Sacco cut herself off": Avrich, *Anarchist Voices*, 123.

360 "Don't pray": Feuerlicht, 409n.

360 "Did you know that your grandfather was executed": Avrich, *Anarchist Voices*, 93.

360 "Your grandfather was a murderer!": Ibid.

360–61 A stormy committee hearing: *Boston Herald*, April 3, 1959, 14.

361   **"for revolutionary purposes"**: Montgomery, *The Murder and the Myth*, 347.

361   **"a human vehicle"**: *Sacco-Vanzetti: Developments and Reconsiderations*, 102.

362   **"Sacco was guilty"**: Max Eastman, "Is This the Truth About Sacco and Vanzetti?" *National Review*, October 21, 1961, 264.

362   **"left-wing intelligentsia"**: William Henry Chamberlin, "Myths Die Hard," *National Review*, July 26, 1966, 734.

362   **"one long sneer"**: Alexander M. Bickel, "Sacco-Vanzetti and the Intellectuals," *New Republic*, April 2, 1966, 25.

362   **"There can be no doubt"**: Michael Musmanno, "Was Sacco Guilty?" *New Republic*, March 2, 1963, 27; and Francis Russell, "Sacco Guilty, Vanzetti Innocent?" *American Heritage*, June 1962, 108.

362   **"will have difficulty believing"**: Trial Transcript, xv.

363   **"the saturation of the trial"**: Ibid., xxi–xxx.

363   **"Fred is embittered"**: Upton Sinclair, "The Fishpeddler and the Shoemaker," *Institute of Social Studies Bulletin* 2, no. 2 (Summer 1953): 24.

363   **"He then told me"**: *Los Angeles Times*, December 24, 2005, B3.

363   **"his brooding on his wrongs"**: Arthur Spiegelman, "Upton Sinclair's Integrity Challenged," Reuters, January 26, 2006.

363   **"Those who believe or declare"**: Musmanno, "Was Sacco Guilty?" *New Republic*, March 2, 1963, 29.

364   **"left completely satisfied"**: Russell, *Tragedy in Dedham*, 303–304.

364   **a rambling ninety-six-page rebuttal**: Joseph Morelli, "Introduceing [*sic*] the Most Famous Case of the World: The Sacco-Vanzetti Case and the Morelli Gang," Sacco-Vanzetti Case Papers, HLS.

364   **" 'We whacked them out' "**: Vincent Teresa with Thomas C. Renner, *My Life in the Mafia* (Garden City, NY: Doubleday, 1973), 45–46.

365   **"Everyone [in the Boston anarchist circle]"**: Russell, *Sacco and Vanzetti: The Case Closed*, 12.

365   **"Sacco c'era"**: Avrich, *Anarchist Voices*, 133.

365   **"any stigma and disgrace"**: Brian Jackson, *The Black Flag: A Look Back at the Strange Case of Nicola Sacco and Bartolomeo Vanzetti* (Boston: Routledge and Kegan Paul, 1981), 89–90.

365   **"We are not here to decide"**: *Boston Globe*, July 20, 1977, 8.

365   **"You would have thought these men"**: Ibid.

366   **the Parmenter and Berardelli families**: Throughout the six years of appeals and protests during the 1920s, the Parmenter and Berardelli families remained silent. In late July 1927, a telegram supposedly sent to Governor Fuller by Sarah Berardelli, the slain guard's wife, was published in several newspapers. It read, in part, I HAVE ALWAYS DOUBTED THAT SACCO AND VANZETTI WERE GUILTY AND I HOPE THAT YOU WILL FREE THEM AND LET THEM GO HOME TO THEIR FAMILIES. Within days, however, Sarah Berardelli told the press she had never sent such a telegram. Parmenter's widow never spoke to the press. According to the *Boston Globe* (April 14, 1927), a high school classmate of Frederick Parmenter Jr. met with Governor Fuller to tell him how the boy had become

a delinquent and his mother a "white-haired, sad faced little lady" after Parmenter's murder. Aside from these two instances, the families and descendants of the slain men have never made a statement regarding the guilt or innocence of Sacco and Vanzetti.

366   "disgraced himself": Ibid.

366   The files revealed: Young and Kaiser, *Postmortem*, 128; FBI Files, 11a-12.

366   FBI files for the summer of 1926: FBI Files, 8–27-57; Young and Kaiser, 131.

367   "an important public service": Abbott Lawrence Lowell to Judge Robert Grant, August 1, 1927, Abbott Lawrence Lowell Papers, Harvard University Archives, Harvard University, Box 1, Folder 1.

367   a memo written by Chief Stewart: Young and Kaiser, 90.

367   "looked exactly alike": Ibid., 107.

367   Both Bullet III and Shell W: Ibid., 113.

Bibliography

ARCHIVES

Baldwin, Roger. "The Reminiscences of Roger Nash Baldwin." Oral History
    Research Office Collection, Columbia University (CUOHROC).
John Dever Papers. Boston Public Library (BPL).
Herbert B. Ehrmann Papers. Harvard Law School (HLS) Library.
Elizabeth Glendower Evans Papers. Radcliffe Institute. Schlesinger Library.
Federal Bureau of Investigation, Sacco-Vanzetti Case, File Number 61-126 (FBI
    Files).
Felicani, Aldino. "The Reminiscences of Aldino Felicani." Oral History Re-
    search Office Collection, Columbia University (CUOHROC).
Felix Frankfurter Papers. Harvard Law School (HLS) Library.
Gardner Jackson Papers. Brandeis University.
Jackson, Gardner. "The Reminiscences of Gardner Jackson." Oral History Re-
    search Office Collection, Columbia University (CUOHROC).
Abbott Lawrence Lowell Papers. Harvard University Archives, Harvard Uni-
    versity.
Massachusetts State Police Papers. Sacco-Vanzetti Case. Massachusetts State
    Archives.
Sacco-Vanzetti Case Papers. Harvard Law School (HLS) Library.
Sacco-Vanzetti Case Papers. Boston Public Library (BPL).
Michael E. Stewart Papers, Boston Public Library (BPL).
Thompson, William G. Massachusetts Lawyer's Dairy, 1925–1927, Boston Pub-
    lic Library (BPL).

MAGAZINES, PAMPHLETS, JOURNAL ARTICLES

"After Two Years." *New Republic,* August 21, 1929, 5–6.
"Anarchists and the Ambassador." *Literary Digest,* November 5, 1921, 9.

Beffel, John Nicholas. "Eels and the Electric Chair." *New Republic,* December 29, 1920, 127–129.

———. "The Sacco-Vanzetti Verdict." *New Republic,* August 10, 1921, 299–300.

Bent, Silas. "Checking Up on the Confession." *Outlook and Independent,* October 31, 1928, 1071–1075.

Bickel, Alexander M. "Sacco-Vanzetti and the Intellectuals." *New Republic,* April 2, 1966, 23–27.

Brown, Don. "So This Is America!" *New Republic,* October 12, 1927, 202–204.

Callahan, Jack. "How I Found Frank Silva." *Outlook and Independent,* October 31, 1928, 1060–1070.

Cannistraro, Philip V. "Mussolini, Sacco-Vanzetti, and the Anarchists: The Transatlantic Context." *Journal of Modern History,* March 1996, 31–62.

Chamberlin, William Henry. "Myths Die Hard." *National Review,* July 26, 1966, 734–735.

"The Cobbler and the Pedler [*sic*] Whose Fates Stir the World." *Literary Digest,* April 23, 1927, 5–6.

Colp, Ralph, Jr. "Bitter Christmas: A Biographical Inquiry into the Life of Bartolomeo Vanzetti." *Nation,* December 27, 1958, 485–500.

———. "Sacco's Struggle for Sanity." *Nation,* August 16, 1958, 65–70.

Cook, Fred J. "Sacco and Vanzetti: The Missing Fingerprints." *Nation,* December 22, 1962, 442–451.

Cook, Waldo L. "Forgetting Sacco and Vanzetti." *Nation,* August 21, 1929, 188–190.

Crawford, Ruth. "On the Trail of Sacco-Vanzetti Abroad." *Nation,* October 5, 1927, 334-336.

Dos Passos, John. *Facing the Chair: Story of the Americanization of Two Foreign Born Workmen.* Boston: Sacco-Vanzetti Defense Committee, 1927.

———. "An Open Letter to President Lowell." *Nation,* August 24, 1927, 176.

Eastman, Max. "Is This the Truth About Sacco and Vanzetti?" *National Review,* October 21, 1961, 261–264.

Ehrmann, Herbert B. "The Bouncer of the Bluebird Inn." *Survey Graphic,* August 1933, 398–403, 431–435.

Evans, Elizabeth Glendower. *Outstanding Features of the Sacco-Vanzetti Case.* Boston: New England Civil Liberties Committee, 1924.

Frankfurter, Felix. "The Case of Sacco and Vanzetti." *Atlantic,* March 1927, 409–432.

"Frank Silva's Story." *Outlook and Independent,* October 31, 1928, 1055–1060.

Goodwin, Frank. "Sacco-Vanzetti and the Red Peril." Speech before the Lawrence Kiwanis Club, June 30, 1927. Boston: Industrial Defense Association, Inc., 1927.

" 'Have Faith in Massachusetts'? Letters from our Readers." *Nation,* September 14, 1927.

Hays, Arthur Garfield. "A Conference with Governor Fuller." *Nation,* September 21, 1927, 285–286.

Holladay, Paula. "I Paraded." *New Republic,* October 19, 1927, 230–235.

Jackson, Gardner. "We Defend Boston!" *Lantern,* February 1928, 3–7.

Kirchwey, George W. "Sacco-Vanzetti." *Nation,* April 20, 1927, 415.

Lyons, Eugene. "Italians in American Courts." *Survey,* November 1921, 237–238.

"Massachusetts the Murderer." *Nation,* August 31, 1927, 192–193.

Meade, Norman G. "Practical Criminology at Work: Some of the Adventures of the Scientific Modern Detective." *Scientific American,* October 1923, 232–233.

Musmanno, Michael. "Was Sacco Guilty?" *New Republic,* March 2, 1963, 25–30.

Musmanno, Michael, and Francis Russell. "Tragedy in Dedham: A Final Note." *American Heritage,* February 1963, 92–93.

O'Brien, Robert Lincoln. *My Personal Relations to the Sacco Vanzetti Case as a Chapter in Massachusetts History.* Boston: self-published pamphlet, 1928.

"$1,000 Prize!" *Nation,* March 26, 1930, 351–352.

"One Year Later." *Lantern,* July-August 1928, 13.

"Our Communist 'Martyrs' Disturbing the World." *Literary Digest,* December 10, 1921, 34–42.

"Our Gray, 21-Inch Lives." *Nation,* December 1, 1956, 470.

Parrish, Michael E. "Sacco and Vanzetti Revisited: Russell and Young & Kaiser." *American Bar Foundation Research Journal* 12, no. 2/3 (Spring/Summer 1987): 575–589.

Pernicone, Nunzio. "Carlo Tresca and the Sacco-Vanzetti Case." *Journal of American History* 66, no. 3 (December 1979): 535–547.

"Press Comment on the Sacco-Vanzetti Execution." *Nation,* September 14, 1927, 252–253.

"Reaffirming the Sacco-Vanzetti Verdict." *Literary Digests,* August 20, 1927, 5–7.

Russell, Francis. "The End of the Myth: Sacco and Vanzetti Fifty Years Later." *National Review,* August 19, 1977, 938–941.

———. "Sacco Guilty, Vanzetti Innocent?" *American Heritage,* June 1962, 5–9, 107–111.

"Sacco-Vanzetti and Boston Common." *Survey,* September 1947, 481.

"The Sacco-Vanzetti Case." *Literary Digest,* August 13, 1927, 9.

Shields, Art. *Are They Doomed?* New York: Workers Defense League, 1921.

"Shipping Lenine's [*sic*] Friends to Him." *Literary Digest,* January 3, 1920, 14.

Sinclair, Upton. "The Fishpeddler and the Shoemaker." *Institute of Social Studies Bulletin* 2, no. 2 (Summer 1953): 1, 23–24.

Somkin, Fred. "How Vanzetti Said Goodbye." *Journal of American History* 2, no. 68 (September 1981): 298–312.

Stark, Louis. "The Grounds for Doubt." *Survey,* October 1, 1927, 38–55.

Sutherland, Sidney. "The Mystery of Sacco-Vanzetti." *Liberty,* March 15, 1930, 38–40, 45–48.

Thompson, William G. "Vanzetti's Last Statement." *Atlantic,* February 1928, 254–257.

"Those Two Men." *Lantern,* August 1929.

"Truth About the Bridgewater Holdup." *Outlook,* October 31, 1928, 1053–1063.

Van Amburgh, Charles, as told to Fred H. Thompson. "The Hidden Drama of Sacco and Vanzetti." *True Detective Mysteries,* April–October 1935.

Vanzetti, Bartolomeo. "Awaiting the Hangman: A Journalistic Lynching." *Official Bulletin of the Sacco-Vanzetti Defense Committee,* August 1926, 1–3.

———. *Background of the Plymouth Trial.* Chelsea, MA: Road to Freedom Group, 1926.

Walled in This Tomb: Questions Left Unanswered by the Lowell Committee in the Sacco-Vanzetti Case. Privately published, 1936.

"What Does the Sacco-Vanzetti Case Teach?" *Literary Digest,* September 3, 1927, 5–7.

"What Other Editors Say—Press and Magazine Comment on the Vanzetti Story." *Outlook and Independent,* November 21, 1928, 1204.

Whyte, William Foote. "Race Conflicts in the North End of Boston." *New England Quarterly,* December 1939, 623–642.

BOOKS

Allen, Frederick Lewis. *Only Yesterday: An Informal History of the 1920s.* New York: Harper and Row, 1931.

Amory, Cleveland. *The Proper Bostonians.* New York: E. P. Dutton, 1947.

Annual Reports of the Commissioner of Correction. Boston: Commonwealth of Massachusetts, 1920–1927.

Avrich, Paul. *Anarchist Voices: An Oral History of Anarchism in America.* Princeton, NJ: Princeton University Press, 1995.

———. *Sacco and Vanzetti: The Anarchist Background.* Princeton, NJ: Princeton University Press, 1991.

Baker, Liva. *Felix Frankfurter.* New York: Coward-McCann, 1969.

Baritz, Loren. *The Culture of the Twenties.* Indianapolis: Bobbs-Merrill, 1970.

Barry, John M. *The Great Influenza: The Epic Story of the Deadliest Plague in History.* New York: Viking, 2004.

Blumenfeld, Harold. *Sacco and Vanzetti: Murderers or Murdered.* New York: Scholastic Book Services, 1972.

Botta, Luigi. *Sacco e Vanzetti: Giustiziata la verità.* Cavallermaggiore, Italy: Edizioni Gribaudo, 1978.

Brown, Richard D., and Jack Tager. *Massachusetts: A Concise History.* Amherst: University of Massachusetts Press, 2000.

Buhle, Mari Jo, Paul Buhle, and Harvey J. Kaye. *The American Radical.* New York: Routledge, 1994.

Cannistraro, Philip, and Gerald Meyer, eds. *The Lost World of Italian-American Radicalism.* Westport, CT: Praeger, 2003.

Carr, Virginia Spencer. *Dos Passos: A Life.* Garden City, NY: Doubleday, 1984.

Cather, Willa. *Not Under Forty.* New York: Alfred A. Knopf, 1936.

Chernow, Ron. *The House of Morgan: An American Banking Dynasty and the Rise of Modern Finance.* New York: Atlantic Monthly Press, 1990.

Coben, Stanley. *A. Mitchell Palmer: Politician.* New York: Columbia University Press, 1963.

Conlin, Joseph R. *At the Point of Production: The Local History of the I.W.W.* Westport, CT: Greenwood, 1981.

Cowan, Geoffery. *The People v. Clarence Darrow: The Bribery Trial of America's Greatest Lawyer.* New York: Times Books, Random House, 1993.

D'Allesandro, Frank M. *The Verdict of History on Sacco and Vanzetti.* New York: Jay Street Publishers, 1997.

Davis, John, ed. *Sacco & Vanzetti.* Melbourne, Australia: Ocean Press, 2004.

Debs, Eugene Victor. *Walls and Bars.* Montclair, NJ: Patterson Smith, 1973.

Delamater, Jerome H., and Mary Anne Trasciatti. *Representing Sacco and Vanzetti.* New York: Palgrave Macmillan, 2005.

Dos Passos, John. *The Best Times: An Informal Memoir.* New York: New American Library, 1966.

———. *The Big Money.* New York: New American Library, 1933.

DuBasky, Mayo. *The Gist of Mencken: Quotations from America's Critic.* Metuchen, NJ: Scarecrow Press, 1990.

Ehrmann, Herbert B. *The Case That Will Not Die: Commonwealth vs. Sacco and Vanzetti.* Boston: Little, Brown, 1969.

———. *The Untried Case: The Sacco-Vanzetti Case and the Morelli Gang.* New York: Vanguard, 1933.

Evans, Harold. *The American Century.* New York: Alfred A. Knopf, 1998.

Felix, David. *Protest: Sacco and Vanzetti and the Intellectuals.* Bloomington: Indiana University Press, 1965.

Feuerlicht, Roberta Strauss. *Justice Crucified: The Story of Sacco and Vanzetti.* New York: McGraw-Hill, 1977.

Financial Report of the Sacco-Vanzetti Defense Committee. Boston, 1925.

Fitzgerald, F. Scott. *The Crack Up.* New York: New Directions, 1945.

Flynn, Elizabeth Gurley. *The Rebel Girl: An Autobiography—My First Life (1906–1926).* New York: International Publishers, 1973.

Fraenkel, Osmond K. *The Sacco-Vanzetti Case.* New York: Alfred A. Knopf, 1931.

Frankfurter, Felix. *The Case of Sacco and Vanzetti: A Critical Analysis for Lawyers and Laymen.* New York: Grosset and Dunlap, 1927.

Frankfurter, Marion Denman, and Gardner Jackson. *The Letters of Sacco and Vanzetti.* New York: Penguin, 1997.

Frost, Richard H. *The Mooney Case.* Stanford, CA: Stanford University Press, 1968.

Gallagher, Dorothy. *All the Right Enemies: The Life and Murder of Carlo Tresca.* New Brunswick, NJ: Rutgers University Press, 1988.

Gambino, Richard. *Blood of My Blood: The Dilemma of the Italian-Americans.* Garden City, NY: Doubleday, 1974.

Gedda, Alberto. *Gridatelo dai tetti: Autobiografia e lettere di Bartolomeo Vanzetti.* Asti, Italy: Editoriale Fusta, 2005.

Gitlow, Benjamin. *I Confess: The Truth About American Communism.* New York: E. P. Dutton, 1940.

Goldberg, David. *Discontented America: The United States in the 1920s.* Baltimore: Johns Hopkins University Press, 1999.

Grant, Robert. *The Chippendales.* New York: Charles Scribner's Sons, 1909.

———. *Fourscore: An Autobiography.* Boston: Houghton Mifflin, 1934.

Greenslet, Ferris. *The Lowells and Their Seven Worlds*. Boston: Houghton Mifflin, 1946.

Guerin, Daniel. *Anarchism: From Theory to Practice*. New York: Monthly Review Press, 1970.

Gunther, Charles O., and Jack Disbrow Gunther. *The Identification of Firearms from Ammunition Fired Therein with an Analysis of Legal Authorities*. New York: John Wiley and Sons, 1935.

Hamilton, Alexander, James Madison, and John Jay. *The Federalist Papers*. New York: New American Library, 1961.

Hart, Albert Bushnell, ed. *Commonwealth History of Massachusetts, Colony, Province, and State*. Vol. 5. New York: States History Company, 1927.

Harvard Class of 1912: Twenty-fifth Anniversary Report. Cambridge, MA: Common Press, 1937.

Haywood, William. *Bill Haywood's Book: The Autobiography of Big Bill Haywood*. New York: International Publishers, 1929.

Hirsch, H. N. *The Enigma of Felix Frankfurter*. New York: Basic Books, 1981.

Historical Statistics of the United States: Colonial Times to 1970, Part 1. Washington, D.C.: U.S. Department of Commerce, 1975.

Howe, Helen. *The Gentle Americans, 1864–1960: Biography of a Breed*. New York: Harper and Row, 1965.

Jackson, Brian. *The Black Flag: A Look Back at the Strange Case of Nicola Sacco and Bartolomeo Vanzetti*. Boston: Routledge and Kegan Paul, 1981.

Joughin, Louis, and Edmund M. Morgan. *The Legacy of Sacco and Vanzetti*. Chicago: Quadrangle Books, 1948.

Kadane, Joseph B., and David A. Schum. *A Probabilistic Analysis of the Sacco and Vanzetti Evidence*. New York: John Wiley and Sons, 1996.

Kennedy, David M. *Freedom from Fear: The American People in Depression and War, 1929–1945*. New York: Oxford University Press, 1999.

LaGumina, Salvatore J., ed. *Wop: A Documentary History of Anti-Italian Discrimination in the United States*. San Francisco: Straight Arrow Books, 1973.

Lash, Joseph P., ed. *From the Diaries of Felix Frankfurter*. New York: W. W. Norton, 1975.

Leuchtenburg, William E. *The Perils of Prosperity: 1914–1932*. Chicago: University of Chicago Press, 1958.

Lyons, Eugene. *Assignment in Utopia*. New York: Harcourt, Brace, 1937.

———. *The Life and Death of Sacco and Vanzetti*. New York: International Publishers, 1927.

Macdougall, Allan Ross. *Letters of Edna St. Vincent Millay*. New York: Harper and Brothers, 1952.

Manchester, William. *Disturber of the Peace: The Life of H. L. Mencken*. Amherst: University of Massachusetts Press, 1986.

Mann, Arthur. *La Guardia: A Fighter Against His Times, 1882–1933*. Philadelphia: J. B. Lippincott, 1959.

Marks, Jeannette. *Thirteen Days*. New York: Albert and Charles Boni, 1929.

Meade, Marion. *Dorothy Parker: What Fresh Hell Is This?* New York: Villard, 1988.

Montgomery, Robert H. *The Murder and the Myth*. New York: Devin-Adair, 1960.

Moquin, Wayne, and Charles Van Doren, eds. *A Documentary History of the Italian Americans*. New York: Praeger, 1974.

Moreno, Barry. *Italian Americans*. New York: Ivy Press Limited, 2003.

Morison, Samuel Eliot. *The Ropemakers of Plymouth: A History of the Plymouth Cordage Company, 1824–1949*. Boston: Houghton Mifflin, 1950.

Murray, Robert K. *Red Scare: A Study in National Hysteria, 1919–1920*. Minneapolis: University of Minnesota Press, 1955.

Musmanno, Michael A. *After Twelve Years*. New York: Alfred A. Knopf, 1939.

Nelson, Victor. *Prison Days and Nights*. Garden City, NY: Garden City Publishing Co., 1933.

Neville, John F. *Twentieth-Century Cause Célèbre: Sacco, Vanzetti, and the Press, 1920–1927*. Westport, CT: Praeger, 2004.

Phillips, Kevin. *Wealth and Democracy: A Political History of the American Rich*. New York: Broadway Books, 2002.

Porter, Katherine Anne. *The Never-Ending Wrong*. Boston: Atlantic Monthly Press, 1977.

Ramella, Franco. *I documenti personali e la storia dell'emigrazione: Le lettere americane di Giovanni Batista Vanzetti, contadino cuneese*. Cuneo, Italy: Rivista dell'Istituto Storico della Resistenza in Cuneo e Provincia, n.d.

Russell, Francis. *Sacco and Vanzetti: The Case Resolved*. New York: Harper and Row, 1986.

———. *Tragedy in Dedham*. New York: McGraw-Hill, 1962.

The Sacco-Vanzetti Case: Transcript of the Record of the Trial of Nicola Sacco and Bartolomeo Vanzetti in the Courts of Massachusetts and Subsequent Proceedings, 1920–7. 6 vols. Mamaroneck, NY: Paul P. Appel, 1969. Referred to in the notes as Trial Transcript.

Sacco-Vanzetti: Developments and Reconsiderations—1979, Conference Proceedings. Boston: Boston Public Library, 1982.

Salvatore, Nick. *Eugene V. Debs: Citizen and Socialist*. Urbana: University of Illinois Press, 1982.

Schactman, Max. *Sacco and Vanzetti: Labor's Martyrs*. New York: International Labor Defense, 1927.

Schlesinger, Arthur M., Jr. *The Age of Roosevelt: The Crisis of the Old Order, 1919–1933*. Boston: Houghton Mifflin, 1957.

Schoener, Allon. *The Italian Americans*. New York: Macmillan, 1987.

Sinclair, Upton. *Autobiography*. New York: Harcourt, Brace and World, 1962.

———. *Boston*. New York: Albert and Charles Boni, 1928.

———. *My Life in Letters*. Columbia: University of Missouri Press, 1960.

Smith, Walker C. *The Everett Massacre: A History of the Class Struggle in the Lumber Industry*. New York: Da Capo, 1971.

Spivak, John L. *A Man in His Time*. New York: Horizon, 1967.

Teresa, Vincent, with Thomas C. Rennor. *My Life in the Mafia*. Garden City, NY: Doubleday, 1973.

Thoreau, Henry David. "Civil Disobedience." In *The Selected Works of Thoreau*. Boston: Cambridge Editions, Houghton Mifflin, 1975.

Tomasi, Lydio F., ed. *The Italian in America: The Progressive View, 1891–1914.* New York: Center for Migration Studies, 1972.

Topp, Michael M. *The Sacco and Vanzetti Case: A Brief History with Documents.* New York: Palgrave Macmillan, 2005.

Trager, James. *The People's Chronology.* New York: Henry Holt, 1994.

Trent, Lucia, and Ralph Cheyney, eds. *America Arraigned.* New York: Dean and Co., 1928.

Tuchman, Barbara. *The Proud Tower: A Portrait of the World Before the War, 1890–1914.* New York: Macmillan, 1966.

Urofsky, Melvin I., and David W. Levy, eds. *Letters of Louis D. Brandeis—Volume V (1920–1941): Elder Statesman.* Albany: State University of New York Press, 1978.

Vanzetti, Bartolomeo. *Il Caso Sacco e Vanzetti: Lettere ai familiari.* Rome: Editori Riuniti, 1971.

Vorse, Mary Heaton. *A Footnote to Folly.* New York: Farrar and Rinehart, 1935.

Weeks, Robert P., ed. *Commonwealth vs. Sacco and Vanzetti.* Englewood Cliffs, NJ: Prentice-Hall, 1958.

Who's Who in Massachusetts 1940–41. Boston: Larkin, Roosevelt and Larkin, 1940.

Wilkie, Richard W., and Jack Tager. *Historical Atlas of Massachusetts.* Amherst: University of Massachusetts Press, 1991.

Wilson, Edmund. *The American Earthquake: A Documentary of the Twenties and Thirties.* New York: Octagon, 1971.

Woodcock, George, ed. *The Anarchist Reader.* Glasgow: Fontana/Collins, 1977.

Yeomans, Henry Aaron. *Abbott Lawrence Lowell: 1856–1943.* Cambridge, MA: Harvard University Press, 1948.

Young, William, and David E. Kaiser. *Postmortem: New Evidence in the Case of Sacco and Vanzetti.* Amherst: University of Massachusetts Press, 1985.

Zinn, Howard. *La Guardia in Congress.* Ithaca, NY: Cornell University Press, 1958.

THESES AND DISSERTATIONS

Haight, Laura Ann. "Tenders of the Flickering Flame: Boston Brahmin Women in Defense of Sacco and Vanzetti, 1920–27." Honors Thesis, History and Literature, Harvard and Radcliffe Colleges, March 1, 1984.

FILM AND VIDEO

The Good Shoemaker and the Poor Fish Peddler. Newsreels. Robert D. Farber University Archives and Special Collections, Brandeis University.

Landmark American Trials: Sacco and Vanzetti, 1921. Court TV. World Almanac Video, 2000.

Montaldo, Giuliano. *Sacco e Vanzetti.* Ripley's Home Video, 1971.

WEB SITES

The Statue of Liberty–Ellis Island Foundation, Inc. http://www.ellisisland
    records.org.
"The Influenza Pandemic of 1918." http://www.stanford.edu/group/virus/uda/.
Marstar Canada (information on Colt Pistols). http://marstar.ca/c32s.htm.

Index

Grateful acknowledgment is made for permission to reprint excerpts from the following copyrighted works:

"Law Like Love" from *Collected Poems* by W. H. Auden. Copyright 1940 and renewed 1968 by W. H. Auden. Used by permission of Random House, Inc.

Dante Alighieri's Diving Comedy, translated by Mark Musa. Used by permission of Indiana University Press.

The Big Money by John Dos Passos (Harcourt, Brace and Company). Copyright 1936 by John Dos Passos. Copyright renewed 1964 by John Dos Passos. By permission of Lucy Dos Passos Coggin.

"Justice Denied in Massachusetts" by Edna St. Vincent Millay. Copyright 1928, 1955 by Edna St. Vincent Millay and Norma Millay Ellis. Reprinted by permission of Elizabeth Barnett, Literary Executor, The Millay Society. All rights reserved.

Letter from Edna St. Vincent Millay to Governor Alvan T. Fuller, August 22, 1927, from *Letters of Edna St. Vincent Millay*. Copyright 1952 by Norma Millay Ellis. Reprinted by permission of Elizabeth Barnett, Literary Executor, The Millay Society. All rights reserved.

Selections from papers held in the archives and libraries cited on page 413 are used with permission.

Illustration credits: p. 2 *top*, p. 4. *bottom*, p. 5 *top*, p. 6, p. 7, p. 9, pp. 11–16: Boston Public Library/Rare Books Department; p. 2 *bottom*, p. 3, p. 4 *top*: Robert D. Farber University Archives & Special Collections Department, Brandeis University; p. 5 *bottom*: © Corbis; p. 10: Courtesy of Art & Visual Materials, Special Collections Department, Harvard Law School Library.